S0-BQJ-539

John Dewey

The Later Works, 1925–1953

Volume 3: 1927–1928

EDITED BY JO ANN BOYDSTON

TEXTUAL EDITOR, PATRICIA BAYSINGER

With an Introduction by David Sidorsky

Southern Illinois University Press

Carbondale and Edwardsville

The text of this reprinting is a photo-offset reproduction of the original cloth
edition that contains the full apparatus for the volume awarded the seal of the
Committee on Scholarly Editions of the Modern Language Association.

The paperbound edition has been made possible by a special subvention from
the John Dewey Foundation.

The Library of Congress catalogued the first printing of this work (in cloth) as
follows:

Dewey, John, 1859–1952.
    The later works, 1925–1953.

    Vol. 3 has introd. by David Sidorsky.
    Continues The middle works, 1899–1924.
    Includes indexes.

    CONTENTS: v. 1. 1925.—v. 2. 1925–1927.—v. 3. 1927–1928.
    1. Philosophy—Collected works.   I. Boydston, Jo Ann, 1924–.
B945.D41 1981   191   80-27285
ISBN 0-8093-1132-1 (v. 3)

ISBN 0-8093-1492-4 (paperback)

Contents

vi CONTENTS

Introduction
By David Sidorsky

The philosophical essays, the reviews and interpretations of studies in the social sciences, and the political commentary that are gathered together in this volume reflect the currents
of American culture in the years of their original publication,
1927 and 1928, just before the Depression and the changing relationship of America to European society were to transform
profoundly many aspects of American intellectual life. The recognition that this volume reflects its times is heightened by its
several *pièces d'occasion* that range from an evaluation of the
Sacco-Vanzetti verdict, written shortly after the trial, to a discussion of the outlawry of war movement during the negotiating of
the Kellogg-Briand Peace Pact, and from a statement of support
for the presidential candidacy of Al Smith relating to American
morals and religion to impressions and appraisals of Russian
education on a tour of the Soviet Union in 1928.

In the chronology of Dewey's philosophical development the
essays of this volume come between two major formulations of
his thought: *Experience and Nature* of 1925 and *The Quest for
Certainty* of 1929. *Experience and Nature* was the culmination
of Dewey's lifelong effort to construct a naturalistic metaphysics,
in the context of a philosophical tradition in which the formulation of a metaphysics was the mark of comprehensive philosophical outlook. *The Quest for Certainty* was a milestone in
Dewey's interpretation of naturalistic ethical theory, developed
in the context of his conception of philosophy as the most general form of cultural criticism. Dewey's philosophical writings of
1927 and 1928 that are found in this volume are framed, in great
measure, by those two poles of his philosophical interest: looking backward, in a sense, to the defense of naturalistic metaphys-

ics and moving forward to the justification and to the implications for practice of an empirical ethical theory.

For Dewey, an empirical ethics was necessarily connected to the methods and findings of the social sciences whether in psychology, economics, or anthropology. Consequently, the philosophical justification of a naturalistic moral philosophy led Dewey into the discussion of the empirical results of the social sciences and their impact upon social and political philosophy.

Dewey's belief that scientific method, broadly understood, is the sole legitimate arbiter of intellectual inquiry provides a common thread among many of the articles on naturalistic metaphysics or empirical ethical theory and the essays on educational and political topics. It is Dewey's recognition of the unique competence of the natural sciences for understanding the world that excludes any appeal to transcendental or nonnaturalistic entities in metaphysics. It is his commitment to scientific method that suggests that problems of moral decision can be resolved by empirical inquiry on objective matters of fact. And it is Dewey's faith in the application of scientific method that motivates his confidence in intelligent reconstruction of contemporary social and educational institutions.

Yet any emphasis on the coherence of the essays in this volume is a partial truth. The essays often clearly bear the imprint of their time, just as they manifest the style and voice of John Dewey, and share many characteristic features of American pragmatic philosophy. Yet the diversity of the topics belies any systemic unity. The conclusions are too many and varied to derive from any set of philosophical premises. In many of the articles there is the sense of Dewey thinking his way anew through a familiar issue or engaging in polemical debate on the line of controversy drawn by the critic or author with whom he is engaged. The overall impression then is that of work in progress, whether in response to criticisms of his metaphysics, projection of the significance of his moral philosophy, or commentary on political events.

I. *Metaphysics*

The several articles and reviews on metaphysical topics form one of the sustained and unifying themes of this volume.

The most dramatic feature of that discussion of metaphysics is the confrontation between the views of George Santayana and those of Dewey. This originates in Santayana's review of *Experience and Nature*, printed in the Appendix, with the issue joined in Dewey's response to that review in the essay "Half-Hearted Naturalism," and the argument extended in Dewey's review, under the title "Philosophy as a Fine Art," of Santayana's major ontological work *The Realm of Essence*.

This confrontation bears with it a number of elements of historical interest. Both Dewey and Santayana were major figures of the last philosophical generation in Anglo-American thought whose philosophical tradition called for the construction of systematic metaphysical theory. Both were naturalists who viewed their own metaphysical theories as continuous with a naturalist tradition whose great representatives were Aristotle and Spinoza. In a more limited historical focus, both were leading spokesmen of major schools of American thought, of Realism and of Pragmatism, which were themselves efforts to mediate the dilemma of philosophy at the turn of the century. Finally, apart from any historical relevance, there is the rare event of a direct criticism and straightforward rejoinder on a fundamental philosophical issue.

Santayana had suggested that the question at issue "which is the crux of the whole system" of Deweyan naturalism is the "*dominance of the foreground*" (p. 373).[1] For Santayana, Dewey's naturalism appears "strangely unseizable and perplexing" since Santayana's own naturalistic vision is one of the infinite greatness of Nature, as a background that dwarfs its animal or human denizens. The lineage of that naturalism can be traced from Democritus and Lucretius through its expression in Romantic poetry and thought. In that rendering of the naturalistic tradition, atoms and the void or the elements such as fire and water overwhelm human aspirations or knowledge. Human activities attain significance only from the point of view of social convention, in subjective perspective, or by personal assertion of parochial values. Santayana is factually correct when he writes that "Dewey . . . or any other pragmatist" would never be "a naturalist . . . like the old Ionians or the Stoics or Spinoza, or like

1. Page numbers throughout refer to this volume.

those many mystics . . . who, heartily despising the foreground, have fallen in love with the greatness of nature and have sunk speechless before the infinite" (p. 374). Santayana is sympathetic to this kind of naturalistic metaphysics and he believes that "in nature there is no foreground or background, no here, no now, no moral cathedra . . ." (p. 373).

The debate between Dewey and Santayana is especially valuable in clarifying the interpretation of naturalistic metaphysics since both recognized as common ground their rejection of philosophical idealism or any species of nonnaturalism. Thus, Dewey's review of Santayana praises the fact that "in the *Life of Reason*," Santayana "taught or seemed to teach that the realm of ideas and ideals is rooted in nature and forms its apex" (p. 287). Santayana reciprocates in his review of Dewey. Santayana defines naturalism as the belief that "any immaterial things which are recognized shall be regarded as names, aspects, functions, or concomitant products of those physical things among which action goes on" (p. 368). He goes on to state that "it would be hard to find a philosopher in whom naturalism, so conceived, was more inveterate than in Dewey" (p. 369).

Thus, the issue is narrowed to competing naturalistic interpretations of the relationship between "foreground" and "background." For Santayana, the values Dewey claims are objectively present in human experience and action represent an anthropomorphic dominance by the foreground that mark his naturalism as "half-hearted." Conversely, for Dewey Santayana's naturalism is untenably dualistic because of his failure to connect human interests and preferences to their appropriate cause, genesis or background in nature. It is a virtue of a naturalistic philosophy that it provides a framework for demonstrating the "continuities" among the physical, the biological, and the human. As Dewey put it in his rejoinder to Santayana:

To me human affairs, associative and personal, are projections, continuations, complications, of the nature which exists in the physical and pre-human world. There is no gulf, no two spheres of existence, no "bifurcation." For this reason, there are in nature both foregrounds and backgrounds, heres and theres, centres and perspectives, foci and margins (pp. 74–75).

Their disagreement is exhibited consistently in Dewey's and Santayana's competing interpretations of naturalistic metaphysics. It is present in their distinctive readings of the naturalistic tradition and determined their positions within the movements of American philosophy at the turn of the century. Thus, both Dewey and Santayana appreciate that Aristotelian naturalism has insisted that Platonic forms must be understood, in Santayana's phrase, as "names, aspects, functions or concomitant products" of the actualized potentialities of Nature. Dewey stresses the moral aspects of Aristotle's naturalism in which the ends and excellences of human and political life are fulfillments of the functioning of human nature and human association. Consequently, Dewey criticizes Aristotle's acceptance of the contemplative life as the highest form of human activity as deriving from an inappropriate separation of theory and practice in Greek culture. Santayana, however, is prepared to see the contemplation of the order of nature in its intelligible aspect as the appropriate outcome of a naturalistic sensibility.

Similarly, both Dewey and Santayana recognize that Spinoza had projected a vision of metaphysical naturalism in postulating that all events were immanent, and determined, within the order of an inclusive nature. Dewey stresses the implication that there could be no bifurcation between the interpretation of human nature or its social conduct and the understanding of the physical features of the universe. Within such a unitary schema, Spinoza's counsel that men should stoically accept the ordinances of nature seems, for Dewey, a limited approach to the physical and social transformations that human interaction with nature makes possible. For Santayana, however, stoicism is not a fatal defect but one ultimate remedy that the naturalist temperament provides for the inevitable insufficiency of technological or social meliorism.

The common ground of Dewey's and Santayana's naturalistic metaphysics emerges more boldly when placed in the context of the philosophical situation in the first decade of this century. For them, as for their leading contemporaries like James, Moore, Russell, Husserl, or Bergson, philosophy appeared to be impaled on the horns of a dilemma. On the one side, positivists and evolutionists proposed a metaphysics of materialism, supported by the record of progress in the natural and the biological sciences. On the other side, in the dominant dialectical tradition within

Continental, British, or American philosophy, exemplified by Hegelians like Bradley and Royce, Absolute Idealism was justified on the ground that scientific knowledge like all knowledge presupposes the reality of a knowing Mind.

Dewey's commitment to naturalistic metaphysics emerged in this context for it represented his effort to overcome the dilemma posed by the metaphysical views of Materialism and Idealism. With reference to that dilemma, it is instructive to compare his approach to that task with those of his major contemporaries.

Edmund Husserl had managed the escape from the dilemma most adroitly by simply declaring at the outset of *Ideas* (1913) that he was bracketing, that is, suspending judgment between conflicting metaphysical interpretations of reality so that he could get on with an independent investigation of the field of phenomenological immediacy.

G. E. Moore provided in 1903 the most elaborate refutation of Idealism carried out for the sake of affirming the validity of Common Sense and the reality of everyday objects, not in order to vindicate a competing vision of scientific materialism. As Russell wrote:

> [Moore] took the lead in rebellion, and I followed, with a sense of emancipation. Bradley argued that everything common sense believes in is mere appearance; we reverted to the opposite extreme, and thought that *everything* is real that common sense, uninfluenced by philosophy or theology, supposes real. With a sense of escaping from prison, we allowed ourselves to think that grass is green, that the sun and stars would exist if no one was aware of them. . . . The world, which had been thin and logical, suddenly became rich and varied and solid.[2]

Subsequently, when Russell parted philosophical company with Moore, he sought to develop a metaphysics of "neutral monism," which was named in a manner that avoided commitment to the traditional metaphysical polarities. Russell's construction of the external world from the elements of sensations or his the-

---

2. Bertrand Russell, "My Mental Development," in *The Philosophy of Bertrand Russell*, ed. P. A. Schilpp (Evanston and Chicago: Northwestern University, 1944), p. 12.

ory of entities as classes of atomic sense data similarly avoided metaphysical Materialism and Idealism.

Santayana was allied to Moorean Realism in the assertion of the reality of the material objects of the universe. Santayana sought to locate the framework for this Realism beyond Common Sense, however, in the naturalistic evolution of the life of Reason. This permitted Santayana to move between Materialism and Idealism by proposing such bridging formulae as the natural origin of every ideal entity and the potential for ideal fulfillment of every natural thing. As Dewey points out, it was this evolutionary naturalism of the *Life of Reason* of 1905 that seemed to make Santayana's views congruent with those of the pragmatists. Thus, Santayana seemed to provide a functional integration of rationalist and empiricist modes of knowing by proposing that one represented the evolution of "concretions in conception" and the other of "concretions in perception." As Dewey suggests in his review of Santayana's *Realm of Essence*, this was probably not Santayana's own final intention. His ultimate solution was more dualistic and paradoxical. There is both a realm of Matter and a realm of Ideals. Even if the latter do not have material embodiment, their essence can be intuited by minds and consequently must have an appropriate part in a comprehensive ontology.

In this context, it is relevant to note that William James had proposed a definition of pragmatism as a method of mediating between Idealism and Materialism in his *Pragmatism* of 1907. The main feature of that method was the appeal to future consequences as the criterion for acceptance or rejection of a metaphysical position, rather than the demonstration of the necessary truth of metaphysical presuppositions or axioms. James realized that hypotheses like Materialism or Idealism did not readily admit of verification or refutation by standard experimental procedures. His contention was that neither Materialism nor Idealism, because of the determinism implicit in their monistic explanation of the world, could account for the reality of change or for the fact that knowledge affected future outcomes. Accordingly, James argued that only the adoption of a view that was pluralistic and accepted the possibility of freedom—that is, a metaphysics which was an alternative to both Materialism and Idealism—could stand the test of future experience.

While James's views never included a detailed interpretation of this metaphysical alternative, they provide a point of departure for Dewey's metaphysics. It is the recognition of the inadequacy of both Materialism and Idealism in developing an account of how men can control their future that helps explain the tenacity with which Dewey pursued the effort to construct a pragmatic metaphysics throughout his philosophical career from his earliest confrontations with the works of Hegel, Bradley, Royce, Moore, and Russell.

There is an interesting confirmation in this volume of the comparative frame of reference for Dewey's naturalistic metaphysics. During 1927 and 1928, Dewey reviews four books whose subject matter is metaphysics. His discussion of each of them, the previously mentioned *Realm of Essence* of Santayana, Hoernlé's *Idealism as a Philosophy*, Bosanquet's *Science and Philosophy*, and Noble's *Purposive Evolution*, involves Dewey in an examination of the metaphysical options available between Idealism and Materialism, ranging between the positivistic evolutionism of Comte and the immanent Idealism of Hegel, or between Bradley and Spencer.

A detailed formulation of the major characteristics of the alternative of naturalistic metaphysics is not presented in the volume. In the dialectical confrontation with the metaphysical views that Dewey criticizes, its salient features continually appear. For Dewey, the human organism lives, thinks, perceives, and more generally, experiences events, in a natural environment. Successful human adaptation to that environment takes place because men correctly identify the objective conditioning factors of the environment. Further, men are able to transform features of their environment through applying their practical intelligence.

It is Dewey's critical view that traditional metaphysical theories were inadequate. Dewey directed these criticisms against both rationalist metaphysical systems that explained knowledge in terms of rational intuition and those empiricist approaches that interpreted knowledge in terms of the perceptual mirroring of a fixed reality. Both were not able to account for human knowledge as an instrument of adaptation and of control of the environment. An alternative metaphysical theory with a pragmatic or instrumental interpretation of human knowledge is therefore required. Such a metaphysics would be naturalistic, since it would sketch, as Dewey sought to do in *Experience and Nature*, the most generic traits and pervasive facts of human experience in its natural environment.

Significant as this point of view is with reference to the cast of competing metaphysical theories, it was not without its own tensions in the context of Dewey's work and thought. Dewey indicates one source of this tension in the preface he wrote for Sidney Hook's *Metaphysics of Pragmatism* (p. 338). Dewey suggests that in the formulation of a pragmatic metaphysics, it is necessary that some traditional terms like "instrument" or "action" be used with extended or new meanings. The consequence of this is that the pragmatic theses are misinterpreted by those who resist the adoption of such new meanings, or insist on assigning rigid definitions based on previously held philosophies to the key terms of the pragmatist's vocabulary.

There is a more significant source of tension, however, for any metaphysics of pragmatism. The pragmatic interpretation of knowledge as an instrument of adaptation and control implied that only scientific inquiry generated knowledge about the nature of the world. Accordingly, the claims of metaphysics would be formulable only as general platitudes about the human condition or as empirical statements within one of the positive sciences. This anti-metaphysical kernel was visible in the very early pragmatic writings of Charles Peirce. Despite his diverse essays adumbrating an evolutionary idealistic metaphysics, Peirce argued that metaphysical hypotheses must be empirically verifiable in a manner similar to hypotheses of the empirical sciences. Further, Peirce provided a pragmatic definition of reality in which an entity is real if its existence is asserted in a science. The face of reality is therefore progressively disclosed by scientific inquiry alone and would achieve its ultimate reading only at the asymptotic conclusion of the process of inquiry.

Apart from this historical tension within pragmatism between its recognized need for a metaphysical theory and its anti-metaphysical commitment to scientific method as the sole arbiter of all empirical knowledge, there were remarkable contemporaneous surfacings of this issue in 1927 and 1928. It was during those years that the anti-metaphysical views of the Vienna Circle were being formulated in their most extreme form, with some homage offered to their Peircean ancestry. Significantly, 1927 was also the year of publication of Heidegger's *Being and Time*, providing the formal opposition to the logical positivism of Wittgenstein, Carnap, and the other early associates of the Vienna Circle.

The question is not one of the degree of awareness, influence, or involvement Dewey had with the emerging European philosophical movements of the late 1920s or even of the ways in which these represent extensions of such earlier confrontations as those of James with Bergson and Moore, or of Dewey with Russell. The relevant point is that the development of Logical Positivism and of Existentialism transposed the poles of philosophical discourse. Dewey's naturalistic metaphysics ceased to occupy the mediating center between Materialism and Idealism but was challenged along different lines. For the Logical Positivists, their belief, shared by Dewey, that science is uniquely competent to decide all empirical questions led them to propose the replacement of metaphysics by logical or linguistic analysis of the concepts of traditional metaphysical theories. For the Existentialists, their concern with the primacy of human condition, also shared by Dewey, led them toward descriptive and structural accounts of the qualities of subjective experience.

These two movements, which were subsequently to reshape and divide the philosophical landscape, were both unacceptable to Dewey. Despite his commitment to scientific method in philosophy, Dewey argued that linguistic analysis was inadequate, for it viewed philosophy as semantic construction or semantic reformation, rather than as social reconstruction or moral direction for the activities of the culture. And despite his recognition of the central importance of human experience, Dewey rejected Heideggerian Existentialism. On his view, its speculative account of the characteristics of existence, and of their ontological presuppositions, impugns the explanatory and descriptive function of the empirical sciences with the consequence of neglecting the potential of scientific inquiry for social and cultural reform.

These programmatic differences are deep, so that it is particularly noteworthy that the two essays in specific metaphysical analysis that are present in this volume involve clarification of linguistic usage and some descriptive phenomenology of the field of human experience.

The first of these is "Appearing and Appearance" in which Dewey seeks "to give an analytic account of the . . . meaning of appearance . . . eliminating historic misconstructions." This analytic account includes a careful distinction among different meanings of the term "appearance." Thus, "appearing," as opposed to "disappearing," is a phase of temporal presence as in the waxing or waning of the moon or the rising and setting of the sun. Again, an "appearance" is a complete manifestation or showing just as there can be a total concealment or covering up. An appearance can also have a representational function as in the appearance of an actor in a role or of a lawyer for his client. It is Dewey's argument that the cross-treading of the different senses of appearance led to the epistemological and metaphysical confusions of ancient and modern philosophical thought in which the world of appearances is considered a secondary representation or reduplication of the world of reality.

There are remarkable similarities between many of Dewey's examples and those of linguistic analysts, particularly those used by J. L. Austin in his analysis of the vocabulary of perception in *Sense and Sensibilia*. There are even some interesting convergences in the techniques of conceptual clarification including the comparative testing of the usages of "appearing" with "seems" and "looks," or the probing of the ambiguities of the idioms of appearance terms by focusing upon the correlative negative terms. Further, Dewey suggests, for example, that "it may seem like a trick to do away with this 'problem' by substituting specific terms, 'looks,' 'sounds,' 'feels,' for the general term 'appears,' . . ." in a manner which points toward the specific moves that Austin brilliantly devised to undermine the use of the general term "perception." These similarities are not simply a curiosity of intellectual history. They indicate the common ground between a concern with linguistic clarification of the concepts of the metaphysical vocabulary and Dewey's concern with an empirical account of philosophical terminology freed from its systematic incorporation in transcendent metaphysical theories.

Yet Dewey's intentions and those of the language analysts are different. Dewey believes that clarifying the different functions of the terms of "appearance" provides a basis for an empirical account of the processes of knowing. Such an account draws attention to the plural elements in the process. In Dewey's phrase, "knowledge requires as its precondition an appearing object which results from an integrated interaction of all factors, the organism included . . ." (p. 72). Hence he believes that the aim of philosophy goes beyond the unravelling of the conceptual knots in the classic traditions of metaphysics and epistemology. For Dewey, the account of appearance becomes part of a general interpretation of all the phases of interaction between organisms and their environments.

Dewey's confidence in the possibility of a general interpretation of experience is evident in his second metaphysical essay in this volume, "The Inclusive Philosophic Idea." The essay embraces three of his most characteristic themes, and, in particular, suggests the connection between his naturalistic metaphysics and his conception that the central function of philosophy is cultural criticism.

First, the contention that the social is the most inclusive philosophical category is advanced as a way of formulating Dewey's criticism of British empiricism. For Dewey, British empiricism, from Locke to Mill and Bertrand Russell, interpreted reality in terms of atomic "ideas," particularistic "appearances," or discrete "sense data," and hence failed to recognize the associative and holistic character of experience. In this essay, Dewey does not state again the conceptual and practical harm that he believes followed upon this misinterpretation. It was his view, however, that a reformed empiricism that would recognize the reality of associations would provide the basis for an improved understanding of science and of society.

Second, the claim that the social is the "inclusive philosophical idea" is a rejection of any kind of scientific reductionism or monistic scientific explanation of human culture. In denying that the material, the vital, or the mental are the inclusive categories, Dewey is rejecting any ultimate account of human experience in terms of the variables of physics, of biology, or of psychology. This claim raises the question of Dewey's views on the explanatory function of scientific theories or models. It is the particular virtue of some of these theories or models that they select a small number of variables and can assert functional, predictive, and lawlike relations among them within a closed or formal system. Dewey's stress on the social and the holistic that involves the irreducibility of history, culture, or human experience to any schema of theoretical construction implies that the understanding of existence will always be continuous with the expression of everyday experience, and never completely translatable into the formal languages of science. In the light of Dewey's commitment to the applicability of scientific intelligence, what is required is an account of the bridge between scientific theories and his phenomenologically descriptive presentation of social experience.

In a pragmatic sense, however, the claim that the social is a category implies the view that a philosophical metaphysics includes the criticism of culture. The recognition of the "naturalness" of the moral life of man and of the human spirit necessarily leads philosophy into the domain of culture. So Dewey writes in this essay:

> It is a fact rather than a speculation that physical and animal nature are transformed in the process of education and of incorporation in the means and consequences of associated political, legal, religious, industrial, and scientific and artistic institutions (p. 53).

It would follow that a philosopher who is loyal to the most comprehensive philosophical task of naturalistic metaphysics would also be involved in the critical examination of social institutions. Hence there would be no bifurcation between the study of nature in the natural sciences and the examination of human values, preferences, and goals in the social sciences. In this way Dewey can bridge the gap between the traditional view that metaphysics is the pinnacle of philosophical activity and his own view that the primary role of philosophy is the criticism of culture.

II. *Moral Philosophy*

The claim that metaphysics, which has been understood as the attempt to interpret the ultimate nature of things, includes an evaluation of social institutions and human activities is an index of Dewey's belief that the central function of philosophy is cultural criticism. This function of philosophy was, on Dewey's view, not a partisan corollary of a pragmatic or instrumentalist approach. Rather Dewey argued in "Philosophy and Civilization" (the essay, written for the Sixth International Congress of Philosophy, with which this volume opens) that the history of philosophy provides a continuous exposition of the ways in which philosophy has brought the beliefs and values of a culture to critical self-awareness.

In its role of cultural criticism, philosophy has sought to articulate and reconcile the conflicting intellectual traditions of a society. For many Western societies and some Eastern ones, this has involved philosophers in the task of mediating between the intellectual authority of inherited social or religious institutions and the authority of scientific method. For Dewey, such a reconciliation required that the seat of authority on moral issues which had been located in religious absolutism was to be transferred to the empirical and experimental process of scientific inquiry.

Accordingly, Dewey developed an analysis of ethical statements as empirical hypotheses that are to be confirmed or confuted by their consequences in experience. There were diverse sources for this Deweyan analysis. They included the investigation of the important place occupied by disagreement on matters of fact in moral dispute as well as an examination of the way the standards and norms that express traditional moral absolutes evolve or change. More theoretically, they involve an awareness of the differences between empirical propositions of appraisal and emotive expressions of prizing. Dewey's account demonstrates his view that philosophy can seek to integrate the values of a cultural tradition with the challenges of the experimental methods of the sciences.

Dewey also asserted a practical analogue to this empirical theory of ethics in the context of the problems of Western, particularly American, industrial civilization. The conflict which required reconciliation in practice was that between the successful technological application of the methods of the natural sciences, and the inability or refusal to apply scientific inquiry to political, economic, educational, or social contexts. Since societies are unlikely to abandon the fruits of their technology, the gap could only be closed by an ongoing application of experimental methods to moral decision making and to institutional reconstruction.

Thus, both in the theory of empirical ethics and in the shaping of the institutions of an industrial civilization, Dewey asserted confidence in the competence and the potentiality for growth of the social sciences. Appropriately, then, Dewey's philosophical writings through the 1920s and during the years of this volume involve contributions to the social scientific literature, commentary on its method and problems, and appraisals of the significance of its results. The most prominent illustration of this is his review of the works of the pioneers of anthropology and his assessment of the significance of their work for ethics in the essay "Anthropology and Ethics" that was written as a chapter in an anthology on *The Social Sciences and Their Interrelations.*

Certainly the reading of this essay after five decades, but probably even its contemporaneous reading, raises disquieting questions. Despite the great faith Dewey has placed in the process of the social sciences, he documents carefully the limited, and even marginal, significance anthropology thus far has had for ethical philosophy. This suggests a measure of cautionary skepticism regarding Dewey's confidence that anthropological or social scientific inquiry would lead to progress in the theory or practice of ethics.

Dewey's own summary of his conclusions states the problem succinctly:

> Our hasty sketch makes clear that there is still far from being a consensus of opinion regarding the significance for moral theory of anthropological data, or even as to the method by which these data should be utilized. Upon the whole, preexisting differences in moral theories are read over into the data and employed to interpret them (p. 19).

Dewey is able to show that anthropological evidence can be used effectively against those philosophical generalizations which entail strong empirical claims, like some theories of inevitable progress or of economic determinism.

Dewey also adduces significant support from anthropology for the recognition in ethical theory of both elements of moral relativism and of moral universalism. He believes that "relativity in the actual content of morals at different times and places is consistent with a considerable degree of stability and even of uniformity in certain generic ethical relationships and ideals" (p. 22). Dewey believes that the "two forces making for stability" are the "psychological uniformity of human nature with respect to basic *needs*" and the "conditions which must be met in order that any form of human association may be maintained" (p. 22). The methodological question for ethical naturalism which Dewey's essay leaves unresolved emerges from his review of the literature. That question is whether the adequacy of the naturalist interpretation of ethics is to receive confirmation by empirical discovery or whether its truth depends upon the conceptual clarification of moral vocabulary, that is, of its use and distinctive linguistic function in human society.

The question of the significance of conceptual or socially scientific factors in ethical theory is relevant for Dewey's approach to educational or political reform, for example, for progressive education. Generally, there are both conceptual and empirical reasons for any social preference and there were plural grounds for Dewey's championing of progressive education.

One of these grounds was his negative assessment of the traditional American public school with its rigid disciplinary rules, fixed curriculum, and formal hierarchy. As Dewey points out in his essay "Progressive Education and the Science of Education," even without any significant body of theory, it is legitimate to advocate more flexibility in discipline, innovation in curriculum, and informality and greater egalitarianism in personal and staff relations.

A second ground was Dewey's confidence in the possibility of a "science of education," in the sense of cumulative and progressive knowledge derived from a sustained program of experimental research and intellectual inquiry. The possible benefits that may be derived from such studies, including the heightened *esprit* of a professional group of educators, provide significant practical justification for such an approach. It is continuous with Dewey's assertion of heightened expectations from education.

Dewey advocated educational reform in terms of "practical idealism." One such practical formulation of an ideal was: "what the wisest and best of human parents want for their own children, that the community as a whole should want for the children of the community as a whole" (p. 284). Yet an element of Utopianism often entered into the claims of progressive education. One aspect of that Utopianism related to progress in the social sciences and was supported by a tacit Peircean model of scientific inquiry in the field of education.

In such a model, every laboratory research project or experimental class activity could represent an incremental, progressive,

and converging phase toward the ideal of a "science" of education. Yet whatever be the adequacy of the Peircean model in
those natural sciences where conflicting beliefs can be tested by
an appeal to future experimental consequences, the process of
educational theory or practice is not a realization of this model.
In practice, the phenomenon of convergence in social practice
often represents a trend of fashion or taste. This problem is not
restricted to progressive education nor is it overcome by Dewey's
personal integrity that was resistant to any argument based on
intellectual fashion. The problem of the autonomy of social scientific knowledge in contexts of application from societal trends
and fashions is a perennial and recurring one.

Finally, there is a conceptual issue raised by the debate between "traditionalists" and "progressives" in education with reference to the application of social scientific inquiry. The traditional approach to social disorder and to educational authority
is readily formulated. Every society or school is a group of persons bound together by normative laws or rules. In every society,
since the members are human, there will unavoidably be some
violators of the rules for the diverse reasons and motives that
characterize human nature. No special appeal to "original sin"
or even to the immaturity of young students is required in order
to recognize this state of affairs. Hence, there is an inescapable
place for authority, and an inevitable need for force and sanctions to maintain the rules, deter potential violators, and protect
the society.

Many of the progressive educators believed in the conceptual
framework of "causal," that is, scientific, social-psychological
analysis of the phenomenon of social disorder, intended to complement and ultimately—in the ideal school—to replace the traditional system-of-rules approach. With its basis in the vision of
the social sciences, the progressive attitude is that every social
disorder has its root causes. Since these causes are discoverable,
the shift in conceptual framework also shifts the task of social
authority from that of maintaining the rules system against its
violators to that of eliminating the causes of disorder, usually
through reform of the social environment.

Within this framework, every violation by the individual is
traceable causally to inadequacies of the institutional environment. Thus, punishing the person, when it is not an emotional

expression of retributionism, is misdirected toward the symptomatic manifestation of the causal structure. The preferred educational approach is, initially, therapeutic in order to resolve the
psychological causes of individual behavior and, ultimately, the
reformation of the social and economic structures that generate
antisocial behavior.

The dichotomy between the "rules" and the "causal" approaches which emerged in the discussion of progressive education is present in the debate on the problem of freedom and order in liberalism. For a program of "radical" liberalism, the
generalization of the line of the argument is straightforward. It
moves from confidence in the social sciences to the acceptance of
the causal determinism of psychological, social, or economic factors. On this causal basis, the practical imperative of changing
the major institutions of society in order to effect behavioral reform is derived. The issue, accordingly, is not limited to educational theory but is central to the nature of civic order or international stability.

With reference to crime and civic order, for example, one
approach would emphasize the significance of enforcing a system of deterrence of violators through their apprehension and
punishment. The other would stress the attack on the causes of
crime, through therapy or rehabilitation of the perpetrators,
who are themselves "victims" of the relevant causal factors like
poverty, discrimination, inequality, or the "acquisitive society."

A similar divergence is found on the question of international
peace and aggression. With due recognition of the disanalogies
between the civic and the international situations, one view would
stress the importance of a system of deterrence through collective security involving willingness to exercise retaliatory force.
The alternative view would stress the elimination of the causes of
international disorder, characteristically invoking abuses of human rights, or inequitable distribution of natural resources.

These competing points of view formed part of a major debate
within American society on the nature and direction of liberalism. In the 1930s, during the Depression, the debate had its focus
in issues of economic determinism and social reform. In the post-
war period, with the emergence of the United States as a major
world power, the focus of the debate shifted to questions of deterrence in foreign policy. One significant aspect of this debate in
the 1960s was the understanding of civic order as it applied to

the university as a polity or social institution. Throughout the long and ongoing history of this contest for the "soul" of liberalism, both sides have appealed to the thought of John Dewey. His social philosophy has been invoked and interpretations of his approach to moral philosophy have been used in support of both "radical" and "conservative" forms of liberalism.

With specific reference to the present volume, the relevant essay on the nature of liberalism is "Philosophies of Freedom." This essay serves as a strong antidote to any claim that Dewey's championing of the social sciences obscured his sense of individual responsibility or that his support for the idea of freedom as developmental growth weakened his concern for the strategic civil liberties of thought and expression.

In "Philosophies of Freedom," Dewey considers the idea of freedom in terms of the concept of "choice" and of "action." In a characteristically pragmatic gambit, he suggests that the examination of the concept of "choice" should be transferred "from the past to the future, from antecedents to consequences." In such a transfer, Dewey argues, the debate shifts from the question of whether men have an innate free will or are determined, to the recognition that "holding men to responsibility may make a decided difference in their *future* behavior" (p. 94). Dewey applies this point to the "educability" of human beings.

> A child as he grows older finds responsibilities thrust upon him. This is surely not because freedom of the will has suddenly been inserted in him, but because his assumption of them is a necessary factor in his *further* growth and movement (p. 94).

Dewey explicitly distinguishes his approach from that of social determinism.

> In so far as a variable life-history and intelligent insight and foresight enter into it [human action], choice signifies a capacity for deliberately changing preferences. The hypothesis that is suggested is that . . . we have before us the essential constituents of choice as freedom: the factor of individual participation (p. 96).

When Dewey turns to freedom as "action," he outlines the familiar distinction between two senses of liberty. The first is liberty as the right or power to act without governmental inhibition or group obstruction. The second is liberty as the ability to achieve one's ends or purposes that may require public action or institutional support. Advocates of liberty in the first sense have stressed the rights of free speech and free thought while they often neglected appreciation of the social conditions required for the exercise of freedom. Champions of liberty in the second sense have projected ideals of human development while they often neglected the rights of individuals.

Dewey's response to the dilemma is to stress the integration of the concepts of choice and action in the idea of freedom. Accordingly, Dewey's espousal of the idea of freedom in developmental terms is conditioned by the criterion that the development must lead to the further exercise of intelligent choice. In this way, although freedom of speech or other traditional "natural rights" are not absolute properties of human beings, they are necessary, strategic conditions for the functioning of free societies.

For Dewey, this approach is not a compromise between Lockean individualism and Hegelian developmentalism on the problem of liberty. It represents a paradigm of the possibilities available to social criticism when an open-minded empiricism recognizes the significance of the social as a category of experience. Thus, an empirical moral philosophy would not limit itself to a demonstration of ethical naturalism but would develop relevant implications for an improved educational theory or for a more balanced interpretation of liberalism.

III. *Political and Social Commentary*

Dewey's conception of philosophy as an activity of cultural criticism that is continuous with the methods of the empirical sciences has an appropriate personal exemplification in the range and intensity of his own writings on the political and social events of his time. Dewey's work exhibits his belief that a philosophical intelligence can and should approach contemporary social issues disciplined by regard for inclusiveness and coherence among values and informed by empiricism. Yet Dewey is critically aware that he observes, argues, advises, and comments as a person whose preferences, attitudes, and values are the product of his own temperament and experience and reflect his individual attitudes and tastes.

In this activity of criticism of contemporary political affairs, Dewey became the heir of a pragmatic tradition initiated by William James that was carried forward by his own students like Ernest Nagel and Sidney Hook. Since that tradition has fostered significant criticism of American political, economic, and cultural institutions, it is noteworthy that pragmatism has so often been identified by its opponents with the defense and rationalization of American society and culture.

In this volume Dewey scores that view as a myth, refuting Lewis Mumford's charge that "William James gave [the] attitude of compromise and acquiescence a name: he called it pragmatism" (p. 145). The myth of pragmatism as a philosophy of acquiescence to America has diverse roots. One of these may be a biographical accident. Pragmatism was first associated with William James, who was determined to become involved in American cultural life at a time when the question of American residence or of expatriation was significant for many of James's contemporaries or students like Henry James, Santayana, T. S. Eliot, Gertrude Stein, or C. A. Strong. Another root is the simple identification of pragmatism as an American "school" of philosophy which, in the critical view of Bertrand Russell, Georges Sorel, and the Marxists, carried with it an association with other, usually negative, features of American style.

In the case of Lewis Mumford and other cultural critics of American technology, art, or politics, there is discernible a latent motive for their hostility to pragmatism. Dewey, like James before him, was meliorist and reformist in his approach to American society. Mumford and the critics of pragmatism appealed to the vaguely sketched possibility of a more fundamental transformation of American society which would redeem it from the corruption that materialist, capitalist, and individualist history has imposed upon it.

The recognition of this melioristic and reformist attitude in James and in Dewey is consistent with an appreciation of the wide scope and intense severity of their criticism. Dewey does not consider the Sacco-Vanzetti verdict, for example, to be an isolated and tragic miscarriage of justice in a legal system relatively well insulated from prejudicial outcomes. Rather, he believes that the failure to grant clemency represents a moral flaw in "the psychology of the dominant cultivated class of the country" that is "momentous in its bearings" (p. 186).

More generally, in his essay "A Critique of American Civilization," Dewey writes

If one looks at the overt and outer phenomena, at what I may call the public and official, the externally organized, side of our life, my own feeling about it would be one of discouragement. We seem to find everywhere a hardness, a tightness, a clamping down of the lid, a regimentation and standardization, a devotion to efficiency and prosperity of a mechanical and quantitative sort (p. 134).

He continues: "Never have the forces of bigotry and intolerance been so well organized and so active." When he turns from the "domestic political scene" to international matters, Dewey is equally harsh: "That imperialistic policy is now, in an economic form, our dominating note seems to me too evident to need proof" (pp. 135, 136).

This negative survey, as Dewey himself says, reflects his appraisal of the governmental and corporate sectors of American society in the late 1920s. In contrast, Dewey is enthusiastic about the potentialities of the voluntary associations and of the private and less coordinated groups within American culture. Among these groups, Dewey singles out the nascent trade union movement. He also predicts a potentially significant cultural impact by the much greater proportion of the population that is receiving an education. Thus, Dewey criticizes forced "Americanization" and he writes that "in spite of all that is said in depreciation of those from southern and southeastern Europe, I believe that when our artistic renascence comes, it will proceed largely from this source" (p. 141). Dewey is optimistic about the changes that small professional associations of educators, scientists, social workers, and editors will have on a culture which is dominated by narrow and unimaginative corporate and management groups.

This duality of attitude between the public and the private is also found in his discussion of the role the United States should have in world affairs. Perhaps in reaction to his support of American intervention in World War I, Dewey argued against American participation in any European collective security alliance system. On the other hand, Dewey took a leading role, as this volume indicates, in movements to outlaw war, develop popular sentiment in favor of peaceful international relations, and to encourage international legal institutions for the resolution of conflict. Similarly, though Dewey is isolationist on American strategic and geo-political relations he is internationalist in academic exchange, cultural communication, and other movements that foster scientific or cultural cooperation.

A partial confirmation of this duality is found in Dewey's comments on the Chinese civil strife of 1927. Dewey had taught in China for several years and had been involved in the reformation of Chinese education. He is opposed to any American governmental intervention in China on the ground that the indigenous forces within Chinese nationalism should be left to work out their resolution of the conflicts within that society. In this volume, Dewey expresses a similar non-interventionist attitude on Nicaragua and Mexico. (It is relevant to add that the moral dilemma faced by non-interventionists, namely, that inaction may permit or encourage other potentially aggressive powers to carry out their intentions more freely—a dilemma that was posed so sharply for American decision makers in the 1930s by Germany in central Europe and Japan in China—seemed remote in 1927 and 1928.)

Dewey's reports on his visit to the Soviet Union would appear to contradict his preference for the voluntary and the private since he is appraising favorably a society whose public administration had sought to absorb so completely the private sector. Yet Dewey's enthusiasm seems directed mostly to a series of experiments in schools, cooperative factories, churches conserved as museums, or the House of Popular Culture. It is noteworthy that Dewey does not examine the institutions of governance and control in the society and remains critical of the official dogma of communist ideology. Still, it is difficult to avoid the conclusion that Dewey is another one of the long line of men of good will who permitted themselves to respond enthusiastically to the superficially attractive aspects of early Soviet institutions while ignoring the appalling human suffering and the ruthless political coercion endured by the citizens of that society. This conclusion is heightened by the impressionistic character of Dewey's positive assessment and the absence of any detailed or chronological record of the leadership or of the institutions that Dewey is praising.

Three factors, however, may be cited that place this conclusion in the context of the period. First, although the Soviet governmental apparatus violated civil liberties from the outset, and
undertook a systematic purge of the Soviet Academy of Sciences
during the very year of Dewey's visit, there were still areas of Soviet society in 1928 where cultural experimentation and some
degree of personal dynamism were shown. The history of Soviet
film and art until 1928 provides some evidence of this. It is possible therefore that Dewey was correctly reporting on some of the
still vital activities of small segments of Soviet society.

Second, on a comparative basis, Dewey's record is not an extreme one. A philosopher of an extraordinarily analytical austerity, J. L. Austin, visited the Soviet Union in the mid-thirties
and brought back his enthusiastic reaction to Oxford. (Austin
sought to extend his knowledge and asked Isaiah Berlin for recent books written by leading Soviet philosophers. The circuitous consequence of Austin's request to Berlin was their joint
teaching of a seminar on *Mind and the World-Order*, the variant
formulation of the American pragmatic position of C. I. Lewis.
Berlin has written that he believes that this was the first "class or
seminar on a contemporary thinker ever held in Oxford."[3]) Wittgenstein's visit to the Soviet Union in the 1930s led to his recurring expressions of interest in emigrating to that country. There
is nothing in Dewey, for example, that approaches the embarrassment of H. G. Wells's comment on his meeting with Stalin in
1934:

> I have never met a man more candid, fair and honest, and to
> these qualities it is, and to nothing occult and sinister, that he
> owes his tremendous undisputed ascendency in Russia. I had
> thought before I saw him that he might be where he was
> because men were afraid of him, but I realize that he owes his
> position to the fact that no one is afraid of him and every-
> body trusts him.[4]

Third, and most important, during the Moscow Trials, Dewey
agreed to participate in an examination of the evidence. The

3. Isaiah Berlin, *Personal Impressions* (New York: Viking Press, 1981), p. 107.
4. H. G. Wells, *Experiment in Autobiography* (New York: Macmillan Co.,
1934), p. 689.

facts uncovered in that inquiry, apart from confirming his prior criticism of the dogmatic character of Marxist economic determinism, led Dewey to become an informed critic of the repressive institutions of Soviet totalitarianism.

The evaluation of Dewey as a political analyst and social critic turns only secondarily, however, upon his views in foreign policy or on the Soviet Union. Dewey's primary concern is the critical shaping of events in the United States. Ironically, in light of Dewey's constant theme of anti-dualism, his own severe criticism of the public authorities seems to strike too sharp a contrast with his optimism about the voluntary sector. If it is possible to have such high expectations about the private and voluntary groups of a society, then there must be some minimal virtues in the public culture, whether governmental or corporate.

A retrospective view of the United States of the 1920s would seem to support a less dualistic reconsideration: a more realistic recognition of the limitations of the citizens of a democracy and an appreciation that American democracy had been immune from the disastrous regression into totalitarianism that took place in other cultures that had been at the center of Western Enlightenment. Dewey might well concede such a retrospective revision as the sobering moral of the unpredictable devastation of the history of our time, with its corollary levelling effect on his approach: a softening of his critical attitude to American governmental deeds and a lessening of his confidence in American group action.

Yet Dewey's writings on American culture characteristically exhibit a mix of tough-mindedness and of optimism. Consequently, even in retrospect, Dewey's contention could be that his strictures on the America of Coolidge's day were appropriately harsh just as his expectations for education and civic action were legitimate. Dewey believed that the American "spirit" was uniquely open and democratic. In the conclusion of his previously noted forceful critique of American civilization, he wrote:

> If this new spirit . . . does not already mark an attainment of a distinctive culture on the part of American civilization, and give the promise and potency of a new civilization, Columbus merely extended and diluted the Old World. But I still believe that he discovered a New World (p. 144).

Essays

Philosophy and Civilization

Volumes have been written about each term of our theme. What *is* civilization? philosophy? Yet time passes, and ambiguities and complexities cannot be eliminated by definition; we can only circumvent them by begging questions. But as to one of the terms at least, namely, philosophy, we shall frankly make what is begged explicit. A statement of the relations of philosophy to the history of civilization will, after all, only expound, in some indirect manner, the view of philosophy to which one is already committed. Unless this fact is faced, we shall not only beg the issue, but we shall deceive ourselves into thinking that we are setting forth the conclusions of an original inquiry, undertaken and executed independently of our own philosophical conceptions.

As for myself, then, the discussion is approached with the antecedent idea that philosophy, like politics, literature, and the plastic arts, is itself a phenomenon of human culture. Its connection with social history, with civilization, is intrinsic. There is current among those who philosophize the conviction that, while past thinkers have reflected in their systems the conditions and perplexities of their own day, present-day philosophy in general, and one's own philosophy in particular, is emancipated from the influence of that complex of institutions which forms culture. Bacon, Descartes, Kant, each thought with fervor that he was founding philosophy anew because he was placing it securely upon an exclusive intellectual basis, exclusive, that is, of everything but intellect. The movement of time has revealed the illusion; it exhibits as the work of philosophy the old and ever new undertaking of adjusting that body of traditions which constitute the actual mind of man to scientific tendencies and politi-

[First published in *Philosophical Review* 36 (1927): 1–9, from an address to the Sixth International Congress of Philosophy, Harvard University, 15 Sept. 1926.]

cal aspirations which are novel and incompatible with received authorities. Philosophers are parts of history, caught in its movement; creators perhaps in some measure of its future, but also assuredly creatures of its past.

Those who assert in the abstract definition of philosophy that it deals with eternal truth or reality, untouched by local time and place, are forced to admit that philosophy as a concrete existence is historical, having temporal passage and a diversity of local habitations. Open your histories of philosophy, and you find written throughout them the same periods of time and the same geographical distributions which provide the intellectual scheme of histories of politics, industry, or the fine arts. I cannot imagine a history of philosophy which did not partition its material between the Occident and the Orient; which did not find the former falling into ancient, mediaeval, and modern epochs; which in setting forth Greek thought did not specify Asiatic and Italian colonies and Athens. On the other hand, those who express contempt for the enterprise of philosophy as a sterile and monotonous preoccupation with unsolvable or unreal problems, cannot, without convicting themselves of Philistinism, deny that, however it may stand with philosophy as a revelation of eternal truths, it is tremendously significant as a revelation of the predicaments, protests, and aspirations of humanity.

The two views of the history of thought are usually proffered as unreconcilable opposites. According to one, it is the record of the most profound dealings of the reason with ultimate being; according to the other, it is a scene of pretentious claims and ridiculous failures. Nevertheless, there is a point of view from which there is something common to the two notions, and this common denominator is more significant than the oppositions. Meaning is wider in scope as well as more precious in value than is truth, and philosophy is occupied with meaning rather than with truth. Making such a statement is dangerous; it is easily misconceived to signify that truth is of no great importance under any circumstances; while the fact is that truth is so infinitely important when it is important at all, namely, in records of events and descriptions of existences, that we extend its claims to regions where it has no jurisdiction. But even as respects truths, meaning is the wider category; truths are but one class of meanings, namely, those in which a claim to verifiability by their con-

sequences is an intrinsic part of their meaning. Beyond this island of meanings which in their own nature are true or false lies
the ocean of meanings to which truth and falsity are irrelevant.
We do not inquire whether Greek civilization was true or false,
but we are immensely concerned to penetrate its meaning. We
may indeed ask for the truth of Shakespeare's *Hamlet* or Shel-
ley's "Skylark," but by truth we now signify something quite different from that of scientific statement and historical record.

In philosophy we are dealing with something comparable to
the meaning of Athenian civilization or of a drama or a lyric.
Significant history is lived in the imagination of man, and philosophy is a further excursion of the imagination into its own
prior achievements. All that is distinctive of man, marking him
off from the clay he walks upon or the potatoes he eats, occurs in
his thought and emotions, in what we have agreed to call consciousness. Knowledge of the structure of sticks and stones, an
enterprise in which, of course, truth is essential, apart from
whatever added control it may yield, marks in the end but an en-
richment of consciousness, of the area of meanings. Thus scientific thought itself is finally but a function of the imagination in
enriching life with the significance of things; it is of its peculiar
essence that it must also submit to certain tests of application
and control. Were significance identical with existence, were values the same as events, idealism would be the only possible
philosophy.

It is commonplace that physically and existentially man can
but make a superficial and transient scratch upon the outermost
rind of the world. It has become a cheap intellectual pastime to
contrast the infinitesimal pettiness of man with the vastnesses of
the stellar universes. Yet all such comparisons are illicit. We cannot compare existence and meaning; they are disparate. The
characteristic life of man is itself the meaning of vast stretches of
existences, and without it the latter have no value or significance.
There is no common measure of physical existence and conscious experience because the latter is the only measure there is
for the former. The significance of being, though not its existence, is the emotion it stirs, the thought it sustains.

It follows that there is no specifiable difference between philosophy and its role in the history of civilization. Discover and
define the right characteristic and unique function in civilization,

and you have defined philosophy itself. To try to define philosophy in any other way is to search for a will-o'-the-wisp; the conceptions which result are of purely private interpretation for they only exemplify the particular philosophies of their authorship and interpretation. Take the history of philosophy from whatever angle and in whatever cross-section you please, Indian, Chinese, Athenian, the Europe of the twelfth or the twentieth century, and you find a load of traditions proceeding from an immemorial past. You find certain preoccupying interests that appear hypnotic in their rigid hold upon imagination and you also find certain resistances, certain dawning rebellions, struggles to escape and to express some fresh value of life. The preoccupations may be political and artistic as in Athens; they may be economic and scientific as today. But in any case, there is a certain intellectual work to be done; the dominant interest working throughout the minds of masses of men has to be clarified, a result which can be accomplished only by selection, elimination, reduction, and formulation; the interest has to be intellectually forced, exaggerated, in order to be focused. Otherwise it is not intellectually in consciousness, since all clear consciousness by its very nature marks a wrenching of something from its subordinate place to confer upon it a centrality which is existentially absurd. Where there is sufficient depth and range of meanings for consciousness to arise at all, there is a function of adjustment, of reconciliation of the ruling interest of the period with preoccupations which had a different origin and an irrelevant meaning. Consider, for example, the uneasy, restless effort of Plato to adapt his new mathematical insights and his political aspirations to the traditional habits of Athens; the almost humorously complacent union of Christian supernaturalism in the Middle Ages with the naturalism of pagan Greece; the still fermenting effort of the recent age to unite the new science of nature with inherited classic and mediaeval institutions. The life of all thought is to effect a junction at some point of the new and the old, of deep-sunk customs and unconscious dispositions, that are brought to the light of attention by some conflict with newly emerging directions of activity. Philosophies which emerge at distinctive periods define the larger patterns of continuity which are woven in effecting the enduring junctions of a stubborn past and an insistent future.

Philosophy thus sustains the closest connection with the history of culture, with the succession of changes in civilization. It is fed by the streams of tradition, traced at critical moments to their sources in order that the current may receive a new direction; it is fertilized by the ferment of new inventions in industry, new explorations of the globe, new discoveries in science. But philosophy is not just a passive reflex of civilization that persists through changes, and that changes while persisting. It is itself a change; the patterns formed in this junction of the new and the old are prophecies rather than records; they are policies, attempts to forestall subsequent developments. The intellectual registrations which constitute a philosophy are generative just because they are selective and eliminative exaggerations. While purporting to say that such and such is and always *has* been the purport of the record of nature, in effect they proclaim that such and such *should* be the significant value to which mankind should loyally attach itself. Without evidence adduced in its behalf such a statement may seem groundless. But I invite you to examine for yourselves any philosophical idea which has had for any long period a significant career and find therein your own evidence. Take, for example, the Platonic patterns of cosmic design and harmony; the Aristotelian perpetually recurrent ends and grooved potentialities; the Kantian fixed forms of intellectual synthesis; the conception of nature itself as it figured in seventeenth and eighteenth century thought. Discuss them as revelations of eternal truth, and something almost childlike or something beyond possibility of decision enters in; discuss them as selections from existing culture by means of which to articulate forces which the author believed should and would dominate the future, and they become preciously significant aspects of human history.

Thus philosophy marks a change of culture. In forming patterns to be conformed to in future thought and action, it is additive and transforming in its role in the history of civilization. Man states anything at his peril; once stated, it occupies a place in a new perspective; it attains a permanence which does not belong to its existence; it enters provokingly into wont and use; it points in a troubling way to need of new endeavors. I do not mean that the creative element in the role of philosophy is necessarily the dominant one; obviously its formulations have been often chiefly conservative, justificatory of selected elements of traditions and received institutions. But even these preservative systems have had a transforming if not exactly a creative effect; they have lent the factors which were selected a power over later human imagination and sentiment which they would otherwise have lacked. And there are other periods, such as those of the seventeenth and eighteenth centuries in Europe, when philosophy is overtly revolutionary in attitude. To their authors, the turn was just from complete error to complete truth; to later generations looking back, the alteration in strictly factual content does not compare with that in desire and direction of effort.

Of the many objections which may be brought against the conception that philosophy not only *has* a role, but that it *is* a specifiable role in the development of human culture, there are two misconceptions which I wish to touch upon. What has been said, taken without qualifying additions, might suggest a picture of a dominant system of philosophy at each historic period. In fact there are diverse currents and aspirations in almost every historic epoch; the divergence of philosophic systems instead of being a reproach (as of course it is from the standpoint of philosophy as a revelation of truth) is evidence of sincerity and vitality. If the ruling and the oppressed elements in a population, if those who wished to maintain the *status quo* and those concerned to make changes, had, when they became articulate, the same philosophy, one might well be skeptical of its intellectual integrity. The other point is much more important. In making a distinction between meaning and truth and asserting that the latter is but one type of meaning, important under definite conditions, I have expressed the idea as if there might be in the processes of human life meanings which are wholly cut off from the actual course of events. Such is not the intent; meanings are generated and in some degree sustained by existence. Hence they cannot be wholly irrelevant to the world of existence; they all have some revelatory office which should be apprehended as correctly as possible. This is true of politics, religion, and art as well as of philosophy. They all tell something of the realm of existence. But in all of them there is an exuberance and fertility of meanings and values in comparison with which correctness of telling is a secondary affair, while in the function termed science accuracy of telling is the chief matter.

In the historic role of philosophy, the scientific factor, the element of correctness, of verifiable applicability, has a place, but it is a negative one. The meanings delivered by confirmed observation, experimentation, and calculation, scientific facts and principles, serve as tests of the values which tradition transmits and of those which emotion suggests. Whatever is not compatible with them must be eliminated in any sincere philosophizing. This fact confers upon scientific knowledge an incalculably important office in philosophy. But the criterion is negative; the exclusion of the inconsistent is far from being identical with a positive test which demands that only what has been scientifically verifiable shall provide the entire content of philosophy. It is the difference between an imagination that acknowledges its responsibility to meet the logical demands of ascertained facts, and a complete abdication of all imagination in behalf of a prosy literalism.

Finally, it results from what has been said that the presence and absence of native born philosophies is a severe test of the depth of unconscious tradition and rooted institutions among any people, and of the productive force of their culture. For sake of brevity, I may be allowed to take our own case, the case of civilization in the United States. Philosophy, we have been saying, is a conversion of such culture as exists into consciousness, into an imagination which is logically coherent and is not incompatible with what is factually known. But this conversion is itself a further movement of civilization; it is not something performed upon the body of habits and tendencies from without, that is, miraculously. If American civilization does not eventuate in an imaginative formulation of itself, if it merely re-arranges the figures already named and placed, in playing an inherited European game, that fact is itself the measure of the culture which we have achieved. A deliberate striving for an American Philosophy as such would be only another evidence of the same emptiness and impotency. There is energy and activity among us, enough and to spare. Not an inconsiderable part of the vigor that once went into industrial accomplishment now finds its way into science; our scientific "plant" is coming in its way to rival our industrial plants. Especially in psychology and the social sciences an amount of effort is putting forth which is hardly equalled in any one other part of the world. He would be a shameless braggart who claimed that the result is as yet adequate to the activity. What is the matter? It lies, I think, with our lack of imagination in generating leading ideas. Because we are afraid of speculative ideas, we do, and do over and over again, an immense amount of dead, specialized work in the region of "facts." We forget that such facts are only data; that is, are only fragmentary, uncompleted meanings, and unless they are rounded out into complete ideas—a work which can only be done by hypotheses, by a free imagination of intellectual possibilities—they are as helpless as are all maimed things and as repellent as are needlessly thwarted ones.

Please do not imagine that this is a plea in disguise for any particular type of philosophizing. On the contrary, any philosophy which is a sincere outgrowth and expression of our own civilization is better than none, provided it speaks the authentic idiom of an enduring and dominating corporate experience. If we are really, for instance, a materialistic people, we are at least materialistic in a new fashion and on a new scale. I should welcome then a consistent materialistic philosophy, if only it were sufficiently bold. For in the degree in which, despite attendant aesthetic repulsiveness, it marked the coming to consciousness of a group of ideas, it would formulate a coming to self-consciousness of our civilization. Thereby it would furnish ideas, supply an intellectual polity, direct further observations and experiments, and organize their results on a grand scale. As long as we worship science and are afraid of philosophy we shall have no great science; we shall have a lagging and halting continuation of what is thought and said elsewhere. As far as any plea is implicit in what has been said, it is, then, a plea for the casting off of that intellectual timidity which hampers the wings of imagination, a plea for speculative audacity, for more faith in ideas, sloughing off a cowardly reliance upon those partial ideas to which we are wont to give the name of facts. I have given to philosophy a more humble function than that which is often assigned it. But modesty as to its final place is not incompatible with boldness in the maintenance of that function, humble as it may be. A combination of such modesty and courage affords the only way I know of in which the philosopher can look his fellow man in the face with frankness and with humanity.

Anthropology and Ethics

Problems

The relationship of anthropological material to ethics presents a double problem. On the one hand, there is the question of the influence of more primitive practices and ideas upon subsequent development of practice. Tradition and transmission operate perhaps nowhere else as powerfully as they do in morals. This matter, however, belongs to the history of culture, and is too vast a subject to fall under present consideration. One of its phases, however, comes within the theoretical field which is our immediate concern. Many writers tend to exaggerate the differences which mark off the more primitive cultures from those with which we are familiar to-day. Accordingly, when similarities are found they are disposed of as "survivals" of early ideas and customs. As a matter of fact, there is hardly a phase of primitive culture which does not recur in some field or aspect of life to-day. For the most part, tradition does not operate and "survivals" do not occur except where the older beliefs and attitudes correspond to some need and condition which still exist. To put it briefly, the reign of animistic ideas, of the magic and ceremonialism which are sometimes considered to be exclusively or at least peculiarly primitive, is due to modes of feeling, thought, and action which mark permanent traits of human nature psychologically viewed. The important phenomenon is not survival, but the rise of scientific, technological, and other interests and methods which have gradually and steadily narrowed the extent and reduced the power of what is primitive in a psychological sense.

[First published in *The Social Sciences and Their Interrelations*, ed. William Fielding Ogburn and Alexander Goldenweiser (Boston: Houghton Mifflin Co., 1927), pp. 24–36.]

Influence on Theories

The other and narrower question concerns the influence
of knowledge of anthropological and ethnological material upon
the formulation of ethical theories and doctrines. What does
such material have to teach those who now theorize upon moral
problems? What use has already been made by ethical theorists
of this material? Since anthropology is distinctly a recent science, this question is still a relatively new one, and it is not surprising that there is still a great lack of consensus in results.
Indeed, the larger phases of the problem and its conflicting solutions were anticipated long before any such rich store of data
was at hand as now exists. The Greeks came into contact with a
variety of peoples, and their ever avid curiosity was aroused by
the variety and contrariety of practices and beliefs with which
they made acquaintance. They were led to formulate the question whether there was a natural and sure basis of morals, or
whether morals were wholly a matter of "convention," that is, of
local customs, enactments, and agreements; or, as we might say
to-day, whether there was some absolute and unchanging element or whether morals were wholly relativistic. Both answers
were given; and, as to-day, the upholders of the natural or intrinsic view pointed to the fact, or alleged fact, that amid all the diversity there were certain factors common to all peoples. And,
somewhat like theorists of the present time, they were divided in
their explanation of this universal element, some attributing it to
the presence of the same reason in all men—in modern language,
a faculty of conscience or intuition—while others took a more
objective ground and held that certain virtues and rules of obligation were necessarily involved in the constitution of any kind
of community or social life.

Another example of the use by moral theorists of unorganized
anthropological data is found in the lively controversy of the seventeenth and later centuries between the empirical and the a priori schools of philosophy. Thus, we find John Locke (1632–
1704), in his polemic against innate ideas, asserting that "he who
will look abroad into the several tribes of men . . . will be able to
satisfy himself that there is scarce any principle of morality to be
named . . . which is not somewhere slighted and condemned by
the general fashion of whole bodies of men," and citing from re-

ports of missionaries and travelers in support of this proposition. Similar material of a popular rather than a scientific kind supplied the stock argument of relativistic and empirical theories of morals for a long period afterwards.

Kropotkin

The rise of the theory of evolution in the later nineteenth century operated, however, in such a way as to stimulate a more scientific treatment of primitive morals and to promote a systematic, rather than a merely controversial, use of the growing mass of anthropological data. Prince Kropotkin's writings are typical of one phase of the evolutionary school. In his *Mutual Aid* he endeavored to show that reciprocal assistance is a fundamental factor in the evolution of the higher forms of animal life. By emphasizing this factor he found the sub-human basis of morals not in an antagonistic struggle of organisms and species against one another, but in the instincts of sociality developed through cooperation. In his *Ethics, Origin and Development*, he carried this principle further in accounting for the main concepts of human ethics. Primitive man, living in close contact with animals, keen observer of their habits, and attributing to them superior wisdom, was struck with the unified group action exhibited by animals. The first vague generalization made regarding nature was that a living being and its clan or tribe were inseparable. Thus, the instinct of sociability inherited from lower animals was made into a conscious idea and sentiment. Sociality and mutual aid were such general and habitual facts that men were not able to imagine life under any other aspect. The conditions of their own existence were such as to absorb the "I" in the clan or tribe. The self-assertion of "personality" came much later. In the constant, ever-present identification of the unit with the whole, lies the origin of all ethics. Out of it developed the idea of the equality of all members of the tribal whole, which is the root idea of justice, equity.

Kropotkin then endeavors to prove that early peoples had not merely certain lines of conduct which were honored (and their opposites shamed and ridiculed), but also certain modes which were obligatory in principle, and which in fact were rarely violated in practice. He finds, on the basis of the Aleuts of North Alaska, that there were three main categories of obligatory tribal regulation. One concerned the usages established for securing the means of livelihood for each individual and for the tribe as a whole. Then there were the rules relating to the status of members within the tribe; such as rules for marriage, for the treatment of the young and of the old, for education, and the regulations for preventing and remedying acute personal collisions. Finally, there are the rules relating to sacred matters. Kropotkin's general conclusion is that there is no tribe which has not its definite and complicated moral code. His specific conclusion is that there is a definite notion of equity or fairness and means of restoring equality when it has been infringed upon, and also that there is universal regard for life and condemnation of murder within the tribe—that is, of fratricide. The chief limitation of morals in this period is the restriction in most respects to those within the group, though some regulations pertain to inter-tribal relations.

Subsequent development is not altogether of the nature of advance. The absence of adequate inter-tribal regulations led to war, and war strengthened the power of the military leaders, which had an unfavorable effect upon equality and justice. The same effect was produced by the growth of wealth and the division into rich and poor, with increase of industrial skill. Moreover, the elders who were in possession of the tribal traditions in which regulations were contained, tended to form themselves into a distinct and secret class which was the germ of ecclesiastic power. In time this class united its power and authority with that of the rulers established on a military basis. The actual evolution of morals can be studied only in connection with such changes in social life as they specifically take place—that is, within definite social groups. However, there remains the one outstanding fact that notions of good and evil were evolved on the basis of what was thought good and bad for the whole group, not just for separate individuals. It is to be regretted that Prince Kropotkin did not live to undertake such a study himself, as his method of studying moral practices and ideas in definite connection with the life of particular groups is undoubtedly sounder than that of writers who use anthropological data and adopt a purely comparative method, selecting in a miscellaneous group common ideas from different peoples without adequate control by the study of the total situation of each people as an organized whole.

Westermarck

The massive work of Westermarck on *The Origin and Development of the Moral Ideas* presents a larger body of anthropological data in connection with morals than can be found elsewhere, but its value is unfortunately somewhat vitiated by the uncritical adoption of an uncontrolled comparative method. His starting-point is also one-sidedly psychological. He finds that the basic moral factor in evolution springs not from the social relations out of which sentiments and ideas grow, but from the sentiments of praise and blame. These sentiments are akin to gratitude and anger or resentment, but are differentiated from the latter by not being purely personal. They have a disinterestedness and impartiality and quasi-objectivity lacking in the latter, for they are *sympathetic*. That is, they are felt on behalf of others, and of one's self as commanding the sympathetic support of others. Custom is recognized as the great factor in determining the objects and contents toward which sympathetic approval and resentment are directed. Westermarck, however, reasons in a circle in holding that custom is the factor which makes gratitude and resentment impartial and disinterested, while still holding that custom is a moral principle only because its maintenance arouses approval and its breach, resentment. The circle is significant because it follows necessarily from his excessively psychological and subjective starting-point. Westermarck, however, undoubtedly supplements in a desirable way the objective sociological methods of writers like Prince Kropotkin and the French school of Durkheim and Lévy-Bruhl by his introduction of emotional favor and resentment. However, it cannot be said that Westermarck derives his starting-point from an unbiased consideration of anthropological material. He sets out, rather, from contemporary philosophical ethical theory which since the time of Hume has been divided, at least as far as English thought is concerned, into moral theorists who make emotion primary and those who give that position to reason. Kropotkin also was influenced by contemporary issues, as his desire to find equity or equality a primary idea is connected with his bias in favor of economic communism.

Wundt

Wundt makes considerable use of anthropological data in his *Ethics*, but he is even more influenced by the traditions of philosophic ethics. He is especially concerned in showing the importance of reflection, of a somewhat abstract kind, in the development of moral conceptions, and thus to make out that only the *materials* out of which moral conceptions were later formed by scientific and philosophic reflection were found in primitive race-consciousness—not the ideas themselves. He emphasizes the fact that the objects of primitive approbation and blame— which, like Westermarck, he takes to be primary in at least the genetic order—were mainly sensible and outward, while later ideas are reflective and inward. In spite of this fact he holds that man has always had a moral endowment, the germs of later developments being found in early practices and ideas. The actual evolution has been determined by two forces—religious conceptions and social customs and legal norms.

Wundt's bias toward "intellectualism" appears in his notion that the metaphysical element predominates in religions, namely, some kind of theory regarding the universe and human relation to it. So considered, the ideal objects which are involved in religion, especially the ideas of the gods, have served a double moral purpose: they have supplied exemplars and patterns of conduct, and through their connection with a system of rewards and punishments, they have operated as the guardians and executors of moral laws. In custom, also, there is a marked intellectual factor, since human customs involve dependence upon tradition and transmitted material; which means that they demand consciousness of the past and an outlook upon the future. A custom is thus a norm of *voluntary* action. It is intermediate between morality, properly speaking, and law—akin to morals in having at disposal a subjective disposition in the individual to conform, and akin to law in using objective means of compulsion. Gradually the two strains diverged, and only after this divergence can we clearly discriminate morals from law. In detail Wundt considers, in their bearings upon moral development, customs relating to food, habitation, clothing, work, service of others by labor, play, courtesy, rules of intercourse, greeting, etc., and the definite social forms of family, tribal, and civic life. In spite of all change of detail, these *relations* remain constant and thus supply a factor of genuine moral continuity to the variety of customs which history exhibits. Moreover, there are two constants upon the psychological side, namely, reverence and affections. The first finds expression originally on the religious and supernatural side, the latter, on the human side. But they gradually became interconnected. The outcome is that we can mark out three stages of ethical evolution. In the first, the social impulses are confined within a narrow area, and the things which are regarded as virtues are chiefly external qualities that are of obvious advantage. In the second stage, the social feelings, under the influence of religious ideas and feelings which interact with them, come to explicit recognition, and virtues are connected with internal dispositions of a socially directed character, while, however, social objects are limited to local or national groups. In the third stage, the influence of philosophy and religion makes the objects universal, as wide as humanity, and disposition undergoes a corresponding change.

Hobhouse

The subtitle of Hobhouse's *Morals in Evolution* is *A Study in Comparative Ethics*, and in his attempt to trace the development of morality he necessarily draws largely upon anthropological material. Hobhouse regards the idea of *good* as the central and unifying theme of morals, so that the evolution of morals is an evolution of the content assigned to this idea and of the means by which the assigned content is realized. Hobhouse raises more explicitly than other writers the question of the exact relation between sociological and moral development, and concludes that while they are intimately connected, no social development is moral save as it *expresses*, and not merely influences, the idea of good, either in its content or in the area of its application. Thus, most primitive peoples exhibit customs of equal treatment and mutual regard, but since among most peoples these customs existed as a mere fact rather than as a conscious idea, they were submerged by the rise of differences between rich and poor. The Hebrews, on the contrary, grasped the institutions as an idea, and hence were enabled to maintain them against the sociological forces which brought about a division into rich and poor. According to Hobhouse, the factors which have determined ethical evolution have been, first, the form of social organization, and, secondly, the forms of scientific and philosophic thought, including under these headings popular beliefs such as are found in myth and magic. On the social side, morals are correlated respectively with primitive family life, organized clan life, the city-state, the empire, the territorial national state. The intellectual correlation affords an opportunity for a consideration of early animism and magic. In general, the force behind custom, according to Hobhouse, is at first mainly non-ethical, namely, the belief in magic and fear of revengeful spirits. Hence guilt, involving liability to these influences, is removed by non-moral means, such as incantations, purifications, and a technique of appeasements. This stage is paralleled on the social side by the fact that wrongs are first thought of as occasions of vengeance on the part of the injured man's kin, and "justice" arises not for a moral purpose but for the sake of averting, or buying off, a feud which is harmful. But when society gradually became interested in maintaining social peace, it developed an idea of right and wrong, and not simply of harm and liability to vengeance; in a similar way there developed in religion the ideas of spirits who have an interest in protecting the helpless, the guest, the suppliant, and in punishing a murderer simply because he is a murderer. Hobhouse concludes that there are four stages of moral development, or at least one pre-moral, and three ethical. In the first, customary rules obtain, but they have no character of moral laws. Secondly, specific moral obligations are recognized but without being founded on any general moral principle. In the third stage, generalized ideals and standards are formed, but without knowledge of their basis or function. In the fourth, reflection extends to discovering the needs of human life that are served by morals, and the function of serving these needs which forms of conduct, personal and institutional, exercise, so that there is a reflective criterion for judging modes of behavior and institutions which profess to be ethical.

Conclusions

Our hasty sketch makes clear that there is still far from being a consensus of opinion regarding the significance for moral theory of anthropological data, or even as to the method by which these data should be utilized. Upon the whole, preexisting differences in moral theories are read over into the data and employed to interpret them. However, certain converging tendencies may be made out.

First, part of the diversity is due to a desire, which cannot be realized in any case, to differentiate sharply between moral conceptions and practices, on the one side, and manners and economic, domestic, religious, legal, and political relations on the other. In early peoples these traits are so fused that attempts to mark out what is distinctively moral become arbitrary, the writer having to use some criterion which appeals to him at the present time as peculiarly ethical in character. Certain phases of conduct have in the course of time become associated with distinctive, even explicit moral ideas. But this holds for popular practices and beliefs of the present time much less than theoretical moralists suppose. In other words, present as well as early morals are largely a complex blend, and the ideas taken for granted and expounded by theorists have had but little effect on popular consciousness, except when associated with religion and law—which again illustrates a feature of primitive morals. In short, the great demand on the part of moral theory is first an objective study of the types of conduct prevailing in early societies, without any attempt at artificial divisions into morals, religion, law, and manners, and secondly, a history of the transmission and modification of these habits of life, within groups and in their contacts with one another. This is an immense task and will be accomplished but slowly.

Secondly, the emotional factor in conduct is found to be universal and intense. For the very reason, however, that it is a constant, expressing inborn psychological traits, it cannot be appealed to in explanation of differences nor of historical changes. They must be sought for rather in change of institutions and in intellectual changes—theological, philosophical, scientific.

Thirdly, while at various times the effect of modes of industry and commerce upon conduct has been very great, there is no justification for an a priori assumption of economic determinism. As a rule, its importance in early groups is relatively slight, once the demand for necessities has been met. The rise and wane of economic forces in influence is a topic for specific historic study and analysis, the same as that of any other factor. The institution of slavery, for example, has had an undoubted importance for ethics, and the origin of slavery is chiefly economic, since prior to settled agrarian life a slave was more of a liability than an asset. But military conquest, sentiments of honor and superiority, and sexual motives have also played a part in originating human slavery, and the institution once established is persisted in on other than economic grounds, after, indeed, it has become demonstrably an uneconomic device. In general, a purely economic explanation of any primitive social institution, as marriage or myths, is to be regarded with suspicion.

Fourthly, neither side in the controversy as to whether the direction of ethical development has been away from or toward greater individuality, is unambiguously borne out by the facts. The romantic notion of the eighteenth century that the savage is a type of free and independent man, is obviously contradicted by facts. On the other hand, extreme, or at least ambiguous, statements have been made about the enslavement of early men to custom. They were enslaved from *our* standpoint; but they took the customs for granted as part of the necessary conditions of life (just as we, for example, do not feel the necessity of breathing air as a restriction on freedom), and hence probably had less sense of impeded freedom than modern men. For we, with a multiplication of personal wants and aspirations, are much more sensitively aware of constraints. It can also still be said of us that there are many customs which are so much part and parcel of our lives that we are not aware of them, or at least not aware of them as hindrances, while to our descendants they may appear to have been intolerably oppressive. Thus, present economic conditions may appear in the future to have been even more constraining in the case of the well-to-do than among the poor where restriction of freedom is now alone alleged.

No Single Development

The entire question of ethical evolution or progress is often put ambiguously. There is no doubt of the failure to establish uniform and universal stages of moral development. It may also be doubted whether the attempt to discriminate a single continuous line of moral development can be successful when understood in a philosophical sense rather than as literal historic sequences. On the one hand, there are certain basic needs and relations which remain fairly constant. On the other hand, the conditions under which the needs are expressed and satisfied and the relations of man to man are sustained, undergo immense modifications. That there has been, for example, progress in scientific method and knowledge, there can be no doubt; there has been advance in economic invention and control; there has been progress in the complexity and delicacy of legal and political institutions. But these very advances have so complicated conduct, have introduced so many new problems and afforded so many new ways of going wrong, that they cannot be identified with progress in actual morality. These changes have raised the plane upon which conduct operates; they have elevated the quality of ideals and standards; but by this very fact they have multiplied the opportunities for transgressions and shortcomings. Hence the meaning of moral evolution and progress needs to be carefully defined by discrimination between two distinct matters— change of the level upon which all conduct, good and bad alike, goes on, and actual right and wrong in conduct judged by conditions prevailing at the time.

If we speak of the former as a moral evolution we must recognize that it has not been for the most part brought about by distinctively moral causes, but rather by intellectual changes, the operation of new political and economic conditions, and so forth, which have so modified habits of life as to bring about an extension of the scope of previous moral concepts and a refinement of their content. Certain forms of industry and commerce, for example, effect a great widening of the area of human inter-course, and multiply contacts among people previously sepa-rated. In consequence, previous moral ideas as to obligations and rights have to be generalized, and the attempt at generaliza-tion modifies somewhat the nature of the ideas. A like effect is brought about by scientific changes. Thus, the older association of moral practices with certain religious ideas has been broken into more than once by the rise of philosophical and scientific criticism, and in consequence the content of moral ideas has been enlarged and altered so as to be capable of statement inde-pendently of particular religious beliefs. If we use morals in a narrow sense, it probably must be denied that there has been a distinctively moral development; if we use the term in the wider sense, it becomes merged in the general theme of the changes of human culture.

Relativity and Stability

It follows that great relativity in the actual content of morals at different times and places is consistent with a consider-able degree of stability and even of uniformity in certain generic ethical relationships and ideals. Changes have arisen, as just in-dicated, chiefly from sources not usually termed moral in them-selves—science, politics, industry, and art. Within the content of morals proper there are at least two forces making for stability. One is the psychological uniformity of human nature with re-spect to basic *needs*. However much men differ in other respects, they remain alike in requiring food, protection, sex-mates, rec-ognition of some sort, companions, and need for constructive and manipulative activities, and so forth. The uniformity of these needs is at the basis of the exaggerated statements often made about the unchangeability of human nature; it is sufficient to ensure the constant recurrence, under change of form, of cer-tain moral patterns. In the second place, there are certain condi-tions which must be met in order that any form of human associ-ation may be maintained, whether it be simple or complex, low or high in the scale of cultures. Some degree of peace, order, and internal harmony must be secured if men are to live together at all.

In consequence of these two factors of comparative invariance, the extreme statements sometimes made about the relativity of morals cannot be maintained. Yet we do not have to resort to non-empirical considerations to explain the degree of uniformity that is found. There is no society without its modes of shared approval and disapproval, and hence none without an idea of the opposed characters of good and bad. Variations in content are great, but they spring from technological and other methods at command by which needs are satisfied, and from detailed differences in social structure. There is no community which does not regard that which contributes to its social needs and perpetuity as good. There is none which does not strongly condemn conduct which prevents satisfaction of common needs and which renders social relations unstable. Thus, there is universal condemnation of murder, if murder be defined as the taking of the life of a brother, or of a social member within the group. The exceptions that exist are not dissimilar to those which now exist in respect to taking of life by public officials, or in self-defense, or in war. They are simply not thought of as murder. Even the statements which are made about lack of regard for property have to be critically scanned. We have first to know whether and in what respects private property is a contemporary institution, how far thrift is subordinate to generosity, the relative status of the persons involved, and so forth. Till very recently, those who have insisted upon uniformity have usually done so because they thought it was evidence of a common transcendental basis for morals, while those believing in an empirical and a naturalistic basis have felt obliged to seek for and emphasize divergencies. As fast as this motive disappears, we may expect consensus of opinion to grow up concerning uniformity and divergence of morals at different periods, especially if the loose comparative method gives way to a study of the correlations within particular cultures.

Selected References

Bastian, Adolph. *Der Mensch in der Geschichte.*
Dewey, J., and Tufts, J. H. *Ethics*, part I. 1908 [*Middle Works 5*].
Dickinson, Z. C. *Economic Motives*. 1922.
Frazer, J. G. *The Golden Bough*. 3d ed. 1911–25.

Goldenweiser, A. A. *Early Civilization*. 1922.

Harrison, J. E. *Prolegomena to the Study of Greek Religion*. 1908.

Hobhouse, L. T. *Morals in Evolution*. 3d ed. 1915.

Jastrow, Morris. *Aspects of Religious Belief and Practice in Babylonia and Assyria*. 1911.

Kohler, Josef. A series of articles upon "Recht" in various primitive peoples, in the *Zeitschrift für vergleichende Rechtswissenschaft*, XI, XIV, XV.

Kropotkin, P. *Mutual Aid*. 1919.

         Ethics, Origin and Development. 1924 *trans*.

Letourneau, Charles. *L'Évolution de la morale*. 1894.

Maine, Sir Henry. *Early Law and Custom*. 1891 ed.

Maspero, Sir Gaston. *Dawn of Civilization*. 1896.

Petrie, Sir Wm. Flinders. *Religion and Conscience in Ancient Egypt*. 1898.

Post, A. H. *Afrikanische Jurisprudenz*. 1887.

Rée, Paul. *Die Entstehung des Gewissens*. 1885.

Schmidt, L. V. *Die Ethik der alten Griechen*. 1882.

Smith, W. Robertson. *Lectures on the Religion of the Semites*. 1894.

Spencer, Herbert. *Principles of Ethics*, part II. Introduction.

         Principles of Sociology. 1923 ed.

Steinmetz, Sebald. *Ethnologische Studien zur ersten Entwicklung der Strafe*. 1894.

Veblen, Thorstein. *Instinct of Workmanship*. 1914.

Westermarck, E. A. *The Origin and Development of Moral Ideas*. 2 vols. 1908.

Wundt, W. *Philosophische Studien*, vol. IV. 1888.

Body and Mind[1]

There was a time when philosophy, science and the arts, medicine included, were much closer together than they have been since. For both philosophy and the sciences were conceived and begotten of the arts. It was once their aspiration to find their issue in arts; the sciences in arts of the special branches of life and philosophy in the comprehensive art of the wise conduct of life as a whole.

There is a contemporary philosophic movement, popularly known as pragmatism, which, discontented with the current separation of theory and practise, knowledge and action, regards thought and the beliefs which proceed from it as themselves modes of action and strives to envisage them in their directive office in conduct. This movement is often regarded as a heresy, indeed as a novel and peculiarly American heresy indicative of an insensate love of keeping busy, no matter how. But in truth it marks a return to the idea of philosophy which prevailed when reflective thought was young and lusty, eager to engage in combat in the public arena, instead of living a sheltered and protected life. In those days science and philosophy had not parted ways because neither of them was cut loose from the arts. One word designated both science and art: technē. The desire was to command practises that were rational and a reason embodied in practise. During the almost countless ages of prior human history men had pursued the arts thoughtlessly, relying upon the bare accumulation of accidental successes, without paying heed to causes and reasons. In consequence, the arts were routines, devoted to separate ends and meeting only in a common medium of magic and supernatural belief.

1. Read at the Eighty-first Anniversary Meeting of the New York Academy of Medicine, November 17, 1927.

[First published in *Bulletin of the New York Academy of Medicine* 4 (1928): 3–19, and in *Mental Hygiene* 12 (1928): 1–17.]

The Greeks define an epoch in the history of civilization because they turned back to examine these routines and accidents, and made it their business to discover the principles which underlay them in order that they might reincarnate them in a more intelligent pursuit of ends. In liberating the arts from routine and blind accumulation, they gave birth to science; in view of this achievement there arose the idea of an art of life based upon the most comprehensive insight into the relationships between conditions and ends. Medicine was one of the first-fruits of the scientific emancipation, and, since the Greeks recognized the necessity of a sound mind in a sound body for the conduct of life in its wholeness, medicine and philosophy were in close alliance.

The relevant facts are exhibited in the history of the school of Hippocrates. Philosophy appears in it as search for a whole which shall bind together a mass of otherwise disconnected details; while the spirit of science was operative in loving, patient and prolonged search for facts and their significance, and the medical art was the use of the knowledge and insight thus attained. The union of these three things is seen in the school's glorification of technē; in its criticism of other schools of physicians for studying symptoms in isolation and multiplying diseases and remedies; in its emphasis upon prognosis by which was meant not just a prediction of outcome but a reconstruction of the entire course of a disease; in study of health and disease in relation to environment, climate, seasons and seasonal variations, air, water and soil, while the oath of Hippocrates endures as evidence that human and social ties were included in the wide and searching vision. What at first sight may seem to be an attack upon mingling philosophy and medicine turns out upon closer inspection to be an attack upon basing medicine upon a narrow philosophical foundation. For the school, borrowing from Heracleitus, Empedocles and Pythagoras, insisted upon the measured harmony of all elements as the conditions of maintaining and restoring health. As Hippocrates said: "We cannot understand the body without a knowledge of the whole of things." And again, speaking of epilepsy and other disorders regarded as sacred and hence treated by means of magical incantations, he said: "These maladies, like all other things, are divine, and yet no one thing is any more divine than another. For all things alike are divine and yet each one of them has its own natural being and proceeds from a natural cause."

We may indeed now smile at the crudeness of their philosophy and science and in view of this crudeness be led to deplore the connection of philosophy, science and medical art. The disparagement of the union may readily become more pronounced when we consider the later development of various medical schools, the dogmatic, empirical, methodistic and pneumatistic, each allied with a particular school of philosophic thought. But objection is really directed against the crude state of knowledge and culture at the time, a state of which both philosophy and medicine were victims. The philosophic spirit at least kept alive the sense of need for general principles and aided in preventing relapse into the earlier crude empiricism.

This introduction is overlong, and may indeed not seem to be at all an introduction to the special topic of the evening, the relations of body and mind. But it was in the course of such reflections that I was led to this topic as a fitting theme. For the conspicuous trait of the period in which science, philosophy and the arts were closely connected was the sense of wholeness, while the very problem of mind and body suggests the disastrous effect of the divisions that have since grown up. I do not know of anything so disastrously affected by the tradition of separation and isolation as is this particular theme of body-mind. In its discussion are reflected the splitting off from each other of religion, morals and science; the divorce of philosophy from science and of both from the arts of conduct. The evils which we suffer in education, in religion—for example the fundamentalist attack about the evolution of men rests upon the idea of complete separation of mind and body—in the materialism of business and the aloofness of "intellectuals" from life, the whole separation of knowledge and practise:—all testify to the necessity of seeing mind-body as an integral whole.

The division in question is so deep-seated that it has affected even our language. We have no word by which to name mind-body in a unified wholeness of operation. For if we said "human life" few would recognize that it is precisely the unity of mind and body in action to which we were referring. Consequently when we discuss the matter, when we talk of the relations of mind *and* body and endeavor to establish their unity in human conduct, we still speak of body *and* mind and thus unconsciously perpetuate the very division we are striving to deny. I shall make no attempt to consider all the various theories which

have developed in discussing their relation: panpsychism, epiphenomenalism, pre-established harmony, interactionism, parallelism, etc. I shall not even try to prove the unity. I shall beg that
question and devote the time to stating the nature of the unity
and considering some of the causes which work against recognition of it.

I have used, in passing, the phrases "wholeness of operation,"
"unity in action." What is implied in them gives the key to the
discussion. In just the degree in which action, behavior, is made
central, the traditional barriers between mind and body break
down and dissolve. Were this the fit time and place, it could be
shown, I think, that the habit of regarding the mental and physical as separate things has its roots in regarding them as substances or processes instead of as functions and qualities of action. In contrast to such a notion, it is asserted that when we take
the standpoint of human action, of life in operation, body presents itself as the mechanism, the instrumentality of behavior,
and mind as its function, its fruit and consummation. To the interpretation of this statement our further remarks are given.

When we take the standpoint of action we may still treat some
functions as primarily physical and others as primarily mental.
Thus we think of, say, digestion, reproduction and locomotion
as conspicuously physical, while thinking, desiring, hoping, loving, fearing are distinctively mental. Yet if we are wise we shall
not regard the difference as other than one of degree and emphasis. If we go beyond this and draw a sharp line between them,
consigning one set to body exclusively and the other to mind exclusively we are at once confronted by undeniable facts. The
being who eats and digests is also the one who at the same time
is sorrowing and rejoicing; it is a commonplace that he eats and
digests in one way to one effect when glad, and to another when
he is sad. Eating is also a social act and the emotional temper of
the festal board enters into the alleged merely physical function
of digestion. Eating of bread and drinking of wine have indeed
become so integrated with the mental attitudes of multitudes of
persons that they have assumed a sacramental spiritual aspect.
There is no need to pursue this line of thought to other functions
which are sometimes termed exclusively physical. The case of
taking and assimilating food is typical. It is an act in which
means employed are physical while the quality of the act deter-

mined by its consequences is also mental. The trouble is that instead of taking the act in its entirety we cite the multitude of relevant facts only as evidence of influence of mind on body and of body on mind, thus starting from and perpetuating the idea of their independence and separation even when dealing with their connection. What the facts testify to is not an influence exercised across and between two separate things, but to behavior so integrated that it is artificial to split it up into two things.

The more human mankind becomes, the more civilized it is, the less is there some behavior which is purely physical and some other purely mental. So true is this statement that we may use the amount of distance which separates them in our society as a test of the lack of human development in that community. There exists in present society, especially in industry, a large amount of activity that is almost exclusively mechanical; it is carried on with a minimum of thought and of accompanying emotion. There is a large amount of activity especially in "intellectual" and "religious" groups in which the physical factor is at a minimum and what little there is is regretted as a deplorable necessity. But either sort of behavior in the degree of its one-sidedness marks a degradation, an acquired habit whose formation is due to undesirable conditions; each marks an approximation to the pathological, a departure from that wholeness which is health. When behavior is reduced to a purely physical level and a person becomes like a part of the machine he operates, there is proof of social maladjustment. This is reflected in the disordered and defective habits of the persons who act on the merely physical plane.

Action does not cease to be abnormal because it is said to be spiritual and concerned with ideal matters too refined to be infected with the gross matter. Nor is it enough that we should recognize the part played by brain and nervous system in making our highly intellectual and "spiritual" activities possible. It is equally important that we realize that the latter are truncated and tend toward abnormality in the degree that they do not eventuate in employing and directing physical instrumentalities to effect material changes. Otherwise that which is called spiritual is in effect but indulgence in idle phantasy.

Thus the question of the integration of mind-body in action is the most practical of all questions we can ask of our civilization.

It is not just a speculative question; it is a demand: a demand that the labor of multitudes now too predominantly physical in character be inspirited by purpose and emotion and informed by knowledge and understanding. It is a demand that what now pass for highly intellectual and spiritual functions shall be integrated with the ultimate conditions and means of all achievement, namely the physical, and thereby accomplish something beyond themselves. Until this integration is effected in the only place where it can be carried out, in action itself, we shall continue to live in a society in which a soulless and heartless materialism is compensated for by soulful but futile and unnatural idealism and spiritualism. For materialism is not a theory, but a condition of action; that in which material and mechanical means are severed from the consequences which give them meaning and value. And spiritualistic idealism is not a theory but a state of action; that in which ends are privately enjoyed in isolation from means of execution and consequent public betterment.

In insisting upon the need of viewing action in its integrated wholeness, the need of discriminating between different qualities of behavior due to the mode of integration is emphasized, not slurred. We need to distinguish between action that is routine and action alive with purpose and desire; between that which is cold, and as we significantly say inhuman, and that which is warm and sympathetic; between that which marks a withdrawal from the conditions of the present and a retrogression to split off conditions of the past and that which faces actualities; between that which is expansive and developing because including what is new and varying and that which applies only to the uniform and repetitious; between that which is bestial and that which is godlike in its humanity; between that which is spasmodic and centrifugal, dispersive and dissipating, and that which is centred and consecutive. Until we can make such distinctions and make them in a multitude of shades and degrees, we shall not be able to understand the conduct of individuals, and not understanding, shall not be able to help them in the management of their lives. Because of this lack, education will be a guess in the dark; business a gamble in shifting about and circulating material commodities, and politics an intrigue in manipulation. What most stands in the way of our achieving a working technique for making such discriminations and employing them in the guidance of the actions of those who stand in need of assistance is our habitual splitting up the qualities of action into two disjoined things.

It is necessary, however, to be explicit about what is meant in saying that within the unity of behavior body stands for the means and agencies of conduct, and mind for its incorporated fruits and consequences. The bodily phase of action may be approached and studied in two ways. We may take it in its connection with processes which are going on outside the body, the processes which it shares with inanimate things. Or we may take it in connection with what it actually does and effects in the distinctively human medium. The first mode of approach views action in all its modes as a variegated complex of physico-chemical interactions. This kind of study is more than legitimate; it is indispensable. If organic changes are regarded as something unique, cut off from and unlike in kind to those occurring in inanimate nature, we cannot understand them, and therefore cannot direct and modify the manner of their taking place. Only when we identify them with events in inanimate nature does our knowledge in physics and chemistry become available for knowing them; only then do the appliances and techniques that we have developed for control of affairs outside the body become adaptable for use in dealing with what goes on within the body. As long as organic processes and changes are connected with any unique, non-physical force or principle, our knowledge of them is rudimentary and accidental. When they are seen to be shared with processes going on in inanimate nature, all that is discovered about the latter becomes an intellectual tool for systematic knowledge of vital process and the apparatus and technics for directing physical nature are capable of utilization in hygienic, medical and surgical treatment of bodily changes.

If this were the whole of the story, bodily action would be wholly assimilated to inorganic action, and the inclusion of the body in behavior that has mental quality would be impossible. The remainder of the story is that chemico-physical processes go on in ways and by interactions which have reference to the needs of the organism as a whole and thus take on psychical quality, and in human beings at least are in such connection with the social environment as confers upon them intellectual quality. Any notion that human action is identical with that of non-living things or with that of the "lower" animals is silly. It is contradicted by the fact that behavior is so *organized* in human beings as to have for its consequence all that we call civilization, culture, law, arts—fine and industrial, language, morals, institutions, science itself. And by its fruits we know it. Organic processes are thus seen to be the constituent means of a behavior which is endued with purpose and meaning, animate with affection, and informed by recollection and foresight. In the end, the bodily is but a name for the fact that wherever we have consequences, no matter how ideal, there are conditions and means. Materialism does not consist in a full and frank recognition of this fact, but in the isolation of means and conditions from what they actually do.

We have spoken so much of action and behavior that it is needful that we should be explicitly aware of what these words signify. In particular it is indispensable to note that when we are dealing with human behavior, the word designates a kind of behavior in which outcomes of the past and outlook on the future are incorporated; with something longitudinal and not something cross-sectionally lateral. We may isolate a particular organic structure or process for study. In as far as we do so, we regard it as similar to arrangements and processes which are shared with inanimate things. But we cannot understand the organism until we have taken its history into account. We have to know whether we are studying an embryonic, an infantile, a mature or a senescent form. We have to place the particular affair studied in a career of development. In dealing with a special chemical reaction, say that of hydrogen and oxygen in bringing water into existence, we may neglect past history. We select a brief segment for study because we are not concerned with the individuality of the molecules involved; it is enough that what happens is a specimen of something which recurs and is repeated in other situations independently of the individuality of just these molecules. This is precisely the omission we cannot make in studying phenomena of human behavior. A human being carries his past in his habitudes and habituations, and we can rightly observe and understand the latter only as we are aware of the history which is included within them. That the practitioner, physician, psychiatrist and educator, is capable of dealing intelligently with the phenomena which confront him only when he knows something of their life history is a commonplace. And it is not just the life history of the particular symptom of disorder he needs to know but the life history of the individual in whom it appears. It is equally a commonplace that the need of such knowledge of life history as a whole increases in the degree in which the mental phase of disturbance is prominent.

Such facts point to what is signified when it is said that human behavior is longitudinal, not just cross-sectional. It forms a history, an autobiography, not indeed written but enacted. The import of this fact in relation to the mental phase of action should be evident. When it is neglected, any item of behavior is regarded as an immediate lateral cross-section, and thus becomes purely mechanical, and without intellectual and emotional quality. This is precisely what happens when a reflex or specific reaction to a specific stimulus is treated as the unit of behavior, and all other behavior is treated as a compound of such units. Since the simple reflex is devoid of emotional and intellectual quality, it then logically follows that mind is not a property of any behavior. It is a fiction or a meaningless by-product accompaniment like the beauty of a rainbow with reference to a purely physical account of the refraction of light by vapor. To assert, then, that *conscious* behavior is a fiction is to draw a logical deduction from a premise, not to observe a fact. And since the fact of conscious behavior, of observing, analyzing, noting, reasoning, is involved in the whole undertaking, the absurdity of the conclusion shows the falsity of the premise. We know that the structures involved in reflexes are not as matter of fact primitive and original. The converse is true as both phylogeny and ontogeny prove. The beginning is with action in which the entire organism is involved, and the mechanism of reflexes is evolved as a specialized differentiation within an inclusive whole of behavior. The assumption that the nature of behavior is exemplified in a simple reflex is a typical case of the fallacy of neglecting development, historical career. In consequence an account of the mechanism of a particular moment of behavior is converted into an account of behavior itself and of behavior in its entirety. Only in this fashion is the role of the mental in action relegated to the realm of fiction.

The criticism may be broadened to take in the whole reduction of mental phenomena to the stimulus-response type as that reduction obtains in current psychological theory, even among those who do not call themselves behaviorists. There is no doubt that any item of behavior can be stated in terms of a response to a stimulus—just as it may be stated in terms of cause-effect. But as the doctrine is usually employed it omits to consider the one question which is scientifically and practically important: namely, how did an object or situation acquire the capacity to *be* a stimulus? For to be a stimulus in evoking a response is an additive property of physical things. The organism is constantly surrounded by indefinitely numerous conditions which affect it. If we regard them all as stimuli because they enter into causal interaction with the living creature we say in effect that the whole universe is stimulus and also response. Such a view clearly makes the theory worthless for purposes of *analysis*. It is the occurrence of a particular mode of action we are trying to describe and account for, an attempt which implies that some special feature of the environment is so weighted as to operate as stimulus. Now what makes some physical thing or trait a stimulus is the condition of the whole organism at the time, its needs and the kind of behavior in which it is already engaged. And both of these things are longitudinal, historical; they include factors formed in previous life history. Any particular thing at any particular time is a stimulus, evoking an adaptive response and use, only in virtue of the enacted biography of the organism.

There is an attempt to recognize the importance of historical development in some forms of the stimulus-response theory. Present behavior is traced back to original "bonds" in the nervous system which are innate, or to behavior in the form of what are usually called instincts. Thus previous development is nominally taken into account. But such recognition of life history is nominal rather than real. An earlier cross-section of behavior is postulated back of which development is not traced. Consequently the position of the lateral segment in the development of action as a whole is left out. The theory is only a verbal restatement of the compounding of reflex units theory; the only difference is that an "instinct" or a preformed "bond" of stimulus and reaction, is somewhat more extensive and complex than is a reflex. But since it is not sufficiently complex and extensive to take in the needs, demands and disposition of the organism as a whole, the basic fallacy remains the same.

The reference to stimuli proceeding from the environment brings us in effect to the second way in which the account of behavior is rendered so partial and split off that its mental phase has either to be denied as a fiction or else regarded as mysterious and unnatural. For the stimulus-response theory, as usually held, cuts off the environment from behavior. It treats environment simply as an external occasion from which behavior proceeds. Behavior is thus treated exclusively as going on inside the organism, something which is simply set off or initiated by the environment. In reality, the environment is just as much comprised within behavior as are organic processes. Behavior is not just something which goes on *in* a surrounding medium. If it were, behavior could be studied and described as something which goes on in the organism or which goes forth out of it in total neglect of environment, save the reference to some part of the latter as a touch-and-go stimulus. Behavior in fact is a continuous interaction in which environing as well as organic factors are included. This is true even of the functions we often regard as exclusively physiological. We do not just breathe, we breathe air; we do not just digest, we digest foodstuffs. We do not just move the legs and body; we walk on the ground, and from one place to another, so as to obtain a more favorable environment to be incorporated in subsequent behavior.

To describe the structures and processes of the organism in isolation, in their exclusive reference to organic structures, and then call the result an account of behavior, is to omit the most distinctive character of behavior. Sherrington's classic work *The Integrative Action of the Nervous System* marks an epoch in the development of science. What is it which the action of the nervous system integrates? Simply its own self, turning upon itself as a snake is said to swallow its tail? Clearly not, but the behavior of the entire organism of which it is a part. But when and how is the action of the organism integrated? There can be but one answer. It is integrated in the degree that it utilizes and transforms its environment by means of incorporating some element of the latter within behavior. Utilization here signifies that something in the surroundings is rendered a means in the carrying on of some phase of behavior, as assimilation of food and the breathing of air maintains life-behavior itself. Transformation signifies that some part of surrounding conditions is actually changed so that the environment is modified into a form more favorable than before to the maintenance of life-behavior. To describe the action of a part of the nervous system, or of the entire nervous system, or of the entire organism in isolation from the environment included within behavior is like thinking that we can understand a machine, say a loom, if we omit the material, the yarn, upon which it works and the transformation of the material into cloth wrought in the operation. Since the mental, if it can be found anywhere, must be found in behavior which comprises *objects* of desire, thought and affection, to accept the premise which identifies behavior with the action going on inside the organism is to commit ourselves to denial of mental quality as a dialectical conclusion from a premise. Many persons will remain so assured that mental phenomena are actual facts, that they will then prefer to go on believing in them, and will treat them as proofs of a mysterious substance called mind, soul or consciousness. Thus the one-sidedness of the theory about behavior perpetuates the very tradition which a complete account of behavior would eliminate.

The bearing of the one-sided omission of environment in description of behavior upon the reality of the truly mental phase of behavior is most evident when we consider the elimination of the human or social environment. For it is the incorporation of this environment in action which is most intimately and extensively connected with the intellectual and emotional quality of behavior. The question of the role of language and other constructed signs in mind gives a crucial test. I do not question the connection of thinking with speech and other signs. Speech and the use of signs is an affair of behavior. What is questionable is the elimination of relations with other human beings from the account given of language habits and of thinking conceived as "exercised implicitly behind the closed doors of the lips"—in other words as something which goes on subcutaneously, wholly inside the organism. Such a description reduces speech to vocalization or making of sounds, and thinking to a silent exercise of the organs of vocalization and other internal structures. Now the making of sounds is not speech. Sounds issuing from vocalization are speech only when they are used to institute a mode of behavior on the part of another human being which will favorably affect the behavior of the one speaking. Sounds issue from phonograph or radio, sounds which imitate articulate speech. The phonograph does not speak, however. For while the sounds that issue may induce action on the part of others, anticipation of such action does not enter as a factor in its putting forth of sounds. Any modification of the behavior of others which is effected by the sounds emitted by the radio is not incorporated as a factor in *its* behavior. Precisely such inclusion of objective social consequences is what transforms sounds into speech or language, as may be seen from taking any simple case of command, request or advice. Speech is primarily a mode of action by which the behavior of one is so influenced by the expected or hoped for behavior of others as to become an integral part of concerted action.

Thinking as implicit speech is made on the same pattern. It represents the social situation carried over into the habits of the organism. One talks to himself as a way of anticipating objective consequences (that is, consequences into which the environment enters) before they happen, and as a means of eventually securing those that are liked and of averting or avoiding those that are disliked. This renders behavior intelligent, thoughtful. It is all to the good when "consciousness" is thrown overboard as a substance or separate process designated by a noun: for "ness" indicates that the noun is abstract and results from projecting a quality of action into a thing in itself. But the quality of being conscious remains; the difference between behavior that is aware of what it is about and routine or impulse behavior is as marked a factual difference as we can anywhere discover. To deny the reality of meaning in the sense of something mysterious and unnatural, outside of connection with the range of interactions which form behavior, is to the good. But refusal to admit meaning as a quality of behavior is another matter, and one which confutes itself. For the propounders of the doctrine that meaning is non-existent address words on that subject to others; they expect their language to be understood and not be taken as a nonsensical farrago; they anticipate certain consequences in the way of modified behavior to result from understanding and their language behavior is modified by this expectation of response. They take it for granted that some behavior has meaning; this cannot be granted without implying that some behavior, their own for example, in the observations and analyses whose conclusion they present, is conscious: that is, is aware of what it is about, of what it is doing and trying to do. The conception of behavior in its integrity, as including a history and environment is the alternative to a theory which eliminates the mental because it considers only the behavior of the mechanism of action as well as the theory which thinks it ennobles the mental by placing it in an isolated realm.

Thus we are reminded of our beginning, the recall of happier days when the divorce of knowledge and action, theory and practise, had not been decreed, and when the arts as action informed by knowledge were not looked down upon in invidious disparagement with contemplation complete in itself; when knowledge and reason were not so "pure" that they were defiled by entering into the wider connections of an action that accomplishes something because it uses physical means. There are signs that we are perforce, because of the extension of knowledge on one side and the demands of practise on the other, about to attempt a similar achievement on our own account. I close with suggesting the imperative need of such an integration in the art of education, an integration which can become real only as the scientific man, the philosopher, the physician and psychiatrist cooperate.

The art of education is one in which every person is compelled whether he will or not to take an interest, because it so intimately concerns his own conduct. A person may begin with a narrow interest, one that cares only about, say, the education of his own children or of members of his own profession. But he does not go far before he is forced to note that he is building on a sandy foundation because of deficiencies due to earlier education. Professional education has its results limited and twisted because of the general state of education. Surveying that, it appears that its improvement cannot be made secure merely by better training of teachers. Parents, school officials, taxpayers have the last word, and the character of that word is dependent upon their education. They may and do block or deflect the best laid plans. That is the circle in which education moves. Those who received education are those who give it; habits already engendered deeply influence its course. It is as if no one could be educated in the full sense until everyone is developed beyond the reach of prejudice, stupidity and apathy.

There is no possibility of complete escape from this circle. Education returns upon itself in such a multitude of ways as to render out of the question any short cut solution. It is a matter of accelerating momentum in the right direction, and of increasing the effective energy of the factors that make for removing obstacles. Chief among these obstacles are the practises which are associated with the traditional separation of mind and body and the consequent neglect of informed and intelligent action as the aim of all educational development. The division has affected every subject of study, every method of instruction and discipline. More than anything else it explains the separation of theory and practise, of thought and action. The result is a so-called cultural education which tends to be academic and pedantic, in any case aloof from the concerns of life, and an industrial and manual education which at best gives command of tools and means without intelligent grasp of purposes and ends. The consequences of this divided education are writ large in the state of our civilization. The physician meets them in a wide range of induced disorders, to say nothing of waste and incapacitation. The walls which mark the separation are beginning to crack, although they are far from crumbling. From all sides the artificiality of isolation from one another of mind and body are commencing to be seen. There is at least the beginning of cooperation between those who are traditionally occupied with the concerns of mind and those busy with the affairs of the body. The planning of any good school building is an illustrative symbol. Architect, engineer, hygienist, teacher and public official may join forces. But there are still many who should have a say, like the psychologist, who are left out, and such cooperation as there is lacks balance. It would be interesting for example to know what physicians would say of the wisdom of the herding together of thousands of children in our gigantic buildings with the enforced need of dealing with children en masse and the institution of lockstep methods—would say if they were consulted and if they thought their voice would be heeded. The growing interest in pre-school education, nursery schools and parental education, the development of medical inspection, the impact of social hygiene, the institution of school visitors and the use of schools as social centres are other evidences that the isolation of schools from life is beginning to give way because of cooperative action. But not even the most optimistic would hold that we have advanced beyond the outer breastworks. The forces are still powerful that make for centrifugal and divisive education. And the chief of these is, let it be repeated, the separation of mind and body which is incarnated in religion, morals and business as well as in science and philosophy. The full realization of the integration of mind and body in action waits upon the reunion of philosophy and science in art, above all in the supreme art, the art of education.

The Inclusive Philosophic Idea

There are at the present time a considerable number of persons who habitually employ the social as a principle of philosophic reflection and who assign it a force equal and even superior to that ascribed to the physical, vital and mental. There are others, probably a greater number, who decline to take "social" seriously as a category of description and interpretation for purposes of philosophy, and who conceive any attempt so to take it as involving a confusion of anthropology and sociology with metaphysics. The most they would concede is that cultural material may throw light on the genesis and history of human beliefs about ultimate subject-matter. Then it is asserted that it is but a case of the familiar genetic fallacy, the confusion of the history of belief with the nature of that believed, to assign to such an account a place anywhere except within the history of human culture. Such a situation solicits attention; and I desire to state as far as space permits what is the intent of those who attribute genuine philosophic import to the idea of the social.

A start may be conveniently made by noting that associated or conjoint behavior is a universal characteristic of all existences. Knowledge is in terms of related objects and unless it is supposed that relations are a subjective intrusion, or that, *a la* Hume, only *ideas* are associated, relation as the nerve of science correlates with association among things. This fact being noted, we observe that the qualities of things associated are displayed only in association, since in interactions alone are potentialities released and actualized. Furthermore, the manifestation of potentialities varies with the manner and range of association. This statement is only a formal way of calling attention to the fact that we char-

[First published in *Monist* 38 (1928): 161–77, from an address to the Eastern Division of the American Philosophical Association at the University of Chicago, December 1927.]

acterize an element, say hydrogen, not only, as the name implies, in terms of its water-forming potentiality but ultimately in terms of consequences effected in a whole range of modes of conjoint behavior.[1]

These considerations being premised, attention fastens upon the fact that the more numerous and varied the forms of association into which anything enters, the better basis we have for describing and understanding it, for the more complex is an association the more fully are potentialities released for observation. Since things present themselves to us in such fashion that narrower and wider ranges, simpler and more complex ones, are readily distinguished, it would appear that metaphysical description and understanding is demarcated as that which has to do with the widest and fullest range of associated activity. And I remark that if the phrase "degrees of reality" can be given an empirically intelligible meaning, that meaning would seem to depend upon following out the line of thought thus suggested.[2] In short, there appears to be a fairly straight road to the conclusion that a just gauge of the adequacy of any philosophic account of things is found in the extent to which that account is based upon taking things in the widest and most complex scale of associations open to observation.

In making this statement I am not unaware that the opposite method has been pursued and is still recommended by philosophers in good repute: namely, a method based on predilection for ultimate and unattached simples, called by various writers essences, data, etc. The question of whether we should begin with the simple or the complex appears to me the most important problem in philosophic method at the present time, cutting under, for example, the traditional distinctions of real and ideal. Or, if it be said that while perforce we are compelled psychologically and practically to begin with the complex, *philosophy*

1. In case there is objection to the use of the conceptions of potentiality and actualization, it may be pointed out that the same facts may be stated, though as it seems to me more awkwardly, by saying that things in different modes of association occasion different effects and that our knowledge of them is adequate in the degree in which it includes a broad range of effects due to a variety of associated operations.
2. It is perhaps worth while in passing to note also that such concepts as "levels" and "emergence" seem to be most readily definable upon the basis of this consideration.

begins only when we have come upon simples, the problem of method still remains. Are these simples isolated and self-sufficient, or are they the results of intellectual analysis, themselves intellectual rather than existential in quality, and therefore of value only in the degree in which they afford us means of arriving at a better understanding of the complex wholes with which we began? Time forbids consideration of this fundamental question. I content myself with observing that the hypothesis that ultimate and detached simples are the only reals for philosophy seems to be the sole logical alternative to the position that the wider and more complex the range of associated interaction with which we deal the more fully is the nature of the object of philosophic thought revealed to us. Hence, the issue as to method reduces itself to the question whether isolated simples can be asserted without self-contradiction to be ultimate and self-sufficient on their own account. Those who do not accept them as the real, appear committed to the position herein stated.

While the fact of association and of range of associations as determining "degrees of reality" gives us our starting point, it gives *only* a starting point for discussing the value of "social" as a philosophic category. For by the social as a distinctive mode of association is denoted specifically human forms of grouping, and these according to the findings of science appear only late in time. Hence, the objection which readily occurs to mind. The view that "social" in its characteristically human sense is an important category is met with the retort that, on the contrary, it is but a highly special case of association and as such is restricted in significance, humanly interesting of course, but a matter of detail rather than of an important principle. My introductory remarks were intended as an anticipatory reply to such an objection. Association barely by itself is a wholly formal category. It acquires content only by considering the different forms of association which constitute the material of experience. Thus, while it is admitted that society, in the human sense, is a form of association that is restricted in its space-time manifestation, it cannot be placed in contrast with association in general. Its import can be determined not by comparing it with association in its generic formal sense, but only by comparing and contrasting it with other special types of association.

This fact gives what has been said regarding the importance of range and complexity of association as a philosophic measure its special import. If reference to association is to be anything more than a ceremonial and barren act of deference, if it is to be used in an enterprise of philosophic description and understanding, it indicates the necessity of study and analysis of the different modes of association that present themselves in experience. And the implication of our argument is that in such a comparison of definite types of association, the social, in its human sense, is the richest, fullest and most delicately subtle of any mode actually experienced. There is no need to go through the form of discovering, as if for the first time, the different typical modes which are to be compared and contrasted. They have been made familiar enough in the course of thought. Aside from social, whose thoroughgoing admission still awaits adequate acknowledgment, they are the physical, the vital or organic, and the mental. The gist of our problem consists in deciding which of these forms presents the broader and fuller range of associations. Association in general is but a matrix; its filling is the facts of association actually displayed in nature. Indeed, the category of association is but a highly abstract notation of what is formally common to the special modes.

Before coming, however, to this affair of comparison, which constitutes the main topic of this paper, it will be well to clear the ground of certain notions which led to misconstruction and depreciation of the meaning of "social" as a category. A moment ago I referred to the facts of association as they are actually displayed in human life. The reference implied that social facts are themselves natural facts. This implication goes against preconceptions engendered by the common opposition of the physical and the social sciences; by the tacit identification, in other words, of the natural sciences with the purely physical. As far as this idea lingers in the back of the head, social and natural are oppositional conceptions; the attempt to find a key by which to read the cipher of nature in the social is then immediately felt to be absurd; this feeling then operates to effect the contemptuous dismissal of the "social." Denial of opposition between the social and natural is, however, an important element of the *meaning* of "social" as a category; and if anyone is interested in finding out the intent of those who would employ "social" as a philosophic category, that one should begin by asking himself what are the implications of the current separation of natural and social sciences, and whether upon reflection he is willing to stand by them. A denial of the separation is not only possible to a sane mind, but is demanded by any methodological adoption of the principle of continuity, and also, as will be indicated later, by social phenomena themselves. Upon the hypothesis of continuity—if that is to be termed a hypothesis which cannot be denied without self-contradiction—the social, in spite of whatever may be said regarding the temporal and spatial limitation of its manifestations, furnishes philosophically the inclusive category.

A two-fold harm is wrought by the current separation of social and natural science and by accepting the meaning which attaches to social after it has been thus divorced. The chief point at which philosophy may be of aid in the pursuits of the social sciences lies precisely here. In the degree in which what passes for social science is built upon the notion of a gap between natural and social phenomena, that science is truncated, arbitrary and insecure. An analytic survey of the present status of the social sciences would be needed to justify this remark. But there are only a few sociologists who have ventured as yet to assert that there is something distinctive or unique in social phenomena; so we are met with a paradoxical situation in which social phenomena are isolated from physical and organic considerations and yet are explained in physical, organic or psychological terms instead of in characteristically social terms. In psychology the persisting tradition of a purely individualistic and private subject-matter is to be attributed directly to neglect of the social conditions of mental phenomena, while indirectly this neglect goes back to a separation of social from natural: since only acknowledgment of the continuity of the social and the natural provides the intermediary terms which link psychological phenomena with others. Some forms of behaviorism, in reaction against the unnatural isolation of the physical and mental, merely throw the latter overboard entirely, and reduce them to the terms of the material dealt with in purely physical science. In political science may be noted an oscillation between the adoption of non-natural categories, such as a transcendent "will," and the resolution of political phenomena into physical terms of conflict and adjustment of forces. A recent economic writer has asserted that economic science has so neglected the place of technology in industry that a generation has gone forth which, although "educated" in economic science, is almost wholly ignorant of economic affairs.[3] Technology is evidently a matter that connects directly with the development of physical science; the point, instead of being an incidental one, can be shown to be intimately connected with all the sound objections brought against the abstraction of the "economic man." The economic man cannot be set in his place in social phenomena, in his actual relations to legal, political, technological and other cultural institutions, until these are connected with natural phenomena.

These are but too casual and abbreviated hints of the meaning of the assertion that the performance of the service which philosophy might theoretically render to the social sciences waits upon the frank acknowledgment of the social as a category continuous with and inclusive of the categories of the physical, vital and mental.

This reference to the sciences is not to be regarded, however, as implying an adoption of that conception of philosophy which identifies it exclusively with either an analysis or a synthesis of the premises or results of the special sciences. On the contrary, the sciences themselves are outgrowths of some phase of social culture, from which they derive their instruments, physical and intellectual, and by which their problems and aims are set. The only philosophy that can "criticize" the premises of the special sciences without running the danger of being itself a pseudo-science is that which takes into account the anthropological (in its broadest sense) basis of the sciences, just as the only one that can synthesize their conclusions, without running a like danger, is the one which steps outside these conclusions to place them in the broader context of social life.

In now turning to the main point, the social as a ranking philosophic category, on the ground that it is indicative of the widest and richest range of association empirically accessible (and no apology is offered for basing philosophy upon the empirically manifest rather than upon the occult), it is necessary to point out a certain ambiguity of language which because of brevity of exposition, necessarily attaches to our statement. Social *phenomena* are not of themselves, of course, equivalent to

3. Tugwell, *Industry's Coming of Age*, p. vii.

social as a *category*. The latter is derived from the former by means of an intellectual analysis which determines what is their distinctive character. Now I am not here dealing with the important and eventually imperative problem of the category *of* the social, or the determination of the characteristics which constitute the distinguishing nature of the social, but rather with social phenomena *en gross* as comprehending, for philosophic analysis, physical, organic and mental phenomena in a mode of association in which the latter take on new properties and exercise new functions. In other words, I am here implying that social phenomena do as a matter of fact manifest *something* distinctive, and that that something affords the key to a naturalistic account of phenomena baffling philosophic interpretation when it is left out of account. To those who accept this view, the burden of proof as to the value of "social" as a metaphysical category lies upon those who habitually treat its worth as trivial. For what do *they* mean by social phenomena? If social phenomena are not an exemplification upon the widest and most intricate scale of the generic trait of associated behavior or interaction, what do they signify? I see but one kind of answer open to them, covering two alternatives: Either social phenomena are anomalous, an excrescence or intrusion, supervening in an accidental and meaningless way upon other phenomena, or else they have no distinctive import, being in reality *nothing but* physical, vital or psychological phenomena. Does not each of these views contradict the observable traits of social phenomena?

Upon a *prima facie* view, social phenomena take up and incorporate within themselves things associated in the narrower way which we term the physical. It gives a ludicrous result to think of social phenomena merely as lying on top of physical phenomena; such a notion is negated by the most casual observation of the facts. What would social phenomena be without the physical factor of land, including all the natural resources (and obstacles) and forms of energy for which the word "land" stands? What would social phenomena be without the tools and machines by which physical energies are utilized? Or what would they be without physical appliances and apparatus, from clothes and houses to railways, temples and printing-presses? No, it is not the social which is a superficial category. The view is superficial of those who fail to see that in the social the physical is taken up into a wider and more complex and delicate system of interactions so that it takes on new properties by release of potentialities previously confined because of absence of full interaction.

The same consideration applies to the inclusion within the social of the vital or organic. The members of society are living human beings with the characteristics of living creatures; but as they enter into distinctively human associations strictly organic properties are modified and even transformed. Certain physiological factors of sex, of procreation, immaturity and need of care, are assuredly implicated in the functions expressed in family life. But however great the role of animal lust, there is something more in any family association than bare physiological factors. The fact of transformation of the purely organic by inclusion within the scope of human association is so obvious—note the significant case of change of cries into speech—that it has indeed led to belief in the intrusive intervention of unnatural and supernatural factors in order to account for the differences between the animal and the human. The disjunction between the assertion that the human is the merely animal and the assertion that an extraneous force is obtruded is not, however, exhaustive. There remains an alternative which is most fully confirmed by empirical fact, namely that the difference is made when new potentialities are actualized, when the range of interactions that delimits the organic is taken up into the wider and more subtly complex association which forms human society.

Since traits derived from the physical mode have been admitted into philosophy (materialism in other words is at least grudgingly admitted into philosophic companionship); and since organic philosophies, framed on the pattern of vital phenomena, upon conceptions of species, development and purpose, are freely admitted, it seems arbitrary, to say the least, to exclude the social from the role of a legitimate category.

That the mental has a recognized claim to serve as a category of description and interpretation of natural existence is evident in the very existence of idealistic philosophies. There are those who deny the ability of these theories to execute their claim, just as there are those who deny the capacity of the physical and vital to make good. But thought, as well as matter and life, is at least admitted to rank as a respectable figure in the gallery of categories. Now of the mental as of the physical and organic it may be said that it operates as an included factor within social phenomena, since the mental is empirically discernible only where association is manifested in the form of participation and communication. It would therefore appear legitimate to adopt as a hypothesis worthy of being tried out the idea that the ulterior meaning of the mental as well as of the physical and vital is revealed in this form of associational interaction. The implication is not that they have no describable *existence* outside the social, but that in so far as they appear and operate outside of that large interaction which forms the social they do not reveal that full force and import with which it is the traditional business of philosophy to occupy itself.

After this statement of the intent of the enterprise of employing the social as a category, it remains to sketch in a summary fashion a few specimens of its implications which are relevant to the clarification of some outstanding philosophic issues. We may conveniently begin with the matter just referred to, the place of the mental in the existential scheme of things, using for purposes of our discussion as the equivalent of "mental" the fact of *meaning*, whether direct as in cognition of objects, or indirect as in esthetic, affectional and moral relations. The state of philosophic discussion exhibits a dilemma, or rather a trilemma. The mental is viewed (i) as a mysterious intrusion occurring in some unaccountable way in the order of nature; (ii) as illusory, or, in current language, as an epiphenomenon; and (iii) as ontological, whether as a section of being on the same level with the physical section, or as the Being of which so-called physical things are but disguised forms or "appearances." It may be argued that the persistence of the problem and of these widely opposed modes of solution is itself strongly indicative that some factor of the situation, the one which is the key to understanding, has been omitted. In any case, the persistence of these unreconcilable conceptions is a challenge to search for something which will eliminate the scandal of such sharp antagonisms in interpretation. Now when we turn to the social, we find *communication* to be an existential occurrence involved in all distinctively communal life, and we find that communication requires meaning and understanding as conditions of unity or agreement in conjoint behavior. We find, that is, meaning to be not an anomaly nor an accidentally supervening quality but a constitutive ingredient of existential events. We find meaning as a describable, verifiable empirical phenomenon whose genesis, modes and consequences can be concretely examined and traced. It presents itself not as an intrusion, nor as an accidental and impotent iridescence, nor as the reduplication of a structure already inhering in antecedent existence, but as an additive quality realized in the process of wider and more complex interaction of physical and vital phenomena; and as having a distinctive and concretely verifiable office in sustaining and developing a distinctive kind of observable facts, those namely which are termed social. We do not then have to resort to purely metaphysical and dialectical considerations, adopted *ad hoc*, in order to "save" the reality and importance of the mental. The realm of meanings, of mind, is at home, securely located and anchored in an empirically observable order of existence. And this order stands in genetic continuity with physical and vital phenomena, being, indeed, these phenomena taken up into and incorporated within a wider scope of associated interactions. We do not have to read the mental back into the antecedent physical, much less resort to the desperate measure of making it so all-inclusive that the physical is treated as a disguised and illusory "appearance" of the mental. The social affords us an observable instance of a "realm of mind" objective to an individual, by entering into which as a participating member organic activities are transformed into acts having a mental quality.

These considerations are not supposed to demonstrate the truth of the position taken; but they are seriously proposed to indicate a hypothesis which is worthy of trial; as a hypothesis which starts from a *vera causa*, that is, from an empirically verifiable fact, instead of from concepts which have no such observed locus of their own but which are invented simply to account for facts otherwise inexplicable. In the second place, the actual structure of knowledge viewed in relation to the operations by which it is concretely established to be knowledge in the honorific sense, that is as tested and justified, as grounded, instead of as mere opinion and fantastic belief, can be understood only in social terms. By knowledge as grounded I mean belief in relation to evidence that substantiates it. Now the simplest distinction that can be drawn between objects of knowledge in this sense and mere matters of opinion and credulity, or even of thought however internally self-consistent and formally valid, is the distinction between the socially confirmed and the privately entertained. Opinion and theory as long as they are uncommunicated, or as long as, even if communicated and shared, they are unconfirmed in conjoint behavior are at best but candidates for membership within the system of knowledge. To labor this point is to weaken it. It is a truism that science is science because observations, experiments and calculations are so conducted as to be capable of report to others and repetition by others. Now this report and repetition are wholly misconceived when thought of simply as external additions to a thought complete in itself. They signify that thought itself is conceived and developed in such terms as to be capable of communication to others, of understanding by them, and of adoption and utilization in cooperative action. Report, communication, is not a bare emission of thoughts framed and completed in private soliloquy or solipsistic observation. The entire operation of individual experimentation and soliloquizing has been influenced at every point by reference to the social medium in which their results are to be set forth and responded to. Indeed what has been said is an understatement. It is not simply that the characteristic findings of thought cannot pass into knowledge save when framed with reference to social submission and adoption, but that language and thought in their relation to signs and symbols are inconceivable save as ways of achieving concerted action.

In passing, it may also be remarked that the reference to private thought as a *candidate* for knowledge through incorporation into conjoint associated action (which also involves, be it recalled, physical conditions and hence is subject to test by physical consequences), throws light upon and may give the key to another mystery of philosophic speculation—namely the nature of mind as subjective. For the latter when it is interpreted from the standpoint of the social as a category, does not appear as an anomaly, much less as a bogey, an intrusive and wholly undesirable source of error. Thinking and its results present themselves as indeed hypothetical, demanding trial in terms of social action, and hence as subject to error and defeat. But they also offer themselves as having a positive and constructive office. For they are not merely candidates for reception into the social *status quo*, the received and established order of associated behavior; they are rather claimants for a changed social order to be effected in the very action which they promote and by which they are to be tested. Sometimes the claim is narrow, affecting only the behavior of a selected group who are experts in the particular field; sometimes, as in the proposal of new policies, it is wide in the appeal which it virtually makes. But the former type, addressed primarily say to a group of scientific specialists, has a way of expanding; it cannot be kept cooped up; and in any case there is no difference in principle.

In giving illustrations, one is embarrassed by the range of philosophic problems which suggest themselves as receiving illumination and clarification when the social is employed as a category of description and interpretation. We may, however, draw, almost at random, upon the moral field. Consider the recurrent discussion concerning the objectivity of moral distinctions and judgments, with its ceaseless vibration between reduction of them to private preferences, none the less private when they happen to be collectively entertained, and recourse to purely transcendent considerations in order to "secure" their objectivity. It would be dogmatic to assert in this casual allusion that the problem is solved when the social is used as a category, and the social is seen to incorporate the physical, organic and psychological; but no one can reasonably deny that the whole problem takes on a very different aspect when its elements are placed in this context.[4]

An allied topic concerns the "naturalness" of the moral life of man. Those who assert that it is natural are met by the counterassertion that such a view reduces the moral life to a strictly animal plane. This sharp disjunction falls to the ground, however, when the distinctive forms of association characteristic of the life of man in social relations are recognized, for this recognition not only admits but asserts that these relations realize new and unique qualities not manifested in the lesser areas of natural association. A generalization of what is involved in this issue is found in a theory familiar to students of the history of thought. A succession of thinkers, from Herder and Kant to Hegel, have

4. Compare the treatment of the objectivity of esthetic judgments in the article "On the Genesis of the Aesthetic Categories" by J. H. Tufts, *Decennial Publications of the University of Chicago*, Volume III.

asserted that the significance of the history of humanity is found in the struggle of man to emerge from a state in which he was wholly immersed in "nature" to a state in which "spirit" is wholly triumphant, and where triumph involves a sublimated cancellation of the physical and animal. It is submitted that whatever is empirically verifiable in such a doctrine is better stated in terms of the constant remaking of the physical environment and the living organism which occurs when the latter come within the scope of the culture carried in human society. It is a fact rather than a speculation that physical and animal nature are transformed in the process of education and of incorporation in the means and consequences of associated political, legal, religious, industrial, and scientific and artistic institutions. "Spirit" in the doctrine referred to is a transcendent and blind name for something which exhibits itself empirically as that phase of social phenomena called civilization.

The philosophic issues mentioned are cited only as illustrative specimens. They afford at most but a skeleton-like table of contents and a highly incomplete one at that. They are given as indications of a scheme of philosophic description and interpretation that has to be rounded out and filled in in order to realize and to test what is signified by "social" as a philosophic category. It is the historic claim of philosophy that it occupies itself with the ideal of wholes and the whole. It is submitted that either the whole is manifested in concretely empirical ways, and in ways consonant with infinite variety, or else wholeness is but a dialectical speculation. I do not say that the social as we know it *is* the whole, but I do emphatically suggest that it is the widest and richest manifestation of the whole accessible to our observation. As such it is at least the proper point of departure for any more imaginative construings of the whole one may wish to undertake. And in any case it furnishes the terms in which any consistent *empirical* philosophy must speak. Only by whole-hearted adoption of it as a ranking fact and idea can empirical philosophy come into its own, and escape the impotency and one-sidedness which has dogged the traditional sensationalistic empiricism. The commitment of Lockean empiricism to a doctrine that ignored the associative property of all things experienced is the source of that particularistic nominalism whose goal is solipsistic scepticism. In consequence empiricism ceased to be empirical and became a dialectic construction of the implications of absolute particularism. By rebound, it induced recourse to principles of connection extraneously supplied, whether by "synthetic action of thought" or by eternal essences. In the end, these systems rise or fall with the truth of the empirical particularism against which they have reacted. Thus the social as a category is as important in the critical evaluation of recent systems of thought as it is in direct application to problems of matter, life and mind.

Appearing and Appearance

The idea of appearance has played a large and varied role in philosophic thought. In ancient philosophy, it was ontological in character, being used to denote a realm of being which was infected with defect or non-being and hence expressed itself in instability and change. In modern thinking, it has been chiefly an epistemic idea. Ontologically, there is but one kind of being; but this, as it affects the senses, or is itself affected by the faculties and conditions of knowing, becomes subjectivistically altered from its real estate. In both cases the distinction of appearance from reality is, of course, invidious. To an empiricist the distinction, however invalid he may consider it to be metaphysically or epistemologically, must have an empirical basis and origin which are misinterpreted in the traditional doctrines. It is accordingly incumbent upon him to give an analytic account of the origin and role of the meaning of appearance such as will acknowledge the empirical facts while eliminating historic misconstructions.

In its simplest and basic form, "appearance" denotes the fact that some things are at a particular time evident, patent, overt, open, outstanding, conspicuous, in contrast with others which are hidden, concealed, latent, covered up, remote. One of the things which itself soon "appears" or becomes obvious is that there is a connection between what is apparent and what is covert such that what appears has a representative function. It is a revelation, manifestation, exhibition. It can be understood only as a culminating eventuation of something beside itself which may be otherwise hidden—as prophets reveal the will of God—or may be overt in another connection—as trophies exhibit a victory won in war. A further specification of this func-

[First published in *Journal of Philosophy* 24 (1927): 449–63.]

tion is so significant and so common as to deserve a class to itself. We take in the third place something which appears—in the first sense—as the clew to something hidden or unapparent, and as the basis of search for it: as sign, indication, evidence.

I

The primary, innocent neutral meaning of appearance may best be expressed participially, by the word "appearing." The world is so constituted that things appear and disappear; the opposite to appearance is not reality but disappearance. Owing to rotation, the light of a beacon on the seas appears and disappears every so often. Similarly, owing to the rotation of the earth, the sun appears in the morning and disappears at night. In the spring-time leaves appear on the trees; they disappear in winter. Land disappears after a ship has got a distance at sea; another land appears after an interval of days. What is indicated by the term "appearance" is coming into view, sensibly or intellectually—as when the meaning of an obscure passage "dawns" on the mind, or the clew to a desired invention presents itself to an Edison. Appearance signifies conspicuousness, outstandingness, obviousness, being patent, evident in plain view. Its contrast is being obscured, hidden, concealed, absent, remote. A book appears on publication, a king appears once in a while to his subjects, an actor appears daily on the stage. An eclipse of the moon appears at calculable intervals.

If there is a metaphysical problem in the "world of appearances" there must also be one in a "world of disappearances." This correlativity of appearing and disappearing is in reality highly significant; it indicates the existence of a temporal process having phases. The fundamental importance of this temporal characteristic can be better dealt with at a later stage of our own account. At this point, I only want to emphasize that any existential question which arises can only concern stages in some temporal process that includes a cycle of phases. When a thing appears, its hereness and nowness are emphatically realized. If the Aristotelian categories of potentiality and actuality were in vogue, we could well say that appearing marks an actualization of a potential here-now. From any point of view, we must say that it marks a stage in the history of some object having different phases, owing to varied relations to other things. Thus the different appearances of the moon, as it waxes and wanes, are not matters of some unfolding from within any more than they are marks of degrees of reality; they are functions of its movement in relation to the movement of the earth.

It may, however, be objected that the epistemological aspect of the matter can not be so easily disposed of. It will be contended that since an appearance is always to somebody it involves dependence upon the mind or consciousness in or to which a thing appears; for this reason, I suppose, appearances are often called presentations, and presentations are then either identified with states of mind or at least with things modified by mind. But appearance does not denote a total or pervasive character, an intrinsic quality, but a relation which is additive. A lad appears in school; he answers present when the roll is called. No one thinks of supposing that this presence abrogates his being or reduces his reality. It marks a phase of his biography determined by his relations to school, class, and teachers, just as his absence marks a phase determined by other relations, vacation, illness, playing hookey, etc. So a presentation marks the existence of a thing in relation to an organism; the table before me is in view. If I close my eyes, it disappears from view:—a particular relationship ceases, namely, that with a certain part of my organism.

This relation is physical, existential, not epistemic. Its establishment is, indeed, a necessary condition of knowing, but it does not constitute knowledge, in either of its two senses: either as something actually known or as something *to be* known, a theme for inquiry, a subject of an investigation which shall terminate in knowledge. The sun is efficaciously present to the soil it warms, the plants whose growth it effects. Or, taking the case of the organism, its appearance may, just like the sounding of an alarm clock, operate as a signal to begin the round of daily duties. It may, indeed, be known, identified, for just what it is, or it may be present as an occasion of inquiry in order to discover what it is. But knowing in both these senses denotes that something in addition to the original appearance is taking place; that the thing appearing is entering into more complex relationships. In short, while the appearance is a precondition of knowing, it is not a case of knowing. Furthermore, we must note that the relation which determines a thing to appear is definite, specifiable, not wholesale. A table disappears—not absolutely but with respect to sight; when the eyes close, it may still be present to the hand. Failure to bear in mind the definite character of the organic relation that conditions an appearance is largely responsible for treating it as if it involved a unique problem.

II

The second sense of "appearance" is display, exhibition, manifestation, revelation. In some instances this meaning is but an intensification of that just dealt with. A vivid, spectacular, appearance of something is a "show" in an emphatic sense, just as an unusual ball-player or child musician is popularly called a "phenomenon." But in many cases the idea of showing, manifesting, implies something other than the merely striking character of the appearance in question. It calls attention explicitly to the connection between the whole temporal cycle and the phase of it prominent at a particular time in a particular context. This connection is implied in the first sense of appearing. But the idea of manifestation does something more than make the implicit explicit. It designates the appearance as a member of an inclusive *whole*. A display of fireworks may be only a striking appearance. But it may also be a commemoration of a notable event. A procession may be only a vivid pageant; but it may also be a celebration. The presentation is now a representation; it calls to mind a total situation such that *reference* to it gives the appearing object its meaning. It is the appearance *of* something in the sense of expression. Thus a particular act of ill-temper reveals a standing disposition; it is a transient ebullition of something enduring; similarly with a manifestation of greed, a display of courage. An actor appears, but not just in the sense that a man who has been absent is present. Appearance *as* an actor signifies the assumption of a role or part, and this implies the whole, the drama, in which the role is a contributing member. The subject-matter of the role would be, relatively, non-sense by itself and the drama would be defective without the part. A similar context is exemplified when a lawyer appears in behalf of a client. His presence is wholly representative, but it is a necessary phase in the realization of that which is represented. He takes a part in legal proceedings which exhibit a controversy in process of solution. There is thus explicit in appearance as manifestation an added relation. The sun appears and its appearance is a phase of the sun's career. But it does not realize its special status by means of appearing on behalf of anything else, such that its representative office makes a definitive contribution to the whole. If, however, we take the rising of the sun in relation to the constitution of the entire system, the particular event may *then* be said to be a manifestation. On the one hand, it is seen to be a necessary part of the whole, and on the other hand, it can be understood only when it is placed in its relations within the organized system as a whole.

This second meaning leads to a third, the distinctively intellectual one, determining the logical import of "appearance." A representative exhibition may be more or less adequate or perfect— as in the case of lawyer, diplomat, and actor. We say they are or are not true, faithful, to their function. They may *mis*represent. Moreover, in the case of a delegate, a diplomat, credentials are demanded and offered. The question of *claim* and *right* enters in. When an appearance is taken as a manifestation, an organized whole is presupposed. The whole is known and the special place and role of the part is taken for granted. Suppose, however, a doubt arises as to whether the thing appearing is *entitled* to act in behalf of another; a claim is involved which must be investigated before "manifestation" may be predicated. Representative capacity instead of being assumed presents a problem, an inquiry to be undertaken. Yet we must not confuse the nature of the problem. We may assert that it is *false* that a man is an agent or representative of those whom he pretends to appear in behalf of. This does not mean that the "appearance" is false or unreal, but that the objective relations required to confer upon it the role which is claimed are lacking. Are the delegate's credentials in order? What is the nature of the body by whom he was chosen? There is an epistemic relation in the sense of knowledge of the relations which obtain to other objective things, but not an epistemological problem in the usual meaning of epistemology, namely, a direct and unique relation of a thing known to a knower.

A typical case of "appearance" wherein the exact objective

reference which constitutes a representative office (as a contribution in an inclusive whole) is at issue, is found when there is a question of legal liability in certain transactions. Did or did not a certain person "hold himself out" as agent for a certain principal? Or was a man who claimed to be an agent of another in making a certain agreement authorized to do so? Or, putting the two questions together, did he claim a representative character, and if so was he so authorized to act in that manner so that certain obligations are incumbent on a principal? In any such case, there is a question of whether a certain *allegation* was made or implied, and if so whether the relations to other things constituting the whole in question bear out the assertion. There is a problem, and there is inquiry. The solution of the problem one way or another depends upon what relations are discovered to exist to other things. If these objective relations are ignored, then "appearance" is taken to denote a relation to something behind or underneath which is wholly different in *kind* from what appears. The relation is taken in a lump, statically and in a co-existential cross-section. Hence the "reality" of what appears lies in a different realm of being. But in truth what is behind and covert is other things of the same kind but which have to be searched for in order to determine the genuineness of the representative office claimed. What is "back" is homogenous with what appears.

When there is doubt as to an alleged representative relation and it has to be settled by inquiry into connections with other things, we are obviously in a realm where "appearance" has an intellectual significance. What does the appearing thing *signify*? Is the claimed signifying capacity valid? Truth and falsity are involved. In this meaning there are further relations involved than in the second case where manifestation or exhibition is taken as an *undoubted* part of the situation. As the second sense of appearance makes explicit a connection with an inclusive whole, whose various manifestations are determined by the nature of the whole to be a serial order, so the third sense makes explicit the necessity of determining a *right* to inclusion within this whole; or, stated more generally, makes necessary the determination of the interrelated whole of which it is actually a constituent. This determination involves a complex set of relations. In the proposition "The sun appears" there is implied the relation of the event termed "rising" to the sun as an enduring object which passes through a cycle of changes. When we say "The rising of the sun is a manifestation of the structure of the solar system" the relation is to the whole system of which the appearance of the sun at a determinate place and time is a function. The same is true in the proposition "Booth appears in the part of Hamlet," where the drama of Hamlet—or perhaps the entire Shakesperian system—is implied as the inclusive whole; so also in the proposition "Coolidge is the legal president of the United States." But in the last proposition "legal" introduces a relationship which is not explicit in the second sense, as is evident if we imagine the proposition denied. The question of validity, or right, enters in. The system is no longer taken for granted as including the part which "manifests" it in a particular phase but must be sought for. It is also necessary to determine the exact nature of the appearing object which is alleged to be a representative part of the whole.

III

There is involved in the latter determination a triadic set of relations. First, there is the relation which the man in his primary qualities sustains to himself as "holding himself out" as agent or as purporting to be an official. This is a reflexive relation. Secondly, as necessary for the *conclusive* determination of this relation there is the relation of the person claiming the office, role, or part to the principal or those represented. In the third place, depending upon this determination, there is a relation to those with whom he has dealings in virtue of the office. This third relationship constitutes the differential feature of the significance of appearance which is now before us. It is the consequences which follow when the claim to a certain office is legitimate and which do not follow when it is not justified which make it necessary in case of doubt to ascertain the rightfulness of the claim. In virtue of being an officer of the law a man has distinctive dealings with other persons; he has effective connections with them, which he does not have as a human being apart from the representative capacity. There is an obvious difference between Booth playing a certain role and a man *claiming* to be Booth taking the same part. In the first instance, those con-

cerned, those affected by the playing of the part, either like it or
do not like it. But if the claim is proved invalid, they have re-
dress; they can exercise claims in return.

We have selected as typical illustrations instances of persons
who put forth a representative claim. The purpose of the illustrative instances is to prepare the way for an examination of cases
where an appearing object is *taken* to have a particular representative capacity and office, that of being a sign or evidence of
other things: cases where the assertion is not made by a person
on his own account, but is made by the one who takes the thing
as evidence or sign of something else. The same triad of relations
is found in both cases. Hence analysis of the cases in which the
claim is self-asserted instead of depending upon some one's taking or using the appearing object as representative is relevant.
When something is *taken* to be smoke and smoke is taken to be a
sign of fire, there is also found the added and differential trait of
relation to consequences, which consequences differ according
as the representative role is or is not justified. When one takes
the appearing object as a sign of fire, there are reactions and consequences appropriate to fire. Otherwise one merely reacts just
to the appearing object in its own appearing or presented qualities and not as a sign. There is the same difference of treatment
and consequences found in responding just to a sound and to a
sound which is also a word, that is, to which a meaning is assigned, standing for something beyond itself. It is one and the
same whether we say we deal with the whole which includes
the manifestation or with the manifesting object as a member
of the whole; the difference is purely verbal. But in the case of
an appearance as sign or evidence of something else there is the
need of determining how justified or valid is the claimed sign
relationship, since responsive dealing and consequences depend
upon the answer obtained to this question.

IV

The nub of the whole matter turns upon the nature of
the reflexive relationship, the relation which an appearing object
in its intrinsic qualities bears to the properties that capacitate it
to be a sign of something else. That the appearing object is *in*

evidence is a truism; the statement is tautologous. But *of* what is it evidence? The latter question introduces a distinction *within* the thing used as sign, a reflexive relation. That the relation to something else involved in being a sign of it is reflected into the appearing object itself is obvious from the fact that we take things as signs when we do not know *of* what they are signs. This happens in every inquiry, since inquiry implies first that some appearing object is a sign, and secondly that we do not as yet know of what it is a sign or evidence. This mode of taking would be impossible unless there were a distinction and relation set up within the appearing object between itself in its primary qualities and itself in its signifying office: just as a sheriff can neither identify his office as sheriff with all his personal peculiarities, needs, and capacities, nor yet wholly sink the latter in his official capacity. He must distinguish within himself characteristics which belong to him *qua* human being from characteristics belonging to him as officer, and at the same time relate them to each other. Unless he does the latter, his office becomes a purely disembodied function; it can become operative only through traits which belong to him as a human being, his hands, legs, tongue, and wits.

We may take as illustrative evidence the case of a sound used as a sign of something else—as a word in language. A child reacts first to a sound as a sound—as the adult reacts to sounds in a language he does not understand as gibberish or as quasi-musical. Taking it as a sign depends upon not treating it merely as a sound and also upon *not identifying* it with the thing meant. This is the same as saying that one must distinguish it as sound from its properties as signifying. The result is both a degradation and an enhancement. The former affects the sound in its primary existential qualities; the latter the sound as a sign. Mere sound is reduced to a vehicle or carrier; the latter gives the sound dignity and status. A good example is found in mathematical symbols where the direct quality of the appearing object is reduced as near a minimum as is consistent with having any appearance at all in order that there may be gain in effective representative import. Relationships react into the thing used as symbol to redetermine its *prior* estate.

This effect of the reflexive relation is of great importance. It is the clew to understanding the traditional misconstruction of the nature of appearances. The essence of this misinterpretation is that it notes and retains in mind the degradation of immediate existential quality, while it fails to note that this reduction is due to and for the sake of the performance of an office as sign of something else—as in our monetary system a bullion value is reduced existentially to a piece of paper while the paper at the same time gains value as a token of indebtedness. The degradation is taken to be something intrinsic, belonging to an existence as such. The appearing object certainly exists, but lacks self-justifying existence. It is therefore said to be only fragmentary, inherently defective, a puzzling anomaly in the order of being. There inevitably ensues the derogatory valuation of "appearance."

This analysis applies also to the "epistemological" misconstruction of the nature of appearance, though now with especial reference to the second of the triad of relations, that of the relation of the appearing thing as sign of some doubtful object to that of which it is a sign. The *legitimacy* of a case of "holding out" as agent does not depend upon a direct and unique relation of a man to those to whom he holds himself out but upon his antecedent relations to others. So the validity of using a thing as sign of this or that inferred object depends not on its direct relation to the knower, but upon its specific relations to other things. As long as these remain in question, we say that "apparently" it signifies this or that. "It *seems* to do so." "Apparently" and "seeming" have nothing to do with its direct and co-existential relation to the knower, nor with its intrinsic quality as affected by this relation. They designate the doubtful state of an inferred object. Whenever final judgment in inference is suspended an appearing object gains a distinctive intellectual status, such as is conveyed in propositions like: "The bill seems to be counterfeit"; "the patient appears to have typhoid," etc.

Instead of denoting an intrinsic distortion of reality due to relation to a knower, "appearance" here marks a safeguard and precaution characteristic of all careful inferential inquiry. By use of "appears," "seems," attention is called to the as yet uncertain status of the inferred object, while at the same time a record is made of the fact that the thing which appears (in the first sense) has a certain amount of evidential force attached to it. Permit this distinctive phase of partial, inconclusive, representative capacity to be ignored, and "seeming" is inevitably taken to be a quality of what appears, due to relation of the thing in itself to a knower.

V

It is submitted that in the foregoing considerations is found the explanation of the category of "phenomena" as opposed to true realities that is found in Greek thought. Men are now in possession of methods of inquiry which have proved their efficacy to unravel the knots which come along with frustrated inference. There are still, of course, many cases in which we can not complete an attempted inference; when, that is, we can not tell just *what* some thing means although it is undoubted in its existential manifestation. But our technique of inquiry has succeeded in so many cases (and in so many cases we have managed to improve a defective technique until it has proved adequate) that in practise we recognize such cases as instances of blocked inference, and lay the subject-matter aside for further investigation. We employ the subject-matter to define a *problem* for research. But when the distinction between phenomena and noumena as two orders of Being was formulated, there was no technique of experimental analysis. The mechanical and the mathematical instruments of intellectual resolution were both lacking. Consequently, the world was full of anomalies—things which undoubtedly existed, but which could not be understood or duly connected with other things. It was an easy and not unnatural generalization to say that they constituted a realm on their own account. All that could be done, in the absence of methods which would link them into members of a course of events, thereby explaining them, was to *classify* them with one another as "phenomena."

This account is confirmed by the fact that the higher and contrasting realm of being was antithetically conceived to be noumena. Things which appear are present in sense-perception; the eye, ear, hand are the media of their determinate presence. Inferred objects that define their meaning and also constitute their full reality are, on the other hand, *qua* inferred, objects of *thought*. This statement is a truism, inference and thought being synonymous. Now at present our scientific technique is such that we can, speaking generally, experimentally control conditions so that an inferred object may itself be rendered perceptible, if not in its entirety, at least in respect to some of its defining features. The existential subject-matter arrived at by calculation is at least a candidate for observation. When the technique of observational analysis is not adequate to bring the calculated objects into view or render them apparent, they are treated as hypothetical. But Greek methods of inquiry made no provision for the "category" of the hypothetically existent any more than it did for the temporarily problematic. Hence the intelligible object which furnished meaning and stability to the perceptible object was treated as final, not as intermediate. It was intrinsically and wholly the object of thought, the noumenon, while in inference conducted by physical and mathematical methods there is no break in kind between the object which appears and the inferred object. For such inference proceeds by insertion of intermediaries which are sufficiently numerous and compact to be members of a temporal continuum. For lack of such methods, Greek speculation made a single jump from the apparent object to the object of thought; the absence of intermediary connecting links necessarily shoved the latter into a non-temporal realm.

The hard and fast distinction between the perceptible object as mere appearance and the intelligible object as ultimate reality is thus a projection, from a period when methods of inferential inquiry were deficient, into a period when methods actually practised leave no place for the distinction. The important thing to bear in mind is that when an ulterior object of inquiry is constituted, the perceptible or apparent object no longer stands over against what is inferred, but is included along with it in a comprehensive series or an inclusive whole. Any case of physical investigation illustrates what is here asserted. When, for example, the appearances or phenomena termed malaria are satisfactorily understood, they present themselves as part of the life-history of anopheles in connection with the life-history of the creature who is their host. When the inference is completed in the categorical assertion of an object, both the appearing (perceived) thing which has been employed as sign and the inferred (intelligible) object lose the isolation they possess during the process of inquiry and delayed inference. They both become members of an interrelated inclusive whole, so that the category of "manifestation" becomes applicable. A one-to-one relation in isolation between the appearing thing and what it means is characteristic only of the period of doubt and inquiry. The reason why our focal awareness fastens so exclusively upon the perceived or appearing object and the definite inferred or intelligible object is obvious. They are terms in a literal sense, defining terminals of the inclusive whole; nothing is gained by giving attention to the latter. The case is similar to the presence of a locked door and search for its key. The reality is the whole operation of opening the locked door. But the sought-for key is literally the key to this operation, just as the lock defines the problem. As soon as the key which fits is found, the operation takes place as a matter of course. It is passed over in explicit consciousness just because it is taken for granted as that which gives meaning to the key and to the search for it.

VI

We have, however, temporarily turned aside from the explanation of the epistemological misconstruction. Deferred inference, or relation to a missing but signified object, is expressed in such propositions as "This seems to be pure milk (but perhaps it is skimmed milk)." But such propositions as "It looks blue or chalky" have a distinctly different intellectual force. "The man down on the street looks very small from here"—the top of a high building. "That distant mountain appears blue." "The rails seem to converge; the stick appears bent; the coin seems elliptical." Such propositions (which have been made of late the object of much puzzled speculation) have a ready interpretation when taken in their logical status, that is, as involved in the use of appearing things as signs of something else. In the cases previously analyzed it was the inferred object which is merely "apparent," that is apparently but not surely signified. The propositions just stated refer to the way in which the object used as evidence presents itself. They state the appearing object as it appears—in our first neutral sense. But they state it with a purpose—that of defining the exact nature of the evidence at hand. "The stick seems bent in water" does not mean that the appearing object *seems* bent. It means that what appears *is* something bent, though not necessarily the stick; perhaps it is light.

The first step is to put ourselves on guard against depending upon the vague term "seems," "appears." We must specify the respect in which it appears, to eye, ear, touch, smell. If I say that a straight stick rising out of water *looks* bent (implying relation to the eye) I but state an objective fact, verified by a camera, and explained by well-known physical principles. In exactly the same way when I say that a moving whistle *sounds* higher or lower in pitch as it approaches or recedes, I state a fact of relationship to the ear. Incredible as it may appear, a serious problem has been made out of the fact that a fire feels colder as we move away from it. The process of creating the "problem" is as follows. The fire has really but one temperature. How is that fact to be reconciled with the fact that at different distances it *seems* to be of many different temperatures? Of course, it can not; but the statement is so mixed as to be absurd; the problem, not the solution, is at fault. The temperature of the air affected by the fire changes with distance; this is a physical fact, and what is *felt* is the temperature of the air. Thus to say that the fire *feels* colder as we recede is to state an incontrovertible fact; there would be a problem only if it were not so.

It may seem like a trick to do away with this "problem" by substituting specific terms, "looks," "sounds," "feels," for the general term "appears," "seems." But the force of the substitution is to call attention to a specific relation, to that particular part of the nervous organism which is involved as a condition, a physical or causal condition, of the appearance of the thing which is to serve as sign. The propositions under discussion make explicit the exact nature of the thing to be used as evidence, before it is used.

This becomes evident if, instead of stating a definitive or concluded judgment such as "The straight stick looks bent in the water," we say merely "There is present a form which to the eye looks bent," a statement of fact, but of fact about the appearing object irrespective of any inferential use made of it. If we say "The round coin looks elliptical seen from this angle" we again state a correct judgment. If we say "There is present to the eye an elliptical form" we describe the nature of the appearance (in our first sense) preliminary to making inferential use of it. It may be said, however, that we have unduly simplified the situation in getting rid of the alleged problem. It may be objected that the real problem lies in the fact that there are many appearances, and that the question to be answered is which of these, if any, is or corresponds to the real object, a stick or penny. Why, for example, should the circular form, the thing appearing in perpendicular vision, be assigned any superiority over other appearances to the eye? The reply is that it is *not*; the superiority assigned to it is that of being a *better sign*. And that it is such is something learned by experience in making use of various appearing objects as bases of inferring other things.

A man sights with his eye along the edge of a board he has been planing and says "it *looks* straight." This is simply a statement of fact, of the same kind as when he says "it is a board." If he said "it *is* straight," he would have made an inference from what appears to his eye, perhaps a wrong one. When he confined himself to saying "it looks straight" he limits himself to a statement of the nature of what appears and suspends inferential judgment; it is just as if a geologist were to confine his report to saying that there are certain marks on the rock which *suggest* a trilobite, while he refrains from asserting that they *are* a fossil trilobite. In any such case, the one who makes the judgment recognizes in effect that the conditions of the appearing object are complex; they include both the edge of the board and his sensori-cerebral apparatus. Both conditions are involved in the temporal series of which the last term is the appearing object. No epistemic import is assigned to vision, but the visual apparatus is taken for what it is, one of the physically causal conditions of what appears or is present. Distrusting the adequacy of this appearance as sign or evidence, one then resorts to production of another appearance, the process being identical with any physical experiment where conditions are intentionally varied. One runs a finger over the edge and says "It feels uneven here and there." The implication is not that a tactile appearance is more real than a visual, but that for certain purposes it affords a better sign of a sought-for object. If one is still in doubt one may fall back upon mechanical appliances—upon relations to other things instead of relations to the organism—in order to determine that appearance which shall serve as a sign. As actual existence all "appearances" stand on the same level; as signs some are better than others, just as what one witness says is better evidence than what another says, although the utterances of each are equally actual occurrences.

VII

We conclude with a summary. The original and neutral sense of appearance is just that something previously remote, covert or obscure *appears*—comes into view, into actualized presence. When the thing appearing is referred without question to a whole of which it is a related member, it is termed an exhibition, manifestation, display, expression. But often this reference can not be made directly; what it belongs to has to be searched for. The evident object is now treated as evidence; it gains the role of sign or index of something or other. In its reflexive relation it sets a problem to be inquired into. The appearance is now an appearance *of* something whose nature is to be determined by inference from the appearing objects and from others which may be aligned with it. Appearing now takes temporarily the form of seeming rather than of showing. But "seeming" does not signify that something seems to exist, but that a certain *object* seems to be *pointed* to: "seeming" denotes an essayed, but temporarily blocked, inference. Finally, it is often necessary in the interest of control of inference to state the causal conditions of that appearing thing which is used as sign. In this operation, organic conditions of touch, sight, hearing, smell, or taste are specified and "appears" is specified into feels, looks, sounds, smells, tastes thus and so. The process is no different from when a scientist specifies the physical apparatus which he has employed in producing the phenomena which are used as evidence in drawing an inference.

This point is worth dwelling upon. It has been implied throughout that the relation to organic apparatus involved in such terms as "looks," "sounds," "feels," "tastes" is a reference to a causal condition of the production of the particular object which appears, not a reference to a knower, an epistemological reference, and that this relation is specified as a safeguard of the use to be made of it in inference from it. The statement is thus precisely analogous to the pains which a scientific experimenter takes to specify exactly the apparatus through which he obtains the subject-matter from which he infers certain conclusions. If a man uses a microscope in obtaining his evidential subject-matter he tells of its nature and manner of employment so that another can decide *how* the objects were made to appear. The statement that a thing "looks thus and so" is of precisely the same sort; the difference being, on the one hand, the greater degree of refinement of causal condition in the case of the microscope, and on the other hand, the presence of an *organic* mechanism as a condition of the appearance of anything whatever. A similar principle applies to the use of a sense-organ under different conditions and to recourse to various sense organs: not because the appearance conditioned by one is more real existentially than that of any other, or less real than that of the thing inferred, but because in this way subject-matter better for purposes of inference is secured. So, in the laboratory, conditions are intentionally varied and precisely for the same reason: to obtain a fuller amount of evidential material and to use its various phases as means of checking the use of other portions.

The general notion of "appearance" we have broken up into a number of meanings each distinctive in a particular contextual situation. The elimination of traditional misconstruction is procured when we keep these meanings definite, each in its proper place, and do not transfer and mix traits of one with those of another. Four distinctive situations are stated in such propositions as the following: (I) The sun appears (rises, or emerges from a cloud)—the primitive and neutral meaning. (II) The sun's appearing at this place and time is a manifestation of certain characteristics of the structure of the system to which sun and earth belong; a type of proposition which states the conclusion of any completed inquiry accepted as valid knowledge. (III) The sun seems to move (apparently moves) from east to west across a stationary earth; the statement of an inferred object with an intimation of suspense and doubt concerning its correctness, or as preliminary to its rejection and the statement of another inferred total object such as "In reality, the earth rotates and its rotation, while the sun remains stationary with reference to the earth, accounts for the appearing objects which were used (wrongly) as the basis of the other inference." And finally (IV) The sun looks to the eye about the size of a twenty-five cent piece—a statement of a fact which is to serve as part of the matter of an inference as to its actual size, or an inference about its distance, etc.

In denying the metaphysical interpretation of appearance as an inferior order of being, it is not meant, of course, to deny all metaphysical implications in a certain sense of "metaphysical." On the contrary, the argument rests throughout on the fact that existential subject-matter in each of the four types of propositions is a series or temporal order of interrelated elements forming an inclusive whole of which the appearances are members. If this existential fact be denied, some form of bad metaphysics is bound to result. Nor is it implied that no general theory of knowledge is involved. On the contrary, the analysis points to the fact that knowledge requires as its precondition an appearing object which results from an integrated interaction of all factors, the organism included, and that the completed object of knowledge is precisely such an interrelated and self-manifesting whole as includes an appearance.

"Half-Hearted Naturalism"

The ambiguity of philosophic terms and of the conceptions for which the words stand is indicated by the way in which Mr. Thilly cites, approvingly, Mr. Santayana's characterization of my mode of thinking as half-hearted naturalism.[1] To Mr. Santayana, naturalism is a desirable thing; the shortwindedness of my devotion to it is matter for adverse criticism.[2] To Mr. Thilly, my half-heartedness is the saving clause; it intimates an idealistic strain which in spite of myself gives a redeeming touch to what would otherwise be, I suppose, sheer mechanistic materialism. There is no word in the history of thought which carries more varied meanings than "nature"; naturalism shares in its diverse significations.

I am not equipped with capacities which fit one for the office of a lexicographical autocrat, and I shall make no attempt to tell what naturalism must or should signify. But I may take advantage of the opportunity to say what empirical naturalism, or naturalistic empiricism, means to me. I can not hope to offer anything new, or anything which I have not said many times already. But perhaps by concentrating on this one point I may make the tenor of my thinking clearer, and incidentally throw some light on why it appears, from two opposed ends of the philosophic gamut, to be half-hearted.

"In nature," says Santayana, "there is no foreground or background, no here, no now, no moral cathedra, no centre so really

---

1. Thilly, the *Philosophical Review*, Vol. XXXV, p. 532 [this volume, p. 395], in an article entitled "Contemporary American Philosophy." Santayana, *Journal of Philosophy*, Vol. XXII, p. 680 [p. 375], in an article entitled "Dewey's Naturalistic Metaphysics." All further quotations of Santayana are from this article.

2. *Ibid.*: "I am myself a dogmatic naturalist," p. 687 [p. 383].

[First published in *Journal of Philosophy* 24 (1927): 57–64. For articles by Santayana and Thilly to which this is a reply, see Appendixes 1 and 2.]

central as to reduce all other things to mere margins and perspectives" (p. 678 [p. 373]). The statement is dogmatic; I do not say
this in reproach; Mr. Santayana professes himself a dogmatic
naturalist, and everyone, in my conception, must be dogmatic at
some point in order to get anywhere with other matters. But
even a dogmatist may be asked the grounds for his assertion,
not, indeed, in the sense of what proof he has to offer, but in the
sense of what is presupposed in the assertion, from what platform of beliefs it is propounded. I can not think that Santayana
supposes that it is self-evident to others or to himself that nature
is of the sort mentioned. The sweep and import of the statement
is the more striking in that Santayana professes to operate without any metaphysics and is confident that a whole-hearted naturalism is inarticulate, a kneeling, before the unknowable and an
adjuration of all that is human.[3] Since knowledge of nature is not
the ground for Santayana's statements as to its character, their
ground, I take it, is negative and antithetic; the traits denied are
those which are characteristic of human life, of the scene as it
figures in human activities. Since they are found where man is,
they are not, it would seem, attributable to anything but man;
nature, whatever else it is or is not, is just something which does
not have these traits. In short, his presupposition is a break between nature and man; man in the sense of anything more than a
physically extended body, man as institutions, culture, "experience." The former is real, substantial; the latter specious, decep-
tive, since it has centres and perspectives.

To me, then, Santayana's naturalism appears as broken-backed
as mine to him seems short-winded. It is in virtue of what I call
naturalism that such a gulf as Mr. Santayana puts between nature
and man—social or conventional man, if you will—appears incredible, unnatural and, if I am rightly informed as to the history
of culture, reminiscent of supernatural beliefs. To me human affairs, associative and personal, are projections, continuations,
complications, of the nature which exists in the physical and pre-
human world. There is no gulf, no two spheres of existence, no
"bifurcation." For this reason, there are in nature both foregrounds and backgrounds, heres and theres, centres and perspec-

3. "A naturalist instinctively, . . . who, heartily despising the foreground, has
   fallen in love with the greatness of nature and has sunk speechless before the
   infinite" (p. 679 [p. 374]).

tives, foci and margins. If there were not, the story and scene of man would involve a complete break with nature, the insertion of unaccountable and unnatural conditions and factors. To any one who takes seriously the notion of thoroughgoing continuity, the idea of existence in space and time without heres and nows, without perspectival arrangements, is not only incredible, but is a hang-over of an intellectual convention which developed and flourished in physics at a particular stage of history. It is not pragmatism nor any particular philosophical view which has rendered this conception questionable, but the progress of natural science. One who believes in continuity may argue that, since human experience exhibits such traits as Santayana denies to nature, the latter *must* contain their prototypes. The new physics finds them necessary to describe the physical world in its own terms.[4]

There are many occasional statements in Mr. Santayana's expositions which indicate that his agnosticism is not as complete in detail as it is in formal official statement. In discussing specific matters he often suggests that he shares the belief of the ordinary man that human experience, adequately safeguarded by a normal organism and a proper equipment of apparatus and technique, may afford dependable indications of the nature of things that underlie it; that we do not merely fall back on an "animal faith" that there is some adorable substance behind, but that we come to reasonable terms with its constituents and relations. If one generalizes this position, then the main features of human life (culture, experience, history—or whatever name may be preferred) are indicative of outstanding features of nature itself—of centres and perspectives, contingencies and fulfillments, crises and intervals, histories, uniformities, and particularizations. This is the extent and method of my "metaphysics":—the large and constant features of human sufferings, enjoyments, trials,

4. The use of the terms "events" and "affairs" in *Experience and Nature*, which Mr. Santayana finds redolent of a submergence of real "nature" in an all-absorbing human moralism, was dictated by the fact that physical science is now compelled, on its own behalf, to employ, if not these words, at least these ideas. On the philosophical side, it is dictated by the fact that the metaphysics, adhered to as far as I can make out by Santayana, which treats nature as a single substance whose parts and changes as such are illusory, is a flight of metaphysics which is beyond me, and which appears to be a survival of a rationalistic spiritualism which he officially repudiates.

failures and successes together with the institutions of art, science, technology, politics, and religion which mark them, communicate genuine features of the world within which man lives. The method differs no whit from that of any investigator who, by making certain observations and experiments, and by utilizing the existing body of ideas available for calculation and interpretation, concludes that he really succeeds in finding out something about some limited aspect of nature. If there is any novelty in *Experience and Nature*, it is not, I should say, this "metaphysics" which is that of the common man, but lies in the use made of the method to understand a group of special problems which have troubled philosophy.

Experience thus conceived is obviously opposed to the usage of the word in the English psychological tradition, a divergence which I was at some pains to point out in criticizing the latter. I consider myself justified, however, in departing widely from the strain of Locke and Hume and James Mill, because I believe that I am only reverting, with some critical purification, to the implications of its everyday untechnical meaning. Experience, thus conceived, constitutes, in Santayana's happy phrase, a foreground. But it is the foreground *of* nature. If I differ from Santayana as to this latter point, the difference lies in that he thinks of the foreground as a screen which conceals the background; to me it conducts our thought to the background. Apparently he conceives of the foreground as lying between human intuition and experience and the background; to me human experiencing is the foreground, nature's own. He also may think that the background alone is nature to the exclusion of the foreground; I am not sure. But I am sure that the foreground is itself a portion of nature, an integral portion, and that nature is not just the dark abysmal unknown postulated by a religious faith in animality, especially since on such a view animality itself becomes a matter of faith.

Holding these views, the reader may dimly imagine the shock I felt when I read that it is axiomatic with me that "nothing but the immediate is real" (p. 683 [p. 378]).[5] A large portion of

5. Lest silence be taken to imply assent, I state specifically that the positions taken by me are as distant as may be from those attributed to me by Santayana on pp. 685–686 [pp. 380–81]. If I held them I should admit his argument against them to be conclusive, but they are as unreal to me as they are to him. As he says, "practice precludes" any such beliefs, and while I am not as much

Mr. Santayana's article is a dialectic development of the consequences of such a belief, and naturally a destructive one. Since he thinks the view is mine I can only be grateful to him that he did not devote his skillful dialectic to showing that the whole of *Experience and Nature* is a mass of contradictions; the doctrines of "instrumentalism" with its assertion of recurrent identities in nature and of efficacious connections among natural existences, and of knowledge as always mediate and relational, evidently contradict the belief that only the immediate is real. But perhaps lack of interest in my discussion of specific topics on the part of Mr. Santayana saved me from that fate. I repeat, then, that I hold that everything which is experienced *has* immediacy, and that I also hold that every natural existence, in its own unique and brutal particularity of existence, also *has* immediacy, so that the immediacy which characterizes things experienced is not specious, being neither an unnatural irruption nor a supernatural imposition. To *have* traits, however, is not to *be* them, certainly not in any exclusive sense; and a considerable part of my discussion of special topics is an attempt to show that characteristic traits of the subjects dealt with are to be accounted for as "intersections" or "interpenetrations" (I could think of no better words) of the immediate and the nexional or mediatory, just as my criticism of various philosophical theories rests on showing that they have isolated one phase at the expense of the other. That I do not think the immediacy which matters of experience have is specious or non-natural, I freely admit, for a nature that had no immediacy would not even exist, and the precious word "substance" would then turn out to be a synonym for that other word "essence." But perhaps such a naturalism as this is *too* wholehearted to be acceptable.

Mr. Santayana says: "Suppose I say that 'everything ideal

---

of a pragmatist—or at least not the kind of pragmatist—as I am sometimes alleged to be, I am not so witless as to try to unite respect for practice with a belief in the exclusive absoluteness of immediacy. He says: "The dominance of the foreground, avowedly relative, has been turned from a biological accident into a metaphysical principle" (p. 686 [p. 382]). But since I do not regard the foreground as an accident and since I also do not regard the mid-distant biological as an accident with regard to the physical, my "metaphysical principle" is that the related foreground may be taken as a method for determining the traits of the background. Treating the foreground as an "accident" illustrates what to me is *un*natural in Santayana's notions. In lieu of many references which might be made to *Experience and Nature*, I content myself with one, p. 262 [*Later Works* 1:200–201].

emanates from something natural.' Dewey agrees, understanding that everything remote emanates from something immediate. But what I meant was that everything immediate—sensation, for example—emanates from something biological" (p. 685 [p. 381], foot-note). This statement of what I believe is a specific case of the assumption that I hold that only the immediate is real and that the foreground is a foreground of nothing. So I repeat that while "consciousness" is foreground in a preeminent sense, experience is much more than consciousness and reaches down into the background as that reaches up into experience. I agree that the ideal "emanates" from the biological; I have been even criticized by other critics as if I held it to be a mere gaseous emanation from the biological. In reality I think that the ideal, sensation, for example, is as real as the biological from which it emanates, and, expressing a higher meed of the interaction of things than does the biological without sensation, is in so far I will not say more real, but a fuller reality. Nor do I believe that sensation *is* immediate, though it *has* immediacy. It bears within itself connections; it carries something of the remote conditions which call it into existence; otherwise it could never serve as a sign nor have cognitive value. And lest this disclaimer should be interpreted in the sense which Santayana points out in the context, namely, to mean that the *concept* of sensation is derived from biological concepts as terms in discourse, I add that I mean the derivation from the biological of the ideal in a literal existential sense. When Mr. Santayana goes on to say that it emanates from "the largely unknown or humanly unknowable process of animal life," there is indicated, perhaps, a difference. That the biological process and its history of eventuating (*pace* Santayana, for the suggestion of "history" and "event") in sensation is largely *unknown*, is only too evident. But to my mind this ignorance is not because experience interposes a veil, but because experience has not been sufficiently probed for its indications. To Mr. Santayana, if I understand him—and perhaps I do not any better than he does me—experience is such that "humanly unknowable" is his proper phrase. But in that case, why refer to the underlying conditions as biological? Or is it merely that all discourse, since experiential, is specious and conventional, and that one phrase is as good as another over against the abysm of unknowable Substance, God, Matter?

Santayana finds traces of my actual position, in as far as it is identical with his in the matter of the biological basis and substantiation of the ideal, in my implicit behaviorism. But Mr. Santayana always makes it as difficult as possible for anyone to agree with him, and so he criticizes behaviorism as a peculiarly "American" form of externalism. The real gravamen appears to be that Santayana thinks that the behavioristic account of thought in connection with animal functions is bound to deny mind itself. There are psychologists who call themselves behavioristic who doubtless do precisely this thing. Santayana thinks that I must be either a behaviorist in this sense or a speculative egotist, and that my empiricism compels me, in spite of tendencies in the former direction, to become the latter. But the main thesis of *Experience and Nature* is that human experience is intelligent (including, of course, mis-intelligent) and emotional behavior. In other words, I have tried to bring together on a naturalistic basis the mind and matter that Santayana keeps worlds apart. The attempt, I know, is unusual; perhaps it is doomed to frustration, but I should not want that matter prejudged on the basis of my own ineptness. The trial is bound to be made again, and again, and I hope with increasing success. That success is impossible, given Santayana's premises, I am quite aware. But why not change the premises? My dependence upon the social or conventional medium may be too great, but my faith in it does not extend to believing that the last word on matter and mind has been said by it.

Mr. Santayana says that the foreground as conceived by me is a social world, a social medium. This he terms, somewhat invidiously, I think, convention. But, accepting the word "convention," I state what I have already implied, that "convention" is not conventional, or specious, but is the interaction of natural things when that interaction becomes communication. A "sign" may be conventional, as when a sound or a mark on a piece of paper—themselves physical existences—symbolizes other things; but *being* a sign, the sign-function, has its roots in natural existences; human association is the fruit of those roots. I can understand Santayana's idea that the social medium is conventional in a prejudicial sense only as another illustration of that structural dislocation of non-human and human existence which I have called a broken-backed naturalism.

One of the basic contradictions which Santayana might readily have pointed out in my conclusions, if I really hold that only the immediate is real, concerns the social. He says that I have a "tendency to dissolve the individual into his social functions" (p. 675 [p. 370]), which, put in logical language, signifies that I resolve the immediate into the mediate. But since I find in human life, from its biological roots to its ideal flowers and fruits, things both individual and associational—each word being adjectival—I hold that nature has both an irreducible brute unique "itselfness" in everything which exists and also a connection of each thing (which is just what *it* is) with other things such that without them it "can neither be nor be conceived." And as far as I can follow the findings of physics, that conclusion is confirmed by the results of the examination of physical existence itself. Since experience is both individualized and associational and since experience is continuous with nature as background, as a naturalist I find nature is also both. In citing Mr. Santayana's denial that nature has here, now, and perspective, I found myself in stating my own view compelled to use the plural form:— heres, nows, perspectives. I would not draw an inference from the mere use of a word, but Santayana's use of the singular form is suggestive that he thinks experience is something sole and private, and so thinking attributes a similar view to others who use the term. It *is* absurd to confer upon nature a single here, now, and perspective, and if that were the only alternative, I should agree with Mr. Santayana in his denial. But there are an indefinite multitude of heres, nows, and perspectives. As many as there are existences. To swallow them up in one all-embracing substance is, moreover, to make the latter unknowable; it is the logical premise of a complete agnosticism. But such an embrace also makes substance inconceivable, for it leaves nothing for it to absorb or substantiate. Moreover, the things which have heres and nows all interact with one another; they form a world of intercourse and association, though not of that communication which is a fuller exhibition of their connections with one another. If, perchance, I have exaggerated by my manner of speech the associated aspects of experience, it is because the traditional theory of experience dominated by a false psychology (as the traditional view of nature which Santayana reflects is dominated by a false physics) has ignored and denied that phase, assuming, as Mr. Santayana appears to do, a sole and lonely here and now.

It is not my purpose to criticize Mr. Santayana's philosophy, but to make an evidently much-needed statement of what I hold in distinction from what is imputed to me. This intention moves me even when I go on to say that I find two movements and two positions in Santayana which are juxtaposed, but which never touch. In his concrete treatments of any special topic when a matter of controversy to which traditional school labels are attached is in abeyance, he seems genuinely naturalistic; the things of experience are treated not as specious and conventional, but as genuine, even though one-sided and perverse, extensions of the nature of which physics and chemistry and biology are scientific statements. But he has a number of pigeonholes into which every philosophy must go with its appropriate, fixed, and absolute tag attached:—his own philosophy when it becomes self-conscious as well as those of others. When he lets himself go in any body of subject-matter, free from the influence of traditional and professorial labels, I not only learn much from him, but I flatter myself that I am for the most part in agreement with him. But when he deals with a system of thought and finds it necessary to differentiate his own system from it, his naturalism reduces itself to a vague gesture of adoring faith in some all-comprehensive unknowable in contrast with which all human life—barring this one gesture—is specious and illusory. Only in this way can I explain the fact that while I find myself in so much agreement with him he is in such profound disagreement with me. The case seems to resemble that of the Irishman who said the two men looked very much alike, especially one of them. Barring that feature of Mr. Santayana's thought to which exception has been taken, I am happy to be that one.

Meaning and Existence

In their *Meaning of Meaning*, Ogden and Richards relate the following incident quoted from a book entitled *Among Congo Cannibals*, written by J. H. Weeks: "I remember on one occasion wanting the word for Table. There were five or six boys standing around, and tapping the table with my forefinger, I asked, 'What is this?' One boy said it was a *dodela*, another that it was an *etanda*, another stated that it was *bokali*, a fourth that it was *elamba*, and the fifth said it was *meza*." It turned out afterwards that "one boy thought we wanted the word for tapping; another understood that we were seeking the word for the material of which the table was made; another had the idea that we required the word for hardness; another thought we wished for a name for that which covered the table; and the last, not being able, perhaps, to think of anything else, gave us the word, *meza*, table—the very word we were seeking."[1]

The incident appears to me relevant to the first part of the recent article by Professor Hall.[2] In it, following what he takes to be the denotative method that I recommend and try to use in *Experience and Nature*, he selects a number of passages in which I am dealing with meanings, and implies that the selection is equivalent to the "pointing" required by the empirical denotative method. I can not complain that he has dealt severely with them or me, or that he relies upon any merely verbal analysis. But he seems to ignore the fact that "pointing" is not so simple and direct an affair as pointing a finger—or tapping on a table. In *Experience and Nature*, the words "showing" and "finding"

---

1. *The Meaning of Meaning*, p. 174.
2. "Some Meanings of Meaning in Dewey's *Experience and Nature*." *Journal of Philosophy*, Vol. XXV (1928), pp. 169–181 [this volume, pp. 401–13].

[First published in *Journal of Philosophy* 25 (1928): 345–53. For Hall's article to which this is a reply, see Appendix 3.]

are usually added in explanation of "pointing," while this is described, for example, as follows: "Index to a starting point and road which if taken may lead to a direct and ineffable presence."[3] The implication is that any idea, reasoning, theory, hypothesis, is an indication to a road to be taken so that its value is that of stating a method to be used, the value being tested by its capacity to terminate in the situation required. Hence—as the above incident shows—the "denotative empirical method" is not an affair of pointing directly to things (things being inclusive of passages in a book), but of having such ideas as point and lead by use as methods to some directly experienced situation. Hence regard for context is indispensable. Moreover, since the parties in question failed to understand one another because they did not share in a common situation—in one of communication—the anecdote may be taken to illustrate the need of a shared situation whenever the understanding of ideas and symbols enters into question. Hence I make the following comments in the hope that what I say may serve to indicate a road that will lead to and terminate in the *situations* that are designated by the symbol "meaning," and aid in instituting a shared situation and so promote understanding.

I

Reference to Mr. Hall's text shows that he finds diversity and possibly inconsistency in at least five types of cases in which I refer to meanings. Some of the cases overlap, so I shall state them all before proceeding to deal with any of them. First, there are quotations to support the statement that I hold meaning to be *restricted* to communication and that in turn to linguistic behavior.[4] In conflict with this view are quoted statements by me which indicate to Mr. Hall that I accept "meaning" antecedent to

3. *Experience and Nature*, p. 86 [*Later Works* 1:74–75]. The word "ineffable" occasions difficulty. The idea might be expressed by saying "presence in a non-symbolic way." Something can be said *about* a situation so present or "had," but it can not possibly be duplicated by any possible number or combination of symbols.
4. The term "restriction" is not only used by him on p. 170 [p. 402], but is repeated several times with emphasis in his own discussion in the second part of the article.

language and discourse and the social participation based upon them. The second set of quotations concerns the temporal relations of the occurrence of meanings, and seems to indicate that after officially restricting meaning to a future reference, the facts compel me also to introduce "immanent temporal wholes." The third point concerns an apparent inconsistency between the instrumental and the final or consummatory character of meanings. The fourth set of quotations concerns meaning as "referential" and as "immanent." The fifth, as he points out, brings us back to the first point: there are quotations that are taken by Mr. Hall to indicate that I at some times assert that meanings arise in direct interaction of the human organism with a physical environment, apart from any social mediation, or the function of "communication."

Let me state first that my general position is correctly stated by Hall in his second paragraph; namely, I hold that events "acquire meanings" or that "meaning occurs within nature."

1a. *Restriction to Communication.*—Coming to his first point, the assertion I make is that events "acquire" meaning through the fact of communication, which is an observably empirical fact in some phases of human intercourse. But being begotten is quite a different affair from subsequent development. There is not a word quoted by Mr. Hall to indicate that this further growth is "restricted" to conditions of *origin*. To say (as I do say in a passage cited) that "meanings do not *come into being* without language" is neither to say, nor to imply, that conditions of origin are identical with those of all subsequent status. Not only that, but a phrase in a sentence cited says explicitly that "its [language's] consequences react upon other events physical and human, giving them meaning or significance." What is more important than this particular indication of the arbitrary character of Mr. Hall's imputation to me of restriction of meaning to linguistic behavior is the fact that the text of *Experience and Nature* devotes considerable space to showing that after communication has been instituted, its pattern is extended to all sorts of acts and things, so that they become signs of other things. There is nothing original in the idea of "language of nature"; such contribution as I have made to the idea consists simply in finding the locus of the *origin* of the voice and message of natural things in human communication.⁵ What has led Mr. Hall wrong in this particular case of his use of the denotative method is failure to recognize the context of discussion of *origin*, so that in consequence he gives an illegitimate extension of passages that concern genesis to all further developments and functions.

1*b. Qualities and Meanings.*—The notion that, after I have found the origin of meaning in that interaction of natural events that constitutes the distinctive trait of human social life, I attribute meaning to events antecedent to any communication, contains an analogous misconception. (This statement applies to the latter part of the paragraph on p. 170 [p. 402] and also to the entire point made on p. 173 [p. 405].) I certainly hold that there are natural "prerequisites" of the origin of meaning in communication. Among these indispensable preconditions are the immediate qualities called, in psychological terminology, "feelings"; these are, as I have said, the existential basis and "stuff" of meanings. It is only by imputing to me the position that these qualities or feelings are themselves meanings that he can attribute to me inconsistency. That such qualities or feelings exist prior to, and independent of, any language function—even in the widest sense of sign-function—and that they guide behavior in all kinds of subtle ways, I distinctly hold. But I explicitly deny that they are meanings. Mr. Hall may hold they *are* meanings, and he may be able to give such reasons for so holding as to entitle him to the belief. But he is hardly entitled to imply or assert that I hold such a view, and then find inconsistency in my views.⁶

2. *The Temporal Question.*—That events acquire meaning by having their potential consequences identified with them as their

5. The bearing of this point affects Mr. Hall's discussion in the second part of his article, since that is based upon imputing to me quite arbitrarily the "restriction" mentioned. Take for illustration his example from sailing (on p. 174 [p. 407]). It is wholly compatible with my position that wrinkles, etc., in sails should convey to us messages that a particular speech terminology is inadequate to set forth.

6. On p. 173 [p. 405], after quoting from me a statement about qualities, he inserts in brackets after the word "qualities," the phrase "direct meanings—in this case sensations." It is easy to convict any one of inconsistency by attributing to him conceptions which one holds one's self, but which the one criticized repudiates.

properties (as in the case of practically anything designated by a common noun) I certainly hold. I also hold that when it is a question of *critical* search for *valid* meaning, namely, for that meaning we are *entitled* to treat as the genuine meaning of the events in question, we are obliged to have recourse to antecedent conditions. For when a question arises as to what the consequences *really* are, we must take into account a course of events and sometimes a long one.

3. *Instrumental and Final.*—The right determination of meanings thus involves the consideration of "total histories" or "immanent temporal wholes," for while the meaning of existences is constituted by expected or potential consequences, the nature of these consequences can be properly decided only in connection with such larger histories. When such a history is explicitly taken into consideration, the distinction of instrumental and final meanings is made or comes into view. That there are some things which have their meaning determined by use in attaining or accomplishing other things or that are tools, and that some meanings are deliberately determined as means of reaching other meanings, I do not suppose is questioned by any one.

Instrumental meanings also, and obviously, imply as their ulterior goal some meaning *to* which they are instrumental, or a meaning that is final, fulfilling, consummatory. On the basis of any empirical method, there are no meanings which are always and inherently instrumental or final; this is a matter of their status and role in some actual situation. Hence the need for taking a situation as a "total history." Antecedent events as such, or "efficient" events as preparatory conditions, define an instrumental meaning; the last or closing events taken in their meaning with respect to events that have preceded have final meaning. Each is correlative with the other with respect to the temporal course as a whole. A further reason why the relation of meanings in this phase to a "total history" is made much of is the fact that philosophical literature is so filled with instances of sharp separation of instrumental and final. It became necessary in criticism of such views to point out that *any* event, however instrumental, may also be fulfilling with respect to what antecedes; while, since the event with the final meaning is involved in an ongoing course of events, it has in this phase instrumental value. Instead of an inadvertent inconsistency, the reference to "total histories" is thus an integral and consistent part of the entire hypothesis.

4. *Referential and Immanent.*—There is an undoubted ambiguity in the word "meaning" as it is currently used. We say something means something else in the sense of signifying it, being a sign of it. This is equivalent to taking one thing as evidence for something else, a ground for inference to the other thing, as when we say smoke means fire—that is, where smoke is observed, fire is inferred. But events are also clothed with meaning on their own behalf; thus something is directly taken to be "smoke" in the instance just cited; the character of being smoke belongs to the event as it is observed—although in some other case "smoke" might be a character signified or inferred. The words "referential" and "immanent" are used to designate the two uses, so as to avoid the ambiguity that resides in the word as it is ordinarily employed.

Since it will be admitted, I take it, that I did not originate the ambiguity, but found it in the current use of "meaning," the question that arises concerns only the relationship of the two meanings to other phases of my entire hypothesis regarding meaning. (1) The recognition of the two kinds is consistent with the theory of origin in communication; sounds first gain meaning as signs when used to stand for something besides themselves; while in consequence of such repeated use, the things stood for come to be the "immanent" meaning of the sounds in question. (This is the case with the illustration of "cat" used by Mr. Hall on p. 179 [p. 413].) According to my hypothesis, immanent meanings exist in consequence of the repeated successful outcome of referential or evidential meanings. (2) As to the temporal matter, the thing signified in the case of an event as sign is something that is experienced in consequence of an act based upon taking an existence as sign or evidence; it is subsequent or future in the course of experience. But critical testing of the validity of such a meaning involves recourse to larger temporal wholes. (3) Thus the fulfilling or consummatory meaning of a referential case becomes the immanent meaning, the directly taken-for-granted meaning, of subsequent situations. Thus, as far as I can make out, there is no inconsistency in the various parts of the whole theory; they hang together, imply and support one another.

II

The foregoing is meant to cover the first section of Mr. Hall's article, in which he cites various passages of mine; by anticipation it covers also certain portions of his second section as well. There is, however, a point of considerable importance in his second section that has not been touched upon.[7] If I grasp the point of his criticism, it may be put baldly as follows: My treatment has no way of distinguishing events without meaning from others having meaning except as I attribute to the former some nature or character, and thus assign meaning to them. The distinction implies a connecting identity; that identity is itself one of meaning. It is, accordingly, argued that the distinction I have drawn is in reality one between partial, imperfect meaning and a fuller and more inclusive meaning, not between that without meaning and that with meaning. His third section, as I understand it, develops this idea positively. I shall, then, deal with this argument in both its critical or negative aspect and its positive form.

For a reason that will presently appear the portion of his argument based upon a logical analysis of my position will have to be dealt with briefly. That when I think of anything or when anything enters into discourse it in so far acquires meaning, there can be no doubt. And, of course, when events-without-meaning are referred to, that very fact brings them within the field of thought and discourse, and in so far confers meaning upon them, if only the meaning of being without meaning. One could go further: to refer to anything as an *event* is in so far to ascribe character or nature and hence a meaning to it. Of all this, there is no doubt. But to use these considerations as evidence that things have meaning prior to, and independently of, entering into thought or discourse is another matter. Such an argument converts a predicament of discourse into a trait of existence—a somewhat unconvincing procedure. The fact that if one supposes, by way of

---

7. I do not wish to leave the impression that I suppose that there are no laxities or inconsistencies in the treatment of meaning in *Experience and Nature*. There is one such case (but I think only one) in the passages cited by Mr. Hall, and I accept responsibility for that as far as it may have misled Mr. Hall. The exception is the use of the phrase "*sense* of rightness" in the passage quoted by him on p. 170 [p. 402]. There is an undoubted shift here from "qualities" (or "feelings") to qualities with meaning, or "sense."

hypothetical premiss, that there are existences without meaning, they would nevertheless acquire some meaning in virtue of entering into discourse—and in my conception this is precisely what happens—deprives this argument of probative value. It is akin to the argument once used by idealists when they said that the realist's assertion that there are things not related to mind presupposes that things are related to mind.

The positive argument, as I understand it, comes to the following: What signifies, being a symbol, is meaning; what is signified is also meaning, but a larger and more inclusive meaning. Symbol and symbolized are thus related as a partial and a complete meaning; although we rarely if ever attain to the complete meaning, there is always a sense that it is there, and that we might go to it and explore it in at least some greater detail. "The symbol is not a self-contained whole external to and set over against another self-contained whole which is its meaning. No, the symbol is a true part of the meaning" (p. 179 [p. 413]). "The meaning (that which refers) and the meant" are not "separate and external." For example, a sailor in a storm hears a whine, a roar, a crack. "These sounds mean that a sail has been blown out of its bolt ropes. Clearly the sign or symbol is here not external to the signified" (p. 180 [p. 413]).

Let me restate the matter in terms of my own hypothesis. There are two possible cases, those of "referential" and "immanent" meaning. In the former, there is an event that has the meaning of indicating, signifying, being a sign or evidence of something else. This case would be exemplified if the sailor were inexperienced or were a landlubber. He would hear the shriek and crack, and would think it signified something, but he would have to *infer*—use the noise as a symbol—and do something to find out what it signified. If, however, the sailor is experienced, the consequences of his prior-tested and verified inferences enter directly into the object of perception; the noise will *be*, to him, a sail blown out of its bolt ropes. This sort of thing is what is intended by the phrase "immanent meaning,"—precisely the same sort of thing happened in the case of the supposititious landlubber when he identified an event as a noise, a cracking noise, etc. In such cases there is no distinction of something as sign and something else as thing signified; there is a total situation "had," having its direct meaning-content. Upon my hypothesis, how-

ever, there are no "immanent meanings" except in consequence
of the results of prior referential or reflective (inferential) meanings. And the event in its immanent meaning also enters into
some other situation with reference to a part of which it serves as
a sign—in the referential sense. For example, just as the landlubber in hearing the peculiar noise would ask what it signifies,
the sailor will ask, on "knowing" that the sail is blown out,
What next? Or, what shall I do about it?

Returning to Mr. Hall's account, the following difference between it and mine is evident. According to him, the sound *is* intrinsically a meaning. According to me, the sound is something
which is used or taken as a sign, and hence "meaning" is here a
name for the *relation* between it and something else—the relation being the function or office of serving as a sign of something
else. The related is identified and demarcated by the operation of
inference. In the same way, the thing signified is not meaning un-
qualifiedly; it is something *having* meaning; something indicated
and taken as satisfying the requirements of the thing or events
having the signifying role. Of course, the signifying event is not
self-contained; if it were it would not signify; the very meaning
of being a signifying event is that it stands in the *relation* of indicating. And when the inference is completed, there is a "whole,"
a situation in which the distinction between signifying and signified no longer holds; for the completion of the inference is
found in a situation which is directly "had"—the situation "we
go to" and then go from.

In taking the symbol and the thing symbolized as themselves
"meanings" in their own right and behalf, and not because of the
relation they enter into—that of inference,—Mr. Hall to my
mind unwittingly begs the entire issue. Thus he says "the *symbol*
is not a self-contained whole, but is a true part of the meaning."
But the question at issue is already decided when a thing is
termed a "symbol"—to term it a symbol is, of course, to assign
meaning to it. The real issue concerns the conditions under
which a thing *becomes* a symbol—or at least concerns the question whether they *are* symbols inherently or become symbols in
their use as signs or evidence in inference. Consider the following
sentence of Mr. Hall's: "It is the arbitrariness of symbols in language which lends false color to the notion that meaning (that
which refers) and the meant are separate and external" (p. 180

[p. 413]). To call *that which* means meaning and *that which* is meant meaning is simply, I submit, to beg the issue. His statement is open to the obvious reply that he has taken advantage of an elliptical use of language. "Meaning" as "that which refers" is a short expression for some existence that stands as a sign or as ground for inferring something else. "The meant" is a short expression for something in its capacity of being intended or signified in the reference. Mr. Hall's view is that which signifies is intrinsically a meaning, and that it means a meaning. My view is that a *thing* signifies another *thing* in being employed as an evidential sign, and that in this *relation* both acquire meaning. Even in case Mr. Hall's view is right and mine is wrong, the case can not be settled by taking advantage of the ambiguity involved in an elliptic use of language. Then, in the case of "cat" that has come to have immanent meaning and of the sail-blown-out-of-bolt-ropes, we have by my theory the funded immanent result of the successful issue of prior referential or reflective relations. It is necessary, as was pointed out earlier, not to be misled by the ambiguity in the ordinary uses of the word "meaning," and so shift without warning from one sense to the other.

This discussion is not supposed to prove my position or disprove Mr. Hall's. It is intended to make clear the distinction between them, and to make explicit the assumptions on the basis of which Mr. Hall reaches the conclusion that "existence" is itself but a partial meaning within a larger whole of meaning. To my mind his argument is an able and ingenious restatement of the idealistic position as conveyed, for example, in Royce's distinction of external and internal meanings. The topic of meaning is certainly one of the most important in contemporary philosophical discussion, and while I regret that my article is necessarily so controversial, I wish to express my appreciation of the genial temper and acuteness of Mr. Hall's article, and my gratitude to him for giving me the opportunity to restate some points in my own hypothesis in their relations to one another.

Philosophies of Freedom

A recent book on *Sovereignty* concludes a survey of various theories on that subject with the following words: "The career of the notion of sovereignty illustrates the general characteristics of political thinking. The various forms of the notion have been apologies for causes rather than expressions of the disinterested love of knowledge. The notion has meant many things at different times; and the attacks upon it have sprung from widely different sources and been directed toward a multiplicity of goals. The genesis of all political ideas is to be understood in terms of their utility rather than of their truth and falsity."[1] Perhaps the same thing may be said of moral notions; I do not think there is any doubt that freedom is a word applied to many things of varied plumage and that it owes much of its magic to association with a variety of different causes. It has assumed various forms as needs have varied; its "utility" has been its service in helping men deal with many predicaments.

Primary among the needs it has been employed to meet and the interests it has served to promote is the moral. A good deal is assumed in asserting that the centre of this moral need and cause is the fact of choice. The desire to dignify choice, to account for its significance in human affairs, to magnify that significance by making it the centre of man's moral struggles and achievements has been reflected in the idea of freedom. There is an inexpugnable feeling that choice *is* freedom and that man without choice is a puppet, and that man then has no acts which he can call his very own. Without genuine choice, choice that when expressed in action makes things different from what they otherwise would be, men are but passive vehicles through which ex-

1. *Sovereignty*, by Paul Ward, p. 167.

[First published in *Freedom in the Modern World*, ed. Horace M. Kallen (New York: Coward-McCann, 1928), pp. 236–71.]

ternal forces operate. This feeling is neither self-explanatory nor self-justificatory. But at least it contributes an element in the statement of the problem of freedom. Choice is one of the things that demands examination.

The theoretical formulation for the justification of choice as the heart of freedom became, however, involved at an early time with other interests; and they rather than the unprejudiced examination of the fact of choice determined the form taken by a widely prevalent philosophy of freedom. Men are given to praise and blame; to reward and punishment. As civilization matured, definite civil agencies were instituted for "trying" men for modes of conduct so that if found guilty they might be punished. The fact of praise and blame, of civil punishment, directed at men on account of their behavior, signifies that they are held liable or are deemed responsible. The fact of punishment called attention, as men became more inquiring, to the ground of liability. Unless men were responsible for their acts, it was unjust to punish them; if they could not help doing what they did, what was the justice in holding them responsible for their acts, and blaming and punishing them? Thus a certain philosophy of the nature of choice as freedom developed as an apologia for .an essentially legal interest: liability to punishment. The outcome was the doctrine known as freedom of will: the notion that a power called will, lies back of choice as its author, and is the ground of liability and the essence of freedom. This will has the power of indifferent choice; that is, it is equally free to choose one way or another unmoved by any desire or impulse, just because of a causal force residing in will itself. So established did this way of viewing choice become, that it is still commonly supposed that choice and the arbitrary freedom of will are one and the same thing.[2]

It is then worth while to pause in our survey while we examine more closely the nature of choice in relation to this alleged connection with free will, free here meaning unmotivated choice.

2. Doubt may be felt as to the assertion that this interpretation of freedom developed in connection with the legal motif. The historic connecting link is found in the invasion of moral ideas by legal considerations that grew up in the Roman Empire. The association was perpetuated by the influence of Roman law and modes of moral thought, and even more by the incorporation of the latter in the theology and practices of the Christian Church, the nurse of morals in Europe.

Analysis does not have to probe to the depths to discover two serious faults in the theory. It is a man, a human being in the concrete, who is held responsible. If the act does not proceed from the man, from the human being in his concrete make-up of habits, desires and purposes, why should *he* be held liable and be punished? Will appears as a force outside of the individual person as he actually is, a force which is the real ultimate cause of the act. *Its* freedom to make a choice arbitrarily thus appears no ground for holding the human person as a concrete being responsible for a choice. Whatever else is to be said or left unsaid, choice must have some closer connection with the actual make-up of disposition and character than this philosophy allows.

We may seem then to be in a hopeless dilemma. If the man's nature, original and acquired, makes him do what he does, how does his action differ from that of a stone or tree? Have we not parted with any ground for responsibility? When the question is looked at in the face of facts rather than in a dialectic of concepts it turns out not to have any terrors. Holding men to responsibility may make a decided difference in their *future* behavior; holding a stone or tree to responsibility is a meaningless performance; it has no consequence; it makes no difference. If we locate the ground of liability in future consequences rather than in antecedent causal conditions, we moreover find ourselves in accord with actual practice. Infants, idiots, the insane, those completely upset, are not held to liability; the reason is that it is absurd—meaningless to do so, for it has no effect on their further actions. A child as he grows older finds responsibilities thrust upon him. This is surely not because freedom of the will has suddenly been inserted in him, but because his assumption of them is a necessary factor in his *further* growth and movement.

Something has been accomplished, I think, in transferring the issue from the past to the future, from antecedents to consequences. Some animals, dogs and horses, have their future conduct modified by the way they are treated. We can imagine a man whose conduct is changed by the way in which he is treated, so that it becomes different from what it would have been, and yet like the dog or horse, the change may be due to purely external manipulation, as external as the strings that move a puppet. The whole story has not then been told. There must be some practical participation from within to make the change that is effected significant in relation to choice and freedom. From *within*—that fact rules out the appeal, so facilely made, to will as a cause. Just what is signified by that participation by the human being himself in a choice that makes it really a choice?

In answering this question, it is helpful to go, apparently at least, far afield. Preferential action in the sense of selective behavior is a universal trait of all things, atoms and molecules as well as plants, animals and man. Existences, universally as far as we can tell, are cold and indifferent in the presence of some things and react energetically in either a positive or negative way to other things. These "preferences" or differential responses of behavior, are due to their own constitution; they "express" the nature of the things in question. They mark a distinctive contribution to what takes place. In other words, while changes in one thing may be described on the basis of changes that take place in other things, the *existence* of things which make certain changes having a certain quality and direction occur cannot be so explained. Selective behavior is the evidence of at least a rudimentary individuality or uniqueness in things. Such preferential action is not exactly what makes choice in the case of human beings. But unless there is involved in choice at least something continuous with the action of other things in nature, we could impute genuine reality to it only by isolating man from nature and thus treating him as in some sense a supra-natural being in the literal sense. Choice is more than just selectivity in behavior but it is *at least* that.

What is the more which is involved in choice? Again, we may take a circuitous course. As we ascend in the range of complexity from inanimate things to plants, and from plants to animals and from other animals to man, we find an increasing variety of selective responses, due to the influence of life-history, or experiences already undergone. The manifestation of preferences becomes a "function" of an entire history. To understand the action of a fellow-man we have to know something of the *course* of his life. A man is susceptible, sensitive, to a vast variety of conditions and undergoes varied and opposed experiences—as lower animals do not. Consequently a man in the measure of the scope and variety of his past experiences carries in his present capacity for selective response a large set of varied possibilities. That life-history of which his present preference is a function is complex.

Hence the possibility of continuing diversification of behavior: in short, the distinctive *educability* of men. This factor taken by itself does not cover all that is included within the change of preference into genuine choice, but it has a bearing on that individual participation and individual contribution that is involved in choice as a mode of freedom. It is a large factor in our strong sense that we are not pushed into action from behind as are inanimate things. For that which is "behind" is so diversified in its variety and so intimately a part of the present self that preference becomes hesitant. Alternative preferences simultaneously manifest themselves.

Choice, in the distinctively human sense, then presents itself as one preference among and out of preferences; not in the sense of one preference already made and stronger than others, but as the formation of a new preference out of a conflict of preferences. If we can say upon what the formation of this new and determinate preference depends, we are close to finding that of which we are in search. Nor does the answer seem far to seek nor hard to find. As observation and foresight develop, there is ability to form signs and symbols that stand for the interaction and movement of things, without involving us in their actual flux. Hence the new preference may reflect this operation of mind, especially the forecast of the consequences of acting upon the various competing preferences. If we sum up, pending such qualification or such confirmation as further inquiry may supply, we may say that a stone has its preferential selections set by a relatively fixed, a rigidly set, structure and that no anticipation of the results of acting one way or another enters into the matter. The reverse is true of human action. In so far as a variable life-history and intelligent insight and foresight enter into it, choice signifies a capacity for deliberately changing preferences. The hypothesis that is suggested is that in these two traits we have before us the essential constituents of choice as freedom: the factor of individual participation.

Before that idea is further examined, it is, however, desirable to turn to another philosophy of freedom. For the discussion thus far has turned about the fact of choice alone. And such an exclusive emphasis may well render some readers impatient. It may seem to set forth an idea of freedom which is too individual, too "subjective." What has this affair to do with the freedom for which men have fought, bled and died: freedom from oppression and despotism, freedom of institutions and laws? This question at once brings to mind a philosophy of freedom which shifts the issue from choice to action, action in an overt and public sense. This philosophy is sufficiently well presented for our purposes in the idea of John Locke, the author, one may say, of the philosophy of Liberalism in its classic sense. Freedom is *power to act* in accordance with choice. It is actual ability to carry desire and purpose into operation, to *execute* choices when they are made. Experience shows that certain laws and institutions prevent such operation and execution. This obstruction and interference constitutes what we call oppression, enslavement. Freedom, in fact, the freedom worth fighting for, is secured by abolition of these oppressive measures, tyrannical laws and modes of government. It is liberation, emancipation; the possession and active manifestation of *rights*, the right to self-determination in action. To many minds, the emphasis which has been put upon the formation of choice in connection with freedom will appear an evasion, a trifling with metaphysical futilities in comparison with this form of freedom, a desire for which has caused revolutions, overthrown dynasties, and which as it is attained supplies the measure of human progress in freedom.

Before, however, we examine further into this notion in its relation to the idea of choice already set forth, it will be well to consider another factor which blended with the political *motif* just mentioned in forming the classic philosophy of Liberalism. This other factor is the economic. Even in Locke the development of property, industry and trade played a large part in creating the sense that existing institutions were oppressive, and that they should be altered to give men power to express their choices in action. About a century after Locke wrote this implicit factor became explicit and dominant. In the later eighteenth century, attention shifted from power to execute choice to power to carry *wants* into effect, by means of free—that is, unimpeded—labor and exchange. The test of free institutions was the relation they bore to the unobstructed play of wants in industry and commerce and to the enjoyment of the fruits of labor. This notion blended with the earlier political idea to form the philosophy of Liberalism so influential in a large part of the nineteenth century. It led to the notion that all positive action of government is oppressive; that its maxim should be Hands Off; and that its action should be limited as far as possible to securing the freedom of behavior of one individual against interference proceeding from the exercise of similar freedom on the part of others; the theory of *laissez-faire* and the limitation of government to legal and police functions.

In the popular mind, the same idea has grown up in a noneconomic form, and with the substitution of instincts or impulses for wants. This phase has the same psychological roots as the economic philosophy of freedom, and is a large part of the popular philosophy of "self-expression." In view of this community of intellectual basis and origin, there is irony in the fact that the most ardent adherents of the idea of "self-expression" as freedom in personal and domestic relations are quite often equally ardent opponents of the idea of a like freedom in the region of industry and commerce. In the latter realm, they are quite aware of the extent in which the "self-expression" of a few may impede, although manifested in strict accordance with law, the self-expression of others. The popular idea of personal freedom as consisting in "free" expression of impulses and desire— free in the sense of unrestricted by law, custom and the inhibitions of social disapprovals—suggests the fallacy inhering in the wider economic concept, suggests it in a more direct way than can readily be derived from the more technical economic concept.

Instincts and impulses, however they may be defined, are part of the "natural" constitution of man; a statement in which "natural" signifies "native," original. The theory assigns a certain intrinsic rightness in this original structure, rightness in the sense of conferring upon impulses a title to pass into direct action, except when they directly and evidently interfere with similar selfmanifestation in others. The idea thus overlooks the part played by interaction with the surrounding medium, especially the social, in generating impulses and desires. These are supposed to inhere in the "nature" of the individual when that is taken in a primal state, uninfluenced by interaction with an environment. The latter is thus thought of as purely external to an individual, and as irrelevant to freedom except when it interferes with the operation of native instincts and impulses. A study of history would reveal that this notion, like its theoretically formulated congeners in economic and political Liberalism, is a "faint ru-

mor" left on the air of morals and politics by disappearing theological dogmas, which held that "nature" is thoroughly good as
it comes from the creative hand of God, and that evil is due to
corruption through the artificial interference and oppression exercised by external or "social" conditions.

The point of this statement is that it suggests the essential fallacy in the elaborate political and economic theories of freedom
entertained by classic Liberalism. They thought of individuals as
endowed with an equipment of fixed and ready-made capacities,
the operation of which if unobstructed by external restrictions
would be freedom, and a freedom which would almost automatically solve political and economic problems. The difference between the theories is that one thought in terms of natural rights
and the other in terms of natural wants as original and fixed. The
difference is important with respect to special issues, but it is
negligible with respect to the common premise as to the nature
of freedom.

The liberalistic movement in each of its phases accomplished
much practically. Each was influential in supplying inspiration
and direction to reforming endeavors that modified institutions,
laws and arrangements that *had* become oppressive. They effected a great and needed work of liberation. What were taken to
be "natural" political rights and "natural" demands of human
beings (natural being defined as inherent in an original and native fixed structure, moral or psychological) marked in fact the
sense of new potentialities that were possessed only by limited
classes because of changes in social life due to a number of causes.
On the political side, there was the limited class that found its activities restricted by survivals of feudal institutions; on the economic side, there was the rise of a manufacturing and trading
class that found its activities impeded and thwarted by the fact
that these same institutions worked to protect property-interests
connected with land at the expense of property-interests growing
out of business and commerce. Since the members of the two
classes were largely identical, and since they represented the
new moving forces, while their opponents represented interests
vested and instituted in a past that knew nothing of these forces,
political and economic liberalism fused as time went on, and in
their fusion performed a necessary work of emancipation.

But the course of historic events has sufficiently proved that they emancipated the *classes* whose special interests they represented rather than human beings impartially. In fact, as the newly emancipated forces gained momentum, they actually imposed new burdens and subjected to new modes of oppression the mass of individuals who did not have a privileged economic status. It is impossible to justify this statement by an adequate assemblage of evidence. Fortunately it is not necessary to attempt the citation of relevant facts. Practically every one admits that there is a new social problem, one that everywhere affects the issues of politics and law; and that this problem, whether we call it the relation of capital to labor, or individualism versus socialism, or the emancipation of wage-earners, has an economic basis. The facts here are sufficient evidence that the ideals and hopes of the earlier liberal school have been frustrated by events; the universal emancipation and the universal harmony of interests they assumed are flagrantly contradicted by the course of events. The common criticism is that the liberal school was too "individualistic"; it would be equally pertinent to say that it was not "individualistic" enough. Its philosophy was such that it assisted the emancipation of individuals having a privileged antecedent status, but promoted no general liberation of all individuals.

The real objection to classic Liberalism does not then hinge upon concepts of "individual" and "society."

The real fallacy lies in the notion that individuals have such a native or original endowment of rights, powers and wants that all that is required on the side of institutions and laws is to eliminate the obstructions they offer to the "free" play of the natural equipment of individuals. The removal of obstructions did have a liberating effect upon such individuals as were antecedently possessed of the means, intellectual and economic, to take advantage of the changed social conditions. But it left all others at the mercy of the new social conditions brought about by the freed powers of those advantageously situated. The notion that men are equally free to act if only the same legal arrangements apply equally to all—irrespective of differences in education, in command of capital, and the control of the social environment which is furnished by the institution of property—is a pure absurdity, as facts have demonstrated. Since actual, that is, effective, rights and demands are products of interactions, and are not found in the original and isolated constitution of human nature, whether moral or psychological, mere elimination of obstructions is not enough. The latter merely liberates force and ability as that happens to be distributed by past accidents of history. This "free" action operates disastrously as far as the many are concerned. The only possible conclusion, both intellectually and practically, is that the attainment of freedom conceived as power to act in accord with choice depends upon positive and constructive changes in social arrangements.

We now have two seemingly independent philosophies, one finding freedom in choice itself, and the other in power to *act* in accord with choice. Before we inquire whether the two philosophies must be left in a position of mutual independence, or whether they link together in a single conception, it will be well to consider another track followed by another school of thinkers who also in effect identify freedom with operative power in action. This other school had a clear consciousness of the dependence of this power to act upon social conditions, and attempted to avoid and correct the mistakes of the philosophy of classic Liberalism. It substituted a philosophy of institutions for a philosophy of an original moral or psychological structure of individuals. This course was first charted by Spinoza, the great thinker of the seventeenth century. Although the philosophy of Liberalism had not as yet taken form, his ideas afford in anticipation an extraordinarily effective means of criticizing it. To Spinoza freedom was power. The "natural" rights of an individual consist simply in freedom to do whatever he *can* do—an idea probably suggested by Hobbes. But what *can* he do? The answer to that question is evidently a matter of the amount of the power he actually possesses. The whole discussion turns on this point. The answer in effect is that man in his original estate possesses a very limited amount of power. Men as "natural," that is, as native, beings are but parts, almost infinitesimally small fractions, of the whole of Nature to which they belong. In Spinoza's phraseology, they are "modes" not substances. As merely a part, the action of any part is limited on every hand by the action and counteraction of other parts. Even if there is power to initiate an act—a power inhering in any natural thing, inanimate as well as human—there is no power to carry it through; an action is immediately caught in an infinite and intricate net-work of *inter-*

actions. If a man acts upon his private impulse, appetite or want and upon his private judgment about the aims and measures of conduct, he is just as much a subjected part of an infinitely complex whole as is a stock or stone. What he actually does is conditioned by equally blind and partial action of other parts of nature. Slavery, weakness, dependence, is the outcome, not freedom, power and independence.

There is no freedom to be reached by this road. Man has however intellect, capacity of thought. He is a mode not only of physical existence but of mind. Man is free only as he has power, and he can possess power only as he acts in accord with the whole, being reinforced by its structure and momentum. But in being a mode of mind he has a capacity for understanding the order of the whole to which he belongs, so that through development and use of intellect he may become cognizant of the order and laws of the whole, and insofar align his action with it. Insofar he shares the power of the whole and is free. Certain definite political implications follow from this identification of freedom with reason in operation. No individual can overcome his tendencies to act as a mere part in isolation. Theoretic insight into the constitution of the whole is neither complete nor firm; it gives way under the pressure of immediate circumstances. Nothing is of as much importance to a reasonable creature in sustaining effectively his actual—or forceful—reasonableness as another reasonable being. We are bound together as parts of a whole, and only as others are free, through enlightenment as to the nature of the whole and its included parts, can any one be free. Law, government, institutions, all social arrangements must be informed with a rationality that corresponds to the order of the whole, which is true Nature or God, to the end that power of unimpeded action can be found anywhere. It would be difficult to imagine a more complete challenge to the philosophy of Locke and the Liberalistic school. Not power but impotency, not independence but dependence, not freedom but subjection is the natural estate of man—in the sense in which this school conceived "the natural." Law, however imperfect and poor, is at least a recognition of the universal, of the interconnection of parts, and hence operates as a schoolmaster to bring men to reason, power and freedom. The worst government is better than none, for some recognition of law, of universal relationship, is an absolute prerequisite. Freedom is not obtained by mere abolition of law and institutions, but by the progressive saturation of all laws and institutions with greater and greater acknowledgment of the necessary laws governing the constitution of things.

It can hardly be said that Spinoza's philosophy either in its general form or in its social aspect had any immediate effect—unless it was to render Spinoza a figure of objurgation. But some two centuries later a phase of reaction against the philosophy of Liberalism and all the ideas and practices associated with it arose in Germany; and Spinoza's ideas were incorporated in deed in a new metaphysical scheme and took on new life and significance. This movement may be called institutional idealism, Hegel being selected as its representative. Hegel substituted a single substance, called Spirit, for the two-faced substance of Spinoza, and restated the order and law of the whole in terms of an evolutionary or unfolding development instead of in terms of relations conceived upon a geometrical pattern. This development is intrinsically timeless or logical, after the manner of dialectic as conceived by Hegel. But externally this inner logical development of a whole is manifested serially or temporally in history. Absolute spirit embodies itself, by a series of piecemeal steps, in law and institutions; they are objective reason, and an individual becomes rational and free by virtue of participation in the life of these institutions, since in that participation he absorbs their spirit and meaning. The institutions of property, criminal and civil law, the family and above all the national state are the instrumentalities of rationality in outward action and hence of freedom. History is the record of the development of freedom through development of institutions. The philosophy of history is the understanding of this record in terms of the progressive manifestation of the objective form of absolute mind. Here we have instead of an anticipatory criticism and challenge of the classic liberal notion of freedom, a deliberate reflective and reactionary one. Freedom is a growth, an attainment, not an original possession, and it is attained by idealization of institutions and law and the active participation of individuals in their loyal maintenance, not by their abolition or reduction in the interests of personal judgments and wants.

We now face what is admittedly the crucial difficulty in framing a philosophy of freedom: What is the connection or lack of

connection between freedom defined in terms of choice and freedom defined in terms of power in action? Do the two ways of
conceiving freedom have anything but the name in common?
The difficulty is the greater because we have so little material to
guide us in dealing with it. Each type of philosophy has been
upon the whole developed with little consideration of the point
of view of the other. Yet it would seem that there must be some
connection. Choice would hardly be significant if it did not take
effect in outward action, and if it did not when expressed in
deeds make a difference in things. Action as power would hardly
be prized if it were power like that of an avalanche or an earth-
quake. The power, the ability to command issues and consequences, that forms freedom must, it should seem, have some
connection with that something in personality that is expressed
in choice. At all events, the essential problem of freedom, it
seems to me, is the problem of the relation of choice and unimpeded effective action to each other.

I shall first give the solution to this problem that commends
itself to me, and then trust to the further discussion not indeed to
prove it but to indicate the reasons for holding it. There is an
intrinsic connection between choice as freedom and power of action as freedom. A choice which intelligently manifests individuality enlarges the range of action, and this enlargement in turn
confers upon our desires greater insight and foresight, and makes
choice more intelligent. There is a circle, but an enlarging circle,
or, if you please, a widening spiral. This statement is of course
only a formula. We may perhaps supply it with meaning by first
considering the matter negatively. Take for example an act following from a blind preference, from an impulse not reflected
upon. It will be a matter of luck if the resulting action does not
get the one who acts into conflict with surrounding conditions.
Conditions go against the realization of his preference; they cut
across it, obstruct it, deflect its course, get him into new and perhaps more serious entanglements. Luck may be on his side. Circumstances may happen to be propitious or he may be endowed
with native force that enables him to brush aside obstructions
and sweep away resistances. He thus gets a certain freedom,
judged from the side of power-to-do. But this result is a matter of
favor, of grace, of luck; it is not due to anything in himself.
Sooner or later he is likely to find his deeds at odds with condi-

tions; an accidental success may only reinforce a foolhardy impulsiveness that renders a man's future subjection the more probable. Enduringly lucky persons are exceptions.

Suppose, on the other hand, our hero's act exhibits a choice expressing a preference formed after consideration of consequences, an intelligent preference. Consequences depend upon an interaction of what he starts to perform with his environment, so he must take the latter into account. No one can foresee all consequences because no one can be aware of all the conditions that enter into their production. Every person builds better or worse than he knows. Good fortune or the favorable cooperation of environment is still necessary. Even with his best thought, a man's proposed course of action may be defeated. But in as far as his act is truly a manifestation of intelligent choice, he learns something:—as in a scientific experiment an inquirer may learn through his experimentation, his intelligently directed action, quite as much or even more from a failure than from a success. He finds out at least a little as to what was the matter with his prior choice. He can choose better and *do* better next time; "better choice" meaning a more reflective one, and "better doing" meaning one better coordinated with the conditions that are involved in realizing his purpose. Such control or power is never complete; luck or fortune, the propitious support of circumstances not foreseeable is always involved. But at least such a person forms the habit of choosing and acting with conscious regard to the grain of circumstance, the run of affairs. And what is more to the point, such a man becomes able to turn frustration and failure to account in his further choices and purposes. Everything insofar serves his purpose—to be an intelligent human being. This gain in power or freedom can be nullified by no amount of external defeats.

In a phrase just used, it was implied that intelligent choice may operate on different levels or in different areas. A man may, so to speak, specialize in intelligent choices in the region of economic or political affairs; he may be shrewd, politic, within the limit of these conditions, and insofar attain power in action or be free. Moralists have always held that such success is not success, such power not power, such freedom not freedom, in the ultimate sense.

One does not need to enter upon hortatory moralization in order to employ this contention of the great moral teachers for the sake of eliciting two points. The first is that there are various areas of freedom, because there is a plural diversity of conditions in our environment, and choice, intelligent choice, may select the special area formed by one special set of conditions—familial and domestic, industrial, pecuniary, political, charitable, scientific, ecclesiastic, artistic, etc. I do not mean of course that these areas are sharply delimited or that there is not something artificial in their segregation. But within limits, conditions are such that specialized types of choice and kinds of power or freedom develop. The second (and this is the one emphasized by moral teachers in drawing a line between true and false power and freedom), is that there *may* be—these moral idealists insist there *is*—one area in which freedom and power are always attainable by any one, no matter how much he may be blocked in other fields. This of course is the area they call *moral* in a distinctive sense. To put it roughly but more concretely: Any one can be kind, helpful to others, just and temperate in his choices, and insofar be sure of achievement and power in action. It would take more rashness than I possess to assert that there is not an observation of reality in this insight of the great teachers of the race. But without taking up that point, one may venture with confidence upon a hypothetical statement. If and inasfar as this idea is correct, there is one way in which the force of fortunate circumstance and lucky original endowment is reduced in comparison with the force of the factor supplied by personal individuality itself. Success, power, freedom in *special* fields is in a maximum degree relatively at the mercy of external conditions. But against kindness and justice there is no law: that is, no counteracting grain of things nor run of affairs. With respect to such choices, there may be freedom and power, no matter what the frustrations and failures in other modes of action. Such is the virtual claim of moral prophets.

An illustration drawn from the denial of the idea that there is an intimate connection of the two modes of freedom, namely, intelligent choice and power in action, may aid in clearing up the idea. The attitude and acts of other persons is of course one of the most important parts of the conditions involved in bringing the manifestation of preference to impotency or to power in action. Take the case of a child in a family where the environment formed by others is such as to humor all his choices. It is made easy for him to do what he pleases. He meets a minimum of resistance; upon the whole others cooperate with him in bringing his preferences to fulfillment. Within this region he seems to have free power of action. By description he is unimpeded, even aided. But it is obvious that as far as he is concerned, this is a matter of luck. He is "free" merely because his surrounding conditions happen to be of the kind they are, a mere happening or accident as far as his make-up and his preferences are concerned. It is evident in such a case that there is *no growth* in the intelligent exercise of preferences. There is rather a conversion of blind impulse into regular habits. Hence his attained freedom is such only in appearance: it disappears as he moves into other social conditions.

Now consider the opposite case. A child is balked, inhibited, interfered with and nagged pretty continuously in the manifestation of his spontaneous preferences. He is constantly "disciplined" by circumstances adverse to his preferences—as discipline is not infrequently conceived. Does it follow then that he develops in "inner" freedom, in thoughtful preference and purpose? The question answers itself. Rather is some pathological condition the outcome. "Discipline" is indeed necessary as a preliminary to any freedom that is more than unrestrained outward power. But our dominant conception of discipline is a travesty; there is only one genuine discipline, namely, that which takes effect in producing habits of observation and judgment that ensure intelligent desires. In short, while men do not think about and gain freedom in conduct unless they run during action against conditions that resist their original impulses, the secret of education consists in having that blend of check and favor which influences thought and foresight, and that takes effect in outward action through this modification of disposition and outlook.

I have borrowed the illustration from the life of a child at home or in school, because the problem is familiar and easily recognizable in those settings. But there is no difference when we consider the adult in industrial, political and ecclesiastic life. When social conditions are such as to prepare a prosperous career for a man's spontaneous preferences in advance, when things are made easy by institutions and by habits of admiration

and approval, there is precisely the same kind of outward freedom, of relatively unimpeded action, as in the case of the spoiled
child. But there is hardly more of freedom on the side of varied
and flexible capacity of choice; preferences are restricted to
the one line laid down, and in the end the individual becomes
the slave of his successes. Others, vastly more in number, are
in the state of the "disciplined" child. There is hard sledding for
their spontaneous preferences; the grain of the environment, especially of existing economic arrangements, runs against them.
But the check, the inhibition to the immediate operation of their
native preferences no more confers on them the quality of intelligent choice than it does with the child who never gets a fair
chance to try himself out. There is only a crushing that results in
apathy and indifference; a deflection into evasion and deceit; a
compensatory over-responsiveness to such occasions as permit
untrained preferences to run riot—and all the other consequences which the literature of mental and moral pathology has
made familiar.

I hope these illustrations may at least have rendered reasonably clear what is intended by our formula; by the idea that freedom consists in a trend of conduct that causes choices to be more
diversified and flexible, more plastic and more cognizant of their
own meaning, while it enlarges their range of unimpeded operation. There is an important implication in this idea of freedom.
The orthodox theory of freedom of the will and the classic theory of Liberalism both define freedom on the basis of something
antecedently given, something already possessed. Unlike in contents as are the imputation of unmotivated liberty of choice and
of natural rights and native wants, the two ideas have an important element in common. They both seek for freedom in something already there, given in advance. Our idea compels us on
the other hand to seek for freedom in something which comes to
be, in a certain kind of growth; in consequences, rather than in
antecedents. We are free not because of what we statically are,
but inasfar as we are becoming different from what we have
been. Reference to another philosophy of freedom, that of Im-
manuel Kant, who is placed chronologically in the generation
preceding that of Hegel and institutional idealism, may aid in developing this idea. If we ignore the cumbrous technicalities of
Kant, we may take him as one who was impressed by the rise

of natural science and the role played in science by the idea of causation, this being defined as a necessary, universal or invariant connection of phenomena. Kant saw that in all consistency this principle applies to human phenomena as well as to physical; it is a law of all phenomena. Such a chain of linked phenomena left no room for freedom. But Kant believed in duty and duty postulates freedom. Hence in his moral being, man is not a phenomenon but a member of a realm of noumena to which as things-in-themselves free causality may be ascribed. It is with the problem rather than the solution we are concerned. How one and the same act can be, naturalistically speaking, causally determined while transcendentally speaking it is free from any such determination is so high a mystery that I shall pass it by.

But the *problem* as Kant stated it has the form in which it weighs most heavily on contemporary consciousness. The idea of a reign of law, of the inclusion of all events under law, has become almost omnipresent. No freedom seems to be left save by alleging that man is somehow supra-natural in his make-up—an idea of which Kant's noumenal and transcendental man is hardly more than a translation into a more impressive phraseology.

This way of stating the problem of freedom makes overt, explicit, the assumption that either freedom is something antecedently possessed or else it is nothing at all. The idea is so current that it seems hopeless to question its value. But suppose that the origin of every thought I have had and every word I have uttered is in some sense causally determined, so that if anybody knew enough he could explain the origin of each thought and each word just as the scientific inquirer ideally hopes to explain what happens physically. Suppose also—the argument is hypothetical and so imagination may be permitted to run riot—that my words had the effect of rendering the future choices of some one of my hearers more thoughtful; more cognizant of possible alternatives, and thereby rendering his future choices more varied, flexible and apt. Would the fact of antecedent causality deprive those future preferences of their actual quality? Would it take away their reality and that of their operation in producing their distinctive effects? There is no superstition more benumbing, I think, than the current notion that things are not what they are, and do not do what they are seen to do, because these things have themselves come into being in a causal way. Water is what it *does* rather than what it is caused by. The same is true of the fact of intelligent choice. A philosophy which looks for freedom in antecedents and one which looks for it in consequences, in a developing course of action, in becoming rather than in static being, will have very different notions about it.

Yet we cannot separate power to become from consideration of what already and antecedently is. Capacity to become different, even though we define freedom by it, must be a present capacity, something in some sense present. At this point of the inquiry, the fact that all existences whatever possess selectivity in action recurs with new import. It may sound absurd to speak of electrons and atoms exhibiting preference, still more perhaps to attribute bias to them. But the absurdity is wholly a matter of the words used. The essential point is that they have a certain opaque and irreducible individuality which shows itself in what they do; in the fact that they behave in certain ways and not in others. In the description of causal sequences, we still have to start with and from existences, things that are individually and uniquely just what they are. The fact that we can state changes which occur by certain uniformities and regularities does not eliminate this original element of individuality, of preference and bias. On the contrary, the statement of laws presupposes just this capacity. We cannot escape this fact by an attempt to treat each thing as an effect of other things. That merely pushes individuality back into those other things. Since we have to admit individuality no matter how far we carry the chase, we might as well forego the labor and start with the unescapable fact.

In short, anything that is has something unique in itself, and this unique something enters into what it does. Science does not concern itself with the individualities of things. It is concerned with their *relations*. A law or statement of uniformity like that of the so-called causal sequence tells us nothing about a thing inherently; it tells us only about an invariant relation sustained in behavior of that thing with that of other things. That this fact implies contingency as an ultimate and irreducible trait of existence is something too complicated to go into here. But evidence could be stated from many contemporary philosophers of science, not writing with any thought of freedom in mind, but simply as interpreters of the methods and conclusions of science, to the effect that the laws leave out of account the inner being of things, and deal only with their relations with other things. Indeed, if this were the place and if I only knew enough, it could be shown, I think, that the great change now going on in the physical sciences, is connected with this idea. Older formulas were in effect guilty of confusion. They took knowledge of the relations that things bear to one another as if it were knowledge of the things themselves. Many of the corrections that are now being introduced into physical theories are due to recognition of this confusion.

The point needs an elaboration that cannot here be given if its full import for the idea and fact of freedom is to be clearly perceived. But the connection is there and its general nature may be seen. The fact that all things show bias, preference or selectivity of reaction, while not itself freedom, is an indispensable condition of any human freedom. The present tendency among scientific men is to think of laws as statistical in nature—that is, as statements of an "average" found in the behavior of an enormous number of things, no two of which are exactly alike. If this line of thought be followed out, it implies that the existence of laws or uniformities and regularities among natural phenomena, human acts included, does not in the least exclude the item of choice as a distinctive fact having its own distinctive consequences. No law does away with individuality of existence, having its own particular way of operating; for a law is concerned with relations and hence presupposes the being and operation of individuals. If choice is found to be a distinctive act, having distinctive consequences, then no appeal to the authority of scientific law can militate in any way against its reality. The problem reduces itself to one of fact. Just what *is* intelligent choice and just what does it effect in human life? I cannot ask you to retraverse the ground already gone over. But I do claim that the considerations already adduced reveal that what men actually cherish under the name of freedom is that power of varied and flexible growth, of change of disposition and character, that springs from intelligent choice, so there is a sound basis for the common-sense practical belief in freedom, although theories in justification of this belief have often taken an erroneous and even absurd form.

We may indeed go further than we have gone. Not only is the presence of uniform relations of change no bar to the reality of freedom, but these are, *when known*, aids to the development of that freedom. Take the suppositious case already mentioned. That my ideas have causes signifies that their *rise*, their *origin* (not their nature), is a change connected with other changes. If I only knew the connection, my power over obtaining the ideas I want would be that much increased. The same thing holds good of any effect my idea may have upon the ideas and choices of some one else. Knowledge of the conditions under which a choice *arises* is the same as potential ability to guide the formation of choices intelligently. This does not eliminate the distinctive quality of choice; choice is still choice. But it is now an intelligent choice instead of a dumb and stupid one, and thereby the probability of its leading to freedom in unimpeded action is increased.

This fact explains the strategic position occupied in our social and political life by the issue of freedom of thought and freedom of speech. It is unnecessary to dwell by way of either laudation or exhortation upon the importance of this freedom. If the position already taken—namely, that freedom resides in the development of preferences into intelligent choices—is sound, there is an explanation of the central character of this particular sort of freedom. It has been assumed, in accord with the whole theory of Liberalism, that all that is necessary to secure freedom of thought and expression, is removal of external impediments: take away artificial obstructions and thought will operate. This notion involves all the errors of individualistic psychology. Thought is taken to be a native capacity or faculty; all it needs to operate is an outer chance. Thinking, however, is the most difficult occupation in which man engages. If the other arts have to be acquired through ordered apprenticeship, the power to think requires even more conscious and consecutive attention. No more than any other art is it developed internally. It requires favorable objective conditions, just as the art of painting requires paint, brushes and canvas. The most important problem in freedom of thinking is whether social conditions obstruct the development of judgment and insight or effectively promote it. We take for granted the necessity of special opportunity and prolonged education to secure ability to think in a special calling, like mathematics. But we appear to assume that ability to think effectively in social, political and moral matters is a gift of God, and that the gift operates by a kind of spontaneous combustion. Few would perhaps defend this doctrine thus boldly stated; but upon the whole we act as if that were true. Even our deliberate education, our schools are conducted so as to indoctrinate certain beliefs rather than to promote habits of thought. If that is true of them, what is not true of the other social institutions as to their effect upon thought?

This state of things accounts, to my mind, for the current indifference to what is the very heart of actual freedom: freedom of thought. It is considered to be enough to have certain legal guarantees of its possibility. Encroachment upon even the nominal legal guarantees appears to arouse less and less resentment. Indeed, since the mere absence of legal restrictions may take effect only in stimulating the expression of half-baked and foolish ideas, and since the effect of their expression may be idle or harmful, popular sentiment seems to be growing less and less adverse to the exercise of even overt censorships. A genuine energetic interest in the cause of human freedom will manifest itself in a jealous and unremitting care for the influence of social institutions upon the attitudes of curiosity, inquiry, weighing and testing of evidence. I shall begin to believe that we care more for freedom than we do for imposing our own beliefs upon others in order to subject them to our will, when I see that the main purpose of our schools and other institutions is to develop powers of unremitting and discriminating observation and judgment.

The other point is similar. It has often been assumed that freedom of speech, oral and written, is independent of freedom of thought, and that you cannot take the latter away in any case, since it goes on inside of minds where it cannot be got at. No idea could be more mistaken. Expression of ideas in communication is one of the indispensable conditions of the awakening of thought not only in others, but in ourselves. If ideas when aroused cannot be communicated they either fade away or become warped and morbid. The open air of public discussion and communication is an indispensable condition of the birth of ideas and knowledge and of other growth into health and vigor.

I sum up by saying that the possibility of freedom is deeply grounded in our very beings. It is one with our individuality, our being uniquely what we are and not imitators and parasites of others. But like all other possibilities, this possibility has to be actualized; and, like all others, it can only be actualized through interaction with objective conditions. The question of political and economic freedom is not an addendum or afterthought, much less a deviation or excrescence, in the problem of personal freedom. For the conditions that form political and economic liberty are required in order to realize the potentiality of freedom each of us carries with him in his very structure. Constant and uniform relations in change and a knowledge of them in "laws," are not a hindrance to freedom, but a necessary factor in coming to be effectively that which we have the capacity to grow into. Social conditions interact with the preferences of an individual (that *are* his individuality) in a way favorable to actualizing freedom only when they develop intelligence, not abstract knowledge and abstract thought, but power of vision and reflection. For these take effect in making preference, desire and purpose more flexible, alert, and resolute. Freedom has too long been thought of as an indeterminate power operating in a closed and ended world. In its reality, freedom is a resolute will operating in a world in some respects indeterminate, because open and moving toward a new future.

Philosophy

No question can be stated where everything is questioned. Ability to formulate a problem depends upon something which is admitted. Now what is taken for granted in the present inquiry is that men live in a world that is undergoing extensive and accelerated change, and that physical science and technological industry are the causes of this change. On the basis of this admission as to the character of contemporary civilization, the question is: What is implied for philosophy? Can philosophers stand aloof, indifferent and immune; or does this state of affairs say something to them, and say it so urgently that its voice must be hearkened to? It is proposed to answer the interrogation in the affirmative. The answer rests upon another premise which is taken to be admitted. It is taken for granted that philosophical problems and the theories suggested for their solution take their rise out of some social medium, past or present. The authentic subject-matter of philosophy is found in some state of culture, although all civilizations are sufficiently complex to provide quite diverse subject-matters to different thinkers. But a philosopher draws upon that element of culture which is most congenial— or most hostile—to his own temperament and desires, whether it be the contemporary scene, Greece, India, or mediaeval Europe. Realistic content is derived positively from what is there; idealistic content is derived by way of recoil from the defects, perversions, and evils of the social medium.

The tendency of many philosophers to withdraw into the past and the remote—always easier to idealize—does not mark a private idiosyncrasy. The past furnishes an atmosphere in which imagination thrives and thought is less bound down; while the

[First published in *Whither Mankind: A Panorama of Modern Civilization*, ed. Charles A. Beard (New York: Longmans, Green and Co., 1928), pp. 313–31.]

continuity of present civilization with that of the past necessitates this recourse. Ever since the time of the Greeks, European culture has been a borrowed one. The bases and chief values of life have been alien, not indigenous. Rome went in debt to Greece and the Orient; mediaeval culture owed everything that was ordered and supremely prized to Greece, Rome, Judea, and Alexandria; the civilization we call modern has been a struggle to accommodate the outcome of these borrowings to new elements. Philosophers have oscillated between efforts to strike a balance, to repudiate the debts, to declare bankruptcy, and sometimes, though less often, to liquidate what is owed and establish the solvency of modern life. In a civilization largely built out of alien traditions, it is not surprising that thinkers have been more concerned about transmitted borrowings than about contemporary and novel factors. Bacon and Descartes set out with avowal of independence and originality, but even they conducted their intellectual enterprises on capital drawn from sources they nominally rejected.

Tension between old and new has, however, been sufficient to influence the course of philosophic thought since the sixteenth century. Curiously enough, the tension has been least felt in the New World, in the United States. The scene in which new factors have had the most unrestricted sway in fact, has been that in which thinkers, excepting a few outside of professional bounds, have lived most contentedly upon borrowed capital. The more, it would seem, actual life has been transformed by the application of natural science in industry and commerce, the more professional philosophers have ignored the contemporary situation and devoted themselves to manipulation of portions of the European tradition torn from its living context. The result is the thin meagreness of American contributions to the reflective thought of mankind. There is manifest neither the vitality that springs from acceptance of a living tradition that retains significance by struggle with forces which attack and would undermine it, nor that which might spring from appreciative concern with forces that actually dominate contemporary life.

Some European philosophies have been refuges framed for consolation and compensation. But these cities of emotional and moral refuge were at least sought out because of realization of imminent peril. Other philosophies have been deliberate protests against the inherited tradition; they have been revolutionary in intent. Others have given themselves to the task of reconciliation and mediation. In consequences, these European philosophies have been pregnant with meaning in their own social contexts. It is possible for a French historian to write a history of French philosophy with titles drawn from characteristic social movements. British philosophy until the nineteenth century was a deliberate attempt to supply a creed for liberalism and social reform, and its reliance upon German thought in the latter nineteenth century was an attempt to discover adequate means for counteracting disintegrative results of the earlier liberalism as that was carried into action. German thought, conventionally the most speculative and otherworldly of all European systems, has been either a social apologia elaborated by a highly technical apparatus, or a program of social revolution. As for Russia—there every social movement, conservative or radical, has openly, even flagrantly, linked its program with some mode of philosophic doctrine. An American student is bewildered to find, for example, that Lenin considered it necessary as part of his practical movement to engage in heated polemic against every German philosophic doctrine, however innocently theoretical it looks in our perspective, that deviates from orthodox dialectical materialism.

In contrast with the vitality of European philosophies, American professional philosophy has taken with utmost seriousness intellectual formulations extracted from their actual setting. It has played with them in detachment. American philosophies were idealistic, realistic, or pragmatic of this or that shade, without leaving in their wake a ripple in American life. Santayana, the only American thinker who has systematically employed even reaction against the American scene as a factor in framing his philosophy, is of Spanish origin and no longer lives in the country. William James is the outstanding exception to what has been said, in that he used intellectually as much of the distinctively American tradition as had in his day come to any consciousness of itself. But he probably had more influence abroad than at home and is here still criticized as uttering in effect a supine glorification of what is least worthy in American life. Otherwise, one has to go beyond philosophic bounds, to Emerson, Thoreau, Walt Whitman, to find a critical evaluation and report of the American scene.

The situation as described shows many signs of loosening, of breaking up. Such detachment cannot go on indefinitely. If the actual scene does not offer a sufficient challenge, that of the chorus of European critics does. The challenge is not one that should produce apologetic justification; much less petulant retort. It is a challenge to understanding. What *is* our materialism, our commercialism, our narrow practicality, our childish immaturity, our impatient preoccupation with hurry and movement? What *is* our alleged "practical idealism," our devotion to "social service," our curious combination of individualism with collectivistic standardization and conformity? What is the meaning of our union of ideals of peace and regard for the rights of self-determination of other people with an expansion that looks to the outsider remarkably like familiar economic imperialism? Whence and why our combination of complacency and restless discontent? Whence and why our multiplication of regulative laws conjoined with practical lawlessness? Why are our politics and our thinking so legalistic and our practice a matter of taking short-cuts across all legal boundaries? And so on indefinitely.

The challenge is the more peremptory because, if our European critics be correct, Europe, and probably the Orient, are themselves being "Americanized," so that what we are now the world in general is coming to be. For this fact (or prophecy— with whatever truth it may contain) recalls attention to the central fact that the force most active in contemporary life is growth of habits congruous with natural science and still more with the technological application of its discoveries. Practically every phase of our present technique of industry and commerce has its roots in some discovery made somewhere in some laboratory by some scientist engaged in physical or chemical research. Indeed, the connection is now so obvious to the "practical" man that a characteristic feature of our recent industrial life is the development within business itself of richly subsidized laboratories, the number of which is put at some five hundred, and the more important of which are engaged in "pure" research. We cannot discriminate, even if we should like to, the scientific phase of present civilization from its technological phase.

This intimate union of science and technology, realized in mechanical civilization, is a challenge to our most cherished philosophic tradition. For the outstanding feature of the classic tradition is the separateness of knowledge and practice, a separation in which adjectives of praise and honor are attached to the former and those of depreciation to the latter. European philosophy early in its career committed itself to a celebration of the contemplative life. The rise of natural science did not seriously disturb the tradition. Philosophers went on interpreting knowledge by means of the earlier concepts of its exclusively contemplative nature long after actual knowledge in its most authentic form had adopted experimental methods, in spite of the fact that experimentation depended upon the invention and use of physical tools and machines. The dependence of the worker in the factory upon mechanical devices is no greater than that of the worker in the laboratory. The latter consciously employs an elaborate apparatus of theory and theoretical calculations of which the factory worker is innocent. But the latter can ignore this auxiliary intellectual apparatus only because for him it is already physically incarnate in the machines he operates. The machine is the authentically embodied *Logos* of modern life, and the import of this fact is not diminished by any amount of dislike to it.

Philosophy has, however, been little affected by the transformation of the ways in which men actually pursue knowledge. It has remained, as far as possible, true to conceptions formulated more than two thousand years ago in Greece, when the experimental method was not dreamed of; when indeed the absence of mechanical appliances made the method impossible. Philosophy has paid deference to science; but its obeisances have been made rather to the conclusions of science than to its method. As far as the nature of the knowing operation and function is concerned, philosophers have disputed whether knowledge is a direct grasp and intuition of real things, or whether the only things directly known are impressions and ideas in the mind. They have disputed whether sensation or reason is the basic guarantee of knowledge. But the schools have retained the notion that in any case knowing is a matter of some contact or intercourse between mind on one side and things on the other, a contact and intercourse independent of the needs and instrumentalities of practical activity. At first sight this fact may seem of little importance save to professional philosophers. But in reality it involves two of the most significant problems of common humanity, and begs the question as to their solution. For there is contained in it an issue as to the nature of truth and as to the organ by which it is achieved. There is also included an assumption as to the nature of the "practical" that identifies it with the merely utilitarian or the commercial and the politic, to the neglect of any ideal content. The endeavor to pour the new wine of knowledge into old bottles of traditional notions as to the contemplative essence and function of knowing signifies in effect that ideas and intelligence inhabit a self-enclosed realm, and that vital human affairs are conducted by turning to personal and class account such conclusions of science as lend themselves to pecuniary gain and power over others.

Critics of our present social régime often assume that the evils of our industrial civilization are the exclusive products of the reign of mechanical technology. It seems to be inherent in human nature to want a deity to worship and a devil to abhor. Machinery has become the devil of a wide-spread cult. But the indictment overlooks the fact that our existing institutions and interests have their roots in the past, and that the use we make of mechanical instrumentalities is not due to these instruments alone but to their entanglement with a texture of beliefs and ideals that matured in a pre-industrial age. In such a condition there is more petulance than enlightenment in charging evils to machines and industry. The only thing certain is that, when men think and believe in one set of symbols and act in ways which are contrary to their professed and conscious ideas, confusion and insincerity are bound to result, and that in this chaos the unregenerated elements of man, lacking direction, avidly snatch at those immediate and nearby goods which present themselves as attainable. It would be absurd to hold philosophy responsible for the divided estate of civilization; it shows rather a reflection of the division in life itself. But unreconstructed philosophy gives an intellectual formulation of the division, and perpetuates it by the rational justification it thereby seems to provide. However slowly the ideas of thinkers filter into popular consciousness, the first move in straightening out, on the intellectual side, the tangle, in clarifying the confusion, lies with thinkers. They must set their own house in order before they can furnish any plans and specifications for a better integration of the activities of men. This fact seems to me to define the connection of philosophy in America with civilization.

Classic Greek philosophy and the mediaeval synthesis at least reflected the conditions and aspirations of their own times in a coherent system of beliefs. Their ideas could be used to formulate a warrant and goal for their own conduct and institutions. The resultant religious-philosophic organization of beliefs permeated men's minds and was congruous with their deepest hopes and fears. It supplied the greatest need of man, that of an authority by which to live. The central point in this system of authority was the conviction that knowledge is obtained by direct contact of mind with reality, supplemented by revelation; that the knowledge so attained by reason and faith would bring about, when projected into the happier estate of life after death, a direct possession and enjoyment of the ultimate reality, God. That is, a theory of knowledge which isolated both its method and its outcome from practical action was the essence of the classic theory, and the theory had authority, since it laid down both the goal of life and the means of attaining the goal.

The traditional theory received a shock from the rise of new methods in physical science. Everyone is familiar with the struggle induced by the incompatibility of traditional astronomy, the "science" which underlay and justified commonly accepted beliefs about earth, heaven, and hell, with the astronomy of Copernicus and Galileo. We are familiar with a similar although less bitter conflict going on today in the realm of ideas about living creatures, plants and animals. The opposition to each other of fundamentalist and modernist is the latest expression of the results of a shock felt in the sixteenth century. Familiarity with these facts does not of itself, however, induce familiarity with a more important consideration. These special conflicts are but the outward and visible signs of an inner conflict that concerns the very nature of what is to be accepted as knowledge and truth, and the methods by which this knowledge and truth are to be attained. Since such truth—and the method of obtaining it—is the seat of ultimate authority, or affords the warrant of man's ultimate allegiances, the conflict reaches down to the depths of belief and to the patterns of conduct and institutions bound up with belief.

Hence it was practically inevitable that modern thought should make the problem of knowledge its central problem. It would require a long and technical discussion to prove the statement previously made that consideration of this problem has been dominated by retention of notions formed in a period in which experimental inquiry was non-existent. I can cite only an illustration or two. An illuminating instance is found in the formulation given to the problem. Is knowledge possible and if so how? What are its limits and extent? The answer to the latter question which the actual pursuit of knowledge would have suggested is: Knowledge is possible as far as we can develop instrumentalities of inquiry, measurement, symbolization, calculations, and testing. This is perhaps the one answer that has not been given. Solution of the question as to the legitimate extent of knowledge has been sought on the basis of inherited premises as to the nature of mind, of sensations, of concepts, and the relation, physical and epistemological, of mind to the nature of reality as pre-defined; that is, as thought of in a way that was independent of the results of inquiry.

There is something ironical in the very statement of the problem of the possibility of knowledge. At the time when science was advancing at an unprecedented rate, philosophers were asking whether knowledge was possible. And when the answer was in the affirmative, it was justified on the basis of notions about mind, sensation or reason. The straightforward course would seem to have been an examination of the procedures by which knowledge is obtained in actual practice. Men discover how it is possible to walk or talk or fly by examining how these things are actually done. What other way is there by which to find out how knowledge is possible? That this road represents the one road which was *not* taken may have some other explanation than that philosophers are so made that they naturally take the most back-handed approach to anything. The real explanation is that they have been primarily occupied with reconciling tradition with the new movement of science. From the standpoint of tradition, a report of how knowledge *is* obtained would so contradict inherited ideas of mind, in its isolation from the body and other agencies of practical action, as to constitute a serious and perplexing issue. Philosophers were not a unique class. They reflected the control which tradition, engrained in institutions as well as in beliefs, had over the minds of men even when their practice ventured into previously untried fields in ways incompatible with the tradition.

One further illustration may be drawn from an allied field. The deepest problem of modern ethical philosophy has been the reconciliation of human freedom with that phase of science which is called "the reign of law." All sorts of solutions have been propounded, from denial of the reality of freedom to the postulation of a realm above nature by entrance into which man's moral freedom is secured. Attention to the practical scene of contemporary human activity would have given an entirely different turn to the discussion. For every phase of technological civilization shows that an advance in knowledge of natural uniformities and necessary conditions increases man's working freedom, namely, control of nature, enabling him to harness natural energies to his own purposes. This operative power may not correspond to the traditional definition of freedom, for that originated in days when man was so enslaved to natural conditions that he could conceive of freedom only as escape from the bondage they imposed. But it is at least an appreciable part of what men actually want under the name of freedom. The freedom thus gained moreover is poorly thought of when it is conceived merely as increased liberty to realize desires already stirring in men. Its more considerable phase is the release of new desires, the creation and projection of previously unheard of purposes. It was the sense of this new kind of freedom, freedom to want and strive for all kinds of new possibilities, that expressed itself in the feeling of living in a new world lending itself to indefinite progress. This fact brings us to a consideration of that degradation of the idea of the "practical" which has been noted. As far as the traditional idea of the isolation of mind from natural conditions, and the superiority of mind to these conditions, persisted, the feeling assumed, of necessity, a romantic form. As far as actual practice was concerned, the new control was mainly used for personal material advantage.

Thus the traditionalist has a ready retort. He may claim that to offer *this* freedom, freedom to conceive and execute desires, as if it signified what man justly cherishes as true freedom, is only to exemplify the degradation of values and ideals which has been wrought by industrial civilization. For, according to traditional pigeon-holes, all desires that are capable of concrete realization fall within the strictly economic field, within the area of wants for material things and for material prosperity. What of spiritual freedom, of freedom in respect to things which are the dignities and ennoblements of human life; art, religious communion and adoration, the untethered flight of moral aspirations? What better proof can be found, it is asked, of the degeneration effected by industrial civilization than that liberation of economic wants by material means should be proposed as if it were relevant to significant human freedom?

The question reaches far. Before it is considered, it will be well to deal with another objection of a limited nature.

The position taken exemplifies, it may be urged, a complacent contentment with existing industrial conditions. Instead of extension of human control over purposes and their realization, machine-made and machine-bound civilization has deprived men of leisure and led to use of such leisure as they possess in mad search for amusement and foolish display. It has brought not freedom but enslavement to the machine. Work has been deprived of joy; artistic feeling has been eliminated from its performance and its products. The masses have been condemned to become appendages to the machines they tend; and those released from this fate manifest their boasted freedom for the most part only in holding the activities of others in thrall. It is only heartless indifference which can behold in such a state of affairs a gain in human freedom.

The facts that underlie this indictment are undeniable. They are not to be wholly disposed of by setting against the indictment the deplorable state of the masses in all ages, or by pointing out that distance and ignorance effect an easy idealization of their estate in the past. It is more to the point to inquire how far the evils pointed to are solely chargeable to the machine and how far they are due to perpetuation of modes of desire, habits of thought, and institutions that developed in the delightful agrarian and feudal age. For the consciousness of the evil conditions under which masses live, the recognition of them as something humanly abhorrent, as something against which conscience and will should revolt, is itself a product of industrial civilization. One does not find the revolt in earlier civilizations; one does not find it in those parts of the earth which have as yet not come under the industrial blight. The peculiar thing is not the enslavement of masses of mankind to the necessities of making a hardly-won precarious livelihood; that has existed at all times and places. The distinctive thing is increased consciousness of this state of affairs and discontent with it; the belief that it is unjust and unnatural; the conviction that it is a monster to be extirpated. Such an attitude could not have risen until industrial civilization had sufficiently advanced to bring with it the perception of the possibility of a free life upon a higher level for all mankind; until command of natural energies by means of machinery had enabled imagination to conceive of leisure for all. The state of things which is now emphasized as the product of industrial civilization was through long ages taken for granted as part of the natural, the necessary, yes, the providential, order of things.

The modern democratic movement in its broad sense provides the background for our "humanitarian" aspirations. The machine age has resulted in a transference of the locus of the ideal of a larger and more evenly distributed happiness and leisure from heaven to earth. This is true even though the attainment of the ideal is as much beset with doubt in the earthly as in the otherworldly scheme. The facts represented in this transference are closely connected with the issue involved in the belief that industrial civilization inevitably degrades the higher interests of men, offering us at best greater liberty to procure material comfort and ease at the expense of the values which mark off the life of man from that of beasts. The trouble with this objection is that it proves—or assumes—too much. The possession of physical means for a higher degree of material security would not appear to be inherently hostile to creative effort and appreciative enjoyment in the higher arts and values of life. One would rather suppose that increase of security, even if not extending to possession of a large surplus of wealth, would release imagination and emotion to engage more generously in the pursuit of ideal interests.

I do not claim for a moment that this presumption is as a matter of fact realized in our present civilization. Only a blind man would deny that characteristic traits of present life are a mad scramble for material commodities, a devotion to attainment of external power, and an insensate love of foolish luxuries and idle display. But full acknowledgment of this fact settles nothing; it only sets a problem for inquiry. Why is this so? One possibility is that human nature is running true to form; that our industrial development supplies the means by which the ever dominant factors of human nature get a chance to express themselves: that men are so made that taken en masse they always devote themselves to material power and enjoyment rather than to religion, art, and disinterested science if they have the chance. But the adoption of this explanation indicates that the hold of higher values upon man was always accidental and compensatory. Such an explanation commits us to the idea that human nature is inherently so base that only the holy discipline of privation, sacrifice, and suffering can elevate man above himself. Even if this be so, it makes human nature, not industrial civilization, the cause of the evils complained of. The degradations of industrialism can only signify on this score that at last the natural man possesses the means for displaying himself; the evils of industrial civilization are an effect of the constitution of human nature.

Adoption of this alternative lands us in a desperate case. Those who remain loyal to the spiritual interest may repine, scold, or withdraw into seclusion. But by their own statement there is nothing which can be done about the perverse state of civilization. There is, however, another possibility. The present over-zeal for material goods and prosperity may be the fruit of long ages in which man has been starved and oppressed. It may be chiefly the product of the belauded former ages in which, it is asserted, higher values were held in esteem. In this case, the so-called lower desires of man, his demand for comfort, for enjoyment of material things, his foolish love of power over things and other persons for the mere sake of power, were held in restraint not by devotion to spiritual interests, but by force of surrounding external conditions. The pressure removed, these wants are released into action with an intensity proportionate to the pressure which had previously kept them in. In that case, the present situation is one of transitional unbalance, and it is not entirely utopian to look forward to recovery of a sane equilibrium after the so long inhibited appetites have glutted themselves. The prodigal may return to his father's house bringing with him a wisdom gathered in his own experience, not with mere reiteration of precepts forced upon him from without.

Explanation of some of the outstanding evils of industrialism by reference to an exaggerated rebound from a prior abnormal state raises doubts as to the quality of the values which form our inherited standards. These were directly shared only by a few; most persons had to take them on faith, vicariously and as postponed to a future world. And they could have had little depth of root, or the march of industrialism could not so easily have subverted men's allegiance to them.

The fact is that the standards by which we still conventionally judge not only values but also standards are so traditional, and the elements of that tradition are so far removed from the actualities of modern life, that we are almost wholly at a loss when we attempt to pass critical judgments upon what is now going on. Shall we employ standards that matured in an earlier day? If so, the conclusion is foregone. Since it is by the impact of industrial civilization that these standards have lost their vitality, when we measure industrial civilization by them of course it stands condemned. The condemnation, moreover, is not limited to evils that condemn themselves to any intelligent mind; it extends to industrial and scientific methods wholesale, since they are the causal factors. Shall we then employ standards congenial to, arising from, the new technological and scientific trend? But the difficulty is that they are as yet unavowed and unrevealed. We simply do not know what they are. Some of the ignorance is undoubtedly due to the newness and immaturity of industrial civilization itself. But this ignorance is intensified and complicated by the fact that philosophic thought has chiefly devoted itself to cultivating the older tradition instead of exploring the meaning of actual conditions and the possibilities that may inhere in them. In consequence, a nominal and formal intellectual allegiance to standards which have little relevancy to existing civilization is conjoined with practical surrender to forces we make so little effort to understand. The decline of the operative force of old standards and ideals is attended and confirmed by the withdrawal of philosophy from concern with actualities.

Thus we are brought back to the question of the relation of philosophy to existing civilization in its dominantly industrial character. Unless philosophies are to be Edens of compensatory refuge, reached through an exercise of dialectic ingenuity, they must face the situation which is there. It is their business to bring intellectual order out of the confusion of beliefs. For the confusion of which we have been speaking, due to lack of adjustment between ideas and ideals inherited from an older culture and the dominating interests and movements of present civilization, while not itself philosophical in origin, is both a datum and an opportunity for philosophy. "Acceptance" is an ambiguous word in relation to the office of philosophy. It may signify either acceptance of whatever is a fact *as* a fact, or acceptance of it as a value or even as a measure of value. Any philosophy which does not accept important facts is in that degree a philosophy of escape. This appellation holds, in my opinion, even with respect to those theories which would confine the legitimate business of philosophy to analysis of scientific premises or to synthesis of scientific conclusions, in isolation from the place and function of science in life. It is as an *operative* fact that philosophy has to accept the controlling role of technological industry in contemporary civilization. This acceptance is far from implying commitment to its characteristics as values, but it is precedent to any valid criticism of their value. Otherwise criticism is a complaint, an emotional cry, not an intellectual discrimination.

The discussion may be summarized in saying that industrial civilization presents philosophers with a double challenge. One of its tasks is to discover the full meaning of the experimental methods by which the advances of natural sciences have been made secure. In order to make this discovery, there is needed revision and even surrender of fixed prepossessions regarding the nature of mind, thought, and truth that are transmitted to us from a pre-experimental age. Ideas of these and allied subjects must be developed after the model and the pattern of what competent inquirers actually *do* in the attainment of knowledge of facts and principles. The accomplishment of this task is difficult. But it is of more than technical and professional significance. It signifies what is in effect a new logic in investigation and criticism of social institutions and customs. For this area, the one in which men concretely live, is hardly touched as yet by the experimental habit of mind. Philosophers of the seventeenth century did a great work in liberating physical knowledge from bondage, and in projecting the roads upon which it could move securely forward. There is now a similar opportunity and similar demand for the emancipation of knowledge of social affairs—legal, economic, political, religious. Until the implications of the experimental method are worked out in this field, the scientific revolution begun three centuries ago is incomplete and subject to warping and perversion—as it is now actually twisted and deflected when it reaches the popular consciousness and takes effect in action.

A second task may be suggested by saying that the relation between instrumentalities and consequences, means and ends, must be reconsidered on the basis of the new tools and sources of power which come within human control because of applications of science. Upon the whole the record of the history of philosophy displays a division into things called ends-in-themselves and other things that are mere means, intrinsically indifferent to ends-in-themselves, the ulterior sources of value: into noumenal and phenomenal, physical and ideal, material and spiritual. All such separations root in the separation of ends and means from one another. The ideas of objects to which final worth is assigned are formed with little respect to existent conditions, to the realistic factor. Since the latter supplies the only means for the execution of ideas and the realization of desires and purposes, the outcome is that higher and more far-reaching ends become merely "idealistic"—that is, romantic, sentimental, compensatory. It is as if an engineer despised material and energies on the ground that they are merely material in nature. The issue affects equally the conception and the treatment of the "realistic" factor, things as they exist at a given time. Since they are viewed and used in isolation, they too become rigid and fixed. Regard for actual conditions is thought to imply mere accommodation and conformity. Since, however, desire and purpose, the setting up of aims or ends-in-view remains a constant function of human nature, this attitude signifies, in the outcome, that actual conditions *are* employed as means, but as means for ends that are near at hand, suggested by immediate circumstances, attainable by manipulation, and enjoyable on the existing level. Thus operative and controlling "ends" have little to do with professed and sentimentally worshipped ideals. They are then relatively trivial, and superficial; they consist in utilization of conditions as means to direct enjoyment and direct exercise of power over others. Here is the ultimate source of the confusion, insincerity, meaningless change, and unrest characteristic of so much of industrial civilization.

A philosophy of the relations of means and ends, of the materially existent and the ideally possible, based on the control of agencies and instrumentalities which the new technology has brought with itself, cannot terminate with, as it were, a mere *post mortem* dissection. It supplies impetus; its drive is to the future. It takes effect in restatement of the ideal or spiritual elements that have been contained in the religions, arts, literature, moralities, and polities of our traditional inheritance. They are revised so that they bear an operative relation to the state of affairs through which they are realizable. By the same movement of thought, existent conditions cease to be taken as fixed, changeable only by some external and accidental intrusion; they cease to be models and measures of conduct. It is worth while to recur to the analogy with the scientific situation of the seventeenth century. It produced an array of thinkers who clarified and organized the inchoate efforts of a small number of workers in the fields of astronomy, physics, and chemistry. These thinkers evolved an articulate system of ideas which provided subsequent workers with confidence and courage and gave direction and point to their activities.

In the succeeding century, in the period of the "enlightenment," philosophers turned their attention to man, to human nature and human interests. They saw in the methods and results of the new science the promise of complete control of human institutions and efforts by "reason." They predicted an era of liberation from all the oppressions of the past, since these had been conceived in ignorance and perpetuated in superstition. An era of indefinite progress and unlimited perfectibility was ushered in. The course of events gave the lie to their ardent aspiration. "Reason" did not assume a role of control and direction; it, and the new appliances of science, were seized as tools for the promotion of personal and class power over others and as means of new and frenetic display and enjoyment. It did not turn out bliss to be alive, but rather unregulated competition, conflict, and confusion. In consequence the philosophies of the nineteenth century, as far as we can view them with detachment in the present perspective, were infected with a reactionary spirit. Men looked backward rather than forward. The discovery of history considered as a record of the past was its great intellectual contribution. "Evolution" is an idea which generalizes the discovery of history, and the idea of evolution was elaborated into an idea of cosmic forces which follow their own predestined course, and with respect to which the intervening inventive and directive intelligence of man is of slight account. The most systematic philosophic movement of the century, German idealism, fused this idea with elements drawn from the classic religious and philosophic tradition of Europe so as to effect an intellectual rehabilitation of the latter. Many phases of this movement display nobility; all possess pathos. But the movement was essentially apologetic; it justified the existing state of institutions as a manifestation of some inner absolute Idea or Spirit engaged in the slow process of evolutionary expression. In effect, the philosophies contributed their support to acquiescence and impotence rather than to direction and re-creation, because they gave an inherent ideal value to what exists—inherent in the sense of independent of what deliberate action might make out of the existent.

A philosopher who would relate his thinking to present civilization, in its predominantly technological and industrial character, cannot ignore any of these movements any more than he can dispense with consideration of the underlying classic tradition formed in Greece and the Middle Ages. If he ignores traditions, his thoughts become thin and empty. But they are something to be employed, not just treated with respect or dressed out in a new vocabulary. Moreover, industrial civilization itself has now sufficiently developed to form its own tradition. If the United States is more advanced on the road of industrialized civilization than are Old World countries, the meaning of this tradition should be more legible here than elsewhere. It cannot be read, however, unless it is observed and studied, and it cannot be effectively observed without a measure of intellectual sympathy. Such observation and reflection as discern its meaning—that is its possibilities—*is* philosophy, no matter by what name the discernment is called. If philosophy declines to observe and interpret the new and characteristic scene, it may achieve scholarship; it may erect a well equipped gymnasium wherein to engage in dialectical exercises; it may clothe itself in fine literary art. But it will not afford illumination or direction to our confused civilization. These can proceed only from the spirit that is interested in realities and that faces them frankly and sympathetically.

A Critique of American Civilization

When Robinson Crusoe sat down to make a debit-credit list of his blessings and his troubles, he did it in order to cheer himself up. One has a feeling that when one is engaged in undertaking a somewhat similar appraisal of our civilization, one is doing something of the same sort, indulging in social apologetics. Nor is this the only embarrassment. A person can put down in black and white his financial resources and liabilities, but the result will not shed light upon his state of health and his intellectual and moral well-being. So it is possible to itemize with more or less accuracy certain gains and losses in American life, and yet not know what they import for the prosperity of our social body. There is for example a great gain, a gain of two hundred and fifty per cent in ten years in the number of students in our secondary schools and colleges. But what does it signify? There is a great increase in crime and disregard of law. But what does it mean? Neither the causes nor the consequences of such gains and losses are apparent, and without an insight into reasons and effects, we can hardly even guess what these things portend for good and ill in our civilization. One foreign visitor says a number of nice things about our country, and another one may pass a number of harsh criticisms. We may agree as to the substantial truth of both statements, and experience a glow of pride at one and a sense of irritation at the other. But what do these things mean? Has either of them got below the surface? I should not feel greater assurance if I tried to strike a balance sheet of gains and losses in American civilization.

Fortunately for me this is not my task. It has been accomplished in various fields by those competent to speak, each in his

[First published in *World Tomorrow* 11 (1928): 391–95. Republished, with additions, in *Recent Gains in American Civilization*, ed. Kirby Page (New York: Harcourt, Brace and Co., 1928), pp. 253–76.]

and her own special territory. Yet when I am called upon to try and sum up and to tell what it all comes to in the direction and quality of American life, I experience a profound misgiving. Where are we going? Toward what are we moving? The value of any changing thing lies in its consequences, and the consequences of the present conditions and forces are not here. To make an evaluation is to prophesy, and where is there the astronomer who can predict the future of our social system?

I should not, however, indulge in the expression of these doubts if they were merely personal misgivings. They seem rather to be indicative, evidential, in a peculiar way of the state and prospects of American civilization. By this I mean something more than the platitude that we are in a state of social transition and flux. I mean in the first place, that when we list items of gain and loss in opposite columns, we find paradoxes, contradictions of extraordinary range and depth; and in the second place, that these contradictions are evidence of what seems to be the most marked trait of our present state—namely, its inner tension and conflict. If ever there was a house of civilization divided within itself and against itself, it is our own today. If one were to take only some symptoms and ignore others, one might make either a gloomy or a glowing report, and each with equal justice—as far as each went.

If one looks at the overt and outer phenomena, at what I may call the public and official, the externally organized, side of our life, my own feeling about it would be one of discouragement. We seem to find everywhere a hardness, a tightness, a clamping down of the lid, a regimentation and standardization, a devotion to efficiency and prosperity of a mechanical and quantitative sort. If one looks exclusively at the activities of a great number of individuals in different spheres (and by individuals I mean voluntary groups as well), there is a scene of immense vitality that is stimulating to the point of inspiration. This contradiction between the inner and the outer, the private and the public, phases of our civilization, seems to be its most significant feature; the sense of its existence and scope furnishes the gist of all I have to say.

One finds, I think, the fact of this opposition reflected, at least implicitly, in all the articles that report upon special phases of our life. Let me note, almost at random, some of its obviously visible signs. In domestic politics, there is an extraordinary apathy, indicated not only by abstention from the polls, but in the seemingly calm indifference with which the public takes the revelation of corruption in high places. On the other hand, there was never previously so much publicity, so much investigation and exposure having a genuinely scientific quality. And unless one thinks that the cynical indifference of the public is an evidence of thoroughgoing corruption not merely of some officials and business men, but of the heart of the American people, there is ground for thinking that the prevailing attitude toward political life is itself an indication of a growing sense that our reliance and hope is being increasingly put on agencies that lie deeper than the political; that there is a feeling, as yet inarticulate and groping, that the real needs of the American people must be met by means more fundamental than our traditional political institutions put at our disposal. If, and as far as, our political apathy is due to widespread distrust of the reality, under present conditions, of existing political forms, there is ground for belief that social forces that are much more truly characteristic of our social life than is our inherited political machinery are destined to change the latter, when there will be a revival of political interest, and only then.

The domestic political scene presents a still more obvious contradiction in connection with the matter of intolerance. Never have the forces of bigotry and intolerance been so well organized and so active. It is enough to refer to the Ku Klux Klan, not yet negligible. On the other hand, for the first time in history there is a possibility of the election of a Roman Catholic for the office of the presidency. This contradiction may not seem very significant, but to me at least it seems deeply symptomatic of our entire condition, that which I have called inner division and tension. The very factors that have produced the tightening up and solidifying of the forces of reaction are also producing a more conscious and determined liberal attitude. Organization and outer power still lie with the former; but the latter is in process of fermentation and inner growth, and the future may be on its side. So viewed, I would assign to the fact just cited a significance that taken in isolation it does not possess.

A more important if vaguer illustration of the point is found in the whole situation as regards freedom of thought and speech. It goes without saying that never before in our history have there been such flagrant violations of what one would have supposed to be fundamental in the American system. It is customary to refer this particular reenforcement of reaction to the war. Undoubtedly the reference is correct, and yet the war was an opportunity rather than the decisive cause. The sources lie further back in the development of our regime of control of economic forces. On the other hand, never was the spirit of self-criticism so alert and penetrating. If our complacency has grown more strident and self-conscious, so has our spirit of self-examination and discrimination. This fact has been noted sufficiently in special articles so that there is no need to dwell upon it or cite evidence. If we are our own "best pals" we are now also our own "severest critics." Public and organized censorship and repression has its counterpart in spontaneous and private exploration and exhibition of shortcomings and evils. To all appearance, the age of muckraking has disappeared. But by contrast, that outburst was comparatively external and superficial. It dealt with specific and outward ailments. If the fervor of exposure and condemnation that marked the nineties has vanished, it is also true that the critical spirit has turned inward and is now concerned with underlying intellectual and moral causes.

As I recently read Arthur Garfield Hays' *Let Freedom Ring*, I was of two minds. One was of profound shame and depression that we had so far departed from the principles that were supposed to be the foundation of our political and social structure. But then there is the book itself and still more there is the gallant fight for freedom it records. And I wondered whether, if any previous time exhibited such a record of suppression, it also manifested any more courageous and unremitting battle for the maintenance of civil liberties. And it occurred to me that the consolidation of the energy of the forces of reaction was perhaps a sign of their well-grounded fear that after all, contrary social forces were working against them. After all, blacklists and "keysheets" have some occasion, and the ridiculous fear of the Bolshevizing of our country may be a symptom that those in power are not entirely at ease in their Zion.

In international matters, there is, it seems to me, a like contradiction. That imperialistic policy is now, in an economic form, our dominating note seems to me too evident to need proof. But, in spite of the pious words of the Hughes-Coolidge regime, it is becoming recognized for what it is. Only occasionally perhaps does the protest due to its recognition find effective expression in action, as it did in the case of Mexico noted in the article by Norman Thomas. But nevertheless we are not so somnolent as we once were. Our economic policy in Nicaragua goes marching on with the support of marines; but there was a time when similar interventions (with apologies to our authorities for not calling them "interpositions") went almost without notice, beyond the pious hope that we were instilling some decent fear of God in a lot of semi-savages. Perception of great social changes usually lags far behind the changes themselves, so far behind that it is incapable of modifying their operation. But perception of the growth of economic imperialism is not perhaps so far behind the fact, and consequently so important, as has been the case in other matters. There are some grounds for hoping that it is nearly enough up to date so as to exercise a contemporary influence.

That an immediate effect of the war and of the "peace" in which it issued was to intensify and make more conscious our international isolation, there can hardly be a doubt. Silly as it is, the mere word "international" is suspect in many quarters; it smells of Russia and the Third International. While "Americanization" processes are not so drastic as they were a few years ago, the older immigrants to this country, who arrogate to themselves the title of "Americans," still display fear of late comers. Persons are blacklisted for no greater crime than favoring the outlawry of war or adherence of the United States to the World Court. But on the other side individuals have a much wider and more sympathetic interest in foreign affairs than ever before, and numerous voluntary associations stimulate and feed the interest. If overtly and outwardly we are more nationalistic than at any previous time, we are also, as far as intellectual and moral currents are concerned, more internationally inclined. The entire peace movement is less negative, less merely anti-war and more bent on establishing positive international cooperation. As the chapter on "Advances in the Quest for Peace" notes, it is also much more realistic. While, during the war, a man might find himself in jail for a too emphatic declaration that the causes of the war were economic rivalries, that is now a commonplace of discussion from admirals to the man in the street. It is a great gain that intelligent people now know where to look, what to give attention to, in all cases of international friction. While there is not adequate evidence that this enlightenment is sufficient to withstand organized propaganda in the case of a crisis, it is still true, I think, that glittering generalities about freedom, justice, and an end to all war as the objectives of a war have lost much of their force.

It has long been a moot question how civilization is to be measured. What is the gauge of its status and degree of advance? Shall it be judged by its *élite*, by its artistic and scientific products, by the depth and fervor of its religious devotion? Or by the level of the masses, by the amount of ease and security attained by the common man? Was pre-revolutionary Russia at the acme of European civilization because of its achievements in literature, music and the drama? Or will the new Russia if it succeeds, even at the expense of retrogression in these matters, in elevating the life of the masses, stand at a higher level? As between the two sides to the controversy, there is no common premise, and hence no possibility of a solution. One side can claim to stand for ideal attainments as the ultimate measure and accuse the other side of having a low and merely materialistic criterion. This other side can retort with a charge of aristocratic harsh indifference to the well-being and security of the great number to whom the struggle for life is all important, and inquire what is the value of an art and a science from which most are excluded, or of a religion that for the many is merely a dream of a remote bliss compensatory to the suffering of present evils.

The question is evidently crucial for an appraisal of gains in American civilization. From what base line shall we set out to measure? Those who engage in glorification of American life uniformly point to the fact that the lot of the common man (however poor it may still be from an absolute standard) is at least better than that of his fellow in other countries or at other epochs.

If we ask for the intellectual and ideal content of this common life, the tale is not so reassuring. Even when we have discounted the exaggerations of the now familiar denunciations of the yokelry and the booboisie, enough truth remains to be depressing. It would probably be easy to fill my allotted space with evidences of the triviality and superficiality of life as it is lived by the masses. It is perhaps enough to refer for a good-humored depiction of the scene to Charles Merz's *The Great American Band Wagon*. And if we take achievements in higher culture as our standard of valuation, not even the most optimistic can give our civilization a very high rating. To take one illustration, our physical plant for scientific study is far superior to that of any European country; measured by capital invested, it might even be equal to that of all Europe. The results hardly correspond. The pressure toward immediate commercial application is great, and the popular hero is the inventor, not the investigator and discoverer. Burbank and Edison are names to conjure with, while those of Willard Gibbs and Michelson are faint rumors on a thin air.

The dispute concerns ultimate standards, and hence, as has been said, cannot be settled—except by taking sides. But one can say that in the end the value of elevation of the common man in security, ease and comfort of living is to be viewed as an opportunity for a possible participation in more ideal values; and that there is something defective, to say the least, in a civilization wherein achievements in the former do not terminate in a general participation in spiritual values. To bring about opportunities is to have done much; but if the opportunities are not utilized, the actual outcome is a reproach and condemnation. Here then is the issue: Admitting that our civilization displays a relative superiority in its material basis, what are we likely to build upon it in religion, science and art, and in the amenities and graces of life?

The question is framed with respect to the future. There is some truth in the old saying that we have been too occupied with the material conquest of a continent to occupy ourselves with higher things. But since the former task is fairly accomplished, we may well ask ourselves how it stands with the other part of the saying: that when we get around to it, we shall make "culture hum"? The distinctive pioneer virtues have departed with the pioneer age. Where is the enormous and vital energy that marked this age now directing itself? Survey of the immediate scene would seem to indicate that much of it is going into a frenzied money-making, an equally frenzied material enjoyment of the money that is made, and an imitative "having a good time" on the part of those who haven't made much money. There are those who think that in conquering a continent, our own souls have been subdued by the material fruits of the victory. Prosperity is our God.

The case has been so put as to suggest the worst possibility. There is much to be said on the other side; there are many hopeful signs that might be pointed to. In a series devoted to gains in American civilization, I seem to be emphasizing losses. Yet what has been said may be relevant in at least bringing to the fore the ultimate problem, that of the measure of gain and loss. It is also tributary, I think, to my main point—that we are in the throes of an inner conflict and division. For the situation taken at its worst is that of the overt and public phase of our life, while the things that may be set forth on the other side of the account have to do with forces that are as yet unorganized and inchoate. One may point to our newspaper press and to the type of periodical that one finds on the news-stands as representing the organized aspect of our intellectual life in its public impact. A tabloid, with all that that implies, having a circulation of over a million— almost three times that of the other style of papers—and the multitudes of "confession" magazines, would then seem to tell a large part of the story. But on the other hand there is the unprecedented appearance and astonishing popular welcome of books that popularize and humanize serious subjects. I find this fact to be illustrative of something real and vital which is stirring, and which in the outcome may have a potency greater than that of the factors externally dominant. As an isolated fact, it proves nothing. As a symptom, it is perhaps highly significant. The spontaneous local developments of interest in painting, music, drama, and the vogue of poetry go deeper. "Best sellers" are certainly of much higher average type than a generation ago.

Reference to the educational situation is pertinent at this point. It is unnecessary to review what has already been said by Mr. Sharp in his article. Yet the rapid and intense extension of interest and activity in adult, parental and pre-school education, in education at both ends of the scale, is an indication that cannot be ignored, any more than can the remarkable development of progressive schools. The most extraordinary matter, however, is the expansion of secondary and higher education. No one can tell its cause or import, but in velocity and extent it marks nothing less than a revolutionary change. It used to be said that only one in twenty of the elementary pupils found their way into high school, and only one in a hundred into college. Now the number in the lower schools is only five times that in the secondary schools, and there is one student in a college to twenty in the elementary. And the astonishing thing is that the expansion has occurred at an accelerating rate since 1910. There are for example at least six times as many students in colleges and professional schools as there were thirty years ago, and tenfold more in secondary schools. Let the worst possible be said about the quality of the education received, and it remains true that we are in the presence of one of the most remarkable social phenomena of history. It is impossible to gauge the release of potentialities contained in this change; it is incredible that it should not eventuate in the future in a corresponding intellectual harvest. While, as I have said, it is impossible to determine its causes, it at least shows that we are finally beginning to make good our ideal of equal educational opportunity for all. I believe that a considerable part of the development is due to the rise in status of immigrants of the second and third generation; and in spite of all that is said in depreciation of those from southern and southeastern Europe, I believe that when our artistic renascence comes, it will proceed largely from this source.

The reverse side of the pattern is, of course, the intensification of efforts of special interests to control public and private education for their own ends, mainly under the guise of a nationalistic patriotism. The recent revelations of the efforts of the Electric Light and Power Companies to utilize the schools are much in point. I know of nothing more significant than the fact that the instructions sent out to publicity agents for manufacturing public opinion and sentiment uniformly combine "press and schools" as the agencies to be influenced. In some respects these revelations seem to me more sinister than those of the oil scandals, in that they represent an attempt at corruption of the source of public action. In any case, we have a striking instance of what I have called our inner conflict and tension. Our democracy is at least far enough advanced so that there is a premium put on the control of popular opinion and beliefs. There was a time in history when the few did not have to go through the form of consulting the opinion of the many. Government by press agents, by "counsellors of public relations," by propaganda in press and school, is at least evidence that that time has passed. We have enough government by public opinion so that it is necessary for the economic powers that govern to strive to regulate the agencies by which that opinion is created.

If we ask which forces are to win, those that are organized, that know what they are after and that take systematic means to accomplish their end, or those that are spontaneous, private and scattered—like those that have resulted in the expansion of our higher school population—we have, I think, the problem of our civilization before us. To answer the problem is to engage in prophecy that may well be gratuitous. It goes back to faith rather than to proof by sight and touch. Yet there *are* reasons for hoping for a favorable issue. One of them is the fact that our civilization, whatever else it may be, is one of diffusion, of ready circulation. It is a fancy of mine to picture the essence of our life in terms of the Ford car. On the one side, there is the acme of mechanization, of standardization, of external efficiency. On the other, there is, as the effect, a vast mobility, a restless movement of individuals. The resulting mobility is aimless and blind; it can be easily represented as exhibiting a mere love of movement for its own sake, an abandonment to speed of change for its own sake. But nevertheless the movement, the instability, is there. The industrial forces that would control it for their own purposes automatically, and as by some principle of fate, multiply and intensify it. Thus the division, the tension, increases. A standardized, regimented technology of industry continually releases unexpected and unforeseen forces of individuality. In its effort to control their operation, it redoubles its repressive and mechanizing efforts. Is it a mere compensatory fantasy to suppose that in the process it is inevitably and unwittingly working its own doom? The answer given will depend upon one's conceptions of the ultimate structure of individual human nature, of what its potentialities will do when they are liberated.

It is a trite saying that our social experiment, that of raising the level of the mass, is an unprecedented one. It is impossible, however, to separate the scope of the endeavor from that side of our civilization that is most open to criticism—its devotion to quantity at the expense of quality. It is as true of civilizations as of persons that their defects and their qualities of value go together. Moreover the ideal of mass elevation is intimately connected with the fact of diffusion. Our democratic fathers apparently thought that the desired elevation of the mass would automatically occur if certain political agencies were instituted. By one of the ironies of history, these political agencies are just the thing that lent themselves, indirectly rather than directly, to appropriation and manipulation by the few in possession of ultimate economic power. But meantime the very forces of industry have created mechanisms that operate to bring about diffusion on an unprecedented scale. European critics of our culture often ignore the fact that many of the things they criticize are due to the fact that we have been compelled perforce to undertake the task which Europe shirked. In their animadversions upon our lack in higher culture, they pass over the fact that millions of European immigrants have, and have realized, opportunities here that they never had at home. The mass and quantitative aspect of our civilization has thus a uniquely positive significance. All the facts indicate that if we should attain the higher values by which civilization is to be ultimately measured, it will be by a mass achievement, and not be the work of a chosen few, of an *élite*. It will be by social osmosis, by diffusion.

If, then, I have not touched specifically upon the industrial and technological phase of our life, it is because I regard it as central and dominant. It is the prepared mechanism of diffusion and distribution. And the ultimate question about it is not the distribution of pecuniary incomes that it finally effects. That question is, indeed, of an importance not to be ignored. But its last importance is its bearing upon the distribution of imponderables, the diffusion of education and of a share in the values of intellectual and artistic life. While it is true that devotion to the economic phase of life is materialism, and that so judged our civilization is materialistic, it is also true that we have broken down the agelong old world separation of the material and the ideal, and that the destruction of this dualism is a necessary precondition of any elevated culture that is the property of a people as a whole. The constructive function, that of using the economic and material basis as a means for widely shared ideal ends, is only begun. But it is far enough along to provide what never existed before: operative agencies of diffusion. Even though it be of the nature of prophecy rather than of record, I do not believe that in the long run anything can defeat or seriously deflect the normal diffusion effect of our economic forces.

The tightening-up, the repression, the mechanical standardization, to which allusion has been made, presents the attempt at obstruction and diversion of this normal tendency. The liberation of individual potentialities, the evocation of personal and voluntary associated energies, manifest the actual effect still expressed in a form as inchoate as the effort in the opposite direction is organic. Our faith is ultimately in individuals and their potentialities. In saying this, I do not mean what is sometimes called individualism as opposed to association. I mean rather an individuality that operates in and through voluntary associations. If our outward scene is one of externally imposed organization, behind and beneath there is working the force of liberated individualities, experimenting in their own ways to find and realize their own ends. The testimony of history is that in the end such a force, however scattered and inchoate, ultimately prevails over all set institutionalized forms, however firmly established the latter may seem to be.

In concluding, let me confess that I am aware that as I have been writing I have been influenced, and unduly so I think, by the mood of self-conscious criticism that has overtaken us. In reality, I believe that we have already accomplished very much in the way of diffusion of culture—whatever that elusive word may signify. It is a part of any humane culture to be concerned to see that others share in it. Our newly acquired self-consciousness makes one hesitant to speak of social service and practical idealism; the overworked words have taken on a somewhat ridiculous color. But it is true that no other people at any other age has been so permeated with the spirit of sharing as our own. If defects go with qualities, so do qualities with defects. The excessive sociability that breeds conformity also makes us uneasy till advantages are shared with the less fortunate. Every significant civilization gives a new meaning to "culture." If this new spirit, so unlike that of old-world charity and benevolence, does not already mark an attainment of a distinctive culture on the part of American civilization, and give the promise and potency of a new civilization, Columbus merely extended and diluted the Old World. But I still believe that he discovered a New World.

The Pragmatic Acquiescence

There are myths and myths. Some are inspiriting; some are benumbing. Nature myths, at least in their first form, inspire because they are spontaneous responses of imagination to the scene that confronts it. Myths of literary criticism and historic interpretation are deadening. They do not enliven; they force subject-matter into ready-made patterns and thus dull sensitivity of perception. Such myths grow up in interpretations of past philosophies and always tend to overlay and conceal the realities of past reflection. They flourish in those literary versions by which the ideas of philosophers reach the public—for philosophers themselves are usually too much preoccupied with the technique, the professional rules, of their calling to have a public—except one another. Even such new movements as pragmatism and instrumentalism already have their accretion of myths which stand in place of the ideas themselves. Probably the unfortunate names themselves invite the creation and encourage the spread of these myths. The names account alike for some of the vogue of the doctrines and for some of the condemnation they receive.

One reading of the myth is embodied in the words which form the caption of what I am writing. They are borrowed from Lewis Mumford's *The Golden Day*; they sum up his essential criticism. "William James," he says, "gave this attitude of compromise and acquiescence a name: he called it pragmatism." Not content with this epithet, he headlines the idea of acquiescence; "the pragmatism that followed it was a paralysis." And again, "pragmatism was a blessed anesthetic." What is denoted by "this attitude"? And in what did James acquiesce? The America of his own time, according to Mr. Mumford, the America of the Gilded Age that followed the Civil War. More concerned with making clear his

[First published in *New Republic* 49 (1927): 186–89.]

pattern than he is with William James he goes as far as to say, "James was only warming over again in philosophy the hash of everyday experience in the Gilded Age." And this of William James, the arch-heretic of his day, the intellectual nonconformist, the constant protester against everything institutionalized in action and belief, the valiant fighter for causes which if not lost were unpopular and conventionally ignored! Such are the exigencies and dangers of a myth. If one were to apply Mr. Mumford's method to his own treatment, one might regard him as the acquiescent prophet of the Slogan Age of the 1920's.

For some reason, Mr. Mumford is fairer to me than he is to William James. But to bring me into line with his formula he has to attribute to me ideas of democracy and of "adjustment" which I not only have never held, but against which I have consistently, if vainly, taught and written. As evidence of a willing surrender on my part to industrial utilitarianism, he cites the following passage from my writings: "Fine art, consciously undertaken as such, is peculiarly instrumental in quality. It is a device in experimentation carried on for the sake of education. It exists for the sake of a specialized use, use being a training of new modes of perception," etc. The reader of the passage would inevitably infer what Mr. Mumford intends him to infer, that the passage represents my view of fine art, namely, that it is merely instrumental in character. But the entire chapter from which it is extracted is a statement that all art which is really fine exhibits experience when it attains completion or a "final," consummatory character, and, while it is urged that such art is also contributory, that to which it is held to be auxiliary is "renewal of spirit," not, it would seem, a base end, and certainly not a utilitarian one. The passage cited is directed against those views of fine art which treat it as an experience apart and for the few, an esoteric experience, instead of as a perfecting of the potentialities of any and all experience. This reference is implied in the quoted phrase "consciously undertaken as such"; it is explicitly stated in words which immediately precede what is cited, namely "seclusive estheticians," the point being that fine art conceived in *their* sense is "instrumental," so that while all value is not denied to it, its value consists in opening "new objects to be observed and enjoyed." The next sentence after those which Mr. Mumford quotes, reads as follows: "This is a genuine service, but only an age of combined confusion and conceit will arrogate to works that perform this special utility the exclusive name of fine art." My literary style must indeed be "fuzzy and formless," as Mr. Mumford calls it, to have led him to assign to me a definition of fine art which I assert indicates combined confusion and conceit.

William James, however, hardly needs defense, certainly not against shaping him to a pattern which inverts his whole spirit and thought, and I do not think that a few more misconceptions of my own ideas are of such importance as to justify writing the present article. What has been said is introductory to an issue which is of genuine significance. What is the relation of criticism to the social life criticized? What, more particularly, is the relation of philosophy to its social medium and generation? I doubt if any competent student of the history of thought would say that there has existed any philosophy which amounted to anything which was merely a formulated acquiescence in the immediately predominating traits of its day. Such things need no formulation, not even an apologetics; they dominate and that is enough for them. Yet there is probably also no historic philosophy which is not in some measure a reflection, an idealization, a justification of some of the tendencies of its own age. Yet what makes it a work of reflection and criticism is that the elements and values selected are set in opposition to other factors, and those perhaps the ones most in evidence, the most clamorous, the most insistent: which is to say that all serious thinking combines in some proportion and perspective the actual and the possible, where actuality supplies contact and solidity while possibility furnishes the ideal upon which criticism rests and from which creative effort springs. The question whether the possibility appealed to is a possibility of the actual, or is externally imported and applied, is crucial.

There is a sense, then, in which pragmatic philosophy is a report of actual social life; in the same sense it is true of any philosophy that is not a private and quickly forgotten intellectual excrescence. Not that philosophers set out to frame such reports. They are usually too much preoccupied with the special traditions within which their work is done to permit the assumption of any such task. They are concerned with doing the best they can with problems and issues which come to them from the conflict of their professional traditions, which, therefore, are specialized and technical, and through which they see the affairs of the contemporary scene only indirectly and, alas, darkly. Nevertheless being human they may retain enough humanity to be, sub-consciously at least, sensitive to the non-technical, non-professional, tendencies and issues of their own civilizations, and to find in the peculiar characteristics of this civilization subjects for inquiry and analysis. In any case, it is as necessary as it is legitimate that their methods and results should, in their leading features, be translated out of their proper technical context and set in a freer and more public landscape. The product of the dislocation may surprise no one more than the author of the technical doctrines. But without it the ulterior and significant meaning of the doctrines is neither liberated nor tested. The office of the literary and social critic in dealing with the broader human relationship of specialized philosophical thinking is, accordingly, to be cherished. But the office is a difficult one to perform, more difficult to do well than that of technical philosophizing itself, just as any truly liberal human work is harder to achieve than is a technical task. Preconceptions, fixed patterns, too urgent desire to point a moral, are almost fatal. A pattern is implied in such critical interpretation, but it must be tridimensional and flowing, not linear and tight.

What, then, is to be said of pragmatism and of instrumentalism when they are viewed as reflective reports of the American scene? More specifically, admitting a certain connection between the thought of James and the pioneer phase of American life and between instrumentalism and our industrialism, how is that connection to be understood? Mr. Mumford recognizes that the reflection by James of pioneer life is genuine and significant as far as it goes. But, he says, a "valuable philosophy must take into account a greater range of experience than the dominating ones of a single generation." Doubtless: nevertheless the dominating tendencies of two or three centuries may reveal to a genial mind something of vast significance for all generations. Their very exaggeration may disclose something hitherto concealed, while the lack of that something may have introduced such distortion and thinness into the earlier intellectual picture that its disclosure operates as a transformation. Mr. Mumford says that James lacked a Welt-Anschauung. No sentence he could have uttered affords such a measure of his competency to state the relation which the thought of James bore to pioneerdom. The idea of a universe which is not all closed and settled, which is still in some respects indeterminate and in the making, which is adventurous and which implicates all who share in it, whether by acting or believing, in its own perils, may appear to Mr. Mumford a commonplace, and not to be reckoned as a Welt-Anschauung. But one who has not studied James patiently enough to learn how this idea is wrought into his treatment of all special topics, from the will to believe to his pluralism, from his radical empiricism to his moral and religious ideas, has not got far in knowledge of James. That the controlling Welt-Anschauung does not appear in formal and pompous logical parade in discussion of special topics may not make the task of the would-be critic easy. But the style shows how genuinely and spontaneously the leading idea pervades his thinking. No other mode of literary presentation could have been so faithful to the central thought.

Perhaps one has to be old enough to recall, with some fullness of impression, the intellectual atmosphere in which James's work was carried on to realize that James brought with him not only a Welt-Anschauung but a revolutionary one. His professional contemporaries did not even trouble to criticize his philosophy; it was enough to laugh. Was it not self-evidently a more or less delightful whimsy of a tyro in philosophy who happened at the same time to be temperamentally something of a genius in psychology? Not until he gathered together the ideas which long previously he had profusely scattered in his other writings under the rather unfortunate title of pragmatism did he receive serious attention. And long after "pragmatism" in any sense save as an application of his Welt-Anschauung shall have passed into a not unhappy oblivion, the fundamental idea of an open universe in which uncertainty, choice, hypotheses, novelties and possibilities are naturalized will remain associated with the name of James; the more he is studied in his historic setting the more original and daring will the idea appear. And if perchance the future historian associates the generation of the idea with a pioneer America—in which James had no personal share—that historian may be trusted to see that such an idea is removed as far as pole from pole from the temper of an age whose occupation is acquisition, whose concern is with security, and whose creed is that the established economic régime is peculiarly "natural" and hence immutable in principle.

But America is now industrial and technological, not pioneering. Perhaps the later form of pragmatism called instrumentalism is the anodyne to reconcile the imagination and desire of man to the brutalities and perversions of this aspect of our life? Well, natural science and the technology which has issued from it are dominant tendencies of present culture, more conspicuously prominent in the United States than elsewhere, but everywhere all but universal in scope. That preoccupation with them should, whether consciously or sub-consciously, have played a part in generating "instrumentalism" is a not unreasonable hypothesis. What then? If one confronts this phenomenon and does not withdraw for consolation to the "pillaging" of other climes and epochs, what is to be done with it? It needs criticism, not acquiescence: granted. But there is no criticism without understanding. And no matter how much one may draw upon contrasting phases of life, Greek, Indian with Mr. Santayana, or the Golden Day of Emerson, Thoreau and Whitman with Mr. Mumford, for aid in this understanding, it is also true that without an understanding of natural science and technology in their own terms, understanding is external, arbitrary, and criticism is "transcendent" and ultimately of one's own private conceit.

Words, especially epithets, in philosophy are far from self-explaining. But the term "instrumentalism" might suggest to a mind not too precommitted, that natural science and technology are conceived as instruments, and that the logical intellect of mind which finds its congenial materials in these subjects is also instrumental—that is to say, not final, not complete, not the truth or reality of the world and life. Instruments imply, I should suppose, ends to which they are put, purposes that are not instruments which control them, values for which tools and agencies are to be used. The record of philosophy doubtless presents instances of almost utter self-contradiction and self-stultification. But it would require a mind unusually devoid both of sense of logic and a sense of humor—if there be any difference between them—to try to universalize instrumentalism, to set up a doctrine of tools which are not tools for anything except for more tools. The counterpart of "instrumentalism" is precisely that the values by which Mr. Mumford sets such store are the ends for the attainment of which natural science and all technologies and industries and industriousnesses are intrinsically, not externally and transcendentally, or by way of exhortation, contributory. The essential and immanent criticism of existing industrialism and of the dead weight of science is that instruments are made into ends, that they are deflected from their intrinsic quality and thereby corrupted. The implied idealization of science and technology is not by way of acquiescence. It is by way of appreciation that the ideal values which dignify and give meaning to human life have themselves in the past been precarious in possession, arbitrary, accidental and monopolized in distribution, because of lack of means of control; by lack, in other words, of those agencies and instrumentalities with which natural science through technologies equips mankind. Not all who say Ideals, Ideals, shall enter the kingdom of the ideal, but those who know and who respect the roads that conduct to the kingdom.

The Fruits of Nationalism

Like most things in this world which are effective, even for evil, Nationalism is a tangled mixture of good and bad. And it is not possible to diagnose its undesirable results, much less to consider ways of counteracting them, unless the desirable traits are fully acknowledged. For they furnish the ammunition and the armor which are utilized as means of offense and defense by sinister interests to make Nationalism a power for evil.

Its beneficent qualities are connected with its historical origin. Nationalism was at least a movement away from obnoxious conditions—parochialism on one hand and dynastic despotism on the other. To be interested in a nation is at least better than to restrict one's horizon to the bounds of a parish and province. Historically, Nationalism is also connected with the decay of personal absolutism and dynastic rule. Loyalty to a nation is surely an advance over loyalty to a hereditary family endued in common belief with divine sanctions and covered with sacrosanct robes. Much of superstitious awe and foolish sentiment has indeed passed over into Nationalism, but nevertheless the people of a country as a whole are surely a better object of devotion than a ruling family. Except where national spirit has grown up, public spirit is practically non-existent. In addition to these two historical changes, Nationalism is associated with the revolt of oppressed peoples against external imperial domination. If one wants to see one of the most potent motive forces in creating nationalism, one has only to consider the Greece of fifty years ago, the Ireland of yesterday and the China and India of today.

It is not to the present purpose to consider these gains; but it is to the point that without them Nationalism could not be perverted to base ends. The passionate loyalties which have been

[First published in *World Tomorrow* 10 (1927): 454–56.]

produced by struggle for liberation from foreign yokes, by the sense of unity with others over a stretch of territory wider than the parish and village, by some degree of participation in the government of one's own country, furnish the material which, upon occasion, make the spirit of a nation aggressive, suspicious, envious, fearful, acutely antagonistic. If a nation did not mean something positively valuable to the mass of its citizens, Nationalism could not be exploited as it is in the interest of economic imperialism and of war, latent and overt. Carlton Hayes has convincingly pointed out that Nationalism has become the religion of multitudes, perhaps the most influential religion of the present epoch. This emotion of supreme loyalty to which other loyalties are unhesitatingly sacrificed in a crisis could hardly have grown to its high pitch of ardor unless men thought they had found in it the blessings for which they have always resorted to religious faith: protection of what is deemed of high value, defense against whatever menaces this value, in short an ever present refuge in time of trouble.

But institutionalized religion is something more than a personal emotion. To say it is institutionalized is to say that it involves a tough body of customs, ingrained habits of action, organized and authorized standards and methods of procedure. The habits which form institutions are so basal that for the most part they lie far below conscious recognition. But they are always ready to shape conduct, and when they are disturbed a violent emotional irruption ensues. Practices, after they are adopted, have to be accounted for and explained to be reasonable and desirable; they have to be justified. Hence, along with the emotions and habits, there develops a creed, a system of ideas, a theology in order to "rationalize" the activities in which men are engaged. Faith in these ideas, or at least in the catch-words which express them, becomes obligatory, necessary for social salvation; disbelief or indifference is heresy. Thus Nationalism starting as an unquestioned emotional loyalty, so supreme as to be religious in quality, has invaded the whole of life. It denotes organized ways of behavior and a whole system of justificatory beliefs and notions appealed to in order to defend every act labelled "national" from criticism or inquiry. By constant reiteration, by shaming heretics and intimidating dissidents, by glowing admiration if not adoration of the faithful, by all agencies of education and propaganda (now, alas, so hard to distinguish) the phrases in which these defenses and appeals are couched become substitutes for thought. They are axiomatic; only a traitor or an evilly disposed man doubts them. In the end, these rationalizations signify a complete abdication of reason. Bias, prejudice, blind and routine habit reign supreme. But they reign under the guise of idealistic standards and noble sentiments.

Any one who reads the laudations of patriotism which issue from one source and the disparagements which proceed from another group must have been struck by the way in which the same word can cover meanings as far apart as the poles. The word is used to signify public spirit as opposed to narrow selfish interests. When so employed patriotism is a synonym for intense loyalty to the good of the community of which one is a member; for willingness to sacrifice, even to the uttermost, in its behalf. So taken, it surely deserves all the eulogies and reverence bestowed upon it. But because of nationalistic religions and its rationalization, the test and mark of public spirit becomes intolerant disregard of all other nations. Patriotism degenerates into a hateful conviction of intrinsic superiority. Another nation by the mere fact that it is other is suspect; it is a potential if not an actual foe. I doubt whether there is one person in a hundred who does not associate a large measure of exclusiveness with patriotism; and all exclusiveness is latent contempt for everything beyond its range. The rabies that exultantly sent Sacco and Vanzetti to death is proof of how deeply such patriotism may canker. It extends not only to foreign nations as such, but to foreigners in our own country who manifest anything but the most uncritical "loyalty" to our institutions. Thousands upon thousands of the most respectable element in the community believed they were exhibiting patriotism to the nation or to Massachusetts when they urged the death of men who were guilty of the double crime of being aliens and contemners of our forms of government.

Were it not for facts in evidence it would be hard to conceive that any sane man could parade the motto: "My country right or wrong." But, alas, one cannot doubt that the slogans conveyed the feeling which generally attaches to patriotism. That public spirit, an active interest in whatever promotes the good of one's country, is debased and prostituted to such a use, is chargeable to Nationalism; and this fact stands first in its indictment.

It is a trait of unreasoning emotion to take things in a mass and thereby to create unities which have no existence outside of passion. Men who pride themselves upon being "practical" and "concrete" would be incensed beyond measure if they were told that the Nation to which they yield such unquestioning loyalty is an abstraction, a fiction. I do not mean by this statement that there is no such thing as a Nation. In the sense of an enduring historic community of traditions and outlook in which the members of a given territory share, it is a reality. But the Nation by which millions swear and for which they demand the sacrifice of all other loyalties is a myth; it has no being outside of emotion and fantasy. The notion of National Honor and the role which it plays is a sign of what is meant. Individual persons may be insulted and may feel their honor to be at stake. But the erection of a national territorial State into a Person who has a touchy and testy Honor to be defended and avenged at the cost of death and destruction is as sheer a case of animism as is found in the records of any savage tribe. Yet he would be a thoughtless optimist who is sure that the United States will not sometimes wage a war to protect its National Honor.

As things now stand and as they are likely long to remain there is really such a thing as national interest. It is to the interest of a nation that its citizens be protected from pestilence, from unnecessary infection; that they enjoy a reasonable degree of economic comfort and independence; that they be protected from crime, from external invasion, etc. But Nationalism has created a purely fictitious notion of national interests. If a large gold field were located just over the border of Alaska, thousands of American breasts would swell with pride, as thousands would be depressed if it happened to lie in British territory. They would feel as if somehow they were personal gainers, as if the Nation to which they belong had somehow integrally promoted its interests. The illustration is somewhat trivial. But the spirit which it indicates is responsible for the acquiescence, if not the active approval, with which the new Coolidge version of international law with respect to property rights of American citizens in foreign countries has been received. For the gist of his revolutionary edition of international law (if he says what he means and knows what he means) is that any property right or property interest of any private citizen or any corporation in a foreign country (doubtless with the tacit understanding that it is not one of the Great Powers) is a National Interest to be protected when necessary by national force.

The culmination of Nationalism is the doctrine of national sovereignty. Sovereignty was originally strictly personal or at least dynastic. A monarch held supreme power; the country was his proper domain or property. The doctrine is historically explicable as part of the transition out of feudalism and the weakening of the power of feudal nobles in the growth of a centralized kingdom. The doctrine was also bound up with the struggle of State against Church and the assertion of the political independence of the secular ruler from the authority of ecclesiastics. As historians have clearly shown, the doctrine of the divine right of kings originally meant that secular monarchs had at least the same kind of divine commission as had Pope or Archbishop. But with the rise of modern territorial states the idea and attributes of Sovereignty passed over from the ruler to the politically organized aggregate called the Nation.

In so doing, it retained all the evils that inhered in the notion of absolute and irresponsible personal power (or power responsible only to God and not to any earthly power or tribunal) and took on new potencies for harm.

For disguise it as one may, the doctrine of national sovereignty is simply the denial on the part of a political state of either legal or moral responsibility. It is a direct proclamation of the unlimited and unquestionable right of a political state to do what it wants to do in respect to other nations and to do it as and when it pleases. It is a doctrine of international anarchy; and as a rule those who are most energetic in condemning anarchy as a domestic and internal principle are foremost in asserting anarchic irresponsibility in relations between nations. Internationalism is a word to which they attach accursed significance, an idea to which by all the great means at their disposal they attach a sinister and baleful significance, ignoring the fact that it but portends that subjection of relations between nations to responsible law which is taken for granted in relations between citizens. The doctrine is not of course carried to its logical extreme in ordinary times; it is mitigated by all sorts of concessions and compromises. But resort to war as the final arbiter of serious disputes between nations, and the glorification of war through identification with patriotism is proof that irresponsible sovereignty is still the basic notion. Hence I spoke in terms of the popular fallacy when I referred to the "right" of a state to do as it pleases when it pleases. For *right* is here only a polite way of saying power. It was usual during the World War to accuse Germany of acting upon the notion that Might makes Right. But every state that cultivates and acts upon the notion of National Sovereignty is guilty of the same crime. And the case is not improved by the fact that the judges of what National Sovereignty requires are not actually the citizens who compose a nation but a group of diplomats and politicians.

Patriotism, National Honor, National Interests and National Sovereignty are the four foundation stones upon which the structure of the National State is erected. It is no wonder that the windows of such a building are closed to the light of heaven; that its inmates are fear, jealousy, suspicion, and that War issues regularly from its portals.

Imperialism Is Easy

In common, I imagine, with large numbers of my fellow countrymen, I had long entertained in a vague way the notion that imperialism is a more or less consciously adopted policy. The idea was not clearly formulated, but at the back of my head was the supposition that nations are imperialistic because they want and choose to be, in view of advantages they think will result. A visit to Mexico, a country in which American imperialism is in the making, knocked that notion out of my head. The descent to this particular Avernus is unusually easy. Given, on one hand, a nation that has capital and technical skill, engineering and financial, to export, plus manufacturers in need of raw material, especially iron and oil, and, on the other hand, an industrially backward country with large natural resources and a government which is either inefficient or unstable, or both, and it does not require intention or desire to involve the first nation in imperialistic policies. Even widespread popular desire to the contrary is no serious obstacle. The natural movement of business enterprise, combined with Anglo-American legalistic notions of contracts and their sanctity, and the international custom which obtains as to the duty of a nation to protect the property of its nationals, suffices to bring about imperialistic undertakings.

Imperialism is a result, not a purpose or plan. It can be prevented only by regulating the conditions out of which it proceeds. And one of the things which most stands in the way of taking regulatory measures is precisely the consciousness on the part of the public that it is innocent of imperialistic desires. It feels aggrieved when it is accused of any such purpose, then resentful, and is confusedly hurried into dangerous antagonisms, before it perceives what is happening. The charge of imperialistic

[First published in *New Republic* 50 (1927): 133–34.]

desires sounds strange even to the group of men who have created the situation in which they appeal to their home country for
intervention. All they want, as they indignantly assert, is protection of life and property. If their own government cannot afford
that protection, what is it good for anyway?

In Mexico, and presumably in other Latin-American states,
conditions are exacerbated by the extended meaning which has
been given the Monroe Doctrine. In this widened meaning it has
become one of the chief causes of the growing imperialism of the
United States. Investors and concession holders from European
countries are estopped from appealing to their own countries for
intervention to give them protection. Pressure is consequently
brought to bear upon the United States. Unless we act, we are a
dog in a manger. We won't do anything ourselves, and we won't
let anybody else do anything. Thus the United States has become
a kind of trustee for the business interests of other countries. As
one consequence, the animosity which might otherwise be distributed among a number of countries is consolidated, and then
directed at the United States. About the most promising thing
which could happen would be for our people to realize, with viv-
idness, the Spanish-American view of the Monroe Doctrine. We
still, for the most part, pat ourselves upon the back complacently
for upholding it. We think of it as a benevolent measure for
which all Central and South America is, or should be, grateful to
us. We do not take into account the change of conditions in these
states; their growth in power and national consciousness, which
makes them resent being treated as infants under our tutelage.
We are not aware of the change in conditions brought about by
our development into a nation possessed of enormous capital
seeking investment, a fact which makes the countries to the
south much more afraid of us than they are of Europe. In consequence, the sacred doctrine has become entangled with all the
forces which plunge us into imperialistic dangers.

The average citizen of the United States has little knowledge of
the extent of American business and financial interests in Mexico. It does not occur to him that, from the standpoint of intelligent Mexicans, that country is, or was, in great danger of
becoming an economic dependency of this country. As things
went under the Díaz régime, the Mexicans might have awakened
some morning and found their natural resources, agricultural

and grazing lands, mines and oil wells, mainly in the hands of foreigners, largely Americans, and managed for the profit of investors from foreign countries. I well remember how one indignant legal representative of American business concessionaires contrasted the present régime with that of Díaz. He said: "Díaz had a standing order that any complaint from any American citizen was to be settled the same day it was made." This was his naïve tribute to the Díaz administration. In contrast with it, the Calles régime naturally appears to Americans with investments as something unspeakable.

I would not say that it gives no cause for legal complaint; I would not say that it does not afford many an occasion for protest. From the Mexican standpoint, the government is fighting for control of its own country, as much as if it were at war, and too scrupulous a regard for legal technicalities might mean defeat. An unusually frank Mexican ex-official said to an American business man: "Of course, we have to handicap you by legislation and administration in every way we can. You are much abler and more experienced in business than we are; if we don't even up some other way, you will soon own the whole country." Such things indicate the ease with which the relations of an industrially advanced and a backward country ultimately drift into situations where the vested legal rights which have grown up are confronted by a vigorous national sentiment, and then can hardly be maintained without appeal for governmental intervention.

The ease with which imperialism follows economic exploitation is indicated by the almost unanimous sentiment of Americans resident in Mexico, including those who do not own concessions and who are not directly affected by the new laws. They would deny, and as far as their conscious intent is concerned, deny sincerely, for the most part, any imperialistic taint. What they want is simply "protection" for American rights. Judging from conversations, the objects of their dislike stand in about the following order: in the first rank, they are irritated with Americans having no business interests, who come down there for a few weeks, talk with plausible Mexicans, and, with the usual prejudice against "Wall Street," go away more or less pro-Mexican. Locally, such visitors would be gladly consigned to a lethal chamber. They are said to be completely ignorant, and yet they assume to know more about the right relations between

Mexico and the United States than "we do who have lived here many years, and know the facts about the persecution of Americans and the disregard for their rights." President Wilson was not one of this class, but he succeeded in winning the equal dislike of American residents and of Mexicans, of the latter by his action, and of the former by his talk against concessionaires, a talk which "encouraged Mexican Bolshevism."

Next in order comes irritation with the American State Department, based on the fact that while "it is always writing notes, it never does anything." There is little doubt on the Mexican side of the line as to what "doing something" means. Superpatriots, on this side, may suppose that it signifies a show of force such as has taken place in Nicaragua. On the spot, they know that it means not only war and continued guerrilla strife, but taking control of the government, and managing Mexican affairs for a number of years. To be sure, there is the usual pious talk, also quite sincere as far as the consciousness of many Americans is concerned. We should, of course, set up a model of administration, multiply schools, and after we had shown the Mexicans how a state should be managed, should turn it over to them, in good running order. It is not difficult for the American who has been expatriated for a number of years to idealize the honesty and efficiency of our own government, in contrast with the corruption, inefficiency and, above all, instability, which have obtained in Mexico. The favorite idea, which is even shared, it is rumored, in diplomatic quarters, is that Great Britain and the United States shall unite in this benevolent undertaking. Was this in Mr. Hearst's mind when he made his recent touching appeal for closer cooperation between this country and Great Britain?

An American oil man, who knows his Mexico well, one of the adventurous type which is personally more attractive than the smug legalistic, told us that they did not ask for the support of the State Department; all they wanted was to be let alone. He said, as an indication of how well they could take care of themselves, that at one time all was in readiness for three independent states in Mexico, one including Vera Cruz, another Tampico, and a third the lands in the north, next to the American border, where immigrants from this side had settled. At Tampico, he said, 2,000 American workmen, engaged in the oil industry, were furnished with rifles. There was perhaps some romantic exaggeration in the tale, but there was also a residuum of fact. Of course, these revolutions were not to be undertaken by Americans, but by dissatisfied Mexicans. Unfortunately, the State Department said No.

Third in the order of dislike, as far as talk goes, comes the Calles government.

Below this state of mind, instances of which might be given indefinitely, is the conflict between Anglo-American institutional psychology, especially with reference to charters, contracts and other legal points, and the Spanish-Latin temper. The two mix no better than oil and water, and unfortunately there is no great disposition to discover and use any emulgents. As usually happens with small colonies in a foreign country, the native "Anglo-Saxon" psychology stiffens up, instead of relaxing. The years of civil war, of chaos and destruction, which Mexico has gone through, make it easy for outsiders to maintain an attitude of superiority and aloofness. The supposed principle of international law by which it is the duty, rather than simply the right, of a nation to come to the protection of the rights of its nationals when they are disregarded, makes the conflict of interests and of traditions a serious menace to peace. Our constitutional system is an additional source of danger. Congress must be consulted before war can be declared. But the President is the Commander of the Army and Navy, and it is only too easy to create a situation after which the cry "stand by the President," and then "stand by the country," is overwhelming.

Public opinion has spoken with unusual force and promptitude against interference in Mexico. But the causes of the difficulty, the underlying forces which make for imperialistic ventures, are enduring. They will outlast peaceful escape from the present crisis, supposing we do escape. Public sentiment, to be permanently effective, must do more than protest. It must find expression in a permanent change of our habits. For at present, both economic conditions and political arrangements and traditions combine to make imperialism easy. How many American citizens are ready for an official restatement of the Monroe Doctrine? How many are willing to commit the country officially to the statement that American citizens who invest in backward foreign countries do so at their own risk?

"As an Example to
Other Nations"

On March 9, 1918, Mr. S. O. Levinson published in the *New Republic* an article entitled "The Legal Status of War." It put forward the first public proposal for the outlawing of war. In April of last year, M. Briand in a public speech stated that "France is willing publicly to subscribe to an engagement with the United States tending to outlaw war (using an American expression) between the two nations." Not long afterwards, he showed that his statement was not a casual, irresponsible remark, by officially transmitting, as Foreign Minister of France, to our own State Department, the suggestion that the two nations should, by solemn compact, completely renounce war as an instrument of policy with respect to each other, binding themselves to settle all disputes of whatever nature by pacific means. A few months ago Secretary Kellogg replied, suggesting a multilateral treaty instead of a bilateral one, and the making of an effort to secure the adherence of all the principal powers.

The immediate effect of this reply was to check the bilateral treaty; the ultimate fate of both proposals now lies on the lap of the gods. But whatever the eventual outcome—and there are good grounds, as we shall see, for hoping that the negotiations have not come to an *impasse*—history records few more dramatic incidents. Within ten years an idea of the most far-reaching character of any ever put forth as to international relations, an idea developed by a private citizen without official connections, one promoted without the backing of any large and well financed organization, and one promptly condemned as utopian, has made its way into responsible negotiations between two great powers. One would have to look far to find a parallel.

[First published in *New Republic* 54 (1928): 88–89. For reply by James T. Shotwell, see Appendix 4; for Dewey's rejoinder, see pp. 168–72.]

The reception of Secretary Kellogg's note by Briand and by the European press has made one fact clear, henceforth written upon the record so plainly that it cannot be effaced. The proposal of a many-sided treaty was declared unwelcome because it conflicted with war-engagements assumed by members of the League of Nations to other nations of the League. Those who objected to the entrance of the United States into the League on the ground that it committed us, under articles Ten and Sixteen, to participation in European wars, and who met with hot denials from friends of the League, may find some satisfaction in the now officially established confirmation of their position.

The *New York World* will not be suspected of hostility to the League. In its editorial columns of January 12 of this year, speaking of Secretary Kellogg's counter-proposal, it said: "It was suggested that all the nations subscribe to a treaty renouncing war. A more accurate description of this proposal would have been to call it a treaty to renounce the Covenant of the League of Nations, the Treaty of Locarno and all the French defensive alliances in Europe. For the whole European political system today is based on the theory *not* of renouncing war as an instrument of policy but of *pledges to wage war* against any nation which disturbs the peace." (Italics not in the original.) It would be impossible to state the situation more accurately. Just what would have happened, however, if any opponent of our entry to the League had drawn this contrast between the American and the European system? The same editorial of the *World* condemned the Secretary of State's proposal as absurd and amateurish, as a source of irritation, and as leading to a sure fiasco. To quote again from the editorial, "The European idea is to maintain the *status quo* by a general guarantee to make war upon any nation which attacks the *status quo* by force." There are those who will think that Mr. Kellogg's proposal was not inept if it made perfectly clear the fact that the European "idea" is of the sort stated—although there is no reason for supposing that the desire to bring about such a clarification was the intention of his suggestion. From now on, we at least know where Europe stands and where we stand with reference to her commitment by war pledges to the *status quo*.

Nevertheless, I am not willing to think that the European commitment to the war system is so irretrievable that there is a deadlock which makes impossible any systematic cooperation of the United States with Europe in the interest of peace. In an important article by Senator Borah in the *New York Times* of February 5, he makes some points which seem to have escaped notice. In the first place, he points out that Briand's original proposal would be estopped by the reasoning he employs against a multilateral treaty. For if the United States were to engage in war against a signatory member of the League and the League Council decided our war was unjustifiable, France's obligation to the League would compel her to take up arms against us, and her treaty with us would be a scrap of paper. More important, however, is the constructive point which he makes. Supposing, he argues, that a multilateral treaty were signed not only by the chief powers but also by the lesser nations who are supposed to stand especially in need of guarantees of security. Supposing, further, that some signatory nation violated its treaty compact by attacking a nation which is a member of the League. By every rule of the binding force of contracts, a violation by one party releases other parties from their obligations under its terms. It would be a simple matter to insert a clause to that effect in the multilateral treaty. The obligations of the nations which are members of the League would thus be met; they would be free to come to the aid of the nation that was attacked. The United States and other non-League members would be free to take whatever stand they judged desirable under the circumstances. In short, there is a simple way out of the seeming *impasse*: work to make the treaty more, instead of less, inclusive.

It would seem as if the only logical course for France to pursue were to join with the United States in securing as many signatory nations as possible, since a sufficiently wide range of adhering nations would both cover the renunciation of war as an instrument of national policies, and permit nations that are members of the League to carry out all their obligations to it. Such a move, instead of "torpedoing the League," could not fail to strengthen its position. Moreover, such action on the part of France would be wholly in line with Briand's original proposal. For, as Senator Borah reminds us in the article referred to, that proposal suggested that the treaty between France and the United States would serve "as an example to other nations."

In his reply to Mr. Kellogg's proposal to extend the treaty of outlawry of war to other nations, Briand, however, introduced an idea not contained in his first proposal: namely, the outlawing of "aggressive" war. And a considerable portion of American pacific opinion has been inveigled into a belief that definition of what constitutes aggression is the necessary first step, to be followed by an outlawing of the nation which then engages in aggression as that has been defined. This notion has gained such wide currency that League obligations are now frequently spoken of as if they were based on mutual agreement to attack an aggressor nation. This is, however, sheer confusion; there is nothing about an "aggressor nation" in the covenant. Moreover, although the definition is often proposed as a much needed improvement in the idea of outlawing war, it evinces an almost total lack of comprehension of that idea. War is at present an institution legalized under existing international law. To outlaw the institution of war is a radically different thing from outlawing a nation. Use of the latter conception shows that those who employ it are still thinking and talking in terms of legalized war.

The injection of the idea of outlawing "aggressive war"—i.e., of outlawing an aggressor nation—needs to be accounted for. It is not at all hard to find the explanation. The passage already cited from the *World* reads: "To maintain the *status quo* by a general guarantee to make war upon any nation which attacks the *status quo*." In this phrase is contained the reality of any definition of "aggression" that would be satisfactory to France. That nation is the aggressor that strongly questions the *status quo*; in other words, that questions the settlements made by the war treaties. The diplomacy of the great European powers is quite adequate to the task of declaring a nation an aggressor which agitated vigorously for their revision, even if it did not take up arms to secure the revision. Under actual conditions, the treaty engagements of France with Poland and Czechoslovakia outside the League, engagements which Briand now urges against the possibility of becoming a party to multilateral treaties, take on a sinister aspect. There can be no doubt of the pious intent of the American group which is so devoted to defining "aggression" as a preliminary to the outlawry of an aggressive nation. But when it is noted that the European *status quo* is that fixed by the Paris war treaties, and that the League is the armed guardian of the settlement thus arrived at, the proposal to make the United

States a party to a treaty which outlaws "aggression" is simply, from the European point of view, to make it a party to guaranteeing the results of the war treaties, with all their injustices. I fear the aspirations of the American group are far removed in their conception of "aggression" from the realities of the European situation, as these are used to define "aggression" by France and her allies.

That the reference in the *World* editorial to guaranteeing by armed force the *status quo* was not ill-considered is made perfectly clear by earlier editorials in that journal. Under the date of December 3 it said: "Substitute the word 'revision' for the word 'aggression' and the words 'maintenance of the Paris treaties' for the word 'security,' and you have the real meaning of this interminable debate." It is accordingly surprising to find the *World*, together with a section of the American internationally minded group, now supporting Briand's position as against Mr. Kellogg's. In a further editorial of January 14, the *World* said: "The League, the Locarno Treaty and the various alliances are all built on the idea not of renouncing war but of waging war against any nation which disturbs the peace—that is, an aggressor nation." Since the *World* at least is under no illusions as to the identity in the minds of France and her allies of "disturbing the peace" with striving for revision of the Paris treaties, why is it that the *World* does not bring its great influence to bear against the Briand injection of aggression? There appears to be but one course for American lovers of peace, namely, to get firmly and unanimously behind Kellogg's proposal for a general treaty of renunciation of war, and thereby execute the spirit of Briand's original idea of setting an example to the nations of the world. If the nations do not intend to embrace the opportunity thus afforded, it can only be because they propose to reserve to themselves the right to use war in promoting their national ambitions. If such be the case, it is just as well to have no treaties which disguise the real situation and which lull lovers of peace into a wholly delusive notion of the prospects of peace.

Rejoinder to James T. Shotwell

Sir: It is not easy to guess just what is the basis of criticisms, from the American side, of Kellogg's proposal to Briand of a multilateral treaty renouncing war as an instrument of policy, such as are implied in the reply of Professor Shotwell to my recent article. They seem somewhat vague, as if there were something unexpressed in the background. I take it, however, that it is not so much an objection to the multilateral feature as it is to refusal to commit this nation in advance of further negotiations to a renunciation of "aggressive" war and to a reservation in favor of "defensive" war. The halt and possible *impasse* appear to turn on the matter of definitions.

Even so, the ground of objection is not altogether clear. For in his correspondence, Professor Shotwell makes a distinction between commitment to a definition, and the question of what acceptance of the definition practically imports, in case some nation is adjudged an aggressor under the definition. For, according to him, the definition is independent of measures to be taken practically beyond removing the aggressor nation from the protection of international law. But since it is not stated what follows practically from this exemption, and the measures to be taken against the aggressor are still left open, this would seem to render the matter of definition an academic exercise. However, it is not possible to suppose that the group objecting to the position of our State Department would halt the negotiations for a purely academic reason. Moreover, Professor Shotwell expressly says there is an important practical distinction between the demand for definitions, and the suggestion of Senator Borah that if a nation violated the terms of the multilateral treaty, other signatory nations would be automatically released from their obli-

[First published in *New Republic* 54 (1928): 194–96. For Shotwell's article to which this is a rejoinder, see Appendix 4.]

gations, and hence be free to take such measures as they then desired. Senator Borah's suggestion thus left the members of the League free to fulfill whatever obligations are incumbent upon them under the terms of the League against an "aggressor" nation. I am not able to see the consistency between Professor Shotwell's two arguments. If all that is wanted is an academic definition, academic because involving no specified practical consequences, the proposal of our State Department, interpreted in the light of Senator Borah's suggestion, goes further than the definition; for it permits the members of the League to fulfill any obligations they may have to engage in a cooperative defensive war. If it is more than academic, it, and the suggestion of Borah to which objection is taken leave matters upon exactly the same footing as far as members of the League are concerned. Is it then unreasonable to suppose that the unexpressed desire that is back of the objection is that the United States should commit itself to the same obligations to take action against an "aggressor" nation that devolve upon the League members? In this case, the insistence upon definitions springs from a desire to have the United States make a commitment under the terms of a definition that it has so positively refused to assume in an open manner.

It is, however, a striking fact that the League itself has so far refused, through its most important members, to define just what action will be taken in case of violation of its provisions by one of its members. Various attempts have been made to define these measures, but so far they have come to naught. The net result is that, up to the present, members of the League practically reserve to themselves freedom of decision and action—being in this respect in a position not unlike that of the United States and other non-League members. If, then, the matter of a definition to be incorporated in the negotiations and treaties is practically important, insistence upon it as a precondition signifies not only that the United States should do under the cover of a definition what it has so far refused to do openly, but also that it should be the instrument—or tool—of bringing about commitments which the European nations have themselves refused to undertake. Admission of this desire would explain the objections of the American groups, and relieve them of the vagueness which so far clings to them.

For it is argued that the hesitation of the European powers is due to the isolation of the United States, since no great power, and certainly not Great Britain, could afford to pledge itself to action that might involve it in difficulties with our own country. Hence, various efforts to induce this country by some indirect means—of which the Capper resolution is a sample—to agree to abide by the decision of the League as to an aggressor nation and not insist upon such rights as might otherwise appertain to it as a neutral. Viewed in this light, the insistence upon prior definitions becomes intelligible. It may, however, be understandable without being reasonable.

For it is not sensible to seek the end of American cooperation in the peace of the world by means that are impossible of adoption. There is not, in my judgment, the slightest probability that the United States will take indirectly, *via* the elaboration of definitions, action that will deprive it in advance of freedom of judgment and decision with respect to a future European war. Nor, as has been argued in the editorial columns of the *New Republic* several times of late, is it in the interest of Europe itself that we should do so. For the practical effect would be to give the victorious European nations security respecting the *status quo* instituted by the post-war treaties; commitment in advance on our part would cut the nerve of any disposition on their part to consider a readjustment in the interest of justice and secure an enduring peace.

The only practical issue is whether there is some means of engaging the action of the United States on the side of cooperation for international peace that does not tie us in advance to support of existing European settlements. The proposal of our State Department affords just such an opportunity; it is accordingly discouraging to note that, instead of obtaining unanimous and hearty support, it is the subject of criticism from an important American peace group. Opposition from this side can only have the effect of encouraging European foreign offices to cherish wholly illusory hopes of drawing the United States into commitment to support the *status quo* in Europe. Since these hopes are illusory, any action from this side that encourages them defers, by just that much, our active cooperation, in any official way, in the cause of peace. This is a responsibility which I should think American lovers of peace would be slow to assume.

Failure in American backing, represented by criticisms which virtually support Briand's position, sets back active American cooperation in the cause of peace, because the criticisms demand a kind of action on the part of this country which public opinion here has rejected, and also because they encourage European nations to continue in a false course in their efforts to enlist our aid. They also, in making agreement upon definitions a precondition of action in renouncing war, rest upon a misconception of the true order of procedure. The idea put forth by Secretary Kellogg, if accepted by European powers, is in any case a preliminary to conference and negotiations. These future negotiations define the place and time for consideration of niceties and refinements of phraseology. If perchance it should develop during these negotiations that the European nations decline to enter into any renunciation of war that does not commit both them and us to "defensive" war in support of the *status quo*, the responsibility for failure would not rest with us. But why make that assumption in advance? Why not go ahead on the assumption that their desire for peace is genuine? Why not trust to the future instead of assuming on their part an unqualified adherence to the present system?

It is, of course, absurd to suppose that acceptance by European nations of the Kellogg proposal for a multilateral treaty outlawing war as a means of settling disputes could be anything but a preliminary. Criticism of Senator Borah's proposal as being irresponsible in respect to consequences, completely overlooks the fact that he is already pledged to the idea of revision of international law and to the institution of a world court with positive jurisdiction. Why, then, this insistence upon definitions in advance, instead of trusting to the future negotiations to make the necessary revisions of present international law, and to future action of conferences and the world court? It seems infinitely wiser to trust to the realities of a moving and developing situation, when the idea of renunciation of war has been accepted as a foundation, than to pin faith to definitions made in advance.

I do not pretend to know just how far such future international conferences would succeed in working out certain definitions. The courts have refused to define fraud, just because no definition can be framed which would not leave loopholes through which ingenuity could creep. The law relies upon the facts revealed in a particular case in order to decide the presence or absence of fraud. The same thing might or might not occur with definitions of defensive and aggressive war. But in any case, it is the part of any realistic devotion to the cause of international peace to trust to future developments rather than to any magic inhering in antecedent definitions. If there is no general will to peace, nothing will be securely guaranteed in any case, definitions or no definitions; if there is such a desire it will be expressed in subsequent negotiations, conferences; in the revision of law and in the working of the supreme court of the nations, infinitely better than by fixed formal definitions made in advance. Again I ask: What is behind the insistence upon definitions as a precondition of further action?

Outlawing Peace by Discussing War

Public opinion adjusts itself slowly to any proposed novel project in human relationships. Habit is even more solidly entrenched in beliefs, in modes of thinking and understanding, than in outer actions. Much of the current reaction to the Briand reply concerning the renunciation of war by a far-reaching multilateral treaty, illustrates the mental inertia by means of which old ideas are used to interpret a new idea, even though the latter is antithetical to them. Adherents of the "outlawry" policy have often said that the greatest difficulty in the way of getting an intelligent hearing for that idea comes from the fact that imagination, even when supposedly envisaging the situation after the legitimacy of war is renounced, projects into the picture the present situation in which war is the legalized ultimate method of settling disputes.

This statement is confirmed by the reaction of a considerable number to the new status given the outlawry idea by the Briand reply. Instead of its being discussed in terms of the situation that should and may come about when nations have solemnly agreed "never to seek the settlement of any difference or conflict of whatsoever nature or origin save by pacific means," it is largely discussed in terms of war—of what would happen if one of the signatory nations should violate its pledge and go to war! It would be hard, I think it would be impossible, to find a better illustration of the hold that the habit of thinking of international relations in terms of war has acquired. Similarly, when the relation of the League of Nations to the proposal is discussed, the thing chiefly put to the fore is not the stimulation and reinforcement it may give the work of the League in seeking out appropriate pacific means of settling disputes, but its effect on the actual

[First published in *New Republic* 54 (1928): 370–71.]

or implied war-making powers of the League! This way of looking at the question it is fashionable to call "realistic." It strikes
me as the stupidity of habit-bound minds.

An amusing trait of the discussion is that when the relation of
the League through its members to a nation waging a war is under consideration, the argument assumes that all nations bound
by a treaty to go to war will keep their word. But when it is a
question of a treaty to settle disputes by other methods than war,
the chief consideration is the probability that nations—always,
of course, the other nations—will *not* keep their word, even
though given in the most comprehensive and most far-reaching
international document ever drawn.

Treaties to make war have, it would seem, an irresistibly attractive and binding force; treaties not to make war are in all
probability scraps of paper.

The *New York World* has reduced to a formula the idea that
Europe, through the League, is committed to the policy of sustaining peace by treaties which provide for going to war, and
that Europe shows no sign of doubting that these treaties will be
sacredly observed. It speaks well for the candor of the *World*
that, although a supporter of the idea that the United States
should enter the League, it presents the function of the League in
the form least palatable to the American public—including most
of the American supporters of the League. Although I do not
happen to be personally a supporter of the policy the *World* advocates, I do not think it is true that the business of keeping
peace by waging a joint war is the chief of the League's functions
with respect to peace; I should suppose that even those who regard this as a necessary measure in some contingency, look on it
as a desperate last resort, instead of the League's main concern.
The formula reappears, however, in a *World* editorial of April 11.
The editorial says: "Europe is organized on the principle of
maintaining peace by waging war against the nation which starts
a war. Europe has not the slightest intention of abandoning that
principle."

I do not profess to have any mandate to speak for Europe as to
what it is willing or unwilling to do. Without assuming any such
lofty role, a layman like myself may, however, doubt whether the
"principle" in question is thought, even by the nations who have
hesitatingly and ambiguously committed themselves to it, to be

one upon which a vast continent can be "organized." A layman may entertain a modest doubt whether a vague and as yet uncertainly formulated willingness to wage war in common is exactly a principle of organization. Entertaining the doubt, one may venture to go on to doubt whether the *World*'s further statement, based on this premise of Europe's determined refusal, covers the whole case or the most important phase of the effect of Briand's last reply. It says: "M. Briand has led Mr. Kellogg around by polite but perfectly logical steps to a point where the proposal to outlaw war has become really a proposal to define the policy of the United States toward the League." To one who is not wholly bound by the habit of thinking of international relations in terms of war, it seems that a truer statement would be that the negotiations have come around (with perhaps Mr. Kellogg doing a considerable part of the leading) to a point where the United States and the nations in the League will have to discuss the nature and operations of the procedures and mechanisms by which the common agreement to settle disputes by pacific means can be converted into an effective reality.

To say this is only to repeat the statement that the very essence of the position which Briand has accepted is that the negotiations for a multilateral treaty must terminate in some plan for finding and employing peaceful means in lieu of warlike ones for settling disputes. There may be those, whose ideas do not get beyond headlines, who suppose that the signing of a treaty in general terms would end the whole matter. It is hard to believe that any responsible statesman entertains that idea. Certainly every active proponent of the outlawry idea has always held that any such general statement would, and could, be but a preliminary to providing adequate means for reaching pacific adjustments. It could be but a preliminary for further negotiations respecting arbitration, conciliation, conference, revision of international law to comply with its terms, a world court and so on.

The harm that is done in discussing the present status of the negotiations as if they mainly concerned some future war lies just here. The harm and danger are practical. The American public, and possibly some Senators, need to be prepared for subsequent efforts that will have to be made in order to provide the necessary pacific means of adjustment of disputes. Discussion in terms of what would happen in case of war distracts attention from this essential need. If discussion does not prepare the public mind for the necessity and we are caught unawares, then when the treaty has been negotiated, we may well be in for another failure, a failure humiliating to our national self-respect and tragic in its consequences for the world.

Justice Holmes and the
Liberal Mind

When men have realized that time has upset many fighting beliefs, they may come to believe even more than they believe the very foundations of their own conduct that the ultimate good desired is better reached by free trade in ideas—that the best test of truth is the power of the thought to get itself accepted in the competition of the market, and that truth is the only ground upon which their wishes safely can be carried out. That, at any rate, is the theory of our Constitution. It is an experiment, as all life is an experiment.[1]

Were I to select a single brief passage in which is summed up the intellectual temper of the most distinguished of the legal thinkers of our country, I think I should choose this one. It contains, in spite of its brevity, three outstanding ideas: belief in the conclusions of intelligence as the finally directive force in life; in freedom of thought and expression as a condition needed in order to realize this power of direction by thought, and in the experimental character of life and thought. These three ideas state the essence of one type, and, to my mind, the only enduring type, of liberal faith. This article proposes, then, to consider the identity of the liberal and the experimental mind as exemplified in the work of Justice Holmes.

If it were asserted that Justice Holmes has no social philosophy, the remark would lend itself to misconstruction, and, in one sense, would not be true. But in another sense, and that in which

---

1. Quoted from a citation of Justice Holmes' dissenting opinion in the Abrams free speech case in Felix Frankfurter's article on "Mr. Justice Holmes and the Constitution," the December, 1927, number of the *Harvard Law Review*. I am glad to take this opportunity to express my indebtedness to this article. Such quotations in the present article as are not taken from it are drawn from the volume of the *Collected Legal Papers* of Justice Holmes.

[First published in *New Republic* 53 (1928): 210–12.]

the idea of a social philosophy is perhaps most often taken, it would be, I think, profoundly true. He has no social panacea to dole out, no fixed social program, no code of fixed ends to be realized. His social and legal philosophy derives from a philosophy of life and of thought as a part of life, and can be understood only in this larger connection. As a social philosophy, "liberalism" runs the gamut of which a vague temper of mind—often called forward-looking—is one extreme, and a definite creed as to the purposes and methods of social action is the other. The first is too vague to afford any steady guide in conduct; the second is so specific and fixed as to result in dogma, and thus to end in an illiberal mind. Liberalism as a method of intelligence, prior to being a method of action, as a method of experimentation based on insight into both social desires and actual conditions, escapes the dilemma. It signifies the adoption of the scientific habit of mind in application to social affairs.

The fact that Justice Holmes has made the application, and done so knowingly and deliberately, as a judge, and in restriction to legal issues, does not affect the value of his work as a pattern of the liberal mind in operation. In his own words: "A man may live greatly in the law as well as elsewhere; there as well as elsewhere his thought may find its unity in an infinite perspective; there as well as elsewhere he may wreak himself upon life, may drink the bitter cup of heroism, may wear his heart out after the unattainable. All that life offers any man from which to start his thinking or his striving is a fact. And if this universe is one universe, if it is so far thinkable that you can pass in reason from one part of it to another, it does not matter very much what that fact is. . . . Your business as thinkers is to make plainer the way from some thing to the whole of things; to show the rational connection between your fact and the frame of the universe." Justice Holmes has shown fondness for the lines of George Herbert:

Who sweeps a room as for Thy laws,
Makes that and th' action fine.

But he takes it as having "an intellectual as well as a moral meaning. If the world is a subject for rational thought it is all of one piece; the same laws are found everywhere, and everything is connected with everything else; and if this is so, there is nothing

mean, and nothing in which may not be seen the universal law."
The field which Justice Holmes has tilled is a limited one, but
since he has "lived greatly in it," his legal and social philosophy
is great, not limited. It is an expression of the processes and issues of law seen in an infinite perspective; that of a universe in
which all action is so experimental that it must needs be directed
by a thought which is free, growing, ever learning, never giving
up the battle for truth, or coming to rest in alleged certainties, or
reposing on a formula in a slumber that means death.

"The Constitution is an experiment, as all life is an experiment." According to the framework of our social life, the community, the "people," is, through legislative action, the seat of
social experiment stations. If Justice Holmes has favored giving
legislative acts a broader and freer leeway than has, in repeated
instances, commended itself to fellow judges, it has not been because he has always thought the specific measures enacted to be
wise; it is not hard to see that in many cases he would not have
voted in favor of them if he had been one of the legislators. Nor
is his attitude due to a belief that the voice of the people is the
voice of God, or to any idealization of popular judgment. It is
because he believes that, within the limits set by the structure of
social life (and *every* form of social life has a limiting structure),
the organized community has a right to try experiments. And in
his ken, this legal and political right is itself based upon the fact
that experimentation is, in the long run, the only sure way to discover what is wisdom and in whom it resides. Intellectual conceit
causes one to believe that his wisdom is the touchstone of that of
social action. The intellectual humility of the scientific spirit recognizes that the test can only be found in consequences in the
production of which large numbers engage. Time has upset so
many instances of fighting private wisdom that, even when one's
own wisdom is so mature and assured that for one's own self it is
the very foundation of one's own conduct, one defers to the beliefs of others to the extent of permitting them a free competition
in the open market of social life. Judicial decisions amply prove
that it demands courage as well as a generosity beyond the scope
of lesser souls to hold that "my agreement or disagreement has
nothing to do with the rights of a majority to embody their opinions in law," and to declare that "constitutional law like other
contrivances has to take some chances."

The faith that, within certain large limits, our social system is one of experimentation, subject to the ordeal of experienced consequences, is seen in Justice Holmes' impatience with the attempt to settle matters of social policy by dialectic reasoning from fixed concepts, by pressing "words to a drily logical extreme." "There is nothing I more deprecate than the use of the Fourteenth Amendment beyond the absolute compulsion of its words to prevent the making of social experiments that an important part of the community desires." "It is important for this court to avoid extracting from the very general language of the Fourteenth Amendment a system of delusive exactness." It is impossible to state in any short space the full practical implications of Justice Holmes' repeated warnings against "delusive exactness," where exactness consists only in fixing a concept by assigning a single definite meaning, which is then developed by formal logic, and where the delusion consists in supposing that the flux of life can be confined within logical forms. "The language of judicial decision is mainly the language of logic. And the logical method and form flatter that longing for certainty and repose which is in every human mind. But certainty generally is illusion, and repose is not the destiny of man. Behind the logical form lies a judgment as to the relative worth and importance of competing legislative grounds. . . . You can give *any* conclusion a logical form." "To rest upon a formula is a slumber, that prolonged, means death."

Yet nothing could be further from truth than to infer that Justice Holmes is indifferent to the claims of exact, explicit and consistent reasoning. In reality, it is not logic to which he takes exception, but the false logic which is involved in applying the classic system of fictitious fixed concepts, and demonstratively exact subsumptions under them, to the decision of social issues which arise out of a living conflict of desires. What he wants is a logic of probabilities. Such a logic involves distinctions of degree, consideration of the limitation placed upon an idea which represents the value of one type of desire by the presence of ideas which express neighboring, but competing interests. These requirements can be met only by employing the method borrowed, as far as possible from science, of comparison by means of measuring and weighing. He objects to domination of law by classic logic in the interest of a logic in which precision is material or quantitative, not just formal. To rely on deduction from a formal concept of, say, liberty as applied to contract relations is but a way of hindering judges from making conscious, explicit, their reasons of social policy for favoring the execution of one kind of desire rather than another. Thus the formal logic becomes a cover, a disguise. The judgment, the choice, which lies behind the logical form is left "inarticulate and unconscious . . . and yet it is very root and nerve of the whole proceeding." "I think the judges themselves have failed adequately to recognize their duty of weighing considerations of social advantage. The duty is inevitable, and the result of the often proclaimed aversion to deal with such considerations is simply to leave the very ground and foundation of judgments inarticulate and unconscious." Formal logic has become a mask for concealing unavowed economic beliefs concerning the causes and impact of social advantage which judges happen to hold. It is hard to imagine anything more *illogical* than leaving the real premises for a conclusion inarticulate, unstated, unless it be the practice of assigning reasons which are not those which actually govern the conclusion.

Upon the positive side, Justice Holmes has left us in no doubt as to the logical method he desires to have followed. "The growth of education is an increase in the knowledge of measure. . . . It is a substitution of quantitative for qualitative judgments. . . . In the law we only occasionally can reach an absolutely final and quantitative determination, because the worth of the competing social ends which respectively solicit a judgment for the plaintiff or the defendant cannot be reduced to number and accurately fixed. . . . But it is of the essence of improvement that we should be as accurate as we can." In deprecating the undue share which study of history of the law has come to play, he says that he looks "forward to a time when the part played by history in the explanation of a dogma shall be very small, and instead of ingenious research we shall spend our energy on the study of ends to be attained and the reasons for desiring them." More important than either a formal logical systematization of rules of law or a historical study of them is "the establishment of its postulates, from within, upon *accurately measured* social desires instead of tradition." And so he says in another address: "For the rational study of the law the black-letter man may be the man of the present, but the man of the future is the man of statistics and the master of economics." Summing it all up: "I have had in mind an ultimate dependence [of law] upon science because it is ultimately for science to determine, as far as it can, the relative worth of our different social ends. . . . Very likely it may be with all the help that statistics and every modern appliance can bring us there will never be a commonwealth in which science is everywhere supreme. But it is an ideal, and without ideals what is life worth?"

There is a definitely realistic strain in the thinking of Justice Holmes, as there must be in any working liberalism, any liberalism which is other than a vague and windy hope. It is expressed in his warning against the delusive certainty of formal logic, against taking words and formulas for facts, and in his caution to weigh costs in the ways of goods foregone and disadvantages incurred in projecting any scheme of "social reform." It is found in his belief that intelligent morals consist in making clear to ourselves what we want and what we must pay to get it; in his conception of truth as that which we cannot help believing, or the system of our intellectual limitations. It is seen in his idea of a rule of law as a prediction where social force will eventually impinge in the case of any adopted course of conduct. At times, his realism seems almost to amount to a belief that whatever wins out in fair combat, in the struggle for existence, is therefore the fit, the good and the true.

But all such remarks have to be understood in the light of his abiding faith that, when all is said and done, intelligence and ideas are the supreme force in the settlement of social issues. Speaking in commemoration of the work of Justice Marshall, he remarked: "We live by symbols. . . . This day marks the fact that all thought is social, is on its way to action; that, to borrow the expression of a French writer, every idea tends to become first a catechism and then a code; and that according to its worth an unhelped meditation may one day mount a throne, and . . . may shoot across the world the electric despotism of an unresisted power." Again and again he says that the world is today governed more by Descartes or Kant than by Napoleon. "Even for practical purposes theory generally turns out the most important thing in the end." Just because facts are mighty, *knowledge* of facts, of what they point to and may be made to realize, is mightier still.

We live in a time of what is called disillusionment as to the power of ideas and ideals. The seeming eclipse of liberalism is part of this distrust. To believe in mind as power even in the midst of a world which has been made what it is by thought devoted to physical matters, is said to evince an incredible naïveté. To those whose faith is failing, the work of Justice Holmes is a tonic. His ideas have usually been at least a generation ahead of the day in which they were uttered; many of his most impressive statements have been set forth in dissenting opinions. But patience as well as courage—if there be any difference between them—is a necessary mark of the liberal mind. I do not doubt that the day will come when the principles set forth by Justice Holmes, even in minority dissent, will be accepted commonplaces, and when the result of his own teachings will afford an illustration of the justice of his faith in the power of ideas. When that day comes, the spirit of Justice Holmes will be the first to remind us that life is still going on, is still an experiment, and that then, as now, to repose on any formula is to invite death.

Why I Am for Smith

My reasons for voting for Governor Smith for President are not, politically speaking, either profound or far-reaching. I mention this fact at the outset because it has definite bearing on the reason why I am voting for him, namely, because I think his election—and even his campaign if he is not elected—will have a humanizing *social* effect. It is too much to hope that it will eliminate the hypocrisies and humbugs which occupy so much space in our American social life today, but I am confident it will reduce these abnormal swellings. If I had any special confidence in what can be accomplished by any party, with reference to our specifically political needs, I should vote for Norman Thomas, because I think those needs are connected with a much more fundamental facing of the issues of economic reconstruction than we shall obtain from the Democratic party under any conceivable circumstances. But the American people is not ripe to meet this question. Although I wish more power to the campaign of the Socialist party in whatever it may accomplish in preparing the way for this degree of social maturity, the immediate need, as I see it, is to affect the general temper of social discussion among us, and in the direction of introducing some degree of frankness and of humane sympathy. So I shall mention, briefly, some directions in which I think the campaign of Governor Smith—and his election if that should occur—will have this result.

1. I do not regard the final issue of prohibition of manufacture and sale of alcoholic liquors as settled; I believe that in the end, in this particular regard, social welfare is more important than what is called "personal liberty"; and I see no reason to believe that that issue is finally closed. But the present situation is an intolerable one, and perhaps its most intolerable phase is the hypocrisy, political and moral, that has gathered about it. Al Smith

[First published in *New Republic* 56 (1928): 320–21.]

has brought the matter into the open; he has destroyed the atmosphere of secrecy and insincerity that surrounded it; it cannot again be relegated to the hush-hush closet. From sheer gratitude for this clearing of a most poisonous atmosphere—which the Republican party and Mr. Hoover are both breathing and perpetuating—I shall vote for Mr. Smith.

2. The same kind of considerations apply to the question of bigotry and intolerance. That much American sentiment is about as dishonestly insincere in this matter as on the question of liquor, the present campaign is making clear, even if ordinary observation had not made it previously manifest. It is a dreadful thing to have injected into politics what by some perversion of speech is called "religion"; but since there is in our social and intellectual life so much narrow bigotry, it can have only a wholesome effect to get it into the open. The lie contained in it, in its denial of our professed social ideals, will never be dealt with till the issue comes into the open air of publicity.

3. While, as I have already said, I do not expect much in the way of facing fundamental issues from the Democratic party, Mr. Smith's record as Governor is proof of the fact that a humane and sympathetic spirit will at least color their treatment as far as his influence can extend. Administrator for administrator, he is at least the equal of Mr. Hoover, and his extraordinary administrative abilities are as much controlled by a human sense of his fellow beings as Mr. Hoover's are by a hard "efficiency" which works out to strengthen the position of just those economic interests that most need weakening instead of strengthening. I can hardly think of any insincerity greater, whether it is calculated or unconscious, than is involved in the attempt to "sell" Mr. Hoover to the women of the country as a great humanitarian. That he is an efficient administrator of charity and semi-philanthropy in times of emergencies I shall not question. But if he has any human insight, dictated by consciousness of social needs, into the policies called for by the day-to-day life of his fellow human beings, either in domestic or international affairs, I have never seen the signs of it. His whole creed of complacent capitalistic individualism and of the right and duty of economic success commits him to the continuation of that hypocritical religion of "prosperity" which is, in my judgment, the greatest force that exists at present in maintaining the unrealities of our social tone and temper.

Psychology and Justice

Sacco and Vanzetti are dead. No discussion of their innocence or guilt can restore them to life. That issue is now merged in a larger one, that of our methods of ensuring justice, one which in turn is merged in the comprehensive issue of the tone and temper of American public opinion and sentiment, as they affect judgment and action in any social question wherein racial divisions and class interests are involved. These larger issues did not pass with the execution of these men. Their death did not, indeed, first raise these momentous questions. They have been with us for a long time and in increasing measure since the War. But the condemnation and death of two obscure Italians opened a new chapter in the book of history. Certain phases of our life have been thrown into the highest of high lights. They cannot henceforth be forgotten or ignored. They lie heavy on the conscience of many, and they will rise in multitudes of unexpected ways to trouble the emotions and stir the thoughts of the most thoughtless and conventional.

I have no intention of entering into a discussion at large of the many things which are revealed in this new chapter. There is one point to which I confine myself, not, seemingly, very large in itself, but momentous in its bearings: the psychology of the dominant cultivated class of the country as revealed in the report of the Fuller advisory committee. Without disrespect to the important activities which are identified with the names of the men who formed the committee, it is no exaggeration to say that their place in the historic memory of mankind will be settled by the document they have written. And in justice to them, the future will recognize that the document is something more than a personal expression; that it is typical and symbolic, a representation

[First published in *New Republic* 53 (1927): 9–12.]

of the state of mind that must be widespread in the educated leaders of the American public in the third decade of the twentieth century. Because my purpose is limited, I make no attempt to go outside the record, much less to discuss the innocence or guilt of Sacco and Vanzetti. These matters have been dealt with by more competent hands than mine. The attitude, the mental disposition, of the authors of the report, as exhibited in their report, is my theme.

In discussing this matter, the statement of the method followed by the committee in finding the condemned men guilty gives the base-line. They say: "As with the Bertillon measurements or with finger prints, no one measure or line has by itself much significance, yet together they may produce a perfect identification; so a number of circumstances—no one of them conclusive—may together make a proof beyond reasonable doubt." In deciding the men guilty, it is not each item by itself in isolation which counts, but the cumulative effect of all in their mutual bearing. I cite this fact, not to question their statement nor to raise the old controversy regarding circumstantial evidence, but because of its significance in connection with the standard adopted and the method pursued by the committee in dealing with other questions. For these other matters are segregated, both at large and in detail; every item and every topic is treated as an isolated thing, to be disposed of by itself without regard to anything else. The cumulative principle is not only disregarded; it is deliberately departed from. Why? Men, especially men of disciplined and cultivated minds, do not reverse their criterion and procedure without a cause.

The evidence for the sweeping statement just made is found, first, in the plan of treatment adopted in general, the framework of the report; second, in the way in which the considerations falling within the first two divisions are broken up and isolated, and third, in the manner of dealing with a fundamentally important question.

The framework of the report is indicated by the following: "The inquiry you have asked the Committee to undertake seems to consist of answering the three following questions: (1) In their opinion was the trial fairly conducted? (2) Was the subsequently discovered evidence such that in their opinion a new trial ought to have been granted? (3) Are they, or are they not, convinced beyond reasonable doubt that Sacco and Vanzetti were guilty of the murder?" That the first two of these questions were *elements* in the issue with which the committee had to deal, no one will question. Opinions will differ as to whether or not they were called upon to act as a jury and determine and state their own opinion as to the men's guilt or innocence. This difference will depend upon whether, in the light of the world-wide interest in the trial and conviction, men think that the original question of innocence or guilt had or had not in the course of events become, *for the time being*, secondary to the question of administration of justice.

In any event, the segregation of the first two questions, the treatment of the matters of a fair trial and of newly discovered evidence not as *elements* in the issue, but as independent and isolated issues, accounts for the fact that the main issue, as it stands before the world, is not faced. It is not even mentioned. For that issue is whether, taking *all considerations together*, there was or was not reasonable ground for doubt as to a miscarriage of justice in case of the men's immediate execution. The separate treatment of the questions whether the trial already had was fair and whether the newly presented evidence was of value flatly contradicts the cumulative principle accepted and proclaimed in pronouncing the accused guilty. The method fails to face the fact that the two questions have a common and integral bearing upon the main issue, namely, that a miscarriage of justice was reasonably possible if the sentence of death were put into effect forthwith.

The entire procedure was extra-judicial; the very existence of the committee is proof of widely held belief that justice had not, beyond a peradventure, been done; that, irrespective of whether the men were guilty or innocent, there were many circumstances attending the case which indicated that they had not been *proved* guilty. Moreover, any action the committee might recommend, any advice they might give, any conclusions at which they might arrive, were extra-judicial. The governor holds an executive office; he is no part of the judicial system. The appointment of the committee was extra-judicial, and its function was as extra-judicial as its appointment. The governor is entrusted with the task of protecting condemned men against a reasonable degree of a possibility of miscarriage of justice. His is the power to exercise clemency either by pardon or commutation of sentence, not to decide guilt or reverse the action of courts. The office of the committee was to guide the conscience of the governor in the exercise of that function. Why was it, then, that they acted as a jury and as a court, and in so doing adopted strictly legalistic methods of reasoning, even to the point of virtually throwing upon the defense the burden of showing that there was a certainty, not a reasonable possibility, of a miscarriage of justice if the condemned men were at once executed?

Whatever be the answer to this question, the answer to the question as to how they avoided facing the issue is sure. It was done by splitting the issue up into separate questions and disposing of each without any reference to its connection with the others. For, with respect to miscarriage of justice, the question of the old trial and the question of refusal of a new trial in the light of new evidence are, most conspicuously, of a cumulative character. Their net effect, when viewed together, in relation to each other, defined the issue. Why, then, were they treated in complete isolation? The answer can be found only in the attitude with which the issue was approached.

While that attitude is apparent in the framework of the report, with its division into three separate questions, the full force of the isolation in determining the procedure is manifest only when we take up details under the first two heads. By the statement of the report itself, there are six points under each. Are the six points treated as having a force such that, while each by itself is "inconclusive," when taken together they have a probative force as to a reasonable doubt? Such a treatment is not even hinted at. Systematically, each is kept apart from every other, so that the question of cumulative effect may not even arise. The six considerations bearing on the conduct of the original trial include such important points as the bias of the judge, the conduct of the prosecuting attorney in dwelling on the radicalism of the accused, the atmosphere of the court-room, the alleged intervention of federal officials. But each one of these things is taken up as an isolated item, and disposed of in its isolation.

The contrast with the cumulative method used in declaring the men guilty becomes more glaring, the more the details of the two procedures are noted. Under the cumulative procedure, weight is given to the fact that the "general appearance" of Sacco is admittedly "like" that of one of the actual murderers; that his cap bore "a *resemblance* in color and general appearance" to one which he admittedly owned; and that, when arrested, he had in his possession a pistol of the "*kind*" with which the murder was admittedly committed; that, while experts were opposed as to whether the bullet must have been fired from his pistol, the committee are "*inclined* to believe" those who testify it must have been, etc. Try a simple intellectual experiment. What would have become of these separate considerations if the committee had dealt with them by the method of segregation followed in the case of the six considerations adduced to indicate an unfair trial?

There are also six points with respect to the bearing of new evidence upon granting a new trial. One of them was the evidence (not given at the trial), of a bystander, Gould, that the accused men were not the murderers he saw—he being so close to the scene that a bullet passed through his coat lapel. It is also a matter of record that his evidence was not known to the defense at the time of trial. He was known by the prosecution to have been present at the scene of murder, and yet was not called. The committee labor to exculpate the prosecution from the charge of suppression of evidence unfavorable to their case. The method pursued is typical: a highly legalistic argument to whittle down the significance of the admitted facts. Contrast their procedure on this point with that in dealing with a new witness who gave testimony tending to break down Sacco's alibi. Here they remark: "The woman is eccentric, not unimpeachable in conduct; but the Committee believes that in *her* case, her testimony is *well worth* consideration." (The italics, naturally, are not in the original text.) But more significant is their comment that Gould's evidence is "merely cumulative," other eye-witnesses having also testified that the murderers were not Sacco and Vanzetti![1] They do not stop here. They go on to volunteer the remark that "there seems to be no reason to think that the statement of Gould would have any effect in changing the mind of the jury"! Since they can hardly be supposed to mean that the mind of the jury was impervious to evidence, this assumption of the role of jurors

---

1. If it is urged that a court will not grant a retrial on the basis of new evidence that is merely cumulative, the reply hardly helps the case. Since the whole procedure was extra-legal, what is the significance of adoption of a purely legal standpoint?

is indicative of the committee's own attitude, all the more so because the remark about a *former* jury is made in the course of discussion of granting a *new* trial!

But this is but one of the six points adduced. Some of the others were the assertion of Madeiros that he was with another gang when it committed the murder; evidence purporting to show marked prejudice on the part of the foreman of the old jury, under two counts; the testimony of one of the experts for the prosecution that, after he had positively refused to say that the fatal bullet was fired from Sacco's pistol, the prosecuting attorney arranged to have him testify that it was "consistent" with having been so fired. The report itself is the most convincing evidence that can be found of the adoption of the non-cumulative method, as well as of the whittling down of each point, in its isolation, to a minimum, together with magnifying to the utmost all new evidence which fell on the other side. Thus the evidence that the rent in the cap which had been employed as part of its identification with Sacco's is disposed of by saying that it is "so trifling a matter in the evidence in the case that it seems to the Committee by no means a ground for a new trial"—as if it had been argued that, taken by itself alone, it did afford such a ground. This "trifling" matter ceases to be trifling when taken as evidence of the rejection of any recognition of the cumulative principle. Again, when two new experts testified that the fatal bullet was not fired from Sacco's pistol, and two new ones testified that it was, the committee say that, after examining the photographs, they are led to the conclusion "that the latter present the more convincing evidence." In other words, although the question at issue is whether there was ground for a new trial, with a new jury, the committee themselves assume the function of a jury in dealing with new evidence so as to deny the new trial.

The third phase of self-revelation regarding the antecedent attitude of the committee is found in their method of dealing with the radicalism of the condemned men in its alleged effect upon the jury and judge, a radicalism the more heinous because those who professed it were also foreigners. This is the aspect of the case which loomed largest in public attention and interest—it is the basic cause of the committee's existence. In accepting appointment on Governor Fuller's committee, Messrs. Lowell, Stratton and Grant accepted also a responsibility to a public found in every country of the globe. Their own record manifests the way in which they discharged this responsibility. They admit the radicalism; they admit its prejudicial effect in causing illegal arrests and deportations. But they employ these admitted facts only in order to justify the action of the prosecuting attorney! For he had subjected Sacco to a cross-examination "on the subject of his social and political views [which] seems at first unnecessarily harsh and designed rather to prejudice the jury than for the legitimate purpose of testing the sincerity of his statements thereon." In excusing him, they deny that the proof of radicalism did influence the jury! They also admit the bias of the judge on the basis of "indiscreet" conversations out of court, but assert that his bias was not a factor in the conduct of the trial. And the bearing of radicalism upon the conduct of the accused when arrested is ignored. It is next to a psychological commonplace that men, especially men of trained minds, reason in such an inverted fashion only when influenced by some covert factor.

Here are the facts as written in the report. There is no doubt left of the committee's knowledge of the state of public sentiment at the time of the trial and of their knowledge of its actual (not merely possible) effect in bringing about unjust and illegal action. There were "wholesale arrests of Reds—fortunately stopped by Judge Anderson of the United States Circuit Court—in Southeastern Massachusetts." They would hardly have been stopped by the judge and their stoppage have been fortunate, unless they were illegal. Again, "at that time of abnormal fear and credulity, little evidence was required to prove that anyone was a dangerous radical. Harmless professors and students in our colleges were accused of dangerous opinions." The hysteria was so widespread as to extend beyond foreigners and ignorant laborers to college men, teachers and students. And the cross-examination of the prosecuting attorney was of the seemingly harsh and prejudicial character just cited. And it affects the men of the committee as such after a lapse of years in which public opinion has calmed, men who are highly trained, not just the average man such as serves on a jury. Nevertheless, the committee hold that it did not influence the jury living in the midst of the period of fear and credulity, when little evidence was required to convict an accused person of being a Red, and although, instead of little evidence, these jurymen had the fact of radicalism clearly proved, and although they were average men, not trained minds capable of detecting bias and thus, presumably, discounting it!

How is this remarkable result obtained? By two methods, one direct, the other indirect, shifting the issue. The direct procedure lay in questioning the jurors (the ten of them who were accessible) on the subject, and accepting their assurance that they were not influenced by the attitude of the judge and the mode of conduct of the trial. "Each felt sure that the fact that the accused were foreigners and radicals had no effect upon his opinion." These men, in other words, are now sure, an assurance which the committee fully accepts in the most important phase of the trial, that *they* were immune to the prevailing contagion of "fear and credulity," and immune although they had not "little evidence" but convincing proof of "dangerous opinions." Believe it he who can. And disbelief does not involve doubt as to the good faith of any juror in making the statement he made. If, in such an atmosphere, they had been aware of the influence of this force upon their beliefs, they would have been extraordinary men, even more unusual than the members of the committee. If they had been aware of the influence working upon them, they would have been in a position to discount it. Moreover, their statement is made after a period of years, during which their conduct has been the subject of ardent controversy and themselves the object of bitter criticism, so that all their defense mechanisms have been called into action. But the committee accepts their assurance at full value! The committee's belief that the admitted bias of the judge outside the court-room was dropped by him in the court-room, as he might shed an overcoat when he donned judicial robes, evinces an equal disregard of elementary psychological factors.

More self-revealing still is the committee's procedure with reference to the "consciousness of guilt" alleged by the prosecution to be proved by the false statements the prisoners made when arrested. The defense contended their false statements were due to consciousness that they were radicals and foreigners and were due to fear of arrest and deportation. The committee first excuses the seemingly harsh and prejudicial examination of the prosecuting attorney, on the ground that it was necessary for him to test the sincerity of their professed radicalism as explaining their behavior upon arrest. Then not only are the committee certain that the proof the defendants sincerely held these views had no weight with the jury's opinion, but they turn the proof, not to support the men's own explanation of their conduct, but as consistent with, if not actual evidence of, consciousness of guilt! The method by which this is done is perhaps the most extraordinary thing in an extraordinary document.

The argument goes: It was the defendants themselves, when on trial, who made clear their radical views. When they were arrested, there was "in the case of Sacco, no certainty that he held any such views. The United States authorities who were hunting for Reds had found nothing that would justify deportation or any other proceedings against these men." Although there were wholesale arrests, "these men had not been arrested."

Hence the justification of the prosecuting attorney in a seemingly harsh and prejudicial manner of prosecution—which, nevertheless, did not prejudice men at a time of fear and credulity. Moreover, while establishment of the fact that they were radicals, and were arrested at a time of wholesale illegal arrests and deportations, justifies the prosecuting attorney, it has no weight in contravention of the theory of "consciousness of guilt" as displayed upon arrest. The implication is that, instead of acting upon their own knowledge that they were obnoxious radicals, they should have acted upon the lack of certain knowledge on the part of the authorities!

In comparison with the force of elementary psychological considerations, it may seem to weaken the case to refer to another incidental fact. The committee's sole reference to the conduct of Mr. Thompson is that, upon occasion, his conduct indicated that "the case of the defense must be rather desperate" for him to resort to the tactics attributed to him. Well, events, in which the committee had their share, indicate that the plight of the defendants was indeed desperate; and Mr. Thompson, above all others, had occasion to realize how tragically desperate. But, quite apart from the committee's own conviction of the guilt of the accused, it was known to them that Mr. Thompson was equally convinced of their innocence; that he was conservative in his social and political views; that, at great sacrifice of time, of social and professional standing, he had made a gallant fight for the accused out of jealous zeal for the repute of his own state for even-handed justice. Yet their sole reference to him is by way of a slur. I see but one explanation of such lack of simple and seemingly imperative generosity of mind.

One is profoundly humiliated at the revelation of an attitude which, it is submitted, the record amply sets forth, the record placed before the bar of history. The sense of humiliation is akin to that of guilt, as if for a share in permitting such a state of mind as is exhibited in the record to develop in a country that professes respect for justice and devotion to equality and fraternity.

China and the Powers:
II. Intervention a Challenge
to Nationalism

General Crozier has furnished us with an interesting essay on the conditions in China which make it difficult for that country to establish a unified, stable and efficient Government. He has supplemented this account with a briefer essay on the comparative ease with which military conquest of that country could be accomplished. The two statements form the foundation for what is in effect a plea for intervention in China to be undertaken by preferably concerted action of several Great Powers. This intervention is to be wholly altruistic in character, based on desire to help China find her own unity, assist her in development of civil law and administration, free her from the rapacious interference by militarists and officials leagued with them, and is to terminate in turning over a smoothly running Government to the Chinese people. It reads like a dream. If tried, it might turn out a nightmare.

His account of conditions in China, even if once substantially correct as far as it goes, leaves out a fundamentally important fact. He fails to give weight in estimating the probable reception of benevolent intervention by the Chinese to the extraordinary development of national sentiment in recent years. I should not have believed it possible to write about Chinese political affairs and make as little reference as he has done to this feature of the situation. It is quite true that it is not sufficiently strong or well organized to create a unified Government. It may well be years before that goal is reached. But it is powerful enough to bring to naught any such scheme as that proposed.

The probability and the effectiveness of organized resistance to a Government resting upon foreign force is immensely under-

[First published in *Current History* 28 (1928): 212–13. For Crozier's article to which this is a reply, see Appendix 5.]

estimated. It is true the Chinese still lack ability in positive and constructive combination. They have, however, an enormous capacity for negative organization, for resistance. The agitation against foreign interferences carried on in the last few years has already aroused that power into action. Increase of interference would render it an irresistible force. The Chinese are factional; but foreign intervention would weld them into a solid unit, as long as the foreigner was there. General Crozier thinks, apparently on the basis of reports from Hongkong, that they could not successfully unite for even a boycott without assistance from governmental powers, which naturally could not be had with the Government in the hands of foreign agents. Well, I happened to be in China eight years ago at the time the boycott against the Japanese was started. It was started by students. Instead of having support from the Government, the latter was pro-Japanese and set out to suppress the movement by force. In a few short weeks the Cabinet was overthrown; and it is commonly understood that the boycott was so harmful to Japanese interests that it is responsible for the change in Japan's attitude toward China.

Since then things have moved fast and far. The merchants, as well as students, are now organized, while in all industrial centres the workingmen are an organized power. Quite aside from boycotts and means of passive resistance, the proposed scheme of government would be brought to naught by Chinese non-cooperation. Its success would depend upon enlisting Chinese so that they might be educated in modern administrative and legal procedures. The only Chinese that would engage in service in a Government conducted by foreigners, having armed support, would be from the corrupt, self-seeking class. These would be regarded as traitors by their countrymen. The foreign Government would be a mere shell. It might last for years and the Chinese be no nearer self-government than they are today. In fact, with irritation, hatred and union on the basis of hostility to the foreigner it would produce, the last state would be worse than the first.

General Crozier has himself stated so candidly the difficulties in the way of cooperative foreign intervention and of establishing an honest and intelligent Government really managed for the sake of the Chinese people, that it is not necessary to say much about that phase of the matter. As General Crozier says: "The only justification we admit for making use of our strength is the defense of our interests, of the lives and property of our nationals." He regards this as selfish. But it is the only recognized ground, and it is so because the political sense of nations knows how fantastic is the idea of a genuinely benevolent, self-denying, intelligent intervention. At that, interventions already conducted have too often been the causes of predatory aggression and exploitation of peoples subject to it. In the world in which we live General Crozier's ideal of a union of great and imperialistic Powers having the sole purpose of assisting another nation, a nation so unlike in customs and traditions as is China, is a dream.

It took centuries for Western nations to emerge from political conditions not unlike those of China into our present semblance of honest and efficient self-government. It will take time for China to make the transition. She needs our help. But it must come by patience, sympathy and educative effort, and the slow processes of commerce and exchange of ideas, not by a foreign rule imposed by military force.

The Real Chinese Crisis

I should like to emphasize the word *real* in my title. The apparent crisis is that which fills columns in the daily press; foreigners killed, houses looted, security so threatened that foreigners are being concentrated in a few ports and warned to leave the country, the turmoil of war and the barbarities of civil war. Yet in all the rumor, gossip and facts that come to us, there is a frequent note struck, which is a sign, to the discerning, of the real crisis through which China is passing. The entire animus of the latent—in some cases flagrant—propaganda to which we are treated is directed against the nationalistic movement and forces. The Northern forces are invariably let down as easily as possible. Why?

The most direct way to get at the reality of the situation is to inquire what the tone of the news would have been, were it proved that the retreating Shantung troops—whose commander is an ex-bandit—had done the killing and the looting. The answer is that the incidents would surely have been glossed over; they would have been treated as unfortunate concomitants of civil war; it would have been noted that defeated armies were wont, on their retreats, to get out of hand. Doubtless, demands for indemnities would have been made in due course on the Peking government. But we should have had no appeals from Shanghai and London for concerted intervention, for blockades of Chinese ports. In other words, there would have been no clamor for us to take sides with the Cantonese against the Northerners. Just as the news has been colored against the Nationalists, it would have been smoothed over in favor of the Northerners. I cannot imagine anyone who has followed the course of events in China denying this statement.

[First published in *New Republic* 50 (1927): 269–70.]

Again why? What is the significance of this double method in reporting news? If it were true that the Peking government genuinely represents the unity and integrity of China against a band of outlaw rebels, it could be understood. If it were true that there is a stable government in Peking which maintains general and possesses moral and legal authority, the discrimination could be understood. If the Northern troops were, in general, better disciplined and comported themselves in a more orderly way, it could be understood. But it is notorious that each of these suppositions is contrary to fact.

The Peking government has, for many years, been a blind creature in the hands of whatever military overlords happened to be in power. In common with many others, I have seen the President and Cabinet in power thunder against some general, denounce him as a traitor, offer rewards for his head, and, a few weeks later, take it all back, and issue precisely similar edicts against the generals at whose behest the first pronunciamentos were made. I well remember my surprise, when, a newcomer in Peking, I was told by our minister, Mr. Reinsch, in a matter-of-fact way, that the Peking government would not last a month, save for the recognition of foreign powers. It did not take a long residence to convince me that he had revealed no secret of state. In the country at large, the Peking government commanded no authority. Its own supporters kept back its revenues for their own purposes, raised and supported their own troops for their own uses. And this was long before there was an organized popular rebellion against Peking.

No, the explanation of the tone and temper of the news we are receiving lies in the simple fact that the Nationalist government represents a national movement, and that, under the circumstances, any national movement in China is bound to be anti-foreign—against, that is, the special privileges which foreign nationals enjoy because of old treaties. It is not surprising that the mass of foreigners in commercial and industrial centres like Hankow and Shanghai are against the so-called Cantonese revolution. Nor is their opposition wholly to be explained on strictly economic grounds. The American economic stake in China is not large; yet in the large centres, outside of missionary groups, Americans generally share the feelings of the English residents, feelings which centre and flourish in the foreign clubs, where most of the correspondents imbibe their ideas and gather the news they send. The whole mode of life has become bound up with the conditions which were established under the old regime of one-sided privileges. It *is* disturbing to find an old and seemingly settled order shaken at its foundation. That is what is happening in China, and that is the real crisis. China is becoming a nation, in the modern sense of the word.

It requires a good deal of equanimity, of insight and sympathy, in the midst of such a situation, to see things in perspective. It is natural enough for those immediately affected by the formation of a new order to see in it nothing but an anti-foreign manifestation, stirred up by unruly spirits. But it is highly important that those at a distance realize that this anti-foreign phase is but the external aspect of a great internal revolution. A people of four hundred million population, with a continental area, cannot be transformed from a medieval aggregate into a modern nation without tremendous throes. That transformation, preparing for the last ten years, has reached an overt climacteric expression. Unless we in this country bear this fact in mind, we shall have no understanding of what is going on in China.

I received, the other day, a personal letter from an American teaching in a missionary institution in China. His home and personal possessions had been looted. His professional career is interrupted; he will probably have to make a new start in life. Yet he writes: "Ultimately the Nationalists are right. All of us foreigners in China were inextricably bound into an order which a new and enlightened China must do away with. We cannot be bitter because, in their eagerness to destroy that structure, they fail to distinguish the individuals who sustain it." Such magnanimity and far-sightedness may not be expected of all persons who have suffered. But we, who do not suffer, should know that these words state the essence of the whole matter; what I am saying is but an amplification of his statement as a text.

I would not give the impression that the transformation will be complete with a victory of the Nationalist forces, even if they come into possession of Peking. The full task of making over China into a modern state is a work of generations. But we are witnessing a dramatic and critical episode in that transformation, and its consequences, when it is successful, will mark a definite turn in the course of world-history. There are few events in history comparable with it; possibly none in our own day, even the World War. Such a statement, given our habitual provincialism and racial snobbishness, may seem foolishness to the wise. But I doubt if most of the great changes of history were not obscured to their contemporaries by superficial froth and clamor. We think of Asia as outside of our world, and it is hard for us to recognize that any changes going on there are of great importance. But when the changes have produced their consequences, and are seen in historic perspective, it is certain that the reconstitution of the life of the oldest and most numerous people of Asia will stand revealed as at least as significant as the transition of Europe out of medievalism into a modernized culture. Such questions as the bearing of the changes upon the special privileges of a few thousand foreigners, the control of India by Great Britain, and the other features which are now conspicuous, will fall into place as paragraphs in a volume. It is not easy to take a long view of contemporary events. But without such a view, we shall see in the events in China simply sound and fury, a confused medley of passions. This result is not only intellectually unfortunate; it is practically dangerous. For it marks a disposition upon which race and color prejudice and deliberate propaganda operate disastrously. Our historic sympathy with China is in danger of being undermined; further untoward events in China might draw us, on the basis of inflammation of emotions due to misunderstandings, into support of European policies which are contrary both to our traditions and to our interests.

Impressions of Soviet Russia

I. Leningrad Gives the Clue

The alteration of Petrograd into Leningrad is without question a symbol, but the mind wavers in deciding of what. At times, it seems to mark a consummation, a kind of completed transmigration of souls. Upon other occasions, one can imagine it a species of mordant irony. For one can picture an enemy of the present regime finding malicious satisfaction in the baptism of this shabby, down-at-heels city with the name of Lenin; its decadent, almost decaying, quality would strike him as sufficient commentary on the Bolshevik claim of having ushered in a new and better world. But one also understands that more than the name of Peter was stamped upon the city which his energetic will evoked. Everything in it speaks of his creative restlessness. Perhaps Peter, the Tsar, was, after all, what he is often called, the First of the Bolsheviki, and Lenin is his true successor and heir.

At all events, in spite of the unkempt town, whose stuccoed walls, with their peeling paint, are a splendid dress in rags, one has the impression of movement, vitality, energy. The people go about as if some mighty and oppressive load had been removed, as if they were newly awakened to the consciousness of released energies. I am told that when Anatole France visited Russia he refused to collect statistics, accumulate data, investigate "conditions." He walked the streets to derive his ideas from the gestures and the faces of the folk. Never having been in the country before, I have no standard of comparison with what was immediately seen. Nevertheless, one has seen the common people of other countries, and I find it impossible to believe that the communicated sense of a new life was an illusion. I am willing to believe what I have read, that there is a multitude of men and women in Russia who live in immured and depressed misery, just

[First published in *New Republic* 56 (14 November 1928): 343–44.]

as there is a multitude in exile. But this other multitude that walks the streets, gathers in parks, clubs, theaters, frequents museums, is also a reality, as is their unbowed, unapologetic mien. The idea forces itself upon one that perhaps the first reality is of the past, an incident of a revolution, and the second reality is of the present and future, the essence of the Revolution in its release of courage, energy and confidence in life.

My mind was in a whirl of new impressions in those early days in Leningrad. Readjustment was difficult, and I lived somewhat dazed. But gradually there emerged one definite impression that has stayed with me and has been confirmed by subsequent experiences. I have heard altogether too much about Communism, about the Third International, and altogether too little about the Revolution; too much about the Bolsheviki, even though the final revolution was accomplished by their initiation. I now realize that any student of history ought to be aware that the forces released by revolution are not functions, in any mathematical sense, of the efforts, much less the opinions and hopes, of those who set the train of events in motion. In irritation at not having applied this obvious historic truth to an understanding of what is taking place in Russia, I would have shifted the blame of my misapprehension to others—I felt resentment at those adherents and eulogists as well as critics and enemies who, I felt, had misled me with constant talk and writing about Bolshevism and Communism, leaving me ignorant of the more basic fact of a revolution—one which may be hinted at, but not described, by calling it psychic and moral rather than merely political and economic, a revolution in the attitude of people toward the needs and possibilities of life. In this reaction I am perhaps inclined to underestimate the importance of the theories and expectations which operated to pull the trigger that released suppressed energies. I am still at a loss in trying to formulate the exact importance of the communistic formulae and the Bolshevist ideals in the present life of the country; but I am inclined to think that not only the present state of Communism (that of non-existence in any literal sense), but even its future is of less account than is the fact of this achieved revolution of heart and mind, this liberation of a people to consciousness of themselves as a determining power in the shaping of their ultimate fate.

Such a conclusion may seem absurd. It will certainly be as offensive to those to whom Marxian orthodoxy constitutes the whole significance of the Russian Revolution as to those who have imbibed the conventional notion of Bolshevist Russia. Yet with no desire to minimize the import of the fate of Bolshevist Marxianism for Russia and for the whole world, my conviction is unshaken that this phase of affairs is secondary in importance to something else that can only be termed a revolution. That the existing state of affairs is not Communism but a transition to it; that in the dialectic of history the function of Bolshevism is to annul itself; that the dictatorship of the proletariat is but an aspect of class-war, the antithesis to the thesis of the dictatorship of bourgeois capitalism existing in other countries; that it is destined to disappear in a new synthesis, are things the Communists themselves tell us. The present state is one of transition; that fact is so obvious that one has no difficulty in accepting it. That it is necessarily a state of transition to the exact goal prescribed by the Marxian philosophy of history is a tenet that, in face of the new energies that have been aroused, smells of outworn absolutistic metaphysics and bygone theories of straight-line, one-way "evolution."

But there is one impression more vivid than this one. It is, of course, conceivable that Communism in some form may be the issue of the present "transition," slight as are the evidences of its present existence. But the feeling is forced upon one that, if it does finally emerge, it will not be because of the elaborate and now stereotyped formulae of Marxian philosophy, but because something of that sort is congenial to a people that a revolution has awakened to themselves, and that it will emerge in a form dictated by their own desires. If it fails, it will fail because energies the Revolution has aroused are too spontaneous to accommodate themselves to formulae framed on the basis of conditions that are irrelevant—except on the supposition of a single and necessary "law" of historical change.

In any case, Communism, if one judges from impressions that lie on the surface in Leningrad, lies in some remote future. It is not merely that even the leaders regard the present status as only an initial step, hardly complete even as a first step, but that the prevailing economy is so distinctly a money economy to all outward appearances. We used to speculate what would have been our impression if we had arrived in Leningrad with no knowledge of past events and no antecedent expectations as to its economic status. It was, of course, impossible to denude the mind sufficiently of prior prepossessions to answer the query. But I had a strong feeling that, while I should have been conscious of a real psychological and moral difference from the rest of the world, the economic scene would not have seemed especially unlike that of any European country that has not yet recovered from the impoverishment of war, foreign and civil, blockade and famine.

At first, the impression was one of poverty, though not of dire want; rather a feeling that perhaps there was something to be said for all being poor alike, as if the only communism were that of sharing a common lot. But it did not require much time to enable the eye to make distinctions. One readily discriminated, by means of attire and bearing, at least four classes, or perhaps one should say grades, of the kind one meets in any large city of the world. The extremes are not so marked, especially on the side of luxury and display. The classes shade into one another more than one would find to be the case in New York or London. But the distinctions are there. Although fairly long lines are seen waiting at some shops, especially where food is sold, there are no marked signs of distress; the people are well nourished; theaters, restaurants, parks and places of amusement are thronged—and their prices are not cheap. The store windows are filled with the same kind of goods one sees anywhere, though usually of the quality associated with cheap bazaars, children's toys and cheap jewelry drawing the larger crowds at the windows, here as elsewhere. What money there is—and, as I have said, in quality if not quantity there is a purely money economy—is evidently in easy circulation.

I have confined myself to the impressions of the early days, at least to those which subsequent events deepened and confirmed, and to impressions that came directly and upon the surface, unaffected by questions, explanations and discussion. Special knowledge, gained later by more definite inquiry, put some of the earlier impressions in a modified light. Thus one learned that the chief reason why people spend money so freely, and on amusements as well as necessities, is because the entire political control is directed against personal accumulation, so that money counts as a means of direct and present enjoyment, not as a tool of future action. Similarly, as one goes below the surface, one's first impressions of the similarity of the economic system to that of any impoverished country is modified by knowledge that, while the regime is distinctly capitalistic, it is one of government rather than private capitalism. Yet these subsequent modifications converted impressions into ideas rather than annulled the first impressions themselves. The net result for me was that a definite reversal of perspective in preconceptions was effected. The sense of a vast human revolution that has brought with it—or rather that consists of—an outburst of vitality, courage, confidence in life has come to the front. The notion that the Revolution is essentially economic and industrial has in the same degree moved to the background—not that it is, even as far as it has already gone, insignificant, but that it now appears, not as the cause of the human, the psychological, revolution, but as an incident of it. Possibly it is only because of dullness that I did not reason out this conclusion at home. Looking back and judging in the light of history, it is perhaps just what one should have expected. But since the clamor of economic emphasis, coming, as I have said, from both defenders and enemies of the Bolshevik scheme, may have confused others as it certainly confused me, I can hardly do better than record the impression, as overwhelming as it was unexpected, that the outstanding fact in Russia is a revolution, involving a release of human powers on such an unprecedented scale that it is of incalculable significance not only for that country, but for the world.[1]

1. Comments made since the original appearance of these sentences have shown me that my remarks upon the subordinate character of the economic phase of the revolution are too sweeping. I should not think of denying that the political aspect of the economic revolution in elevating labor, especially the interests of the factory workers, from the bottom of the social scale to the top is an integral factor in the psychological and moral transformation. [Note added in republication.]

Impressions of Soviet Russia

II. A Country in a State of Flux

I tried in my first article to give some account of the total feeling aroused in me by the face of Russian life as I saw it in Leningrad. It ought to be easier (and probably more instructive) to forgo the attempt to convey a single inclusive impression, in order to record, in separate fashion, ideas or emotions aroused by this or that particular contact. But the accomplishment of this latter task is made difficult by the fact that, without a prolonged stay, wide contacts and a knowledge of the language, accurate information is hard to come by. One gets about as many views as there are persons one converses with, even about things that might be supposed to be matters of fact; or else one finds questions evaded in an embarrassed way. (For some reason, this latter statement is much truer of experiences in Leningrad than in Moscow. Some things mentioned only in a whisper in the former city were loudly proclaimed in the latter; the atmosphere of avoidance changed to that of welcoming discussion. I do not know why this should have been so, but perhaps the pall of the past with its ruthlessness still hangs over one city, while the energy that looks to the future is centered in the other.)

For example, although one's chief concern is not with economic conditions, one naturally has a certain curiosity about that aspect of affairs, and asks questions. Here are a multitude of shops, selling to customers, to all appearances, for money and a money profit like similar shops in other parts of the world. How are they stocked and managed? How many are government-owned; how many are cooperative and what is the relation of cooperative undertakings to the State? How many are private enterprises? How is honest public accountability secured? What is the technique for regulating the temptation to profiteer on the

[First published in *New Republic* 57 (21 November 1928): 11–14.]

side? The questions seem natural and innocent. But it was not easy to find their answers, nor did the answers, when given, agree very well with one another. In part, the explanation is simple enough; I did not apply to persons who were sufficiently interested to be well informed; any traveler knows how easy it is anywhere in the world to amass misinformation. But along with this fact and behind it there was a cause that seems to me of general significance, one that should be known and reckoned with in any attempt at appraisal of Russian affairs. Its nature may be illustrated by an answer that was often given me at first in reply to questions about the nature of cooperative stores; namely, that they were in effect merely government shops under another name. Later on, through access to more authoritative sources, I learned that the fact of the case was quite to the contrary; not only has the cooperative movement grown eight-fold since its very promising beginnings before the War, but its management is primarily of the autonomous, classic Rochdale type.[1] From a certain point of view, perhaps one more important than that which I entertained during my visit, a report upon the development and prospects of cooperative undertakings in present-day Russia would be more significant than anything I have to say. But I am not an economist, and my purpose in alluding to this matter is not that of giving economic information. What I learned from my experience in this matter (rendered typical by a variety of similar experiences) is the necessity of giving an exact dating to every statement made about conditions in Soviet Russia. For there is every reason to believe that the misinformation I received about the status of cooperative undertakings in Russia was not only honestly given, but was based on recollection of conditions that obtained several years ago. For there was a time when the whole industrial structure of Russia was so disorganized, from the World War, the blockade and civil war, that the government practically took over the management of the cooperatives. (Even of this period it is important to know that the latter jealously safeguarded in legal form their autonomy by formally voting, as if they were their own independent decisions, the measures forced upon them by the government.) This state of affairs no longer

1. This refers to the internal management of the cooperatives. Ultimate price-control is of course in the hands of the government. [Added note.]

exists: on the contrary, the free and democratically conducted cooperative movement has assumed a new vitality—subject, of course, to control of prices by the State. But ideas and beliefs formed during that period got into circulation and persist. Were I not convinced that the instance is typical, so typical that a large part of what passes for knowledge about Soviet Russia is in fact only reminiscence of what was the condition at some time during some phase of affairs, I should not dwell upon it at such length.

This necessity for exact dating of every statement made about Russian conditions, if one is to have any criterion of its value, is indicative of a fact—or a force—that to my mind is much more significant than most of the "facts"—even when they are really facts—that are most widely diffused. For they indicate the extent to which Russia is in a state of flux, of rapid alterations, even oscillations. If I learned nothing else, I learned to be immensely suspicious of all generalized views about Russia; even if they accord with the state of affairs in 1922 or 1925, they may have little relevancy to 1928, and perhaps be of only antiquarian meaning by 1933. As foreigners resident in the country frequently put it to me, Russia lives in all its internal problems and policies from hand to mouth; only in foreign politics is there consistency and unity. In the mouths of those sympathetic with what is going on in Russia, the formula had a commendatory implication; the flux was a sign that those who are managing affairs have an attitude of realistic adaptation to actual conditions and needs. In the mouths of the unsympathetic, the phrase implied incapacity on the part of the rulers, in that they had no fixed mind of their own, even on important matters. But the fact of change, whether favorably or unfavorably interpreted, remained outstanding and unchallenged. In view of current notions (which I confess I shared before my visit) about the rigidity of affairs in Russia, I am convinced that this fact of change and flux needs all the emphasis that can possibly be given it.

While my preconception as to the rigidity of affairs in Russia was the one which turned out most contrary to facts, it may not be one that is widely shared. But there are other preconceptions—most of which I am happy to say I did not share—which seem after a visit even more absurd. One of them is indicated by the question so often asked both before and after the visit: How did the party dare to go to Russia?—as if life there were rude, disorderly and insecure. One hesitates to speak of this notion to an intelligent public, but I have found it so widely current that I am sure that testimony to the orderly and safe character of life in Russia would be met with incredulity by much more than half of the European as well as the American public. In spite of secret police, inquisitions, arrests and deportations of *Nepmen* and *Kulaks*, exiling of party opponents—including divergent elements in the party—life for the masses goes on with regularity, safety and decorum. If I wished to be invidious, I could mention other countries in Eastern Europe in which it is much more annoying to travel. There is no country in Europe in which the external routine of life is more settled and secure. Even the "wild children" who have formed the staple of so many tales have now disappeared from the streets of the large cities.

Another warning that appears humorous in retrospect is that so often given by kindly friends, against being fooled by being taken to see show places. It is hard to exercise imagination in one environment about conditions in a remote and strange country; but it now seems as if it would not have required great imagination to realize that the Russians had enough to do on their own account without bothering to set up show establishments to impress a few hundred—or even thousand—tourists. The places and institutions that were "shown" us—and the Leningrad Society for Cultural Relations had prepared a most interesting program of sightseeing—were show-places in the sense that they were well worthy of being shown. I hope they were the best of their kind, so as to be representative of what the new regime is trying to do; there is enough mediocrity everywhere without traveling thousands of miles to see it. But they exist for themselves, either because of historic conditions, like the old palaces and treasures, or because of present urgent needs. Some of the resorts for workers' vacation periods on the island in the Neva River had a somewhat perfunctory air; the old palatial residence, now used as a workers' summer club-house, seemed to have no special active functions. The much advertised "Wall-newspaper" seemed, when its contents were translated, much like what would elsewhere have been less ambitiously called a bulletin board. But such episodes only brought out by contrast the vitality of other institutions, and the gay spontaneity of the "Wall-newspapers" in the children's colonies and homes.

Of the "sights" contained in the official program, the one enduringly impressed in memory is a visit to a children's colony in a former Grand Duke's summer palace in Peterhof—up the Neva from Leningrad. The place marks the nearest approach of the White Armies to Leningrad; the buildings were more or less ruined in the warfare, and are not yet wholly restored, since the teachers and children must do the work; there is still need in some quarters for hot water and whitewash. Two-thirds of the children are former "wild children," orphans, refugees, etc., taken from the streets. There is nothing surprising, not to say unique, in the existence of orphan asylums. I do not cite the presence of this one as evidence of any special care taken of the young by the Bolshevik government. But taken as evidence of the native capacity of the Russian stock, it was more impressive than my command of words permits me to record. I have never seen anywhere in the world such a large proportion of intelligent, happy and intelligently occupied children. They were not lined up for inspection. We walked about the grounds and found them engaged in their various summer occupations, gardening, bee-keeping, repairing buildings, growing flowers in a conservatory (built and now managed by a group of particularly tough boys who began by destroying everything in sight), making simple tools and agricultural implements, etc. Not what they were doing, but their manner and attitude is, however, what stays with me—I cannot convey it; I lack the necessary literary skill. But the net impression will always remain. If the children had come from the most advantageously situated families, the scene would have been a remarkable one, unprecedented in my experience. When their almost unimaginable earlier history and background were taken into account, the effect was to leave me with the profoundest admiration for the capacities of the people from which they sprang, and an unshakable belief in what they can accomplish. I am aware that there is a marked disproportion between the breadth of my conclusion and the narrowness of the experience upon which it rests. But the latter did not remain isolated; though it never recurred in the same fullness, it was renewed in every institution of children and youth which I visited. And in any case, I feel bound to let the statement stand; its seemingly exaggerated quality will at least testify to the depth of the impression I received of the intrinsic capacity of the Russian people, of the release the Revolution has effected, of the intelligence and sympathetic art with which the new conditions are being taken advantage of educationally by some of the wisest and most devoted men and women it has ever been my fortune to meet.

Since I am dealing only with impressions received at first hand and not with information proceeding from systematic inquiries, I shall conclude with selecting two other impressions, each of which happened to arise apart from any official guidance. The hours of several days of leisure time before the arrival of the party of fellow American educators in Leningrad were spent in the Hermitage. Of this museum as a treasure house of European painting it is unnecessary to speak. Not so of the human visitors, groups of peasants, working men, grown men and women much more than youth, who came in bands of from thirty to fifty, each with a leader eager and alert. Every day we met these bands, twenty or thirty different ones. The like of it is not to be seen anywhere else in the world. And this experience was not isolated. It was repeated in every museum, artistic, scientific, historical, we visited. The wondering question that arose in me the first day, whether there was not a phase of the Revolution, and a most important one, which had not before dawned upon me, became, as time went on, almost an obsession. Perhaps the most significant thing in Russia, after all, is not the effort at economic transformation, but the will to use an economic change as the means of developing a popular cultivation, especially an esthetic one, such as the world has never known.

I can easily imagine the incredulity such a statement arouses in the minds of those fed only by accounts of destructive Bolshevik activities. But I am bound in honesty to record the *bouleversement* of the popular foreign impression which took place in my own case. This new educative struggle may not succeed; it has to face enormous obstacles; it has been too much infected with propagandist tendencies. But in my opinion the latter will gradually die of inanition in the degree in which Soviet Russia feels free and secure in working out its own destiny. The main effort is nobly heroic, evincing a faith in human nature which is democratic beyond the ambitions of the democracies of the past.

The other impression I would record came from a non-official visit to a House of Popular Culture. Here was a fine new building in the factory quarter, surrounded by recreation grounds, provided with one large theater, four smaller assembly halls, fifty rooms for club-meetings, recreation and games, headquarters for trade unions, costing two million dollars, frequented daily—or rather, nightly—by five thousand persons as a daily average. Built and controlled, perhaps, by the government? No, but by the voluntary efforts of the trade unions, who tax themselves two percent of their wages to afford their collective life these facilities. The House is staffed and managed by its own elected officers. The contrast with the comparative inactivity of our own working men and with the quasi-philanthropic quality of similar enterprises in my own country left a painful impression. It is true that this House—there is already another similar one in Leningrad—has no intrinsic and necessary connection with communistic theory and practice. The like of it *might* exist in any large modern industrial centre. But there is the fact that the like of it does *not* exist in the other and more highly developed industrial centres. There it is in Leningrad, as it is not there in Chicago or New York;[2] and there it is in a society supposedly rigidly managed by the State on the basis of dogmatic theory, as an evidence of the vitality of organized voluntary initiative and cooperative effort. What does this mean? If I knew the answer, perhaps I should have the beginning of an understanding of what is really going on in Soviet Russia.

2. The Amalgamated Center in Chicago should perhaps be excepted.

Impressions of Soviet Russia

III. A New World in the Making

Two remarks were frequently heard in Leningrad. One was that that city was an outpost of Europe, rather than truly Russian; the other was that Moscow is authentic Russia and is semi-oriental. I should not venture to put my brief experience against these statements, but it may be of some use to tell wherein it differed. Leningrad, while in no sense oriental, hardly struck me as European, and present-day Moscow, at least, appeared ultra-western. As to the first city, its architects were indeed imported from Italy, and perhaps intended to reproduce a European city. But if so, the spirit of the place entered their minds and took control of their hands and they constructed something of which they had no prescience. And the *genius loci*, the lustrous sky, the illimitable horizon, the extravagant and tempestuous climate, did not remind me of any Europe previously known. As to Moscow, while there is something semi-oriental in its physical structure and while orientals throng portions of the city, its psychic aspect and figure are far from what is associated with the slow-moving and ancient East. For in spirit and intent, Moscow is new, nervously active, mobile; newer, it seemed to me, than any city in our own country, even than a frontier town.

Of the two cities, it was Leningrad that seemed ancient. Of course, history tells a different story, and if I were writing as an historian or antiquarian, I should speak differently. But if one takes Moscow immediately, as it presents itself to the eye and communicates itself to the nerves, it is a place of constant, restless movement, to the point of tension, which imparts the sense of a creative energy that is concerned only with the future. In contrast, Leningrad speaks, even mournfully, of the past. We all

[First published in *New Republic* 57 (28 November 1928): 38–42.]

know a certain legend appropriate to the lips and pen of the European visitor to America: here is a land inhabited by a strangely young folk, with the buoyancy, energy, naïveté and immaturity of youth and inexperience. That is the way Moscow impressed me, and very much more so than my own country. There, indeed, was a life full of hope, of confidence, almost hyperactive, naïve at times and on some subjects incredibly so, having the courage that achieves much because it springs from that ignorance of youth that is not held back by fears born from too many memories. Freed from the load of subjection to the past, it seems charged with the ardor of creating a new world. At one point the comparison fails. Running through the *élan*, there is a tempering sense of the infinite difficulty of the task which had been undertaken (I speak of the educational leaders with whom alone we had contact). It cannot be said that they are depressed, but they appear, along with all their hopeful enthusiasm, as if borne on contending currents that make it uncertain whether they will come to the port they envisage, or be overwhelmed. The union of spontaneity and humor with fundamental seriousness may or may not be a Russian trait; it certainly marked the men and women who are carrying the load of creating, by means of education, a new mentality in the Russian people.

Our stay in Moscow thus differed markedly from the Leningrad visit. The latter was more of the nature of sight-seeing carried on under most favorable auspices, leaving us to form our own ideas from what we saw and had contact with. But Moscow is more than a political centre. It is the heart of the energies that go pulsing throughout all Russia, that Russia which includes so much of Asia as well as of Europe. Hence it was that in Moscow one had the feeling as one visited various institutions that one was coming into intimate contact, almost a vicarious share, in a creative labor, in a world in the making. It was as if, after having seen in Leningrad monuments of the past and some products of the present, we were now suddenly let into the operative process itself. Naturally the new experience modified as well as deepened the Leningrad impressions that I have already recorded. The deepening was of the sense of energy and vigor released by the Revolution; the modification was a sense of the planned constructive endeavor which the new regime is giving this liberated energy.

I am only too conscious, as I write, how strangely fantastic the idea of hope and creation in connection with Bolshevist Russia must appear to those whose beliefs about it were fixed, not to be changed, some seven or eight years ago. I certainly was not prepared for what I saw; it came as a shock. The question that has most often been asked me (along with the question whether there is any freedom there), is whether there is anything constructive going on. The currency of the question indicated the hold that the reports of the destructive character of Bolshevism still have upon the public imagination, and perhaps increases the obligation incumbent upon one who has experienced a different face to events, to record the effect of that experience. So, before speaking of the more positively significant aspect of constructive effort, it may be worth while to say (what, indeed, so many visitors have already stated) that in the great cities, what impresses one is the conserving, rather than the destructive, character of the Revolution. There is much more in the England that has come to us from Henry the Eighth of the sort that is associated with Bolshevist rage than there is in Moscow and Leningrad. Having just come from England and with the memories of ruin and vandalism fresh in mind, I often wished that there might be prepared for the special benefit of the die-hard Anglo-Saxon mind (which is American as well as British) an inventory of the comparative destruction of art and architecture in the revolutions of the two countries. One positive sign of interest in conservation is the enormous enlargement and multiplication of museums that has occurred in Russia. For the establishment of museums and the pious care of historic and artistic treasures are not the sort of thing that prevails where the spirit of destruction is supreme. There are now almost a hundred museums in Moscow alone, and through the country, in provincial towns, they have multiplied under the present regime more than five times, while the efforts to render their treasures accessible and useful to the people have kept pace with the numerical increase.

Contrary, again, to the popular myth, this work of conservation has included the temples of the Orthodox Church and their art treasures. All that has been said of the anti-clerical and atheistic tendencies of the Bolshevist is true enough. But the churches and their contents that were of artistic worth are not only intact, but taken care of with scrupulous and even scientific zeal. It is true that many have been converted into museums, but to all appearances there are still enough to meet the needs of would-be worshipers. The collections of ikons in museums in Leningrad and Moscow are an experience which repays the lover of art for a voyage to these cities. In the Kremlin the aid of experts, antiquarians, scholars of history, chemists has been enlisted in beginning the work of highly important restoration. There was, indeed, a "restoration," of the type with which one is too familiar, undertaken in the old regime; the lovely primitives of the frescoes were, for example, gaudily repainted by "artists" of a higher-grade house-painting sort. This work is now undoing; meretricious ornaments, the product of a combination of superstition, too much money and execrable taste, are stripped off. When the work is completed, the Bolshevist regime, in spite of seemingly more urgent demands on time and money, will have recovered in its pristine charm one of the great historic monuments of the world.

Were it not for the popular impression of Bolshevist Russia as given over to mad destructiveness, such things would perhaps be worthy only of passing note. But as things stand, they take on a significance which is typical. They are symbolic not only of constructive activity, but of the direction in which, to my mind, this work of construction is vital: the formation of a popular culture impregnated with esthetic quality. It is no accident that Lunacharsky, to whom, most of all, the careful conservation of the historic and artistic treasures of Russia is due, is the Commissar of Education. For while a revival of interest in artistic production, literary, musical, plastic, is characteristic of progressive schools all over the world, there is no country, unless it be possibly Mexico, where the esthetic aim and quality so dominates all things educational as in Russia today. It pervades not only the schools, but that which, for the lack of a better word, one must call "adult education"—ludicrously insufficient as is that term, in the meaning it derives from activities in our own country, to convey the organized widespread diffusion and expansion taking place in the country of "destructive" Bolshevism. There is a peculiar tone of irony that hangs over all the preconceptions about Russia that one finds current, and which one has come unconsciously more or less to share. But perhaps the contrast between the popular notion of universal absorption in materialistic economy and the actual facts of devotion to creation of living art and to universal participation in the processes and the products of art strikes the ironic note most intensely.

I write, as perhaps I should remind the reader more frequently, from the angle of educational endeavor; I can speak of Russia with any degree of confidence only as the animating purpose and life of that country are reflected in its educational leaders and the work they are attempting. The reader will naturally ask a question which I have often addressed to myself: How far is the impression gained in this particular reflection a just one with reference to the spirit and aim of Soviet Russia as a whole? That one gets from this particular point of view an idea of that spirit and aim in its best and most attractive, because most constructive, aspect, I freely recognize. But while conceding that the picture formed in this particular reflection is purer and clearer than one could or would get from studying the political or the economic phases of life, I must also record my conviction that it is fundamentally a truer picture as well. It is, of course, impossible for me to cite objective evidence that would justify the reader in sharing this conviction. I may, however, indicate the nature of the grounds upon which there gradually grew up in my own mind the belief that one can appreciate the inner meaning of the new Russian life more intimately and justly by contact with educational effort than with specific political and industrial conditions.

Some of the grounds may be classed as negative: the failure of what I have read, when written from an exclusively political and economic point of view, to convey a sense of reality in comparison with what was personally felt and seen from the educational side. The books contain, some of them, much more information than I shall ever possess; they are written, some of them, by men who know the Russian language and who have had wide contacts. If, then, I indulge in the presumption of trusting my own impressions rather than their reports in some vital matters, it is not because I think they have—again, some of them—wilfully falsified; nor, indeed, because of what they say, but rather because of what they do not say, what they have left out, and which I am sure is there. Consequently, these works affect me as marked by a certain vacuity, an emptiness due to an insensitiveness to what is most vitally significant. They present static cross-sections isolated from the movement which alone gives them meaning.

These remarks are doubtless too indefinite, too much at large, to be illuminating. Possibly they may gain definiteness by reference to a particular book, and I select Karlgren's *Bolshevist Russia*. There is no doubt of the competency of the author's knowledge of the language, or his assiduity in collecting data; I do not question the honesty of his aims; the authenticity of most of his material is vouched for by the fact that it is derived from Bolshevist sources. Why not, then, accept his almost wholly unfavorable conclusions? In part because the book does not sufficiently date its material; it does not indicate the special context of time and conditions under which the evils reported occurred. But in greater part because I fail utterly to get from the book the sense of the quality of moving events which contact with these events gives. In consequence, admitting that all of the evils complained of existed at some time and place, and that many of them still exist, the total effect is dead, empty, evacuated of vital significance. Take, as one instance, the very fact that Bolshevist sources are themselves drawn upon for the mass of damning facts. The net effect of this material is one thing when taken by itself, as a pile of ultimate isolated facts which are self-explanatory. It is quite another thing when taken as evidence of a characteristic tendency. For when one looks for some positive and ruling endeavor with which the collection and publication of these condemnatory data are connected, one finds himself in the presence of a deliberate and systematic effort at exploration and self-examination which is unparalleled in other countries. And in turn one finds this movement to be connected with a belief in the reality of a science of society, as a basis for diagnosis of social ills and projection of constructive change. One may not believe in the alleged "science," but disbelief does not alter the fact that one gets a dead and distorted idea from the report of isolated facts, however authentic, until they have been brought into relation with the intellectual movement of self-criticism of which they are a part.

The positive reason for attaching primary significance to this intellectual movement, and for thinking of it as educational, is the fact that by the necessities of the case the central problem of the Soviet leaders is the production of a new mentality, a new "ideology," to employ one of the three or four words that one hears the most frequently. There can be no doubt of the tenacity with which the dogma of "economic determinism" is held to; it is an article of faith that the content and temper of ideas and beliefs which currently prevail are fixed by economic institutions and processes. But it is not true that the prevalent Marxian economic materialism denies efficacy to ideas and beliefs—to the current "ideology," whatever that is. On the contrary, it is held that, while originally this is an effect of economic causes, it becomes in time itself a secondary cause which operates "reciprocally." Hence, from the Communist standpoint, the problem is not only that of replacing capitalistic by collectivistic economic institutions, but also one of substituting a collective mentality for the individualistic psychology inherited from the "*bourjui*" epoch—a psychology which is still ingrained in most of the peasants and most of the intellectuals as well as in the trading class itself. Thus the movement is caught in a circular predicament, only it would be officially described as an instance and proof of "dialectic." *Ultimate* popular ideology is to be determined by communistic institutions; but meantime the success of their efforts to introduce these institutions is dependent upon ability to create a new mentality, a new psychological attitude. And obviously this latter problem is essentially one of education. It accounts for the extraordinary importance assumed in the present phase of Russian life by educational agencies. And in accounting for their importance, it enables one to use them as a magnifying glass of great penetrating power by which to read the spirit of events in their constructive phase.

An incidental confirmation of the central position, during the present state of "transition," of educational agencies is the omnipresence of propaganda. The present age is, of course, everywhere one in which propaganda has assumed the role of a governing power. But nowhere else in the world is employment of it as a tool of control so constant, consistent and systematic as in Russia at present. Indeed, it has taken on such importance and social dignity that the word propaganda hardly carries, in another social medium, the correct meaning. For we instinctively associate propaganda with the accomplishing of some special ends, more or less private to a particular class or group, and correspondingly concealed from others. But in Russia the propaganda is in behalf of a burning public faith. One may believe that the leaders are wholly mistaken in the object of their faith, but their sincerity is beyond question. To them the end for which propaganda is employed is not a private or even a class gain, but is the universal good of universal humanity. In consequence, propaganda is education and education is propaganda. They are more than confounded; they are identified.

When I speak, then, of educational agencies, I mean something much wider than the operation of the school system. Of the latter as such, I hope to write something later. But here I am concerned with it only as a part of the evidence that the essential constructive work of present-day—or "transitional"—Russia is intrinsically educational. In this particular aspect, the work of the schools finds its meaning expressed in words one often hears: "Nothing can be done with the older generation as a whole. Its 'ideology' was fixed by the older regime; we can only wait for them to die. Our positive hope is in the younger generation." But the office of the schools in creating a new "ideology" cannot be understood in isolation; it is part of a "reciprocal" operation. Political and economic changes and measures are themselves, during the present period, essentially educational; they are conceived of not only as preparing the external conditions for an ulterior Communistic regime, but even more as creating an atmosphere, an environment, favorable to a collectivistic mentality. The mass of the people is to learn the meaning of Communism not so much by induction into Marxian doctrines—although there is plenty of that in the schools—but by what is done for the mass in freeing their life, in giving them a sense of security, safety, in opening to them access to recreation, leisure, new enjoyments and new cultivations of all sorts. The most effective propaganda, as the most effective education, is found to be that of deeds which raise the level of popular life, making it fuller and richer, while associating the gains as indissolubly as possible with a "collective" mentality.

I may perhaps best sum up the difference between my Leningrad and Moscow impressions by saying that in the latter place the notion of the present as a "transition" took on a new significance. My feeling when I left Leningrad, put baldly, was that the Revolution was a great success, while Communism was a frost.

My experience in Moscow did not alter the latter impression to the extent of convincing me that there is in practice any more actual Communism than I had supposed that there was. But those experiences convinced me that there is an enormous constructive effort taking place in the creation of a new collective mentality; a new morality I should call it, were it not for the aversion of Soviet leaders to all moral terminology; and that this endeavor is actually succeeding to a considerable degree—to just what extent, I cannot, of course, measure.

Thus the "transition" appears to be in considerable degree a fact. Towards what it is a transition seems to me, however, a still wholly undetermined matter. To the orthodox Marxian, the goal is, of course, certain; it is just the Communistic institutions his special philosophy of history requires. But personally, I am strongly of the impression that the more successful are the efforts to create a new mentality and a new morality of a cooperative social type, the more dubious is the nature of the goal that will be attained. For, I am wholly inclined to believe, this new attitude of mind, in just the degree in which it is really new and revolutionary, will create its own future society according to its own desires and purposes. This future society will undoubtedly be highly unlike the regime characteristic of the western world of private capital and individual profit. But I think the chances are that it will be equally unlike the society which orthodox Marxian formulae call for.

I hope the tone of what I have written makes it clear that I am dealing with impressions rather than with matters capable of any objective proof. I can readily understand that I may put a higher estimate on the value and validity of my personal impressions than I can expect anyone else to do. But even if my impressions are not only inadequate, which they are sure to be, but also quite wrong, I feel bound to record the one impression which my contacts in Moscow wrote most indelibly in my mind: the final significance of what is taking place in Russia is not to be grasped in political or economic terms, but is found in change, of incalculable importance, in the mental and moral disposition of a people, an educational transformation. This impression, I fear, deviates widely from the belief of both the devotees and the enemies of the Bolshevik regime. But it is stamped in my mind and I must record it for what it is.

Impressions of Soviet Russia

IV. What Are the Russian Schools Doing?

I gave in my last article some reasons for believing that in the "transitional" state of Russia chief significance attaches to the mental and moral (*pace* the Marxians) change that is taking place; that while in the end this transformation is supposed to be a means to economic and political change, for the present it is the other way around. This consideration is equivalent to saying that the import of all institutions is educational in the broad sense—that of their effects upon disposition and attitude. Their function is to create habits so that persons will act cooperatively and collectively as readily as now in capitalistic countries they act "individualistically." The same consideration defines the importance and the purpose of the narrower educational agencies, the schools. They represent a direct and concentrated effort to obtain the effect which other institutions develop in a diffused and roundabout manner. The schools are, in current phrase, the "ideological arm of the Revolution." In consequence, the activities of the schools dovetail in the most extraordinary way, both in administrative organization and in aim and spirit, into all other social agencies and interests.

The connection that exists in the minds of Soviet educators between the formation of attitudes and dispositions by domestic, industrial and political institutions and by the school may perhaps be indicated by reference to the account given, by one of the leaders of the new education, of his own development. His efforts at educational reform date back to the early years of this century, when he joined with a fellow Russian (who had been connected with the University Settlement in New York City) in conducting a social settlement in the working men's quarter in Moscow. Naturally they were compelled to operate along non-

[First published in *New Republic* 57 (5 December 1928): 64–67.]

political lines and in the neutral fields of children's clubs, recreation, health, etc.; in fact, in the familiar fields of our own settlements of the distinctively philanthropic type. Even so, they met with constant opposition and embarrassment from the old regime. For example, the educator who told this story was one of the first to introduce football into Russia; in consequence, he spent several months in jail. For the authorities were convinced that there could be only one object in playing the game: namely, to train young men so that they could throw bombs more accurately! (Incidentally, I may remark that the spread of sports and games is one of the characteristic features of existing social life; one Sunday afternoon, for example, we attended a trotting match sponsored by the horse-breeding department of the government commissariat of agriculture, and a soccer match, each having an audience of fifteen to twenty thousand persons.) In 1911, wishing a broader field, he started an educational experimental station in the country, some eighty or a hundred miles distant from Moscow, getting assistance from well-to-do Russians of liberal temper. This school, so I was informed, was based on a combination of Tolstoy's version of Rousseau's doctrine of freedom and the idea of the educational value of productive work derived from American sources.

The story thus far is of some historical significance in indicating some of the causal factors in the present Soviet educational system. But its chief value depends upon a further development; especially the effect upon the minds of educational reformers of the constant opposition of established authority to even the most moderate and non-political efforts at educational reform and amelioration of the condition of the working population. The educator of whom I am speaking began as a liberal reformer, not a radical but a constitutional democrat. He worked in the faith and hope that the school, through giving a new type of education, might peacefully and gradually produce the required transformations in other institutions. His pilgrim's progress from reforming pedagogue to convinced communist affords a symbol of the social phase of the entire Soviet educational movement. In the first place, there was the striking and unescapable fact that those reforming and progressive endeavors which were hampered in every possible way by the Tsar's regime were actively and officially promoted by the Bolshevist regime, a fact that certainly influenced many liberal intellectuals to lend their cooperation to the Bolshevist government. One of them, not a party member, told me that he thought those intellectuals who had refused to cooperate wherever they could with the new government had made a tragic mistake; they had nullified their own power and had deprived Russia of assistance just when it was most needed. As for himself, he had found that the present government cleared the way for just the causes he had had at heart in the old regime, and whose progress had always been hopelessly compromised by its opposition; and that, although he was not a Communist, he found his advice and even his criticism welcomed, as soon as the authorities recognized that he was sincerely trying to cooperate. And I may add that, while my experience was limited, I saw liberal intellectuals who had pursued both the policy he deplored and the one he recommended. There is no more unhappy and futile class on earth than the first, and none more fully alive and happy—in spite of narrowly restricted economic conditions, living quarters, salaries, etc.—than the second.

This first consideration, the almost unimaginable contrast between the career and fate of social aspirations under the old regime and under the Soviet government, is something to which I, at least, had not given due weight in my prior estimates of Bolshevist Russia. And I imagine there are many who, while they are aware in a general way of the repressive and despotic character of the Tsar's government, unconsciously form their appraisal of the present Russian system by putting it in contrast with an imaginary democratic system. They forget that for the Russian millions the contrast is with the system of which alone they have had actual experience. The Russian system of government at the present time is like that to which the population has been accustomed for centuries, namely, a personal system; like the old system, it has many repressive traits. But viewed in the only way which the experience of the masses makes possible for them, it is one that has opened to them doors that were formerly shut and bolted; it is as interested in giving them access to sources of happiness as the only other government with which they have any acquaintance was to keep them in misery. This fact, and not that of espionage and police restriction, however excessive the latter may be, explains the stability of the present government, in spite of the comparatively small number of Communists in the country. It relegates to the realm of pure fantasy those policies for dealing with Russia that are based on the notion that the present government is bound to fall from internal causes if only it can be sufficiently boycotted and isolated externally. I know of nothing that is more indicative of the state of illusion in which it is possible for isolated groups to live than the fact that, of five or six Russian dailies published by the émigrés in Paris, three are devoted to restoration of the monarchy.

I have become involved in a diversion, though one naturally suggested by the marvelous development of progressive educational ideas and practice under the fostering care of the Bolshevist government—and I am speaking of what I have seen and not just been told about. However, the second factor that operated in the transformation of the educator (whose history I regard as typical and symbolic) takes us out of the region of reforming and progressive ideas into that of communism proper. It is the factor that would, I am sure, be emphasized by every Communist educator rather than that which I have just mentioned. The frustration of educational aims by economic conditions occupied a much larger place in the story of the pilgrim's progress from pedagogy to communism than did explicit and definite political and governmental opposition. In fact, the latter was mentioned only as an inevitable by-product of the former. There are, as he puts it, two educations, the greater and the smaller. The lesser is given by the school; the larger, and the one finally influential, is given by the actual conditions of life, especially those of the family and neighborhood. And according to his own story, this educator found that the work he was trying to do in the school, even under the relatively very favorable conditions of his experimental school, was undone by the educative—or miseducative— formation of disposition and mental habit proceeding from the environment. Hence he became convinced that the social medium and the progressive school must work together, must operate in harmony, reinforcing each other, if the aim of the progressive school was not to be constantly undermined and dissipated; with the growth of this conviction he became insensibly a Communist. He became convinced that the central force in undoing the work of socialized reform he was trying to achieve by means of school agencies was precisely the egoistic and private ideals and methods inculcated by the institution of private property, profit and acquisitive possession.

The story is instructive because of its typically symbolic character; if it were expanded, it would also lead into an account of the definite content of Soviet school activities in the concrete. For as far as the influence of this particular educator is concerned (and it extends very far), the subject-matter, the methods of teaching, and the spirit of school administration and discipline are all treated as ways of producing harmony of operation between concrete social conditions—taking into account their local diversity—and school procedures. My contacts were not sufficiently prolonged to enable me, even if space permitted, to give an adequate report of the structure and technique of this work of harmonization. But its general spirit may at least be suggested. During the transitional regime, the school cannot count upon the larger education to create in any single and wholehearted way the required collective and cooperative mentality. The traditional customs and institutions of the peasant, his small tracts, his three-system farming, the influence of home and Church, all work automatically to create in him an individualistic ideology. In spite of the greater inclination of the city worker towards collectivism, even his social environment works adversely in many respects. Hence the great task of the school is to counteract and transform those domestic and neighborhood tendencies that are still so strong, even in a nominally collectivistic regime.

In order to accomplish this end, the teachers must in the first place know with great detail and accuracy just what the conditions are to which pupils are subject in the home, and thus be able to interpret the habits and acts of the pupil in the school in the light of his environing conditions—and this, not just in some general way, but as definitely as a skilled physician diagnoses in the light of their causes the diseased conditions with which he is dealing. So this educator described his philosophy as "Social Behaviorism." Whatever he saw, a mode of farming, farm implements, style of home construction, domestic industry, church building, etc., led him to ask for its probable effect upon the behavior of those who were subject to its influence. On the other hand the teacher strove to learn, whenever he was confronted with any mode of undesirable behavior on the part of a pupil, how to trace it back to its definite social causation. Such an idea, however illuminating in the abstract, would, of course, remain barren without some technique to carry it into effect. And one of the most interesting pedagogical innovations with which I am acquainted is the technique which has been worked out for enabling teachers to discover the actual conditions that influence pupils in their out-of-school life; and I hope someone with more time than I had at command will before long set forth the method in detail. Here I can only say that it involves, among other things, discussions in connection with history and geography, the themes of written work, the compositions of pupils, and also a detailed study throughout the year of home and family budgets. Quite apart from any economic theory, communistic or individualistic, the results are already of great pedagogical value, and promise to provide a new and fruitful method of sociological research.

The knowledge thus gained of home conditions and their effect upon behavior (and I may say in passing that this social behaviorism seems to me much more promising intellectually than any exclusively physiological behaviorism can ever prove to be) is preliminary to the development of methods which will enable schools to react favorably upon the undesirable conditions discovered, and to reinforce such desirable agencies as exist. Here, of course, is the point at which the socially constructive work of the school comes in. A little something will be said about this later in detail, when I come to speak of the idea of "socially useful" work as a criterion for deciding upon the value of "projects"—for Soviet education is committed to the "project method." But aside from its practical working out, it is also interesting in that it locates one of the burning points of present Russian pedagogical theoretical education. For there is still a school that holds that educational principles can be derived from psychology and biology—although the weight of citations from Marx is now eclipsing their influence—and that correct educational methods are bound to produce the desired effect independently of concrete knowledge of domestic and local environment.

I have dwelt too long on certain general considerations, at the expense of any account of what schools are actually doing and how they are doing it. My excuse is that, in relation to the entire Russian situation, it is these generic points of social aspiration and contact that are significant. That which distinguishes the Soviet schools both from other national systems and from the progressive schools of other countries (with which they have much in common) is precisely the conscious control of every educational procedure by reference to a single and comprehensive social purpose. It is this reference that accounts for the social interlocking to which I referred at the outset. The point may be illustrated by the bearing of school activity upon the family institution as that is conceived by the orthodox Marxian socialists. That thorough-going collectivists regard the traditional family as exclusive and isolating in effect and hence as hostile to a truly communal life, is too familiar to require rehearsal. Apart, however, from the effect of the oft-recited Bolshevist modifications of marriage and divorce, the institution of the family is being sapped indirectly rather than by frontal attack; its historic supports, economic and ecclesiastical, are weakened. For example, the limitation of living quarters, enforced in Russia as in other countries by the War, is deliberately taken advantage of to create social combinations wider than that of the family and that cut across its ties. There is no word one hears oftener than *Gruppe*, and all sorts of groups are instituted that militate against the primary social importance of the family unit. In consequence, to anyone who looks at the matter cold-bloodedly, free from sentimental associations clustering about the historic family institution, a most interesting sociological experimentation is taking place, the effect of which should do something to determine how far the bonds that hold the traditional family together are intrinsic and how far due to extraneous causes; and how far the family in its accustomed form is a truly socializing agency and how far a breeder of non-social interests.

Our special concern here is with the role of the schools in building up forces and factors whose natural effect is to undermine the importance and uniqueness of family life. It is obvious to any observer that in every western country the increase of importance of public schools has been at least coincident with a relaxation of older family ties. What is going on in Russia appears to be a planned acceleration of this process. For example, the earliest section of the school system, dealing with children from three to seven, aims, in the cities, to keep children under its charge six, eight and ten hours per day, and in ultimate ideal (although far from present fact) this procedure is to be universal and compulsory. When it is carried out, the effect on family life is too evident to need to be dwelt upon—although at present even in Moscow only one-tenth of the children of this age are in such schools. Nor does the invasion of family life stop at this point in dealing with young children. There are in contemplation summer colonies in the country, corresponding to our fresh-air homes for children from slums, in which children from these all-day "kindergarten" schools will spend a large part of the summer months. Some of the summer colonies are already in existence; those visited compare favorably with similar institutions anywhere, with respect to food, hygiene, medical attention and daily nurture. Now, it would be too much to say that these institutions are deliberately planned with sole reference to their disintegrating effect upon family life; there are doubtless other more conspicuous causes. They are part of a whole network of agencies by means of which the Soviet government is showing its special care for the laboring class in order to gain its political support, and to give a working object-lesson in the value of a communistic scheme. One derives from this, as from many other social undertakings, the impression that the Soviet authorities are trying to forestall, in a deliberately planned and wholesale manner, those consequences of industrialization which in other countries have crept upon society piecemeal and unconsciously. For every large industrial centre in any western country shows that in fact the effect of machine industrialization has been to disintegrate the traditional family. From this point of view, the Russian government is doing on a large scale what private philanthropy has done in our cities by means of *crèches*, etc. But even when these allowances are made, it remains true that we have here a striking exemplification of the conscious and systematic utilization of the school in behalf of a definite social policy. There are many elements of propaganda connected with this policy, and many of them obnoxious to me personally. But the broad effort to employ the education of the young as a means of realizing certain social purposes cannot be dismissed as propaganda without relegating to that category all endeavor at deliberate social control.

Reference to this phase of Soviet education may perhaps be

suitably concluded by a quotation from Lenin that has become a part of the canonical scriptures of Bolshevist educational literature. For it indicates that, were it necessary, official authority could be cited for the seemingly extreme statements I have made about the central position of the schools in the production of a communist ideology as a condition of the successful operation of communist institutions. "The school, apart from life, apart from politics, is a lie, a hypocrisy. Bourgeois society indulged in this lie, covering up the fact that it was using the schools as a means of domination, by declaring that the school was politically neutral, and in the service of all. We must declare openly what it concealed, namely, the political function of the school. While the object of our previous struggle was to overthrow the bourgeoisie, the aim of the new generation is much more complex: It is to construct communist society."

Impressions of Soviet Russia

V. New Schools for a New Era

The idea of a school in which pupils, and therefore, studies and methods, are connected with social life, instead of being isolated, is one familiar in educational theory. In some form, it is the idea that underlies all attempts at thorough-going educational reform. What is characteristic of Soviet education is not, therefore, the idea of a dovetailing of school activities into out-of-school social activities, but the fact that for the first time in history there is an educational system officially organized on the basis of this principle. Instead of being exemplified, as it is with ourselves, in a few scattering schools that are private enterprises, it has the weight and authority of the whole regime behind it. In trying to satisfy my mind as to how and why it was that the educational leaders have been able in so short a time to develop a working model of this sort of education, with so little precedent upon which to fall back, I was forced to the conclusion that the secret lay in the fact that they could give to the economic and industrial phase of social life the central place it actually occupies in present life. In that fact lies the great advantage the Revolution has conferred upon educational reformers in Russia, in comparison with those in the rest of the world. I do not see how any honest educational reformer in western countries can deny that the greatest practical obstacle in the way of introducing into schools that connection with social life which he regards as desirable is the great part played by personal competition and desire for private profit in our economic life. This fact almost makes it necessary that in important respects school activities should be protected from social contacts and connections, instead of being organized to create them. The Russian educational situation is enough to convert one to the idea that only in

[First published in *New Republic* 57 (12 December 1928): 91–94.]

a society based upon the cooperative principle can the ideals of educational reformers be adequately carried into operation.

The central place of economic connections in the dovetailing of school work with social life outside the school is explicitly stated in the official documents of Commissar Lunacharsky. He writes: "The two chief present problems of social education are: (1) The development of public economy with reference to Socialist reconstruction in general and the efficiency of labor in particular; (2) the development of the population in the spirit of Communism." The aims of education are set forth as follows: "(1) The union of general culture with efficiency of labor and power to share in public life; (2) supply of the actual needs of national economy by preparation of workers in different branches and categories of qualifications; (3) meeting the need of different localities and different kinds of workers."

Like all formal statements, these propositions have to be understood in the light of the practices by which they are carried into effect. So interpreted, the fact that among the aims the "union of general culture with efficiency of labor" precedes that of supply of special needs through preparation of workers assumes a significance that might not otherwise be apparent. For perhaps the striking thing in the system is that it is not vocational, in the narrow sense those words often have with us, namely, the technical training of specialized workers. On the contrary, such training is everywhere postponed and subordinated to the requirements of general culture, which is, however, itself conceived of in a socially industrial sense; that is to say, as discovery and development of the capacities that enable an individual to carry on in a cooperative way, work that is socially useful, "socially useful" being conceived in the generous sense of whatever makes human life fuller and richer. Perhaps the easiest way to grasp the spirit of the industrial connections of school work with general social activities is to take the utterances of our own Manufacturers' Association on the same topic and then reverse them. Preparation for special occupations is deferred to the stage of special schools called *Technicums*, which can be entered only after seven years of the public "unified" school have been completed. These schools are called "polytechnic," but the word is a misleading one in its ordinary English associations. For with us it signifies a school in which individual pupils can select and pursue any one of a considerable number of technologies, while in the Russian system it signifies a school in which pupils, instead of receiving a "mono-technical" training, are instructed in the matters which are fundamental to a number of special industrial techniques. In other words, even in the definitely vocational schools, specialized training for a particular calling is postponed until the latest years, after a general technological and scientific-social foundation has been laid.

As far as could be determined, there are two causes for the adoption of this broad conception of industrial education, in identification with the general culture appropriate to a cooperatively conducted society. One is the state of progressive educational theory in other countries, especially in the United States, during the early formative years after the Revolution. For a leading principle of this advanced doctrine was that participation in productive work is the chief stimulus and guide to self-educative activity on the part of pupils, since such productive work is both in accord with the natural or psychological process of learning; and also provides the most direct road to connecting the school with social life, because of the part played by occupations in the latter. Some of the liberal Russian educators were carrying on private experimental schools on this basis before the Revolution; the doctrine had the prestige of being the most advanced among educational philosophies, and it answered to immediate Russian necessities.

Thus from an early period the idea of the "school of work" (*Arbeit-schule, école du travail, escuela d'acción*) was quite central in post-revolutionary school undertakings. And a main feature of this doctrine was that, while productive work is educative *par excellence*, it must be taken in a broad social sense, and as a means of creating a social new order and not simply as an accommodation to the existing economic regime.

This factor, however, accounts only for the earlier period of the growth of Soviet education, say, up to 1922 or 1923, a period when American influence, along with that of Tolstoy, was upon the whole predominant. Then there came in a reaction, from a Marxian standpoint. The reaction, however, did not take the form of discarding the notion of productive work as central in schools. It only gave the idea a definitely socialistic form by interpreting the idea of work on the basis of the new estate of the worker brought about by the proletarian revolution. The change was a more or less gradual one, and even now there is hardly a complete transition or fusion. But the spirit of the change is well indicated in the words of one of the leaders of educational thought: "A school is a true school of work in the degree in which it prepares the students to appreciate and share in the ideology of the workers—whether country or city." And by the worker is here meant, of course, the worker made conscious of his position and function by means of the Revolution. This transformation of the earlier "bourgeois reforming idea" through emphasis upon the ideology of the labor movement thus continued and reinforced the earlier emphasis upon the general idea of the connection of the school with industry.

This report is necessarily confined to a statement of general principles: the skeleton would gain flesh and blood if space permitted an account of the multifarious threads by which the connection between the schools and cooperatively organized society is maintained. In lieu of this account I can only pay my tribute to the liberating effect of active participation in social life upon the attitude of students. Those whom I met had a vitality and a kind of confidence in life—not to be confused with mere self-confidence—that afforded one of the most stimulating experiences of my life. Their spirit was well reflected in the inscription which a boy of fourteen wrote upon the back of a painting he presented me with. He was in one of the schools in which the idea just set forth is most completely and intelligently carried out, and he wrote that the picture was given in memory of the "school that opened my eyes." All that I had ever, on theoretical grounds, believed as to the extent to which the dull and dispirited attitude of the average school is due to isolation of school from life was more than confirmed by what I saw of the opposite in Russian schools.

There are three or four special points that call for notice in the identification established between cultural and industrial education. One of them is suggested by the official statement regarding the meeting by the schools of local conditions and needs. Soviet education has not made the mistake of confusing unity of education with uniformity: on the contrary, centralization is limited to the matter of ultimate aim and spirit, while in detail diversification is permitted, or rather encouraged. Each province has its own experimental school, that supplements the work of the central or federal experimental stations, by studying local resources, materials and problems with a view to adapting school work to them. The primary principle of method officially laid down is that, in every topic, work by pupils is to begin with observation of their own environment, natural and social. (The best museum of natural and social materials for pedagogical purposes I have ever seen is in a country district outside of Leningrad, constructed on the basis of a complete exhibit of local fauna, flora, mineralogy, etc., and local antiquities and history, made by pupils' excursions under the direction of their teachers.)

This principle of making connections with social life on the basis of starting from the immediate environment is exemplified on its broadest scale in the educational work done with the minority populations of Russia—of which there are some fifty different nationalities. The idea of cultural autonomy that underlies political federation is made a reality in the schools. Before the Revolution, many, most of them had no schools, and a considerable number of them not even a written language. In about ten years, through enlisting the efforts of anthropologists and linguistic scholars—in which branch of science Russia has always been strong—all the different languages have been reduced to written form, textbooks in the local language provided, each adapted to local environment and industrial habits, and at least the beginnings of a school system introduced. Aside from immediate educational results, one is impressed with the idea that the scrupulous regard for cultural independence characteristic of the Soviet regime is one of the chief causes of its stability, in view of the non-Communist beliefs of most of these populations. Going a little further, one may say that the freedom from race- and color-prejudice characteristic of the regime is one of the greatest assets in Bolshevist propaganda among Asiatic peoples. The most effective way to counteract the influence of that propaganda would be for western nations to abandon their superiority-complex in dealing with Asiatic populations, and thereby deprive Bolshevism of its contention that capitalism, imperialistic exploitation and race prejudice are so inseparably conjoined that the sole relief of native peoples from them lies in adoption of Communism under Russian auspices.

The central place of human labor in the educational scheme is made manifest in the plan for the selection and organization of subject-matter, or the studies of the curriculum. This principle is officially designated the "complex system." Details appropriately belong in a special educational journal, but in general the system means, on the negative side, the abandonment of splitting up subject-matter into isolated "studies," such as form the program in the conventional school, and finding the matter of study in some total phase of human life—including nature in the relations it sustains to the life of man in society. Employing the words of the official statement: "At the basis of the whole program is found the study of human work and its organization: the point of departure is the study of this work as found in its local manifestations." Observations of the latter are, however, to be developed by "recourse to the experience of humanity—that is, books, so that the local phenomena may be connected with national and international industrial life."

It is worthy of note that, in order to carry out this conception of the proper subject-matter of study, it is necessary for the teachers themselves to become students, for they must conceive of the traditional subject-matter from a new point of view. They are compelled, in order to be successful, both to study their local environment and to become familiar with the detailed economic plans of the central government. For example, the greatest importance is attached in the educational scheme to natural science and what we call nature-study. But according to the ruling principle, this material must not be treated as so much isolated stuff to be learned by itself, but be considered in the ways in which it actually enters into human life by means of utilization of natural resources and energies in industry for social purposes. Aside from the vitalization of physical knowledge supplied by thus putting it in its human context, this method of presentation compels teachers to be cognizant of the *Gosplan*—that is, the detailed projects, looking ahead over a series of years, of the government for the economic development of the country. An educator from a bourgeois country may well envy the added dignity that comes to the function of the teacher when he is taken into partnership in plans for the social development of his country. Such an one can hardly avoid asking himself whether this partnership is possible only in a country where industry is a public function rather than a private undertaking; he may not find any sure answer to the question, but the continued presence of the query in his mind will surely serve as an eye-opening stimulus.

In American literature regarding Soviet education, the "complex system" is often identified with the "project method" as that has developed in our own country. In so far as both procedures get away from starting with fixed lessons in isolated studies, and substitute for them an endeavor to bring students through their own activity into contact with some relatively total slice of life or nature, there is ground for the identification. By and large, however, it is misleading, and for two reasons. In the first place, the complex method involves a unified intellectual scheme of organization: it centres, as already noted, about the study of human work in its connection on one side with natural materials and energies, and on the other side with social and political history and institutions. From this intellectual background, it results that, while Russian educators acknowledge here—as in many other things—an original indebtedness to American theory, they criticize many of the "projects" employed in our schools as casual and as trivial, because they do not belong to any general social aim, nor have definite social consequences in their train.

To them, an educative "project" is the means by which the principle of some "complex" or unified whole of social subject-matter is realized. Its criterion of value is its contribution to some "socially useful work." Actual projects vary according to special conditions, urban or rural, and particular needs and deficiencies of the local environment. In general, they include contributions to improvement of sanitation and hygienic conditions (in which respects there is an active campaign carried on, modelled largely upon American techniques), assisting in the campaign against illiteracy; reading newspapers and books to the illiterate; helping in clubs, excursions, etc., with younger children; assisting ignorant adults to understand the policies of local soviets so that they can take part in them intelligently; engaging in Communist propaganda, and, on the industrial side, taking some part in a multitude of diverse activities calculated to improve economic conditions. In a rural school that was visited, for example, students carried on what in a conventional school would be the separate studies of botany and entomology by cultivating flowers, food-plants, fruits, etc., under experimental conditions, observing the relation to them of insects, noxious and helpful, and then making known the results to their parents and other farmers, distributing improved strains of seed, etc. In each case, the aim is that sooner or later the work shall terminate in some actual participation in the larger social life, if only by young children carrying flowers to an invalid or to their parents. In one of the city schools where this work has been longest carried on, I saw, for example, interesting charts that showed the transformation of detailed hygienic and living conditions of the homes in a working men's quarter effected through a period of ten years by the boys and girls of the school.

A word regarding the system of administration and discipline of Soviet schools perhaps finds its natural place in this connection. During a certain period, the idea of freedom and student control tended to run riot. But apparently the idea of "auto-organization" (which is fundamental in the official scheme) has now been worked out in a positive form, so that, upon the whole, the excesses of the earlier period are obsolescent. The connection with what has just been said lies in the fact that as far as possible the organizations of pupils that are relied upon to achieve self-discipline are not created for the sake of school "government," but grow out of the carrying on of some line of work needed in the school itself, or in the neighborhood. Here, too, while the idea of self-government developed in American schools was the originally stimulating factor, the ordinary American practice is criticized as involving too much imitation of adult political forms (instead of growing out of the students' own social relationships), and hence as being artificial and external. In view of the prevailing idea of other countries as to the total lack of freedom and total disregard of democratic methods in Bolshevist Russia, it is disconcerting, to say the least, to anyone who has shared in that belief, to find Russian school children much more democratically organized than are our own; and to note that they are receiving through the system of school administration a training that fits them, much more systematically than is attempted in our professedly democratic country, for later active participation in the self-direction of both local communities and industries.

Fairness demands that I should say in conclusion that the edu-

cational system so inadequately described exists at present quali-
tatively rather than quantitatively. Statistically considered, its realization is still highly restricted—although not surprisingly so
when one considers both the external difficulties of war, famine,
poverty, teachers trained in alien ideas and ideals, and the internal difficulties of initiating and developing an educational system
on a new social basis. Indeed, considering these difficulties, one
is rather amazed at the progress already made; for, while limited
in actual range, the scheme is in no sense on paper. It is a going
concern; a self-moving organism. While an American visitor may
feel a certain patriotic pride in noting in how many respects an
initial impulse came from some progressive school in our own
country, he is at once humiliated and stimulated to new endeavor
to see how much more organically that idea is incorporated in
the Russian system than in our own. Even if he does not agree
with the assertion of Communist educators that the progressive
ideals of liberal educators can actually be carried out only in a
country that is undergoing an economic revolution in the socialist direction, he will be forced into searchings of heart and mind
that are needed and wholesome. In any case, if his experience is
at all like mine, he will deeply regret those artificial barriers and
that barricade of false reports that now isolates American teachers from that educational system in which our professed progressive democratic ideas are most completely embodied, and from
which accordingly we might, if we would, learn much more than
from the system of any other country. I understand now as I
never did before the criticisms of some foreign visitors, especially from France, that condemn Soviet Russia for entering too
ardently upon an "Americanization" of traditional European
culture.

Impressions of Soviet Russia

VI. The Great Experiment
and the Future

To sum up one's impressions about Russia is of necessity to engage in speculations about its future. Even the belief that has inspired what I have hitherto written, namely, that the most significant aspect of the change in Russia is psychological and moral, rather than political, involves a look into an unrevealed future. While the belief is doubtless to be accounted for by contacts that were one-sided, with educational people, not with politicians and economists, still there is good authority for it. Lenin himself expressed the idea that with the accomplishment of the Revolution the Russian situation underwent a great transformation. Before it had taken place, it was Utopian, he said, to suppose that education and voluntary cooperation could achieve anything significant. The workers had first to seize power. But when they had the reins of government in their hands, there took place "a radical change in our point of view toward Socialism. It consists in this, that formerly the center of gravity had to be placed in the political struggle and the conquest of power. Now this center of gravity is displaced in the direction of pacific cultural work. I should be ready to say that it is now moving toward intellectual work, were it not for our international relations, and the necessity of defending our position in the international system. If we neglect that phase and confine ourselves to internal economic relations, the center of gravity of our work already consists in intellectual work." He went on to say that the cause of socialism is now, economically speaking, identical with that of the promotion of cooperation, and added the significant words: "Complete cooperation is not possible without an intellectual revolution."

Further testimony to the same effect developed in an interview

[First published in *New Republic* 57 (19 December 1928): 134–37.]

some of us had with Krupskaia, Lenin's widow, an official at the head of one branch of the government department of education, and naturally a person with great prestige. Considering her position, her conversation was strangely silent upon matters of school organization and administration; it was about incidents of a human sort that had occurred in her contact with children and women, incidents illustrative of their desire for education and for new light and life—evincing an interest on her part that was quite congruous with her distinctly maternal, almost house-wifely type. But at the close she summed up the task of the present regime: Its purpose is, she said, to enable every human being to obtain personal cultivation. The economic and political revolution that had taken place was not the end; it was the means and basis of a cultural development still to be realized. It was a necessary means, because without economic freedom and equality, the full development of the possibilities of all individuals could not be achieved. But the economic change was for the sake of enabling every human being to share to the full in all the things that give value to human life.

Even in the economic situation the heart of the problem is now intellectual and educational. This is true in the narrower sense that the present industrial scheme and plan cannot possibly be carried through without preparation of skilled technicians in all lines, industrial and administrative. What Wells said about the world is peculiarly true of Russia; there is a race between education and catastrophe—that is, industrial breakdown. It is also true in the fundamental sense that the plan cannot be carried through without change in the desires and beliefs of the masses. Indeed, it seems to me that the simplest and most helpful way to look at what is now going on in Russia is to view it as an enormous psychological experiment in transforming the motives that inspire human conduct.

There are, of course, two points of view from which it is not a genuine experiment, since its issue is foredoomed. The fanatic of individual capitalistic business for private gain and the Marxian dogmatic fanatic both have the answer ready in advance. According to the first, the attempt is destined to failure; it is fated to produce, in the words of Mr. Hoover, an "economic vacuum"; according to the latter, the transformation from individualism to collectivism of action is the absolute and inevitable result of the working of laws that are as positively known to social "science" as, say, the law of gravitation to physical science. Not being an absolutist of either type, I find it more instructive to regard it as an experiment whose outcome is quite undetermined, but that is, just as an experiment, by all means the most interesting one going on upon our globe—though I am quite frank to say that for selfish reasons I prefer seeing it tried in Russia rather than in my own country.

Both beliefs in their dogmatic form have served a purpose. The first—the "individualistic" philosophy—has enabled men to put up with the evils of the present order of things. If this is as fixed as human nature, and if human nature is built upon the pattern of the present economic order, there is nothing to do but bear up as best we can. The Marxian philosophy gave men faith and courage to challenge this regime. But ignoring both of these dogmatic faiths, I should say that what there is in Russia is an experiment having two purposes. The first and more immediate aim is to see whether human beings can have such guarantees of security *against* want, illness, old age, and *for* health, recreation, reasonable degree of material ease and comfort that they will not have to struggle for purely personal acquisition and accumulation, without, in short, being forced to undergo the strain of competitive struggle for personal profit. In its ulterior reaches, it is an experiment to discover whether the familiar democratic ideals—familiar in words, at least—of liberty, equality and brotherhood will not be most completely realized in a social regime based on voluntary cooperation, on conjoint workers' control and management of industry, with an accompanying abolition of private property as a fixed institution—a somewhat different matter, of course, than the abolition of private possessions as such. The first aim is the distinctly economic one. But the farther idea is that when economic security for all is secured, and when workers control industry and politics, there will be the opportunity for all to participate freely and fully in a cultivated life. That a nation that strives for a private culture from which many are excluded by economic stress cannot be a cultivated nation was an idea frequently heard from the mouths of both educators and working people.

It was at this point that my own antecedent notions—or, if you will, prejudices—underwent their most complete reversal. I had the notion that socialistic communism was essentially a purely economic scheme. The notion was fostered by the almost exclusive attention paid by Socialists in western countries to economic questions, and by the loudly self-proclaimed "economic materialism" of Marxian Communists. I was, therefore, almost totally unprepared for what I actually found: namely, that, at least in the circles with which I came in contact (which, however, included some working men as well as educators), the development of "cultivation" and realization of the possibility of everyone's sharing in it was the dominant note. It turned out, most astonishingly, that only in "bourgeois" countries are Socialists mainly concerned with improving the material conditions of the working classes, as if occupied with a kind of public as distinct from private philanthropy in raising wages, bettering housing conditions, reducing hours of labor, etc. Not, of course, that the present Russian regime is not also occupied with such matters, but that it is so definitely concerned with expanding and enlarging the actual content of life. Indeed, I could not but feel (though I can offer no convincing objective proof) that foreign visitors who have emphasized widespread poverty as a ground for predicting the downfall of the present regime are off the track. In the first place, poverty is so much the historic heritage of the masses that they are not especially conscious of the pinching of this particular shoe; and in the next place, there are large numbers, especially of the younger generation, who are so devoted to the human and moral ideal of making free cultivation universal that they do not mind the pinch; they do not feel it as a sacrifice.

Perhaps I should have been prepared to find this attitude. That the movement in Russia is intrinsically religious was something I had often heard and that I supposed I understood and believed. But when face to face with actual conditions, I was forced to see that I had not understood it at all. And for this failure, there were two causes, as far as I can make out—I am, of course, only confessing my own limitations. One was that, never having previously witnessed a widespread and moving religious reality, I had no way of knowing what it actually would be like. The other was that I associated the idea of Soviet Communism, as a religion, too much with intellectual theology, the body of Marxian dogmas with its professed economic materialism, and too little with a moving human aspiration and devotion. As it is, I feel as if for the first time I might have some inkling of what may have been the moving spirit and force of primitive Christianity. I even hate to think of the time, that seems humanly inevitable, when this new faith will also have faded into the light of common day, and become conventional and stereotyped. I am quite prepared to hear that I exaggerate this phase of affairs; I am prepared to believe that, because of the unexpectedness of the impression, I have exaggerated its relative importance. But all such allowances being made, I still feel sure that no one can understand the present movement who fails to take into account this religious ardor. That men and women who profess "materialism" should in fact be ardent "idealists" is undoubtedly a paradox, but one that indicates that a living faith is more important than the symbols by which it tries to express itself. Intellectual formulae seem to be condemned to have about them something pathetically irrelevant; they are so largely affected by accidents of history. In any case, it is hard not to feel a certain envy for the intellectual and educational workers in Russia; not, indeed, for their material and economic status, but because a unified religious social faith brings with it such simplification and integration of life. "Intellectuals" in other countries have a task that is, if they are sincere, chiefly critical; those who have identified themselves in Russia with the new order have a task that is total and constructive. They are organic members of an organic going movement.

The sense of disparity between the Soviet official theology, the Marxian doctrines, and the living religious faith in human possibilities when released from warping economic conditions, remains. A similar disparity seems to have attended all vital movements hitherto undertaken. They have had their intellectual formulations; but use of the latter has been to provide a protective shell for emotions. Any prediction about the Russian future has to take into account the contradiction and conflict between rigid dogmas on one side and an experimental spirit on the other. Which will win, it is impossible to say. But I cannot but suppose that the Russian people will, in the end, through a series of adaptations to actual conditions as they develop, build something new in the form of human association. That these will be communistic in the sense of the leaders of the Revolution, I doubt; that they will be marked by a high degree of voluntary cooperation and by a high degree of social control of the accumulation and use of capital, seems to be probable. Symbols, however, have a great way of persisting and of adapting themselves to changes in fact, as the histories of Christianity and democracy both show. So, unless there is some remarkable breach of continuity, it is likely that the outcome, whatever it may be in fact, will be called Communism and will be taken as a realization of the creed of its initial authors.

Education affords, once more, the material for a striking illustration of the role of experiment in the future evolution of Soviet Russia. In a region something less than a hundred miles from Moscow, there is a district fairly typical of northern rural Russia, in which there is an educational colony under the direction of Schatzsky. This colony is the centre of some fourteen schools scattered through a series of villages, which, taken together, constitute an extensive (and intensive) educational experiment station for working out materials and methods for the Russian rural system. There is not in my knowledge anything comparable to it elsewhere in the world. As the summer colony was in operation, we had the satisfaction of visiting the station and also noting its effect on the villages that have come under its influence. A somewhat similar undertaking under Pistrak exists in Moscow to deal with the problems of urban workers. It was closed on account of the vacation period, and so my knowledge is less at first hand. But it is in active and successful operation. Then, as has been noted, each province has its own experimental station to deal with specifically local problems. These enterprises are under the government, having its sanction and authoritative prestige. There is also in existence a Supreme Scientific Council having a pedagogical section. The duties of this Scientific Council are in general to form plans for the social and economic development of Russia; the program, while flexible, looks ahead over a term of years and includes much detail based on researches that are continuously conducted. Of this undertaking, probably the first in the world to attempt scientific regulation of social growth, the pedagogical section is an organic member; its business is to sift and audit the results of the educational experiments that are carried on and to give them a form in which they may be directly incorporated into the school system of the country. The fact that both Schatzsky and Pistrak are members of this Council ensures that conclusions reached in the experiment stations receive full attention.

This matter is referred to here rather than in the account of Soviet education to which it properly belongs, in order to suggest, through a concrete example, that, however rigid and dogmatic the Marxian symbols may be, actual practices are affected by an experimental factor that is flexible, vital, creative. In this connection it may be worth while to quote from Pistrak, the words being the more significant because he is a strict party member. "We cannot apply the same rules to every school condition; that procedure would be contrary to the essence of our school. It is indispensable to develop in teachers aptitude for pedagogical creation; without this, it will be impossible to create the new school. The notion that pedagogues are artisans rather than creators seems to us incorrect. Every human being is more or less a creator, and while an individual in isolation may fail to find a creative solution of a problem, in collectivity we are all creators." No one would claim that this ideal of creation is as yet realized, but no one can come in contact with educational activities without feeling that this spirit marks the Russian school leaders to an extent unknown in other countries. In my first article, before coming into any close contact with educational endeavor, I wrote of the feeling of vitality and liberation that was got from contact with the face of the Russian scene. The later educational contacts confirmed this surface impression, while they also left the feeling of being initiated into the definite movement by which the movement of liberation was intensified and directed.

I do not believe that any person's particular guess about the exact form of the outcome of the present Russian movement is of any importance; there are too many unknowns in the equation. If I venture in the direction of a prediction, it is only by way of calling attention to two movements already going on. The factor of greatest importance seems to me to be the growth of voluntary cooperative groups. In the orthodox theory, these form a transition stage on the road to the predestined end of Marxian Communism. Just why the means should not also be the end, and the alleged transitory stage define the goal, is not clear to me. The place occupied by the peasant in Russian life, the necessity of consulting his interests and desires, however disagreeable that consultation is, the constant concessions made to him in spite of official preference for the city factory worker, strengthens belief in the probability of a cooperative rather than a strictly communistic outcome. Side by side with this factor, though of less immediate practical force, I should place the experimental aspect of the educational system. There is, of course, an immense amount of indoctrination and propaganda in the schools. But if the existing tendency develops, it seems fairly safe to predict that in the end this indoctrination will be subordinate to the awakening of initiative and power of independent judgment, while cooperative mentality will be evolved. It seems impossible that an education intellectually free will not militate against a servile acceptance of dogma as dogma. One hears all the time about the dialectic movement by means of which a movement contradicts itself in the end. I think the schools are a "dialectic" factor in the evolution of Russian Communism.

These remarks do not detract from the significance of the Russian revolutionary movement; rather they add, in my mind, to it, and to the need for study of it by the rest of the world. And it cannot be studied without actual contact. The notion that a sixth of the world can be permanently isolated and "quarantined" is absurd enough, though the consequences of acting upon the absurdity are more likely to be tragic than humorous. But it is even more absurd to suppose that a living idea that has laid hold of a population with the force and quality of a religion can be pushed to one side and ignored. The attempt, if persisted in, will result in an intensification of its destructive features and in failure to derive the advantages that might accrue from knowledge of its constructive features. Political recognition of Russia on the part of the United States would not go far in bringing about the kind of relations that are in the interest of both countries and of the world, but it is at least a necessary antecedent step. I went to Russia with no conviction on that subject except that recognition was in line with our better political traditions. I came away with the feeling that the maintenance of barriers that prevent intercourse, knowledge and understanding is close to a crime against humanity.

The phase of Bolshevism with which one cannot feel sympathy is its emphasis upon the necessity of class war and of world revolution by violence. These features of Soviet Russia tend to recede into the background because of the pressure the authorities are under to do a vastly difficult constructive work in Russia itself. But the spirit that produces them is fed by the belief that the rest of the world are enemies of Soviet Russia; that it must be constantly on the defensive and that the best defense is aggressive attack. I do not think that free intercourse with the rest of the world would cause an immediate disappearance of the idea of stirring up civil war in capitalistic countries. But I am confident that such intercourse would gradually deprive the flame of its fuel, and that it would die down. One derives the impression that the Third International is Russia's own worst enemy, doing harm to it by alienating other peoples' sympathy. Its chief asset, however, is non-recognition. The withdrawal of recognition by Great Britain has done more than any other one thing to stimulate the extremists and fanatics of the Bolshevist faith, and to encourage militarism and hatred of bourgeois nations.

I cannot conclude without mentioning one point that is not strictly connected with the remainder of this summary. In times of peace the Third International does, as I have said, more injury to Russia than to other countries. But if there is a European war, it will, I believe, spring to life as a reality in every European nation. I left Russia with a stronger feeling than I had ever had before of the criminal ineptitude of those statesmen who still play with the forces that generate wars. There is one prediction to which I am willing to commit myself. If there is another European war, under present conditions, civil war will add to the horrors of foreign war in every continental country, and every capital in Europe will be a shambles in which the worst horrors of the days of revolution will be outdone.

The Direction of Education[1]

Doubtless many in this audience have been embarrassed in meeting questions put by European visitors concerning the school system of the United States. Foreign students who carry in their minds the systems with which they are familiar and who naturally employ this knowledge as a standard of judgment are perplexed when confronted with American educational institutions. They inquire into our system and they find from their standpoint no system at all but what strikes them as chaos. In one part of the country they find townships almost a law to themselves, and learn that even fractions of civil units called districts enjoy an almost complete educational autonomy. In other regions, they learn that counties are the units of organization; and that while in a few states the state itself exercises considerable regulative and supervisory authority, this authority manifests great diversity in actual operation. While all states lay down certain regulations as to minimum requirements for the length of the school year, certification of teachers, character of school buildings and subjects to be taught, there is often little attention paid to any close supervision that sees to it that these regulations are locally enforced. Actual control is mainly exercised by custom. And of a national system, as they understand it, the visitor finds not more than a trace. Instead of a minister in the national cabinet clothed with the powers every European state takes for granted, he finds hardly more than a clerical bureau gathering and distributing information but without administrative authority.

I have referred to these familiar facts to place before your minds the background of the development of American educa-

1. Address delivered on the occasion of the installation of Dean William Fletcher Russell, Teachers College, Columbia University, April 10, 1928.
[First published in *School and Society* 27 (1928): 493–97.]

tion and to suggest the way in which that development has been
attained. For there has been a growth; there is a record of accomplishment. No one is wholly satisfied, least of all such an audience as is here represented. But nevertheless things have happened educationally in spite of the lack of official leadership and
regulation. Where has direction of the movement come from?
There is of course but one alternative to official or state direction: voluntary and personal leadership, internal ferment and
contagion. What has been done has been largely done by inspiration and stimulation issuing from individuals and from educational centres not clothed with authority to impose on the
schools their ideas and ideals. Education has been mainly promoted by the processes of education rather than by state administration. Ideas have been communicated by word of mouth, by
periodicals, by books and by observation of the efforts and results of other teachers. New ideas and practices in the field of
administration, methods of instruction or subjects of study have
spread rather than been enacted and instituted. The spreading
has taken place by the same sort of contact, radiation, infiltra-
tion and contagion that changes social habits and beliefs in other
fields that do not fall within any governmental regulation.

I am not here to make a comparison of the respective merits of
the two systems, or, if you please, of system and lack of system,
much less to glorify the method which we have for the most part
unconsciously adopted because it corresponded to the conditions
of our social life. I have introduced the contrast only by way of
calling attention to the intellectual and moral responsibilities
that are necessarily involved in our accepted procedure. Exemption of political government and officials from responsibilities
that are elsewhere incumbent upon them places corresponding
responsibilities upon individuals and institutions. With all our
drifting, there must be leadership somewhere, or absence of governmental system will signify lack of all unified and cooperative
educational movement. But leadership that is not official can
only be intellectual and moral leadership. It is not merely leadership *in* education but it is leadership *by* education rather than by
law and governmental authority. Indeed, it is a kind of leadership that gives a new meaning to the word. It is a process of guidance. It takes effect through inspiration, stimulation, communication of ideas, discovery and report of facts, rather than by

decree. It is compelled to trust for the most part to the power of facts and ideas and to the willingness of the community at large to receive and act upon them.

I am probably not divulging anything hidden when I say that these introductory remarks have been framed with a view to calling attention to the opportunity and the responsibility of leadership that a situation like this confers upon an institution like the one in whose interests we have gathered together to-day. It is from institutions like our own that moral and intellectual direction proceeds; and they must continue to exercise this function of guidance if our outward drifting is not to become an inward flux and degeneration. You will not expect from me mere glorification and adulation of our Teachers College. Our loyalty is not so feeble that it has to be fed from such a source. Yet it will not be out of place, if only to remind ourselves of future opportunities and demands, to allude to some phases of the office of moral and intellectual leadership that have already manifested themselves.

Fortunate in its close connection with a great urban university, possessed of a cosmopolitan constituency, and fortunate in the leadership over a long span of years of the beloved retiring dean, a man open and responsive to every social and intellectual demand, gifted with vision and with courage to act upon his vision, and with the cooperative support of an able faculty, representing practically every aspect and interest of our complex social life, Teachers College has flourished in numbers and in other outward signs of prosperity, because it has recognized the need of American education for educative guidance from within, the need of intellectual direction and inspiration. Numbers make an institution big but not great; what has made Teachers College great has been its firm grasp upon an idea, the perception of the public need for educational guidance, and its devotion to the fulfilment of this need.

To enumerate the various fields in which Teachers College has pointed the way to educational advance and directed practical movements to their realization would be like calling the roll of its departments. For when an educational need has shown itself, this institution has answered "Here." To catalogue its achievements would both impose on your time and recite the familiar. To select some as being of superior importance would be invidious. And yet a random mention of a few movements to which Teachers College has lent its powerful support and some of which it may be said to have originated seems necessary in order to indicate the quality and scope of the intellectual and moral service it has rendered in lending direction to American education. There come to mind the development of measurements and tests; the project method; school surveys and study of administration; the transformation of kindergarten theory and practice; the nursery school and the scientific study of pre-school children; domestic science and art and the placing of education of nurses on a more dignified and self-respecting, because more intellectually responsible plane; contributions to industrial training and vocational guidance; to rural schools; to Americanization through education, to religious education, to international phases of education—but why continue? The things mentioned are not spoken of by way of mere congratulation, but as indications of the way in which an educational institution can give voluntary and unofficial direction to an otherwise confused and dispersive scene. Your own minds will readily supply the further illustrations needed to complete and solidify the suggestion.

Although no one a generation ago could have possibly predicted the development of the last thirty years, it is not too much to say that the work is only in its initial stage. Certain things have been demonstrated. It has been proved that education is a proper field for scientific research; that it ranks with any subject as a proper and richly rewarding topic for university study; it has been redeemed from the academic contempt that so long was felt toward pedagogy; especially has its fruitfulness been demonstrated as a means of correlating a vast variety of specialized topics and interests, scientific and social, so as to bring them into vital unity in a human and humane perspective. The training of teachers is no longer a mere matter of equipping students having a somewhat inadequate prior intellectual preparation with the means by which to deal with the immediate problems of the schoolroom. The simple discovery that education is first of all a problem for study, for investigation and research, and a problem so complex and diversified as to demand prolonged and thorough training, marks in itself almost a revolutionary departure from the older attitude.

Indeed, I should be willing to say that this discovery is that which gives Teachers College its distinction. Important as are all the special contributions that have been alluded to, the recognition of the necessity of regarding education in all its phases as an intellectual problem, a philosophical and scientific problem, is the most important. For the attitude contained in this recognition has been the inspiration of these movements and the source of their directive value. To remove education from the plane of opinion, tradition, and routine and to place it on the high plane of intellectual worth and dignity is no easy task, and it will not be accomplished in a generation. The idea that activities like medicine and agriculture are proper fields for scientific exploration and that they can prosper only when conducted upon the basis of the conclusions of patient and prolonged inquiry has pretty well made its way into popular consciousness. I do not think a similar statement can be made as yet regarding education. The air is full of glittering generalities and of sentimental appreciation of its supreme importance, but not of steady and definite realization of its significance as an intellectually grounded art. This fact is natural. Education is the most complex, intricate and subtle of all human enterprises. Its intellectual emancipation and elevation was compelled to wait until other inquiries and sciences, physical, mathematical even, as well as social and psychological, had developed to the point where they could make their contributions. In consequence, the art of education will be the last of the arts to come into its own scientifically.

The pioneering stage of this great idea is not past. This fact is an inspiration, for this stage in any subject is that of greatest ardor and utmost devotion. I congratulate the staff and students of this institution upon the opportunity and the outlook. You are here at a critical juncture. The idea that education is a field of study, observation, experiment and inquiry has been already demonstrated. It remains not only to continue the development of all the special investigations incident to this fact, but to bring the public to the appreciation of its full significance, to make its force felt in every aspect and phase of educational endeavor. I like to think that there is a happy omen for the continued development of this ideal in the instance of academic apostolic succession we are celebrating here to-day. The paternal-filial relationship seen in the change of deans may well symbolize the moving life of Teachers College itself. As one of the older teachers among you, I wish to express my deep sense of the honor I experience in being associated with this ceremony. I like to imagine this association to be also a link in the continuity of the life of this great institution. A long-time friend of the father, it is a happy duty to welcome the son, as a former student, a long-time colleague and I am sure a permanent friend, to the responsibilities, the joys and burdens of his office. You know, without my saying so, Mr. Dean, that in meeting the responsibilities you will have the heartiest cooperation and support of all your colleagues, the students and the alumni. And the latter, the staff, alumni and students, also know without being told that you bring to the execution of your duties the spirit of humanity, of quick and responsive sympathies, combined with full integrity of purpose and a widely cultivated scientific outlook. We bid you affectionate Godspeed and take hope and courage for the future.

Progressive Education and the Science of Education

What is Progressive Education? What is the meaning of experiment in education, of an experimental school? What can such schools as are represented here do for other schools, in which the great, indefinitely the greater, number of children receive their instruction and discipline? What can be rightfully expected from the work of these progressive schools in the way of a contribution to intelligent and stable educational practice; especially what can be expected in the way of a contribution to educational theory? Are there common elements, intellectual and moral, in the various undertakings here represented? Or is each school going its own way, having for its foundation the desires and preferences of the particular person who happens to be in charge? Is experimentation a process of trying anything at least once, of putting into immediate effect any "happy thought" that comes to mind, or does it rest upon principles which are adopted at least as a working hypothesis? Are actual results consistently observed and used to check an underlying hypothesis so that the latter develops intellectually? Can we be content if from the various progressive schools there emanate suggestions which radiate to other schools to enliven and vitalize their work; or should we demand that out of the cooperative undertakings of the various schools a coherent body of educational principles shall gradually emerge as a distinctive contribution to the theory of education?

Such questions as these come to mind on the occasion of such a gathering as this. The interrogations expressed are far from all inclusive. They are one-sided, and intentionally so. They glide over the important questions that may be asked about what these schools are actually doing for the children who attend

[First published in pamphlet form by the Progressive Education Association from an address given to the Association at its Eighth Annual Conference on 8 March 1928.]

them; how they are meeting their primary responsibility—that to the children themselves and their families and friends. The one-sided emphasis is, as was said, intentional. The questions are shaped to take another slant; to direct attention to the intellectual contribution to be expected of progressive schools. The reasons for this one-sidedness are close at hand. It is natural that in your own exchange of experiences and ideas the question slurred over should be prominent. And that pupils in progressive schools are themselves progressing, and that the movement to establish more progressive schools is progressing, I have no doubt. Nor do I think that the old question, once a bugaboo, as to what will happen when the pupils go to college or out into life, is any longer an open one. Experience has proved that they give a good account of themselves; so it has seemed to me that the present is a fitting time to raise the intellectual, the theoretical problem of the relation of the progressive movement to the art and philosophy of education.

The query as to common elements in the various schools receives an easy answer up to a certain point. All of the schools, I take it for granted, exhibit as compared with traditional schools, a common emphasis upon respect for individuality and for increased freedom; a common disposition to build upon the nature and experience of the boys and girls that come to them, instead of imposing from without external subject-matter and standards. They all display a certain atmosphere of informality, because experience has proved that formalization is hostile to genuine mental activity and to sincere emotional expression and growth. Emphasis upon activity as distinct from passivity is one of the common factors. And again I assume that there is in all of these schools a common unusual attention to the human factors, to normal social relations, to communication and intercourse which is like in kind to that which is found in the great world beyond the school doors; that all alike believe that these normal human contacts of child with child and of child with teacher are of supreme educational importance, and that all alike disbelieve in those artificial personal relations which have been the chief factor in isolation of schools from life. So much at least of common spirit and purpose we may assume to exist. And in so far we already have the elements of a distinctive contribution to the body of educational theory: respect for individual capacities, in-

terests and experience; enough external freedom and informality
at least to enable teachers to become acquainted with children as
they really are; respect for self-initiated and self-conducted
learning; respect for activity as the stimulus and centre of learning; and perhaps above all belief in social contact, communication, and cooperation upon a normal human plane as all-
enveloping medium.

These ideas constitute no mean contribution: It is a contribution to educational theory as well as to the happiness and integrity of those who come under the influence of progressive
schools. But the elements of the contribution are general, and
like all generalities subject to varied and ambiguous interpretations. They indicate the starting point of the contribution that
progressive schools may make to the theory or science of education, but only the starting point. Let us then reduce our questions to a single one and ask, What is the distinctive relation of
progressive education to the science of education, understanding
by science a body of verified facts and tested principles which
may give intellectual guidance to the practical operating of
schools?

Unless we beg the question at the outset assuming that it is already known just what education is, just what are its aims and
what are its methods, there is nothing false nor extravagant in
declaring that at the present time different sciences of education
are not only possible but also much needed. Of course such a
statement goes contrary to the idea that science by its very nature
is a single and universal system of truths. But this idea need not
frighten us. Even in the advanced sciences, like those of mathematics and physics, advance is made by entertaining different
points of view and hypotheses, and working upon different theories. The sciences present no fixed and closed orthodoxy.

And certainly in such an undertaking as education, we must
employ the word "science" modestly and humbly; there is no
subject in which the claim to be strictly scientific is more likely to
suffer from pretense, and none in which it is more dangerous to
set up a rigid orthodoxy, a standardized set of beliefs to be accepted by all. Since there is no one *thing* which is, beyond question, education, and since there is no likelihood that there will be
until society and hence schools have reached a dead monotonous
uniformity of practice and aim, there cannot be one single sci-

ence. As the working operations of schools differ, so must the intellectual theories devised from those operations. Since the practice of progressive education differs from that of the traditional schools, it would be absurd to suppose that the intellectual formulation and organization which fits one type will hold for the other. To be genuine, the science which springs from schools of the older and traditional type, must work upon that foundation, and endeavor to reduce its subject-matter and methods to principles such that their adoption will eliminate waste, conserve resources, and render the existing type of practice more effective. In the degree in which progressive schools mark a departure in their emphasis from old standards, as they do in freedom, individuality, activity, and a cooperative social medium the intellectual organization, the body of facts and principles which they may contribute must of necessity be different. At most they can only occasionally borrow from the "science" that is evolved on the basis of a different type of practice, and they can even then borrow only what is appropriate to their own special aims and processes. To discover how much is relevant is of course a real problem. But this is a very different thing from assuming that the methods and results obtained under traditional scholastic conditions form the standard of science to which progressive schools must conform.

For example it is natural and proper that the theory of the practises found in traditional schools should set great store by tests and measurements. This theory reflects modes of school administration in which marks, grading, classes, and promotions are important. Measurement of IQs and achievements are ways of making these operations more efficient. It would not be hard to show that need for classification underlies the importance of testing for IQs. The aim is to establish a norm. The norm, omitting statistical refinements, is essentially an average found by taking a sufficiently large number of persons. When this average is found, any given child can be rated. He comes up to it, falls below it, or exceeds it, by an assignable quantity. Thus the application of the results make possible a more precise classification than did older methods which were by comparison hit and miss. But what has all this to do with schools where individuality is a primary object of consideration, and wherein the so-called "class" becomes a grouping for social purposes and wherein diversity of ability and experience rather than uniformity is prized?

In the averaging and classificatory scheme some special capacity, say in music, dramatics, drawing, mechanical skill or any other art, appears only one along with a large number of other factors, or perhaps does not appear at all in the list of things tested. In any case, it figures in the final result only as smoothed down, ironed out, against a large number of other factors. In the progressive school, such an ability is a distinctive resource to be utilized in the cooperative experience of a group; to level it down by averaging it with other qualities until it simply counts in assigning to the individual child a determinate point on a curve is simply hostile to the aim and spirit of progressive schools.

Nor need the progressive educator be unduly scared by the idea that science is constituted by quantitative results, and, as it is often said, that whatever exists can be measured, for all subjects pass through a qualitative stage before they arrive at a quantitative one; and if this were the place it could be shown that even in the mathematical sciences quantity occupies a secondary place as compared with ideas of order which verge on the qualitative. At all events, *quality* of activity and of consequence is more important for the teacher than any quantitative element. If this fact prevents the development of a certain kind of science, it may be unfortunate. But the educator cannot sit down and wait till there are methods by which quality may be reduced to quantity; he must operate here and now. If he can organize his qualitative processes and results into some connected intellectual form, he is really advancing scientific method much more than if, ignoring what is actually most important, he devotes his energies to such unimportant by-products as may now be measured.

Moreover, even if it be true that everything which exists could be measured—if only we knew how—that which does *not* exist cannot be measured. And it is no paradox to say that the teacher is deeply concerned with what does not exist. For a progressive school is primarily concerned with growth, with a moving and changing process, with *transforming* existing capacities and experiences; what already exists by way of native endowment and past achievement is subordinate to what it may become. Possibilities are more important than what already exists, and knowledge of the latter counts only in its bearing upon possibilities. The place of measurement of achievements as a theory of education is very different in a static educational system from what it is in one which is dynamic, or in which the ongoing process of growing is the important thing.

The same principle applies to the attempt to determine objectives and select subject-matter of studies by wide collection and accurate measurement of data. If we are satisfied upon the whole with the aims and processes of existing society, this method is appropriate. If you want schools to perpetuate the present order, with at most an elimination of waste and with such additions as enable it to do better what it is already doing, then one type of intellectual method or "science" is indicated. But if one conceives that a social order different in quality and direction from the present is desirable and that schools should strive to educate with social change in view by producing individuals not complacent about what already exists, and equipped with desires and abilities to assist in transforming it, quite a different method and content is indicated for educational science.

While what has been said may have a tendency to relieve educators in progressive schools from undue anxiety about the criticism that they are unscientific—a criticism levelled from the point of view of theory appropriate to schools of quite a different purpose and procedure—it is not intended to exempt them from responsibility for contributions of an organized, systematic, intellectual quality. The contrary is the case. All new and reforming movements pass through a stage in which what is most evident is a negative phase, one of protest, of deviation, and innovation. It would be surprising indeed if this were not true of the progressive educational movement. For instance, the formality and fixity of traditional schools seemed oppressive, restrictive. Hence in a school which departs from these ideals and methods, freedom is at first most naturally conceived as removal of artificial and benumbing restrictions. Removal, abolition are, however, negative things, so in time it comes to be seen that such freedom is no end in itself, nothing to be satisfied with and to stay by, but marks at most an opportunity to do something of a positive and constructive sort.

Now I wonder whether this earlier and more negative phase of progressive education has not upon the whole run its course, and whether the time has not arrived in which these schools are undertaking a more constructively organized function. One thing is sure: in the degree in which they enter upon organized constructive work, they are bound to make definite contributions to building up the theoretical or intellectual side of education. Whether this be called science or philosophy of education, I for one, care little; but if they do not *intellectually* organize their own work, while they may do much in making the lives of the children committed to them more joyous and more vital, they contribute only incidental scraps to the science of education.

The word organization has been freely used. This word suggests the nature of the problem. Organization and administration are words associated together in the traditional scheme, hence organization conveys the idea of something external and set. But reaction from this sort of organization only creates a demand for another sort. Any genuine intellectual organization is flexible and moving, but it does not lack its own internal principles of order and continuity. An experimental school is under the temptation to improvise its subject-matter. It must take advantage of unexpected events and turn to account unexpected questions and interests. Yet if it permits improvisation to dictate its course, the result is a jerky, discontinuous movement which works against the possibility of making any important contribution to educational subject-matter. Incidents are momentary, but the use made of them should not be momentary or short-lived. They are to be brought within the scope of a developing whole of content and purpose, which is a whole because it has continuity and consecutiveness in its parts. There is no single subject-matter which all schools must adopt, but in every school there should be some significant subject-matters undergoing growth and formulation.

An illustration may help make clearer what is meant. Progressive schools set store by individuality, and sometimes it seems to be thought that orderly organization of subject-matter is hostile to the needs of students in their individual character. But individuality is something developing and to be continuously attained, not something given all at once and ready-made. It is found only in life-history, in its continuing growth; it is, so to say, a career and not just a fact discoverable at a particular cross section of life. It is quite possible for teachers to make such a fuss over individual children, worrying about their peculiarities, their likes and dislikes, their weaknesses and failures, so that they miss perception of real individuality, and indeed tend to adopt methods which show no faith in the power of individuality. A child's individuality cannot be found in what he does or in what he consciously likes at a given moment; it can be found only in the connected course of his actions. Consciousness of desire and purpose can be genuinely attained only toward the close of some fairly prolonged sequence of activities. Consequently some organization of subject-matter reached through a serial or consecutive course of doings, held together within the unity of progressively growing occupation or project, is the only means which corresponds to real individuality. So far is organization from being hostile to the principle of individuality.

Thus much of the energy that sometimes goes to thinking about individual children might better be devoted to discovering some worthwhile activity and to arranging the conditions under which it can be carried forward. As a child engages in this consecutive and cumulative occupation, then in the degree in which it contains valuable subject-matter, the realization or building up of his individuality comes about as a consequence, one might truly say, as a natural by-product. He finds and develops himself in what he does, not in isolation but by interaction with the conditions which contain and carry subject-matter. Moreover a teacher can find out immensely more about the real needs, desires, interests, capacities, and weaknesses of a pupil by observing him throughout the course of such consecutive activity than by any amount of direct prodding or of merely cross-sectional observation. And all observations are of necessity cross-sectional when made of a child engaged in a succession of disconnected activities.

Such a succession of unrelated activities does not provide, of course, the opportunity or content of building up an organized subject-matter. But neither do they provide for the development of a coherent and integrated self. Bare doing, no matter how active, is not enough. An activity or project must, of course, be within the range of the experience of pupils and connected with their needs—which is very far from being identical with any likes or desires which they can consciously express. This negative condition having been met, the test of a good project is whether it is sufficiently full and complex to demand a variety of responses from different children and permit each to go at it and make his contribution in a way which is characteristic of himself. The further test or mark of a good activity, educationally speaking, is that it have a sufficiently long time-span so that a series of endeavors and explorations are involved in it, and included in such a way that each step opens up a new field, raises new questions, arouses a demand for further knowledge, and suggests what to do next on the basis of what has been accomplished and the knowledge thereby gained. Occupational activities which meet these two conditions will of necessity result in not only amassing known subject-matter but in its organization. They simply cannot be carried on without resulting in some orderly collection and systematization of related facts and principles. So far is the principle of working toward organization of knowledge not hostile to the principles of progressive education that the latter cannot perform its functions without reaching out into such organization.

An exaggerated illustration, amounting to a caricature, may perhaps make the point clearer. Suppose there is a school in which pupils are surrounded with a wealth of material objects, apparatus, and tools of all sorts. Suppose they are simply asked what they would like to do and then told in effect to "go to it," the teacher keeping hands—and mind, too—off. *What* are they going to do? What assurance is there that what they do is anything more than the expression, and exhaustion, of a momentary impulse and interest? The supposition does not, you may say, correspond to any fact. But what are the implications of the opposite principle? Where can we stop as we get away from the principle contained in the illustration? Of necessity—and this is as true of the traditional school as of a progressive—the start, the first move, the initial impulse in action, must proceed from the pupil. You can lead a horse to water but you can't make him drink. But whence comes his idea of *what* to do? That must come from what he has already heard or seen; or from what he sees some other child doing. It comes as a suggestion from beyond himself, from the environment, he being not an originator of the idea and purpose but a vehicle through which his surroundings past and present suggest something to him. That such suggestions are likely to be chance ideas, soon exhausted, is highly probable. I think observation will show that when a child enters upon a really fruitful and consecutively developing activity, it is because, and in as far as, he has previously engaged in some complex and gradually unfolding activity which has left him with a question he wishes to prove further or with the idea of some piece of work still to be accomplished to bring his occupation to completion. Otherwise he is at the mercy of chance suggestion, and chance suggestions are not likely to lead to anything significant or fruitful.

While in outward form, these remarks are given to show that the teacher, as the member of the group having the riper and fuller experience and the greater insight into the possibilities of continuous development found in any suggested project, has not only the right but the duty to suggest lines of activity, and to show that there need not be any fear of adult imposition provided the teacher knows children as well as subjects, their import is not exhausted in bringing out this fact. Their basic purport is to show that progressive schools by virtue of being progressive, and not in spite of that fact, are under the necessity of finding projects which involve an orderly development and interconnection of subject-matter, since otherwise there can be no sufficiently complex and long-span undertaking. The opportunity and the need impose a responsibility. Progressive teachers may and can work out and present to other teachers for trial and criticism definite and organized bodies of knowledge, together with a listing of sources from which additional information of the same sort can be secured. If it is asked how the presentation of such bodies of knowledge would differ from the standardized texts of traditional schools, the answer is easy. In the first place, the material would be associated with and derived from occupational activities or prolonged courses of action undertaken by the pupils themselves. In the second place, the material presented would not be something to be literally followed by other teachers and students, but would be indications of the intellectual possibilities of this and that course of activity—statements on the basis of carefully directed and observed experience of the questions that have arisen in connection with them and of the kind of information found useful in answering them, and of where that knowledge can be had. No second experience would exactly duplicate the course of the first; but the presentation of material of this kind would liberate and direct the activities of any teacher in dealing with the distinctive emergencies and needs that would arise in re-undertaking the same general type of project. Further material thus developed would be added, and a large and yet free body of related subject-matter would gradually be built up.

As I have touched in a cursory manner upon the surface of a number of topics, it may be well in closing to summarize. In substance, the previous discussion has tried to elicit at least two contributions which progressive schools may make to that type of a science of education which corresponds to their own type of procedure. One is the development of organized subject-matter just spoken of. The other is a study of the conditions favorable to learning. As I have already said there are certain traits characteristic of progressive schools which are not ends in themselves but which are opportunities to be used. These reduce themselves to opportunities for *learning*, for gaining knowledge, mastering definite modes of skill or techniques, and acquiring socially desirable attitudes and habits—the three chief aspects of learning, I should suppose. Now of necessity the contribution from the side of traditional schools to this general topic is concerned chiefly with methods of teaching, or, if it passes beyond that point, to the methods of study adopted by students. But from the standpoint of progressive education, the question of method takes on a new and still largely untouched form. It is no longer a question of how the teacher is to instruct or how the pupil is to study. The problem is to find what conditions must be fulfilled in order that study and learning will naturally and necessarily take place, what conditions must be present so that pupils will make the responses which cannot help having learning as their consequence. The pupil's mind is no longer to be on study or learning. It is given to doing the things that the situation calls for, while learning is the result. The method of the teacher, on the other hand, becomes a matter of finding the conditions which call out self-educative activity, or learning, and of cooperating with the activities of the pupils so that they have learning as their consequence.

A series of constantly multiplying careful reports on conditions which experience has shown in actual cases to be favorable and unfavorable to learning would revolutionize the whole subject of method. The problem is complex and difficult. Learning involves, as just said, at least three factors: knowledge, skill, and character. Each of these must be studied. It requires judgment and art to select from the total circumstances of a case just what elements are the causal conditions of learning, which are influential, and which secondary or irrelevant. It requires candor and sincerity to keep track of failures as well as successes and to estimate the relative degree of success obtained. It requires trained and acute observation to note the indications of progress in learning, and even more to detect their causes—a much more highly skilled kind of observation than is needed to note the results of mechanically applied tests. Yet the progress of a science of education depends upon the systematic accumulation of just this sort of material. Solution of the problem of discovering the causes of learning is an endless process. But no advance will be made in the solution till a start is made, and the freer and more experimental character of progressive schools places the responsibility for making the start squarely upon them.

I hardly need remind you that I have definitely limited the field of discussion to one point: the relation of progressive education to the development of a science of education. As I began with questions, I end with one: Is not the time here when the progressive movement is sufficiently established so that it may now consider the intellectual contribution which it may make to the art of education, to the art which is the most difficult and the most important of all human arts?

Why I Am a Member of
the Teachers Union[1]

I think you will all agree with me that Miss Blake may be technically retired as a teacher or principal, but she is not retired either from the Union or from interest in everything that is progressive and straightforward that concerns teachers. I thought, as she was speaking, about who the really retired teachers are. At least, the really "tired" teachers, and the retiring ones. I came to the conclusion that they were the ones who are not the members of the Teachers Union, that they were so tired that they are willing to get behind the shelter of the teachers who do band themselves together to do the actual work; they are too retiring to come forward and take any active part in it themselves.

Now, as to why I am a member of the Teachers Union, the query that comes naturally to my mind is why should I not be? Why should not every other teacher be? But there is one personal element in the situation that I would like to mention. I have found that the spirit of courage, of straightforwardness, of energy, of practical idealism, a sense of justice for all who are in any way wronged or in danger of being wronged, which animates our president, is the animating spirit of the Union; and I have been proud, if for no other reason, to be a member of the Union, so as to be associated with the men and women who are conducting its affairs.

I suppose in raising the question, why be a member of the Teachers Union, the emphasis falls upon the fact that it is a union in the familiar sense of the word, and is affiliated with the American Federation of Labor. One would hardly raise the question today of why be a member of a teachers' organization, like the

1. Address delivered at the Membership Meeting of the Teachers Union of the City of New York, Local No. 5, American Federation of Teachers, on November 18, 1927.

[First published in *American Teacher* 12 (1928): 3–6.]

National Educational Association or an Association of English Teachers or History Teachers or Mathematics Teachers. We don't have to have meetings to discuss the why and the wherefore of that question. So I suppose the point of this particular question is: Why be a member of a labor union which is affiliated with other labor unions, which is federated with them? And, in earlier days, at least, that was the stark objection. As Miss Blake has already said it was lowering the dignity of a profession. It was bringing it down to—just think of it—the level of work.

That reminds me that some years ago when there was a proposal to introduce a Department of Social Work in Columbia University, one of my colleagues objected on the ground that he thought it was a very bad precedent to have "work" in the title of any university department.

When Mr. Linville was speaking last, relative to past discussions in the American Federation of Teachers on the question of admitting educational officials to membership, I was reminded of a very similar discussion in connection with the organization of the American Association of University Professors, which I regret to say has not yet advanced to the point of being affiliated with the Federation of Labor, but which at the same time, is a working, and a somewhat militant organization, not one for purely academic discussion. The same question arose in considering whether the college president should be admitted into the Association. By some coincidence which I don't undertake to explain, the professors present came to the same conclusion that you came to in your organization. And while there was an active minority that thought presidents ought to have the benefit of education by contact with the workers of the Association, the views of the majority were decidedly to the contrary. I expect the time will come when the professors' association will be sufficiently large and sufficiently powerful so that it will feel safe to admit them. They have not reached that point yet, I think.

Well, as to why one belongs to a teachers' organization of this type instead of simply to the other type, it seems to me the answer is obvious. There are plenty of grounds for the meeting of teachers together both in general and in particular branches, for the discussion of topics of academic interest; discussions of improvement in subject matter taught and in methods of teaching. That is all to the good! But there is also room, plenty of room, and need, for an organization which has in view something more than academic purposes. There is need for a working, aggressive organization that represents all of the interests that teachers have in common, and which, in representing them, represents also the protection of the children, and the youth in the schools against all of the outside interests, economic and political and others that would exploit the schools for their own ends, and in doing so, reduce the teaching body to a condition of intellectual vassalage.

If the teachers today especially in our larger centres, are not in the position of intellectual serfs, it is due more, I am confident, to the energetic and aggressive activity of the teachers unions than to any other cause.

In how many of the important, practical issues of the day have these other worthy organizations taken an active part? In the document in preparation which our president has spoken of and of which he was kind enough to send me an advance copy, he mentions the fact that the Teachers Union was the first teachers' organization to protest against the Lusk Law. Probably there were others that did it after the way had been blazed, and it did not require so much courage. It was again the first organization to protest against the bills introduced in the Legislature which would involve a censorship of history teaching and which would have made New York as ridiculous in the eyes of the civilized world as is now a city in the middle west that I won't mention. (I used to live there and I have an affection for it.) It was the first teachers' organization to protest against the prostitution of American Educational Week to militaristic purposes.

Now, these are samples of the kind of thing that a Teachers Union organized for definite practical purposes, and strong in its affiliation with the American Federation of Labor, will undertake in meeting courageously the kind of question that academic organizations are likely to dodge.

What would be the condition of the laboring men and women today if there were no labor unions? I don't mean simply the condition of the people who are in these unions, but the condition of labor generally. One has only to ask the question to know that we should be then contemplating a great tragedy.

Now, the very existence of teachers' unions does a great deal more than protect and aid those who are members of it; and that by the way, is one reason the Teachers Union is not larger. It is because there are so many teachers outside of it who rely and depend upon the protection and support which the existence and the activities of the union give them, that they are willing to shelter behind the organization without coming forward and taking an active part in it.

And if there are teachers here tonight—especially if there are any college teachers, but I am afraid there are not—who are not members of the union, I should like to beg them to surrender the, shall I call it, cowardly position, and come forward and actively unite themselves with those who are doing this great and important work for the profession of teaching.

It is said that the Teachers Union as distinct from the more academic organizations over-emphasizes the economic aspect of teaching. Well, I never had that contempt for the economic aspect of teaching, especially not on the first of the month when I get my salary check. I find that teachers have to pay their grocery and meat bills and house rent just the same as everybody else. I find that the respect in which they individually and collectively are held in the community is closely associated with the degree of economic independence which they enjoy. I find that teachers, more than some other members of the community are expected by the community to maintain a certain fairly high standard of living. And I find that in the end, those who control the money that is behind an institution generally control the rest of the institution as well. So I make no apology for saying that one reason for being a member of the Teachers Union is the fact that it does emphasize the economic aspect of the teaching profession as these other organizations do not, though they have been known, I think, when salary bills were up in Albany to send representatives there. But these other organizations do not persistently and consistently maintain the economic independence of the teacher in all its phases.

It was not the Teachers Union that introduced the idea of a business administration of the schools in the great cities of this country, meaning by a business administration one which subordinates the educational management of the school to the group of the largest taxpayers and tax dodgers. It was not the Teachers Union that introduced the economic factor in education by attempting to keep the teachers' mouths shut on all questions that were of economic interest to all excepting a numerically small group of big business concerns. No, my friends, it was not the teachers or the Teachers Union that introduced these economic elements into the schools, and the problems of their right management.

We live in an industrial age and it is academic folly and mere phantasy to suppose that the conduct of public education can be divorced from the prominence which economic, industrial and financial questions occupy in all other phases of our social life.

The Teachers Union has also been a constant and aggressive force in combatting the efforts of various organized interests (that do not meet simply for academic discussions) to exploit the schools for their own ends. These outside forces that like to use the school for their own purposes are both more numerous and better organized than the general public is aware of. Some reference was made by Mr. Linville to the matter of militarism. Now, as many of you probably know, there has been an active movement in many parts of the country to eliminate compulsory military drill as a part of the curriculum of high schools and colleges, where it does not stop with drill. But there has long been a very determined effort in these institutions to inculcate a warlike spirit, a kind of wild, red-eyed patriotism. (The Bolsheviks don't monopolize all the red there is in the world. Some of these conservative citizens are very red under cover.)

There is also a very well organized and apparently well financed movement which is not contented with putting its case before the public, but which produced a document holding up all people who sponsored this movement, as very dangerous citizens. Miss Jane Addams of Chicago, her name beginning with "A"—headed the list as "the most dangerous woman in the United States." And so they went down through the list. It was really quite a roll of honor, but was a personal attack on each one of these persons made to intimidate them. And it may interest you to know that what caused some of these persons to be mentioned as dangerous citizens was that they favored the repeal of the Lusk Law, and a still more damaging charge was that some of them were said to be members of teachers unions. And another proof of dangerous, red radicalism controlled from Moscow was in several cases that the person named had been friendly to organized labor.

Now that is not a laughing matter. It is ridiculous enough; but these people are organized. Not, as I said before, merely for academic discussion, but to control American education in the interest of militarism which is rapidly becoming a vested economic interest in this country. There are some 3,000 jobs at stake in this matter, among other things. And yet, some persons ask why teachers should organize to carry out a definite program of work, instead of simply for academic discussions of subject matter and methods. It was not teachers, and it was not the American Federation of Labor, that recently proposed (with the nerve to do it under the name of progress and advancement) a program of child labor which would reduce conditions below the level now maintained by the statutes of a very considerable number of the states in the Union. It was another organized body, the National Association of Manufacturers, that made this proposal. Are the interests of teachers in their pupils, not merely the children but also the youth of the country, to be confined to the teaching of textbook subjects and the improvement of methods? Or have the educators of the country at least as much interest in maintaining proper standards of child labor; in keeping reasonably high the age at which they may go to work; in protecting the number of hours per week, and in discriminating between safe occupations and those which are unsafe—as much real interest in this question as the manufacturers have? And have not the teachers an interest which is possibly less pecuniary and economic, a broader and more humane social interest? If they have, why is it not merely their right, but even their duty and responsibility to organize to make themselves effective in securing the interests which should be closest to their hearts?

Now, Mr. O'Hanlon has told you something of the educational record of the American Federation of Labor. A few years ago I went over a good many of the documents in that field and I say without any fear of contradiction that there is no organization in the United States—I do not care what its nature is—that has such a fine record in the program of liberal progressive public education as will be found in the printed records of the American Federation of Labor.

I won't say much about the desirability that teachers should get away from a kind of academic snobbery, for there is academic snobbery as well as financial and social snobbery. And I long ago came to the conviction that this snobbery is back of a considerable part of the objections to teachers unions and to their federation with other bodies of working men and working women. I think that is one reason why their arguments are weak. They can't put that reason in print very well; it has to be left as a kind of tacit emotional appeal. I should like to say a little more, however, about the fact that our whole educational system suffers from the divorce between the head and the hand, between work and books, between action and ideas, a divorce which is symbolized in this segregation of teachers from the rest of the workers who are the great mass of the community. If our programs of study in our schools are still too academic and too pedantic, too remote from contact of life, it is largely because the educators, administrators and the teachers are themselves so far remote from the actual problems of life as they are met by the great mass of the population.

If all teachers were within the Teachers Union and if they were not merely—like myself—here I am making a confession which is not in my subject—somewhat nominal members who try to keep their dues paid, but active working members who came into contact with the labor unions, with the working men of the country and their problems, I am sure that more would be done to reform and improve our education, and to put into execution the ideas and ideals written about and talked about by progressive educators and reformers than by any other one cause whatsoever, if not more than by all other causes together.

Teachers are too far remote from the work of the world; not too close to it. I repeat that is one of the fundamental causes for the perpetuation of the weaknesses in our traditional education.

Let me in conclusion say that the time will come—I am not sure that I will live to see it—when the question will not be, Why should I join the Teachers Union? It will be, Why should I not, or why has not this person and that person done it? The time will come when the principle of organization and cooperation and the recognition of common interests of all of those who work in any way, whether mostly with their head or with their hands, or mostly with their voice, will be so clear that the explanations and the apologies and arguments will have to come from those who are not members of the Teachers Union.

Bankruptcy of Modern Education

Dr. Kirkpatrick has made a valuable contribution to our knowledge of the origin, development and present status of higher education in this country, from the standpoint of its organization and control, and the effects of the system upon the teaching body and students.[1] He has assembled material which is little known regarding the early history of Harvard, Yale, Princeton, William and Mary, and a short-lived institution called "The Log College." The account brings out the fact that there was at the outset a period of wavering between the system of external and non-professional governors, and control by the faculty and graduates, following the English system. He makes it clear that the desire of clergymen to make sure of keeping collegiate instruction orthodox, according to their own notions of right belief, was the decisive factor in establishing the outside trustee government which has now become the regular method of university government. As clergymen were par excellence the educated men of the time, and the largest number of students were those preparing for the ministry, the decision was an easy and probably unconscious one. It must have seemed natural, and did not arouse much protest save by some college tutors, and their protest met with no particular response from the public.

The system thus formed persisted when education became secularized, and the preparation of the clergy became the smallest part of college work. Business men became, except in the smaller denominational colleges, the residuary legatees of the functions of ecclesiastics, and, in any case, given the economic conservatism of the church, an alliance was not hard to effect. The greater part of the book is devoted to an account, of a factual and non-

1. *The American College and Its Rulers*. New York. New Republic, Inc. 1926.
[First published in *Modern Quarterly* 4 (1927): 102–4.]

sensational character, of later developments which have reflected unfavorably upon educational freedom, and to a description of present tendencies of discontent with external, non-professional control, and of the movements toward greater participation in government of faculties and students—"democratic stirrings," as Dr. Kirkpatrick calls them. Under the caption of "The Next Step" he outlines a good plan for the substitution of democratic for autocratic control—what a former colleague of mine once termed "despotism tempered by resignation." Dr. Kirkpatrick's own statements are moderate and he has avoided relying upon gossip and rumor. He gives full credit to the work accomplished by the present system in the extraordinary expansion of physical resources and scholastic opportunities. But like most teachers in higher institutions, he feels that the time has come for bringing college rule into line with democratic institutions.

Unfortunately, the obstacles to achievement of this result are not confined to the institutional inertia which everywhere in life expresses itself, nor to the deliberate desire of men of large business and financial interests to dominate educational policies. As a conscious intention and policy, radicals, in my opinion, usually exaggerate the influence of the latter factor, however it may be as to the unconscious and subtly pervasive influence of the capitalistic system within which today we all live, move and have our being. The more powerful agencies in effecting restriction are found, in my judgment, within our institutions themselves. Dr. Kirkpatrick seems to me to exaggerate the liberal temper of youth. That the "Creator is most free in the youthful part of each generation" is a dubious statement. Speaking generally, youth is curiously conventional in intellectual matters, at least that part of the youth which gets into colleges and universities. College atmosphere, "college spirit," the activities of alumni,—all make for a non-critical complacency with things as they are, intellectually and socially, and for a crude hip-hurrah externalism. Possibly this state of affairs is indirectly connected with the existing system of college government, but independent causes for it readily occur to my mind.

Members of faculties are quite generally, in my opinion, uneasy under the present system and free in their critical remarks. But how far they are actively willing to assume the responsibilities which would attend the abolition of absentee academic landlords and the adoption of the policy of home rule is uncertain. In the larger institutions, faculties have much more extralegal control than the present system officially provides for. But the great enemy is scholastic specialization. Most teachers want to be left alone to do their own work; they kick when their special work is interfered with, but on the whole they are not anxious to take time and thought away from it to give to large educational policies, to say nothing of administrative management. The same sort of reasons that induce half of the electorate to abstain from going to the polls affects college teachers, and creates indifference to educational matters save in a crisis. Again, the departmental system within universities is independent of trustee rule; sharp division of departments, competition of departments for funds to extend their staff and subjects, the frequent autocracy of departmental heads, would have to be dealt with in any comprehensive scheme of emancipation of education. Scholastic specialization and the departmentalization of knowledge breed indifference to larger social issues and objects. I do not mean that a change in governmental machinery is not needed nor that it would accomplish nothing in liberation of inquiry and discussion. But in my judgment the greater need is that teachers see their special subject in the light of human interests and well-being. If that were accomplished, there would be a release of energy and an impetus of intellectual activity which would be practically irresistible, and which would quickly effect a change in forms of control.

What, however, I feel most deeply is that discussion regarding higher education is usually isolated in a misleading way from the general educational system. In my observation, college teachers have much more intellectual freedom than teachers in lower public and private schools, especially high-school teachers. These reach much larger numbers of students and affect them at a more impressionable age than do college instructors. Those who attack the system of college government usually take for granted the established "school-board" rule of public schools as something final and inevitable. Yet it is inserted between municipal government and the staff of teachers in a meaningless and needless way. It is the extreme instance of a control which is neither professional nor genuinely social in character. Aside from lack of share of the teaching staff in the formation of educational policies, there is, I am confident, much more autocracy on the part of superintendents and principals in public schools than by presidents and deans in colleges. Our lower schools are ridden by "administrators"; they are administration mad. An arm's-length efficiency, conducted by typewriters from central offices, reaches into the class-rooms where all the educational work is done, and produces there the inefficiency of irresponsibility and routine. Yet these things mostly go without note or comment. The public seems satisfied, not aware there is anything the matter. I shall see real hope for promotion of educational freedom when the status of academic freedom is no longer regarded as something apart, with which colleges alone are concerned. The problem of securing freedom in education is an integral problem. It concerns the entire system. When it is so viewed, it will receive general attention which is a precondition of any adequate solution. Till then college rule will have to muddle along—such at least is my opinion. That youth *might* be free and creative I do not doubt, but college reaches their minds too late. And of necessity college teaching must be more specialized than that of earlier periods. College teachers will most readily win their own emancipation when they recognize their solidarity with all other teachers. Only a few teachers adhere to the American Federation of Teachers, though such action is the most obvious expression of solidarity. As long as conditions are like those which have existed in the recent West Chester Normal School incident, freedom in university teaching will be precarious. And they are likely to continue till teachers in a body organize to effect recognition of their social function.

The Manufacturers' Association and the Public Schools

Others will undoubtedly speak to you regarding the details of the manufacturers' program in reference to the claims which the association puts forward in its behalf, of its marking an advance in strengthening of the educational interests of children. Instead of speaking of these details, I wish to consider with you the attitude shown by the Manufacturers' Association toward public education in general. I think without going into the specific points of their program, we can judge a good deal as to the probability of those details really being in the direction of progress, by looking at the spirit and attitude in which that association, through its representatives, approaches the whole matter of public education. I don't mean by this that I have any private or confidential information regarding their attitude. I know only what they themselves have put forward in their printed documents; and a striking feature of those documents to which I invite your attention is the fact that they have a tendency to gather and pile together the various criticisms which are made, and made very freely, regarding our school system.

Now it probably is not news to any of you that our school system is not perfect. It has its defects and a good many people have pointed out these defects, and have made some severe criticisms of many points in our public school system. I suppose if I were on trial I might have to plead guilty myself. But there are at least two quite different ways with two quite different ends in view in which these criticisms may be offered. Now I will give you in a moment some samples of their critical attitude, and then ask you to consider what conclusion they draw, what moral they point to? Is it that the Manufacturers' Association, with the very large

[First published in *Journal of the National Education Association* 17 (1928): 61–62, from an address to the National Consumers' League, 28 November 1927.]

resources financial and political which they have at command, should turn in and use their power to improve the public schools until these defects disappear? This is certainly one method of reacting to knowledge of just criticisms, is it not? The fact that evils exist is so much the more reason for effective organization to remedy them and make the schools what they may and should be for the children.

No, that is not the conclusion which is drawn. The conclusion which is implied and rather strongly intimated, though not stated with complete frankness, is that these defects in the public schools afford a reason why a considerable portion of the children should not stay in the schools. In other words, the public schools being so bad, it is quite obvious that the factory, the shop, and the store, would be better places for the children than the school system. I expect if these public-spirited and rich and presumably beneficent gentlemen keep on, that in a few years we shall be reading in the headlines of the papers of the "Great Improvement in Park Avenue Apartments. Fifteen percent gain in children now leaving school and finding a place operating a machine." Or, "Conditions in family life on Fifth Avenue very much better. Large proportion of children now leaving school at between fourteen and sixteen to take positions in the department stores of the city, and some of them engaging in selling newspapers."

For if this argument that the schools have such defects that it is better for a considerable portion of the children to go into factories at an early age has any point at all, it is a point which is entirely independent of the economic status and wealth of the parents. It is an argument which, if it is good for one child, is good for all whether their parents are working people or whether their parents are millionaires. Yet I do not find the recommendation urged upon the well-to-do. I think some of these people who drew up the report are trustees of some of our more important universities; I have not heard them as university trustees engaged in urging that the youth who go to college should seek the superior educational advantages of the factories.

The criticisms made are of the following nature. "The public generally and educators are coming into a distinct doubt if not disappointment as to the progress that is being made in public education."

Then they go on to point out the very large increase in the number of children in the public schools in the last ten or twelve years put by some as high as ten millions, at the very large increase in funds and the high-school attendance increased proportionately, involving an enormous burden of taxation, and so on.

The conclusion then is this: "How far are we progressing in the right way in our educational campaign? Are we making education a fad without an adequate understanding of what education is or should be?" Of course it is entirely proper for any body of people, whether representing the interests of manufacturers or others, to inquire whether our education is becoming a fad. But I think we have the right, since we are seriously interested in the particular problem, to question the motives of this particular body of people in raising the question whether Americans at the present time are in danger of making a fad out of the education of their own children.

What is our next step to be? Is it to say that, because some children are physically backward, they shall be deprived of all of the benefits of medical attention and supervision and care of the public schools and turned over to the tender mercies of factory owners whose chief interest in them is the profit they can make out of their labor? Is that the conclusion? Or is it that, since the mental powers of some are backward as compared with others, therefore, they should have no further education at all but engage in the mechanical, deadening and stupefying work of operating machines for eight hours a day, or forty-eight hours a week, making the same motion over and over again, nobody knows how many thousands of times a day? Or should the Manufacturers' Association do what some other public-spirited citizens have done in developing special schools for the care of more or less backward and defective children, and go forward to see to it that if our present school methods do not adequately meet the needs of these children, the schools be improved until these children are properly taken care of?

Again they ask "Are we grinding out a vast lot of machines without developing the thinking capacity of the child?" If I were a big manufacturer, and I had a whole lot of machines that didn't require any great amount of intelligence to operate and my chief interest were in profits got from the factory, I should rather hope that the answer to that question was in the affirmative—that we are grinding out a lot of machines without developing the thinking capacity of the children. For if their thinking capacity is very highly developed they are not going to take these absolutely routine and deadening jobs of the kind which, in other portions of their report, they recommend that all of the less capable school children, those approaching morons, go into because they can do those things without thinking capacity being required.

I don't quite understand their great eagerness on the one hand that the schools develop thinking capacity, and their desire on the other hand that the children somewhat backward mentally should be turned over to manage the automatic machines. Then there is another old friend in here. I should have felt lost, being a college professor, if this bogie hadn't turned up somewhere: "There is unquestionably an increasing tendency in many of our public schools and colleges to the rankest socialism, really to bolshevism itself."

You will excuse me if I can't say that word with all of the explosive power that should accompany it.

"Many of our teachers not capable of serious thinking, or investigation, are caught by the chaff of bolshevism spread broadcast, and are teaching false doctrines dangerous to the future of America."

The moral is evident. The sooner the children leave school, early enough so they don't get into high school or college, the more they will be protected from these dangerous bolshevistic college professors, and the less dangerous will they be to 20 percent or more annual dividends in the textile industries of the United States, and hence less dangerous to the future of America.

There are defects in our school system. There are evils. There are just criticisms to be made. But what do these things indicate? The reply is that they indicate the necessity of organization of all of the intelligent and humane members of the community to remedy these evils, to make the schools such that all children, whatever the grade of culture or wealth of their parents, whatever their own individual physical and mental capacity, may get full profit from them.

And I submit that, antecedent to the study of the details of their program, when we find a body of men approaching the condition of our public schools with the obvious purpose of using these evils to detract from the significance and importance of

the work of the public schools, that we have a right to be suspicious of any further conclusions or recommendations which
they put forth.

The American people, including American business men, say a
great deal about the practical idealism of America. Now if there
is any one phase of human life in which there is need of idealism
and need that that idealism be practical, it is in the upbringing of
the young. This is the one thing, it seems to me, before which
every serious minded person must stand in awe when he considers the immense issues which are at stake both for individuals
and for the future of society. Any genuinely practical idealism
will go upon the belief that what the wisest and best of human
parents want for their own children, that the community as a
whole should want for the children of the community as a whole.
It is a shame to our supposed idealism in any degree in which we
come short of making any effort to live up to that ideal. I do not
mean that we can at once put it into effect. The desire and the
capacity of the wise and well-to-do members of the community
with reference to their own children will, for a very, very long
time, outrun what the community as a whole can and will do for
its children as a whole. But I do say that, if we cannot carry out
the program, it is at least the part of decency and of humanity to
refrain from adding to the obstacles from which the children of
the more unfortunate and the more backward portions of the
community suffer.

If we cannot actively give to all of the children that which it is
ideal they should have, we may at least refrain from deliberately
adding to the obstacles from which they already suffer. And as
for those who add to the sufferings and trials and difficulties, the
handicaps from which so many, and indeed the mass of our children already suffer, I say as for those who would add to these, I
think the old words of scripture still apply, "that it were better
for them that a millstone be tied about their neck."

Reviews

Philosophy as a Fine Art

The Realm of Essence by George Santayana.
New York: Charles Scribner's Sons, 1927.

Philosophy has its local veers and temporal swerves, but it returns from its oscillations to the central question of the relation of existence and ideas, matter and mind, nature and spirit. The vein of positivism and phenomenalism seems to be temporarily worked out. Contemporary philosophy shows a marked disposition to invade the field which much nineteenth-century thought contemptuously dismissed as "ontological"; it manifests a marked tendency to revert to the issues of Greek and medieval speculation and to inquire into the intrinsic nature of matter and mind, nature and spirit, and their relations with one another. For the first time, after many a long year, there is high discourse of Being and Essence. Among those who engage in this discourse, George Santayana is a conspicuous figure.

In *The Life of Reason*, which established him as one whose thought is to be reckoned with, he spoke primarily as a moralist and as an historian (in terms of what he has since called "literary psychology") of the emergence of the rational life out of the flux of blind sensation and desire. In that work, he taught or seemed to teach that the realm of ideas and ideals is rooted in nature and forms its apex: a flower of nature destined, indeed, never to bear seeds which may themselves take root in nature, but altogether lovely, the end of experience and of human life, in the only intelligible sense of end. It now appears, however, that those who interpreted Santayana in this sense of naturalistic idealism were in error. They took his dramatic reproduction of the course of human history in arriving at a knowledge of ideas and ideals as if it were an account of the generation of those ideals themselves. Following his volume on *Skepticism and Animal Faith*, which was introductory, Mr. Santayana is now putting forth his posi-

[First published in *New Republic* 53 (1928): 352–54.]

tive and, so to say, constructive metaphysics—to which, however, he prefers to give the name ontology. *The Realm of Essence* is the first phase of the wider realm of Being to receive attention.

His fundamental position may, I think, be simply stated without doing it an injustice. His philosophic creed is a variant of an old saying: Render to Caesar the things that are Caesar's and to God the things that are God's. In his thorough-going dualism, the version reads: Render to Essence the things which belong to it and to Nature, or existence or matter or substance (the four terms are equivalents), the things which belong to it. All existence is natural, physical as well as psychical, and Matter is the substance of Nature. The latter is a flux, enduring and contingent, having in itself no character or even characters, much less purpose. Over against the realm of existence stands that of Being, consisting of essences which *are* but which do not *exist*, while existences, since they are in ceaseless change, in flux, are not; they are rather what Plato termed non-Being. Since essences do not exist, they are to be described in terms which are mainly those of negation of the properties ascribed to existence: non-material, eternal (that is, in the sense of non-temporal, not in that of everlasting existence), spaceless, the heaven of Platonic Ideas, the world of Leibnizian possibilities out of which some few are selected for inclusion within existence. These essences are each complete and independent in themselves, wholly individual and yet wholly universal—not general—and they are infinitely numerous.

They are the objects of intuition rather than of proof or reflection. For all thinking, and sense as well, presupposes them as its already intuited objects. Their Being and concrete reality may, however, be indicated by various modes of approach, of which the skeptical, showing that existence as such cannot be sensed or known, is one. There are, however, other roads to a realization that as objects of intuition they are already contained in not only every form of knowledge, but in every form of significant experience. There is the road of dialectic, which is either a construction or an analysis of ideal forms tracing the logical patterns assumed by them. These are the objects and the only objects of *exact* science, of mathematics and logic, while the goal of the natural sciences is to trace these patterns as they are actually exemplified in the flux of nature. They are approached in contemplation, especially in the contemplation of sense. Whenever sense ceases to be worried about its objects in their practical or intellectual implications, it becomes contemplative. The most material thing felt to be beautiful is sublimated into essence; the natural affinity of mind is to essence, not to fact, which is of concern only because the body, in order to preserve itself, has to act and to adapt itself practically and existentially to other existences. The proper affinity of mind to essence, rather than to action and fact, is revealed in the beginning of life in play and at its end in contemplation. The other road mentioned is that of spiritual discipline; the liberation of man from absorption in care for the material and his elevation into regard for the eternal in all its indifferency to his worldly fortunes.

The realm of essence is indifferent and inert; it has no potency nor desire to find a home in existence. But the flux of existence, which alone has power and causality, happens to take on and cast off some of the essences. Thereby it attains determinate characters, and in such ways that man, himself a special part of the flux, may, when made shrewd by experience, read determinate courses of events, and pass in inference from one character of existence to another. Such instances of embodied or exemplified essences define the nature of all knowledge of existence, that of common sense, that of physical science as well, but such knowledge represents a concession which mind makes to the exigent conditions of its own existence rather than expresses its proper nature. When such accommodation to the necessities of existence and to the needs of action is treated seriously and made an end or value of life, mind is prostituted. The true attitude toward nature is that of piety, of deferential respect as to a mother, of good-humored acceptance which appreciates the comedy involved in the absurdity of confining essence within existence, while it is recognized that that very absurdity frees man from any obligation to achieve such incarnation and liberates him for the blessed opportunity of contemplative enjoyment of essence. When the mind engages in this, its true office, spirituality is found. Piety to nature is a necessity, since we cannot escape nature as long as we exist, and it is a debt of gratitude as well; for it is due to the favoring grace of nature that the power of thought and intuition exists. Deference to nature having been courteously paid, mind is liberated to dwell in its true home, the eternal. This is the core of meaning in all religions, however burdened they may be with the superstitious legends about existence; of all morality above the merely prudential, and of all fine art.

I have been obliged to omit many things that students of philosophy will find highly interesting—some of them, perhaps, the most instructive things in the volume. But I have not, I hope, omitted anything essential to the framework of his position, although the captivating qualities of his expression have, alas, evaporated: its lucidity, its union of austerity with charm, its urbanity—in this volume one of form as well as of substance, so that some readers will perhaps miss the touches of malice which have spiced most of his writings. Criticism finds itself in an almost hopeless dilemma. Mr. Santayana habitually employs "dogmatic" as a term of honor. There is perhaps no thinker, certainly no contemporary one, who is so assured, so free from intellectual doubts as he is. Doubts and questionings are as foreign to the spirit of his philosophy as they are irrelevant to the contemplation of essence and the enjoyment of music. Intuition is, he tells us, "absolute apprehension, without media or doubt." Mr. Santayana has such an intuition of his own system, and his ultimate reply to anyone who cannot achieve a similar intuition might well be: So much the worse for you. Yet philosophy is reflection rather than music or poetry, albeit it is fortunate, when it finds a poet like Mr. Santayana to expound it. It is, therefore, supposed to fall within the realm of the true or false, and as such has to submit, as music has not, to certain criteria of material evidence and internal coherence. A dream is sometimes a lovely object of contemplation; man is a fantasy-making animal and the contents of a fantasy are, by Santayana's definition, essences. As philosophy, Mr. Santayana's philosophy, therefore, demands trial by raising questions of matter-of-fact evidence and of internal logical consistency from which as a poem or musical symphony it is exempt, and to him as a thinker it is discourtesy not to raise problems having their source in doubt.

Yet, from the standpoint of Mr. Santayana's own definition of truth, the critic now finds himself in another dilemma. The realm of truth for him is that "segment of that realm of essence which happens to be illustrated in the realm of existence." Yet that part of his system with which he is most concerned, and upon which his whole distinction of naturalism from spirituality turns, is precisely essence which is not, save accidentally, exemplified in existence. Mr. Santayana thus seems to have deprived both himself and a critic of any criterion by which to judge of the truth of his system. Technical criticism would, perhaps, proceed both most justly and most sympathetically by tracing the historic forbears of his doctrines. For even if the genetic method is as irrelevant to ulterior problems as Mr. Santayana's dislike of it holds it to be, yet it is still relevant to human opinions about these ulterior matters. So viewed, his system seems to present a version of the Platonic idea in terms of the Lockeian simple idea—a combination which at once arouses doubt as to the consistency of its components. For while Santayana's assertion, that essence is the direct and indubitable object of every kind of awareness, follows from the definition of idea in Locke as the "immediate object of the mind in thinking" (where thinking covers all which the modern psychologist calls "consciousness"), nothing could be more remote from the stern discipline which in Plato is required in order to turn the eye of the soul to the vision of ideas. I fear that Santayana has made more concessions to the temper of a democratic and easy-going age than he can theoretically approve.

Again, one might point out that the flux, which is, by conception, the great distinction of existence from Being, is by definition unknowable, either by sense or thought. It is an easy transition to the conclusion that the existential flux is itself a pure essence and not an existence nor a trait of existence. This conclusion seems trivially dialectical. But followed out, it might lead us to the conclusion that, since existence has order and relations, and is not mcrc flux, essences are but relations and relational operations extracted from natural existence, which after being sublimated in thought into essences, are restored to an existence from which they were never really separated. For it would be no great task for a thorough-going naturalist to derive every trait of Santayana's essence from the characteristics of any object of thought, as thought deals with nature. The task is made easy by the fact that Santayana himself, in denying all potency to essence, is obliged to ascribe intent and communication to the natural world.

A critic, however, would probably be better advised to trace the consequences of that part of Santayana's doctrine in which he distinguishes between essences as directly possessed in intuition and essences as only intended or implicated. The nature of the former phase of experience is conveyed by him when he says: "The torments suffered by the souls in Dante's *Inferno* are not intuited by the poet or the reader in their intended essence, for then he would be enduring these torments actually." For if this strain be developed, it would appear that not only is sense an organ of apprehension of essence but is its only organ, understanding by "sense" not the desiccated "sensations" of analytic psychology but direct and pregnant realization, in which emotion is also contained. Such direct appreciation is possible only of essences or meanings incarnate in matter or natural existence; the "essences" with which thought deals as matters of intent and implication are not had nor intuited. They have their import in an ulterior intent to realize them in nature. Save as instruments facilitating and directing such embodiment, they are but symbols to be symbolically manipulated: remote, pallid, abstract.

Conceived in terms of this strain of Santayana's philosophy, the realm of essences is but the device of thought for projecting possibilities as yet unrealized in nature; their intellectual status, the question of whether they are fantasies or genuine ideas, is decided by their fitness to direct action in effecting an embodied realization. Such action defines the procedure and aim of art and the arts. The act of art, or incarnation in existence, is thus part of the intent of thought in dealing with "essence." Action stands on the same level as the objects of thought, being but the manifestation of the intent of reference to existence which constitutes them. Essences of the Platonic type are as instrumental as is action itself; they are means of a delayed but potential transformation of natural existence such that it will be enriched by meanings capable of direct yet rational enjoyment. A similar outcome is indicated by the analogies which Santayana frequently draws between the realm of essences and music. For music is the antithesis of essence isolated from existence in sense and nature.

It thus appears that, of the four approaches to genuine and final essence, but one, that of sense, is complete and adequate. The others are preliminary and instrumental, preparing the antecedent machinery which is indispensable to a rich and vital appreciation of the realized potentialities of nature. Which is to say

that *they* are *not* essences but means of approach to natural existence alone possessed of essential, that is, final and self-sufficing,
quality.

Were the foregoing suggestions adequately developed, it would
appear, I think, that one may use the dilemma previously mentioned in order to engage in an examination of Santayana's system from two points of view. One may take his doctrine as an
intellectual system having historic forbears in the various systems which have anticipated him in statement of the two-world
scheme of separate essence and existence. From this point of
view, his doctrine is characterized by all the unresolved problems
and contradictions which have afflicted these historic systems,
plus added ones which are revealed because of his more consistent and austerely precise development of implications. From
this point of view, I shall be surprised if the ultimate fate of the
doctrine is not to effect a *reductio ad absurdum* of the common
premises. But one may also take a more genial path and, setting
out from the kinship of enjoyed possession of essence with appreciation of works of art, be led to interpret the doctrine in
the sense of cancellation of the alleged separation of objects of
thought from nature. The conclusion is that thought and its
characteristic objects are, like bare action or practice, but a
means for a transformation of raw nature into products of art—
into forms of existence which are directly significant and enjoyed. Meanwhile, the works of art created by Mr. Santayana afford so much enjoyment of a high order in their embodiment of
observation and reflection, that the reader is well advised who
emulates Mr. Santayana in abrogation of doubt and question,
and surrenders himself to their enjoyment. For in the end, it is
only the wisdom which is embodied in natural existence which
counts, and the technical wisdom of the ontological and dialectical philosopher of itself drops away. The affinity of mind to pure
essence is disciplinary and preparatory; that intermediate and
instrumental affinity once having been developed, mind turns
spontaneously to its proper object, meaning realized by art in
natural existence.

Philosophy's Search for a Satisfying Vision of Reality

Idealism as a Philosophy by R. F. Alfred Hoernlé. New York: The George H. Doran Company, 1927.

Science and Philosophy and Other Essays by Bernard Bosanquet. New York: The Macmillan Company, 1927.

Professor Hoernlé's book is a veritable pedagogical triumph. And when I say "pedagogical" I have not in mind any of that disparaging flavor which often hangs about the word. The book manifests all the marks of the true teacher. It has clarity, order, a high degree of simplicity of statement considering the difficulty of the subject, contagious enthusiasm in communication and that candor which is so appropriate to the philosopher, but so often lost, alas! in the heat of polemics. The preface says that the intention of the book is "to help a beginner thread his way through the tangled mazes of idealistic theory, and that a student, while having much to add and amplify, should have little to unlearn." And, like all good teachers, the aim is to provide a stimulus and introduction for first-hand study of the authors dealt with and not a substitute for such acquaintance. Mr. Hoernlé has succeeded extraordinarily in accomplishing these purposes. Indeed, he has done more. While the book is primarily intended for those who have a little preliminary knowledge, none of a strictly technical kind, I cannot imagine that professional students will read the book without adding to their insight if not their information.

The book opens with an account of the nature of philosophy itself, giving the setting within which idealistic philosophies fall.

[First published in *New York Times Book Review*, 13 November 1927, pp. 8, 22.]

It is characteristic of the temper and method of the work that its statement of the object and materials of philosophy is approached from the side of the student: "How to study philosophy." This approach makes it clear that philosophy is essentially an act; it is philosophizing, not the acquisition of information. "It is an art to be acquired by practice." The writings of great philosophers supply models; one must, as with other arts, understand and repeat for himself, in his own way, the procedures followed by great masters. Thus one acquires expertness.

This emphasis is wholly consonant with Hoernlé's idea that the goal of philosophy is a "vision of reality which shall satisfy both heart and head" and thus contribute to making man at home in the universe. It also explains why the author in repeating two of the usual statements about philosophical thinking as distinct from that of the special sciences also brings to the foreground two phases often omitted or slurred over. The two commonplaces are, first, that philosophy takes into account the processes of perceiving and judging which the sciences ignore in their preoccupation with subject matter perceived and judged; it reckons with the "subjective" factor which is taken for granted in the special sciences, and, secondly, that philosophy examines the fundamental concepts which each special science presupposes and subjects them to searching criticism with a view to discovering their total coherence with one another as integral members of the whole organism of reality and knowledge.

The two phases often passed over are, first, that while philosophy, like science, seeks general principles, the latter does so in a way which strives to discount emotion and desire, while philosophy aims to effect a transfiguration of particular feelings and desires into forms which are appropriate to the general point of view. To apprehend particular things and events in the light of the whole, is, as with Plato and Spinoza, to effect a conversion of emotion and will, not just to bring about a change in theory. The second point is akin. While philosophizing is distinctly reflective thinking and thus takes one away temporarily from absorption in the processes of direct living, its last term is direct acquaintance with the materials of ordinary experience upon a plane of fuller, more assured and profound possession. Mr. Hoernlé remarks that this view of the office and outcome of philosophy represents the conclusion of that branch of idealism to which he himself adheres. But members of other and non-idealistic schools would, I am sure, accept its spirit, even though they radically disagree as to the exact nature of the deeper and fuller direct acquaintance which is the outcome.

The crux of Hoernlé's discussion is found in his analysis of four types of idealism which need to be discriminated if there is to be either intelligent criticism or acceptance. These are, in addition to the Absolute Idealism (to the author the legitimate and culminating form of idealistic reflection), Spiritual Pluralism, Spiritual Monism and the Critical Idealism formulated by Kant. Spiritual Pluralism is the doctrine that the universe is a society of spirits of diverse kinds and degrees with God as the basis and apex of the society. Berkeley is treated, in one of the best chapters of the book, as the author of this view, and James Ward as its typical recent representative (some of the ambiguities involved in the conception of "idealism" are indicated by the fact that Leibnitz, who was even more explicitly a spiritual pluralist than Berkeley, is the source from which recent "realism" has drawn much of its inspiration). Spiritual Monism is the doctrine that there is a single, impersonal, but spiritual force manifesting itself in all things. Its representatives, as discussed by Hoernlé, are Schopenhauer and Bergson. The character of critical idealism speaks for itself in its association with the name of Kant, though it must be admitted that Kant hardly spoke clearly for himself. Hegel is considered as the author of Absolute Idealism, and Bradley and Bosanquet as its modern representatives.

It is impossible in a review to follow the author into his specific accounts, and criticisms of these different thinkers, although this material forms the substance of the book and is the source of its instructive and enlightening qualities. Suffice it to say that Hoernlé has himself adopted the method he commends to his readers. He has employed the methods and results of the authors selected as models for the development of personal expertness and insight; as the reader traverses the ground in his company as guide, the latter cannot fail, if he is willing to do more thinking than is necessary to absorb a best seller, to gain something of these traits for himself.

The chapters which seem to me to be the best are those on Berkeley and Bosanquet, the latter being written with the ardor, I will not say of discipleship, but of profoundly sympathetic appreciation and acceptance. The chapters likely to be found least satisfactory at least by followers of those philosophies are those about Schopenhauer and Bergson. Hoernlé's understanding rarely fails him, but these authors probably have more to say in connection with their critic's main objection, namely, that the derivation of the diversity of detail in actual phenomena from the one single force is not exhibited, than is recognized; indeed, what is accounted the defect in them is attributed to Bosanquet as a merit, namely, "that we must perceive as actual the distinctions which give life its content." And since the dialectic movement by which Hegel undertook precisely the derivation missing in them is explicitly rejected by Hoernlé, and since Hegel also taught that "the universe is a single spirit of whom or of which all appearances are manifestations," it would seem as if the distinction between Spiritual Monism and Absolute Idealism does not lie just where Hoernlé would put it. Reading between the lines, one finds, I think, that the superiority of Hegel and his followers lies in Hoernlé's eyes in the greater attention of the latter to the logic of thought and in their greater appreciation of the great human institutions of art, religion and the State, which are to them the culminating manifestations of the "one absolute spirit." At all events it is Hoernlé's sympathetic appreciation of these factors which is the finally distinguishing trait of his exposition, critical and constructive.

Mr. Hoernlé, in addition to his ardor in expounding Bosanquet, dedicates the book to his memory. It is fitting that with this review of Hoernlé's own work there should be associated a brief notice to the posthumous collection of Bosanquet's own essays. Hoernlé remarks that Bosanquet drew "from philosophical tradition, from science, from literature, from art (he wrote a history of esthetic doctrines), from social work (he was long actively concerned with the activities of the London Charity Organization), from Politics and religion." This statement is amply confirmed by the volume of collected essays. The editors have classified the material under three main heads, "Logic and Metaphysics" (headed by the essay from which the volume takes its title); "Ethical, Social and Political," "Esthetics." This intimation of a broad range is more than carried out when one looks at the actual material. Inspection justifies the prefatory statement of the editors that "few, if any, of the philosophical writers of his own time can show work of the same range." The editors are also justified in their suggestion that in spite of the diversity of subjects included in the volume, the opening essay holds them together in spirit. For it is a plea for extending the scope and jurisdiction of philosophy to whatever has value for man, to whatever gives "satisfactoriness" to objects, especially to those values of beauty and the good which since the time of Plato have been traditionally included in philosophy along with truth. This view is worked out in contrast to the assertion of Bertrand Russell that philosophy is legitimately concerned only with propositions which like those of mathematics would hold good of all abstractly possible worlds, and that the difference between good and bad, the beautiful and ugly, would not appear in such a purely logical subject matter.

Aside from his positive argument for including within the range of philosophical reflection all the great objects of man's enduring interests, he criticizes Russell's position on the ground that the latter concludes from the fact that philosophy is a theoretical interest that its subject matter must be theoretical—a neat turning against Russell of the criticism he once made of pragmatism, that of arguing as if he who drives fat oxen must himself be fat; though perhaps in this case we should substitute "lean"! His other objection is that you find out what philosophy is only in the course of philosophy, that you can't adequately frame a problem till you know something about the answer, while Russell sets up an antecedent and hence arbitrary limitation prior to philosophizing itself. A possible retort, to the effect that the course of philosophizing itself exhibits the futility and waste involved in any other conception of philosophy than that which Russell advances, is not considered, save by an intimation that Hegel and its followers have demonstrated the opposite. Bosanquet's essays will hardly appeal to as wide an audience as will Hoernlé's skillful guidance through the mazes of idealistic thought, but it will command the attention of professed idealists and of students who approach philosophy from other than the idealistic angle.

The Integration of a Moving World

Purposive Evolution: The Link between Science and Religion by Edmund Noble. New York: Henry Holt and Company, 1926.

Mr. Noble's important book holds together like the universe he writes of. It is not easy to select a passage which, in isolation from its context, sums up its main idea. The following passage is, however, representative: "So far as concrete Nature problems are concerned, the aim of the relational philosophy is to unify the self-maintaining organism with the self-maintaining universe, to revise the theory of natural selection with such an account of the internal factors of organic development as shall separate the process by which intelligent adaptations are accumulated from the process by which they are originated; to universalize so-called 'intelligence' by showing it to be primarily neither a conscious nor even an organic process, but a process rooted in the very nature of power; and finally . . . to derive all organic and inorganic characters—characters of form, characters of motion, characters of mind—from their fountain and source, the power system, the Purposive Universe." Thus the subject-matter of the work is broader than its title. The characteristic thing is the derivation of evolution from the character of the universe conceived as power. "Neither vitality nor consciousness can be traced to really ultimate units: they imply and require collectivity."

It is perhaps a safe guess that Mr. Noble's point of departure was the philosophy of Herbert Spencer. In one aspect, his work may be regarded as Spencer brought down to date and rendered coherent. The task of rendering him coherent is, however, no job of external revision and supplementation. It involves radical revision; not quantitative excision and addition, but a qualitative change which has eliminated surds and wrought a relational mo-

[First published in *New Republic* 51 (1927): 22–24.]

nism. One might find a clue to Mr. Noble's thought in its transformation of "relativity" into relatedness. To Spencer—as, upon
the whole, in the entire historic doctrine of relativity—relations
are a kind of blot and blur upon the face of the absolute; a veil
which comes between us and "reality," a veil which not only conceals but distorts. His was a doctrine of a profound dualism
which terminated inevitably in an equally profound agnosticism.
To Mr. Noble, relatedness, universal and thorough-going, is of
the very nature of things; knowledge is relational not because of
some twist or limitation of the mind, but because mind developing in a related world can operate only in terms of the relations
upon which it depends and which form its proper objects.
"Things conform to us for all the superficial elements of knowledge; for all its fundamental characters knowledge conforms to
things." Knowledge is of the universe itself, and in both senses of
"of"; as proceeding from it, its own doing, and as directed toward and fulfilled in it.

Method and style remind one also of Spencer. Spencer's greatest ability was the power to bring facts together from regions apparently unlike and exhibit them as versions of a common principle. Mr. Noble has an extraordinary command of this device.
His learning is vast, and draws upon widely diversified fields. As
he finds that the basic categories of the universe are likeness and
difference, with likeness so dominating the differences which
lead to change and motion as to result in enduring forms and
structures, so the marshaling of facts outwardly different in
order to elicit an underlying identity is characteristic of his
method. Spencer's marshaling of data drawn from all sources
often leaves me with the impression that, having made his formula, he fits his facts into ready-made pigeon-holes. With Mr.
Noble, I feel that the unification is intrinsic; it is the material
which organizes itself, and Mr. Noble's power is that of perceiving and reporting the organization which is already there. Hence
his volume presents a massive and solid structure which puts
much contemporary philosophizing to shame. Mr. Noble's style
also possesses Spencer's knack of recurrent and cumulative
effect. But his presentation is free from Spencer's inflation and
pomposity.

The idea of relatedness accounts for the frequent opposition
drawn by Mr. Noble between "self-sourced" and "system-

sourced." Putting the matter schematically, the idea which pervades his book is that nothing, whether physical, vital or psychical and mental, is explained until it has been traced back to the fundamental traits of the universe itself, while our errors and fallacies come from isolating a particular subject-matter. "Everywhere the absolute method is the method of ignoring the dependence of the individual object, the single process, on the sum of processes, the system of objects; the relational method is everywhere the method of viewing objects and processes in the light of the totality of objects and processes."

As I have just said, the statement is schematic; it gives only the formula, and as the statement isolates the formula it cannot help being false to it. It is the evidence adduced for the formula and the latter's illuminating application to a variety of perplexing problems which renders Mr. Noble's volume significant. For that reason, I ask the reader to look at this review as bearing much the same relation to the book that a city directory bears to the life of the city. As a substitute, it is as worthless as it is dull. But if a person wants to find out where somebody lives so as to come into direct and actual contact with him, a directory is a very useful thing. And I can but hope that these statements—although an incomplete directory—may guide readers to consult the full statement.

My index will confine itself to the structural skeleton. The universe as a power system is self-maintaining. Space is the extension of power; not, as in the traditional view, an empty vessel which holds things as a pan contains separate peas. Power constitutes space. Its dynamic character as extensive is primarily ether; "ether" is somewhat out of scientific vogue at present. But unless nature is to fall to pieces, any theory must acknowledge some universal linkage in virtue of which the whole pervades the units and the system dominates its members. The universe as power makes time, which is not a container of changes but the changes themselves as dominated by the unity which is manifest in extension. Change implies differences; power manifests itself as stress and re-stress, so that nature is characterized by number. These three basic "categories" explain the conservation of matter and energy, which are not ultimate laws or facts but manifestations of the domination of all changes and units by the whole. "The summated potencies of the universe must be conceived as a power reflowing to the units as a power of conservation." The differential character of energy is exhibited as matter, which is derived from ether under conditions of unequal stresses, which bring about everywhere a cooperation of antagonism. Matter and change are thus correlative.

Power as likeness is the equalized stress or *constitutive* energy termed ether. Matter as differential, or difference, is a state of unequalized stresses which, because of the self-maintaining character of power, tend toward equalization. The tendency is motion, energy in its *kinetic* mode. The domination of the power system in effecting equalization forms rhythm, which is manifested in uniformities of succession and also tends to repetition and uniformity of positions and collocations, to those symmetries manifest in uniformities of extension. Evolution is but the generalization of the character of changes; the "law" of evolution but an expression of the universal mode of all changes in their movement toward equalization of stresses. But differential stresses are equalized only when enduring forms, structures, positions, configurations, relationships, are established. The universe is teleological and "intelligent" in the sense that processes of change go on until they terminate in forms which are internally and externally "adapted," stable and enduring, because fitted in their environment—ultimately the whole system. Interchange, action and reaction, are mechanical when viewed piece-meal; as isolated sequences. In relation to the whole system, or viewed in their integral tendency toward terminal forms which endure because they are interadapted, they are teleological. Resort to special design in nature generally, and to *specific* agencies, vital force, the entelechies of Driesch, etc., in relation to living creatures, is made necessary only by absolutistic isolation of changes from the self-maintaining nature of the universe as power.

An organism bears the same relation to a particular set of changes, those which form life, that the universe sustains to all changes. "The universe is concerned, so to speak, only in conserving power; the organism is concerned in conserving itself, and therefore in conserving all those appliances and processes which it must develop as means to self-maintenance." "What characterizes life activities is thus not 'vital force,' nor yet the physicochemical properties of the molecules engaged, but the power of the all-imposing collective character over each." Thus there is interdependence of structure and process. The organism determines what the directions of least and greatest stress shall be within its own processes. It thus exercises control over them and insures that its structures operate in ways which are ways to ends. Natural selection does not account for the origin of favorable variations nor for their cumulative development in a serviceable direction. When it is used to explain useful adaptations, it shows a "naïve substitution of the results of fitness for the causes of fitness"—the external process of elimination cannot give rise to that "which is left untouched by elimination." The use-advantage which variations exhibit before they are structurally valuable for survival is that of saving energy expended in efforts at self-maintenance. Some difficulty operates to set up a condition of differential stress so that variations are in the direction of minimizing tension. As a self-maintainer, the organism has a set toward everything that is useful for life. Since its self-maintenance can occur only through making use of the environing medium, its variations must, upon the whole, be adaptive. In a universe which contains light and a mobile organism whose self-maintenance depends upon relations to distant conditions, it would be more surprising if the latter did not develop sensitive responsiveness to light than it is that eyes appear. Once started on that route, it pushes every attained advantage to its extreme and sees the job through.

Conscious mind is a further exemplification of the same principle. The universe does not manifest inter-adaptation because presided over by conscious mind; I know of no critical examination of arguments from design, and the various ways of anthropomorphizing and psychologizing nature, as destructively searching as that contained in the first part of Mr. Noble's work. But a universe that maintains itself by directing its changes toward enduring forms is one in which intelligence becomes consciously cognizant of the medium in which it lives. A highly complex motile organism has to make constantly novel responses, no two of which are alike, and, as organization cares for uniform and recurrent relationships, "consciousness is of the sudden, irregular, the unaccustomed"; it works in the direction of finer discrimination. Thus consciousness is not the source and basis of mind, but rather its mobile apex.

In this bare directory, many points of great interest have been entirely passed over, and those probably the points of greatest interest for many readers. The development of Mr. Noble's theme in reference to social life is one of these fields; his treatment of esthetic experience, especially of the functions of rhythm and symmetry in works of art, and of religious experience, must at least be alluded to. His philosophy is genuinely "synthetic" in a sense more profound than Spencer's. He begins with a consideration of our present crisis in science and religion, due to the fact that "man has lost his grip on things which he had when we knew them less and believed in them more." It is a crisis in which religion is pale and defensive because its intellectual basis has been identified with an anthropomorphic view which science has made impossible, and in which science is piece-meal and divisive because it has retained the isolating absolutism of primitive mind, and indeed, in its specializations confined to piece-meal views, has exaggerated its disintegrative tendency until the "mechanical" relations of nature are the only bond it acknowledges. To an extraordinary degree, Mr. Noble's work responds to the demand for unity and wholeness, and in a way which is free from the injection of those subjective factors which have infected most modern philosophic schemes of unification.

I cannot close without expressing my deep admiration for Mr. Noble's work. Mr. Noble is not a professional—or professorial— philosopher. And I hope that academic cliquishness will not militate against his work's receiving the attention which it richly deserves. There is some danger that it is too philosophic for professional scientists and too scientific for professional philosophers, especially as the tide of scientific interest in contemporary philosophy sets in the direction of mathematics, and of mathematics divorced from the world of actuality in which Mr. Noble justly places space, time and number. It is no slight achievement to point out the road by which philosophy can integrate mathematical characters with physical and vital things and relations. And that is but one aspect of the task which he has accomplished, and an aspect incidental to his main purpose. He has pointed the road which will restore to man the sense of living in an integrated world. Whatever the immediate reception of the book, Mr. Noble's work will endure; it is a noble and solid exemplification of his own theme that the stress of differences tends toward enduring form and configuration.

Science, Folk-lore and Control of Folk-ways

Science: The False Messiah by C. E. Ayres. Indianapolis: The Bobbs-Merrill Company, 1927.

Since this book can hardly be reviewed without mentioning its provocative character, I shall say at the outset that the book is a highly provoking one. To traditionalists, whether they be such in science or in religion, the provocation will take the form of irritation, but, I fancy, of an irritation which will find little public expression. Silence is the part of discretion; both because all the king's horses and all the king's men cannot put together the Humpty-Dumptys of cultured superstition which Mr. Ayres has so genially dropped from off their wall of high prestige, and because public notice might call the attention of others to the smash of idols. But in those not hopelessly committed, the book will awaken searchings of heart and mind. Rarely in one book have so many glittering bubbles been so deftly and, in style, so delightfully pricked. Indeed, at times the brilliance and wit of form almost conceal the solidity of substance underneath.

For Mr. Ayres knows his stuff, as the saying goes; and his stuff is philosophy, anthropology and current sociological theorizing. Two ideas borrowed from anthropology dominate the presentation. Civilization consists of folk-lore and folk-ways. This is as true now as it ever was. The notion that we have now, in principle at least, outgrown folk-lore, and have institutions and constitutions instead of folk-ways, is a fantasy. Only content has changed. Customary ways of belief and behavior remain, the one believed and the other practised by the mass of people simply because they are customary, while gathering to themselves the glamor and idealized authority which enable customs to be first endured and then cherished. As far as humanity at large is con-

[First published in *New Republic* 52 (1927): 316–17.]

cerned, the attitude toward science is the same as the earlier attitude toward that which enlightened persons now regard as
mythology and magic:

Oh, let us never, never doubt
What no one can be sure about.

This statement does not mean that science does not have its
own solid basis and claims—among practitioners of science. But
as Mr. Ayres remarks, they were men before they were scientists.
When they come out of the laboratory and observatory, they frequently leave their physical apparatus and mechanical appliances behind them, mentally as well as bodily. They then treat
science as a revelation, and, like all revelations, as offering a gospel of salvation for the ills of mankind. Science then becomes for
them, as well as for the passive populace, a body of folk-lore. In
reality, the history of science is the history of the invention and
use of machines and of a technique, as marvelous as it is elaborate, for employing tools. The machine is the reality of science;
theoretical interpretation may or may not be true; in the end, the
answer is read in some machine more delicate, precise and more
skilfully used than the machine which furnished the material on
which other theories were based. The verifiability of scientific
conclusions signifies that they do not stand alone. They are made
possible by machines, and anyone who operates the machines in
a designated way will get like results.

But science ends as well as begins in machines. Machine technology and industrial civilization are the significant products of
science. These products determine the folk-ways of the civilization in which we live. Whatever the resistance of old folk-ways to
invention and new methods, the lure of the tool is finally com-
pelling. Some immediate utility draws men to its adoption. Beliefs, traditions, ideals, meet almost insuperable direct barriers to
diffusion among alien cultures. Technical material traits find
easier acceptance, and do so largely under the illusion that they
will merely serve some directly felt need, leaving other things, especially the cherished body of folk-ways and lore, intact. Ulterior results are wholly unexpected; men lived for a long time in
the new industrial era, with all its political and intellectual alterations, without suspecting that anything had occurred except
an improvement in methods of spinning and weaving—just as

many people still seem to suppose that the railway and motor-
car portend only easier and more rapid locomotion, and regard
those who call attention to certain other effects as dangerous
radicals instigated by some sinister personal motive. Or, beyond
the immediate utility, the invention is celebrated as a theme for
hymns to progress. In reality, eventual changes in folk-ways are
so extensive that, if men had realized them at the outset, they
would have seemed so devastating that cursing and destruction
would have been their lot.

The new consequences in which science, itself born of respect
for machines as ultimate arbiters of truth about nature, bore
fruit are commonly termed the industrial revolution. But as it is
the nature of science to breed new science, so it is the nature of
machinery to generate new forms of machinery. It is a recurrence
of the old illusion of the eternal stability of what is customary
that makes us regard the present era as stable; we are in the first
act of the drama, not at its climax; it may be doubted whether
the industrial revolution has begun. Anyway, it has not, as yet,
begun to have its way with us, for our institutions, and largely,
our beliefs, are still medieval. The result is a hybrid; our present
civilization is marked by an internal conflict greater than any experienced in any culture of the past. The forces which control
our folk-ways are at odds with those which regulate our folk-
lore, and with the conditions under which folk-ways operate. We
live in a period of dissolution.

Such is the groundwork of the book, too summarily stated.
The rest is a diagnosis, without much prognosis, of the resulting
state of science and philosophy, of intellectual and "spiritual"
life. "The onset of mechanical civilization is the great divide. It is
not a meander in the rivers of civilized life. It is another water-
shed." "Machinery begins by altering the day's routine and ends
by altering the cosmos." Such a pervasive and irresistible influence cannot be quarantined; it cannot be kept isolated in a realm
of business and commerce which does not touch the rest of life.
Mr. Ayres is especially concerned to point out its bearing upon
the state of men's beliefs, and especially upon the idea of science
as the authentic fountain-head of truth. For if "science" is ready
to take credit for improvements and progress, it is also subject to
blame not only as the author of the flagrant evils of our industrial life, but even more of the undermining of the ideas and ide-

als which are the intellectual framework of our traditional religion, morals and politics.

The limits of a review do not permit me to trace in any detail the features of Mr. Ayres' diagnosis. It must suffice to say that he indicates two stages, in the first of which science was "meek and mild," presenting apologies, being concerned to show that its methods and conclusions were safe because in harmony with at least the essential spirit of traditional folk-lore; while in the latter stage it tends to "take command," and be presented as the agency of a steady and systematic progress of humanity by means of a control of nature and society, through knowledge of the truth. With respect to the first point, I confine myself to saying that I am not acquainted with any other account so searching and convincing of the ingenious, but not ingenuous, devices by which it has been sought to sustain an old system of beliefs in the face of methods and results utterly inconsistent with it. He applies his analysis to the intellectual insincerities and roundabout circuits of classic philosophers, as well as to the spiritual message and gospel said to be contained in the new scientific revelation. As for its promise of conducting mankind through the wilderness into the promised land, he points out that "science, if we overlook its importance for machine technology," so far consists of an elaborate apparatus for the display of intellectual curiosities, ending in conclusions which are indeed marvelous in precision and sweep, but yet inherently, for the mass of men, just curiosities. This is the aspect of mere folk-lore. The mysteries can be approached only by initiated adepts, and are accepted by the mass on authority, and because of the prestige of custom and fashion—a glamor which attaches equally to pseudo-science and which gives the latter even greater influence. Meanwhile the fundamental thing is that science delivers only means, instruments. It does not tell men for what ends the means should be used; toward aims and purposes, science maintains benevolent neutrality. "If we want to attain certain ends, science has nothing to say against it, and may be able to provide a vehicle." But social control, if it means anything, means control of the desires and purposes which move men to act—and with respect to them, science is not the driver who holds the reins; it is rather an accidental passenger.

A strictly just evaluation of the net worth of Mr. Ayres' brilliant discussion and penetrating analysis is not easy. For certain of his conclusions appear to be incidental, implied in the tone of his discussion. This is especially true of what seems its pessimistic strain. As an antidote to that easy optimism and supine complacency which is a marked trait of the present time (probably as a compensation, as a protection from realization of ills before which we are still impotent), his pages are well-nigh unrivalled. I do not see how any thoughtful person can demur to his main propositions. He says what is both true and needful to say in his criticisms; he seems to me profoundly correct in his statement of the nature of science, in its relation to tools and as itself a tool. It is well to acknowledge that science can "provide instruments of bringing about various effects never dreamed of before in the history of man. But to determine what had better happen or to oblige us to bring about salubrious effects, science is completely impotent." He is surely right in his perception that future history will be similar to past history: "one long uninterrupted series of crises and problems giving way to more problems and crises to be followed by further problems and crises." The notion of any "control" that will give automatic assurance against the recurrence of crises and problems, or that will provide automatic means for their resolution, is the idlest of fantasies. Each stage of human change, even of betterment, will bring with it, on its own level, its own evils and difficulties; of that fact there can be no doubt.

Yet there are certain considerations, which Mr. Ayres passes over lightly, that must yet be taken into account in a complete reckoning. That the civilization of any period will always be an affair of folk-lore and folk-ways is true enough; it is even truistic. From it, however, as from many truisms, important consequences follow, and these consequences Mr. Ayres has brilliantly exhibited in uncovering the source and nature of many current illusions. But there seems to be also an undercurrent of disparagement of any achievement and trait of civilization just because it will be a phase of folk-lore or of folk-ways. Put so baldly, Mr. Ayres can justly deny holding any such view. But I do not find explicit recognition of the fact that the existence of folk-lore and folk-ways is consistent with an enormous difference in their quality; of the fact that even crises and problems are so affected by this difference that it is better to have them on one level than to be without them on some other plateau. And especially he seems to overlook the possibility that, when all is said and done, that which we must still call scientific *method* may affect the quality of future folk-lore. That, in detail, "science" signifies a highly technical apparatus, esoteric to the mass, is true enough. But there are generic attitudes, like those of facing facts, of analysis, of experimentation, of receiving conclusions hypothetically, which are radically opposed to the dispositions which have supported the folk-lore of the past. It is no easy task to incorporate these newer dispositions in the customary habits of thought and belief. Mr. Ayres supplies plenty of evidence that many scientists fail in so doing, the moment they touch matters of morals, religion and politics. But any implication that the task is hopeless implies an estimate of human nature which paralyzes human effort. Not only hope springs eternal in the human breast, but effort as well. That intelligence, the intelligence represented in scientific method, be incarnated in the ever-renewed springs of human desire and energy, is after all, the problem and crisis of present civilization.

It is true that science supplies instruments, and not the purposes and policies which rule action, and which root in the depths of desire. But the attitudes and general habits which mark scientific method may themselves become an increasingly intense object of desire on the part of an expanding public. And since desire and thought do not dwell apart in non-communicating compartments, the growth of intelligent habits will radiate and affect all other desires. When one considers how the "idealistic" desires of man have, in the past, been drafted into channels the issue of which was, in the end, confusion and error; how the ardent efforts of men have been frustrated by the irrelevance to actual conditions of ends proposed, and all because desire and purpose have been framed in terms aloof from all actual and possible instrumentalities, I find it impossible to believe that science, as the purveyor of instruments, and desire, as the well-spring of aims and ideals, are as insulated and non-interacting as the tenor of Mr. Ayres' discussion seems to imply. Hence I venture to think that Mr. Ayres' searching and convincing criticisms do not plot a new road to a new kind of ivory tower, but state the urgent problem of present civilization in a way which, to those who understand, will be a stimulant and a directive in effort, a clarifier and a purge of desire and purpose.

Things, Thought, Conversation

Possibility by Scott Buchanan. Harcourt, Brace and Company, 1927.

Dialectic by Mortimer Adler. Harcourt, Brace and Company, 1927.

It is customary, I believe, for a reviewer to speak of a first book by a new author as promising. The promise contained in Mr. Buchanan's book is based on solid achievement. It is more than an earnest and pledge of something to come; it is itself a significant intellectual achievement. It provides one of those simplifications of a complicated and far-reaching problem that when once it is made causes one to wonder why it has not been done before, especially as the history of thought is now seen to contain so many and so near approaches to it.

The simplification proceeds from envisaging many (I am tempted to say all) philosophical problems as concerned at their root with the question of the relation of actuality and possibility: an insight that gains added significance when joined with the perception that the predicaments and entanglements of living have their source in the same remarkable intersection of direct and imaginative experience.

"One lives," as the author says, "in one world and believes in another, suffering this and at the same time expecting or desiring that." We are caught in what is actual, but in every such entrapment there is the sense of something beyond, something more and something different—of possibilities. The too usual procedure is to try to live in each world separately and by turns. The philosophic temper consists in an endeavor to see them together in a single perspective. To attain to this vision is to have in one's possession "an organon of intellectual imagination."

The book is a contribution to the formation of such a method, by means of a consideration of the operation of the idea of pos-

[First published in *Nation* 126 (1928): 449–50.]

sibility in three fields: artistic creation, science, and metaphysics. The reach of the simplification effected by Mr. Buchanan is manifested in his seeing the fact that the relation of the actual and the possible is involved equally in art, science, and metaphysics. The upshot is that unreal barriers which commonly divide these three fields, to our intellectual confusion, are broken down. A single method or logic that is operative in all of them is revealed.

As to the first of the three fields, the basic idea of Mr. Buchanan is introduced by means of a distinction between aesthetic form and imaginative form. The former is concerned with content, with the materials of the work of art, which may be the same in an epic or a drama or a novel. Imaginative form consists of certain structures which are universal; the actual subject matter in relation to these forms is, to use his mathematical simile, like the relation which values introduced into a formula bear to a system of variables. This structure of connected and consistent possibilities gives true intellectual form to a work of art; it is similar in kind to the function of hypothesis and theory in science. A novel that is a work of art "spreads a vast canvas of possibility on which actual affairs may be projected and seen in perspective." There are logical compatibilities in the relations of the possibilities presented which have to be observed and displayed as truly as in a scientific project. The subordination of actual details to the intrinsic logic of these possibilities measures the degree of intellectual form achieved. The immense scope of the realm of possibilities decrees that there may be an immense variety of artistic creations—provided each is true to the pattern of relations among possibilities imposed by its own type.

It is in virtue of the coherent, or logical, relations involved in any structure of possibilities that elements of imagination become symbols of the actual so as to be capable of truth and falsity. When we pass from enjoyment of the canvas of possibilities, with the actual figures and scenes it contains, to the status of possibility as applied to the actual and as tested by the application, we move from art to science. "When imaginative or aesthetic possibility takes on responsibility, it becomes scientific." Any scientific construction, like any work of art, projects a set of actual existences upon a canvas of possibilities; the latter, since they are possibilities, are connected with imagination rather than with observation. "Facts" in isolation from the system of ordered possibilities are a heap of scraps rather than a science. The difference between art and science lies not in the presence or absence of this imaginative form, but in its testing by application, in which it is discovered whether the possibilities are capable of symbolizing the actualities in question, and in the special care taken with the interrelations of the elements of the structure of possibility. These must present, first, a set of constants that represent the conditions to be met; second, a field of variations or a class of particulars; and third, a rule of order or set of relations defining the co-variations in this field. In so far we have a formal or mathematical science. This is changed into physical or existential science when the structure of possibilities is employed to describe some actual individual. It is true or "real" in so far as it then symbolizes some actual state of affairs. The fallacy which so often enters into the interpretation of science consists in taking this intellectual or theoretical form to exist, or to be a part of actuality, in the same sense as are the things which it is used to symbolize. Such a view converts symbols into things symbolized, a structure of possibilities into a physical fact. The worth of theoretic apparatus depends not upon its being itself existent but upon its *applicability* to actualities.

Discussion passes into the metaphysical realm when the problem of the relation of possibility to actuality is envisaged in its general form. Possibility sometimes means power, potency, this being displayed in the region of the concrete and actual; and sometimes it means intellectual or logical possibility, with the coherences and consistencies therein involved. Confusion of the two senses has played havoc with metaphysics; for it often takes advantage of the ambiguity to identify actual potentiality in existence with a system of ideal possibility. Idealistic metaphysics is a typical case of this confusion. Realistic systems are often involved in the same confusion, but in the opposite sense. They treat logical possibilities as part of the system of physical or psychical actuality. Mr. Buchanan has here provided us with a keen weapon of philosophic criticism, so keen that one almost wonders at the restraint with which he employs it.

This notice hardly covers more than the first half of the book. But it may give the reader some inkling of why Mr. Buchanan is to be congratulated on having done a first-class piece of much needed intellectual work. My mind recurs to the idea of simplification and clarification. Doubtless debate will long go on regarding the relation of real and ideal, thought and things, essence and existence, in connection with morals, science, the theory of knowledge, and metaphysics. But reduction of the issues to the one central issue of the relation of the actual and the possible is a liberating achievement. Even those who do not accept Mr. Buchanan's proposals and conclusions should find his method a solvent of many ambiguities and an eliminator of many confusing irrelevancies. There is meat in the book for immediate consumption; it offers seeds with which to sow many a flourishing intellectual garden.

Mr. Adler's book is also published in the valuable and growing International Library of Psychology, Philosophy, and Scientific Method. The jackets of the two books suggest they should be read in conjunction, and each has a number of cross-references to the other. Mr. Adler's book, in spite of its many interesting suggestions, does not seem to me to move quite on the plane of the other. It is concerned with an important practical problem, the conduct of fruitful dispute, of intellectual conversation about some question in controversy or at least in doubt. It is an attempt to analyze the logic of this universally recurring situation so as to state the conditions under which controversial discussion may contribute to enlightenment. To my mind the chief defects of the analysis spring from the attempt to mark off too fixedly the field of dispute and its logic from that of empirical inquiry on the one hand and the logic of mathematics on the other. His statement that "empirical or scientific thinking has received thorough formulation" is a surprising one. I should have said that the logic bearing on such thinking is thoroughly infected with uncertainty and controversy; there is not even any agreed-upon theory as to the nature and basis of induction. His statement is made incidentally, to be sure, but it exhibits the ground on which alone Mr. Adler can differentiate as rigidly as he has done the field of controversy from that of empirical inquiry. It underlies his basic thesis that appeal to fact is irrelevant to dialectic, or the logic of controversy. There is a sense in which this is formally true; but surely one fruit of dialectic, and its most precious one, is not mere clarification of ideas but the kind of clarification which makes evident what sort of facts are to be looked for and how and where to search for them in order to settle the matter under dispute. If criticism were made from the side of empirical logic it would take the form of saying that doubt and rival possible interpretations are as much a part of scientific inquiry as they are of social debate.

In consequence, the reviewer has found the most significant part of Mr. Adler's book in what he refers to as "very much the least important" of its three parts, namely, the empirical description of argumentative dispute. Here we have an account of language and the complications involved in its use, and a statement of the obstructions in human nature to effective and fruitful discussion, together with suggestions as to how these difficulties may be reduced and natural barriers surmounted. This section is full of shrewd observations and helpful insights; the book was well worth writing for its sake alone. The more formal portion, and that which Mr. Adler seems most to prize, suffers, to my mind, from too much borrowing from mathematical logic, in spite of the distinction theoretically set up between it and the logic of dispute. Were it not for the sharp barrier instituted between dialectic and the method of empirical inquiry, the polemic element would not be so emphasized. It would, in fact, when the personal and emotional element of strife and desire for victory is eliminated, reduce itself to that consciousness of possible alternatives which is present in all thinking. In an interesting chapter Mr. Adler presents the idea that the genuine subject matter of philosophy is the realm of possibilities and that therefore its method is dialectic. He says in this connection many significant and true things about philosophy and philosophies, but here also he seems to me to turn an isolation of the realm of ideas which is a necessary preliminary to a consideration of its relation to the actual world into an unnecessarily fixed separation. Unless the latter question is somewhere faced, philosophies are but logically organized fantasies, and one is superior to another only with respect to its internal coherence.

Both books are evidence of growing vitality and independence on the part of the younger American philosophers. They will stand critical comparison with the best European contributions to the library in which they appear. The editor of the series merits grateful recognition for the independence he shows in the selection of material and writers and for his willingness to give new writers a chance to find an audience.

The Way to Think

The Art of Thinking by Ernest Dimnet. New York: Simon and Schuster, 1928.

Some books lend themselves to reviewing; they seem made for that purpose even more than to read. Abbé Dimnet's little book is not one of these. He gives ferments rather than recipes; he has practiced the art of thinking until its product is itself a work of art. Before a work of art one is likely to be dumb or to indulge only in ejaculations; and when asked why one likes it, to reply "Go and see for yourself." That is the way I feel about this genial and witty book. I would say to the reader "Taste it, try it for yourself. Keep it close at hand, read a page or two, a paragraph, opening at random. Browse about in it; read it consecutively. Keep it on a bedside table and read it to compose your mind at night and to arouse it in the morning." And in answer to the question "Why?" the best reply I can make is still "Try it and see." For the book is compact with the wisdom gathered in years of observation of himself and of others.

The reader finds in it suggestions of ways by which to estimate the quality of his own thinking. The suggestions probe deep, and unless one is willing to face himself he would do better to confine himself to the easier task of checking the list of qualities in some efficiency chart. The reader finds also an account of the causes that have produced a decline in native turn for genuine thought—for all normal children up to ten years of age or so, can think, because they see for themselves. And after the diagnosis of disease, there are remedies provided, "Helps to Thinking." One may at first be disappointed in finding the secret of the entire art put in a sentence: "The Art of Thinking is the art of being oneself." But if one comes back to the book often enough, and if after tasting frequently one absorbs and digests, that one will, I am confident, find in his interpretation of the sentence a

[First published in *Saturday Review of Literature* 5 (1928): 423.]

revelation of himself that will lead him, if he will only permit it to do so, to serener intellectual heights than he has known.

There are at least a dozen of suggestions offered, any one of which, if taken, will lead to improvements of mental habitudes. Among them are "conjuring up a suitable background"; reading only what gives the greatest pleasure; going repeatedly over what one already knows, and so on. But the point that I think I cherish most highly is that Abbé Dimnet has had the courage to insist on the connection between capacity of thinking and the qualities that are usually called moral. He does not preach, but no one can read the book in the spirit in which he recommends that every book should be read, and not realize that sluggishness, parasitical dependence upon others, slackness of taste, and similar defects of character cause more deficiences of mind than do lacks that are distinctly intellectual in origin. If there are those fortunate enough not to need any of the counsels that the author gives, I still urge them to read the book if only to make the acquaintance of an experienced and deeply wise personality.

Politics and Human Beings

Man and the State by William Ernest Hocking.
New Haven: Yale University Press, 1926.

The Science and Method of Politics by G. E. G.
Catlin. New York: Alfred A. Knopf, 1927.

It is not easy to give a just account and estimate of Professor Hocking's book. The work is too rich and varied in contents for that. With no parade of learning, it is informed with great scholarship. Knowledge extends not only to the diversity of theory which complicates historic political philosophy, but to political events past and contemporary. While Mr. Hocking is a clear and vigorous writer, his plan calls for a certain diffuseness of treatment. Like a good teacher, he raises certain issues, suggests certain tentative conclusions, returns to the main problems with added material, introduces new material and opposed conceptions, makes his original suggestions more definite, and so on. These pedagogical traits which make for the education of the reader—provided he is willing to do some thinking as he reads—do not conduce to a summarized review. The attempt to present an outline results, more than is usually the case, in producing a skeleton which lacks the flesh and blood of the original.

In fine, the book is a presentation of the theory of the state which derives from the doctrines of German idealism, especially Hegel, which see in the state an externalization of will and reason. But the idealistic account is edited in a modern version. There is no recourse, in form, to the Absolute. The start is made from psychological conceptions and empirical material and without at any point exhibiting overt resort to metaphysical considerations. Yet the latter remain, to my mind, the sources of the ultimate premises. One who, like the present writer, accepts a different philosophy, can only say that, given the premises, Mr. Hocking has presented the conclusions in the form least re-

[First published in *New Republic* 50 (1927): 114–15.]

pellent, most seductive, to modern empirical ideas—or prejudices, if you will.

His general formula is: "The form of the state's aim is the making of history; its substance is the making of men." History-making has two phases, the "commotive," by which the diverse impulses of men are brought into united purpose and action, making and remaking of groups; and "term-making," the arbitrative process of the judiciary and of legislation. The state, as the fullest and widest interpenetration of promoter and adjuster, is the maker of history. What is common to both functions is survey and revision of bare impulse by reflection, which, in introducing a common purpose, unifies, generalizes and renders permanent. Thus the commotive process takes the form of will, and the term-making the form of reason. Because men have to think about their manifold group-life as a *whole*, the outcome is the state, the objectified purpose and reason of men.

Here, implicitly, is the first of the unexamined fundamental premises, the idea of a necessary, inclusive and dominating totality. The point of view necessarily makes Hocking hostile to the theories which put emphasis upon groups, and which conceive the state as one among many forms of grouping. But I cannot see that, at bottom, his adverse criticisms rest upon anything more than an assumption of comprehensive totality. The assumption becomes explicit in his treatment of the purpose of the state. Here, too, the argument rests upon the unquestioned premise of monism. It is not enough to discover the functions actually exercised by states. These, according to him, are but fragments of a single unifying aim, which must be brought to light if we are to understand the state. Because of the all-inclusive character of the state and the oneness of its purpose, the state is the source and guarantee of all that is valid and valuable in every form of social life. The state is "a permanent order, an available storehouse of acquired wisdom, the conquest of disorder by peace, and of chance by impersonal reason and justice."

An empiricist, of a cynical turn, might remark that waging war instead of conquest by peace, and the maintenance and the interests of one class at the expense of those of other classes, rather than impartial justice, have been in fact the most characteristic phenomena of states. But it may at least be urged that Mr. Hocking exhibits an unrestrained tendency to assume that all values due to all forms of association, when they are reflected upon, are the work of the state. Thus, in relation to all other grouping, he says that the state is the means of making permanent all those which should, in the eye of reason, be permanent, and transient all those which ought to pass. He says that the emancipation of individuals from the overweening claims of special groups is the deed of the state. "The evolution of the state . . . makes individuals aware of themselves as ultimate denominators of all social groups." The conclusion follows logically from the assumptions of totality and monistic unity. Its agreement with facts is another matter. It is certainly arguable that the consequences of value which Hocking attributes to the state may be ascribed to other social conditions which have produced both modern states and the goods upon which he rightly sets store. The idea that forces, ultimately non-political, have generated states, groups and the liberation of individuals is certainly simpler than Hocking's imputation of all results to the state.

That the making of men is the substance of the state's aim is a conclusion reached largely on psychological grounds, involving the same premise of unity and totality. The "quest for power" is the fundamental and unifying thing in human nature. It is an instinct which is in all instincts. It is vital impetus itself; the craving for potency is life. Power is also part of every good end which the operation of the will to power achieves. But the will demands a permanent effect, and this can be secured only through a circuit of individual wills which gives unity and comprehensiveness—once more the state.

In conclusion, it should be said that Mr. Hocking's purpose is not the adulation of the state per se. Ultimate emphasis falls upon individuals. Each individual is a "micro-state." The state is the indispensable means of their realization of themselves, and as an indispensable means it is also an integral part of their achievement of themselves. Whether or not the underlying import of the Hegelian theory was to justify the power of the national state, the charge cannot be brought against Hocking. Rather, I should say, possessed of a philosophy which demands an objectified reason and will, he fastens upon the state to meet the specification.

Mr. Catlin's book is brilliantly written. Brilliance, however, implies reflection from a surface, while his account of the problem and method of a science of politics has depth and reach. His purpose is pragmatic, as Hocking's is not. He is not concerned with what the state *is* in essence and external idea, but with the question of how men are to control political forces for their good instead of being hurried by them to evil and catastrophe. The problem of control is central in his entire treatment. It leads him to commence with a discussion of the nature of history. For "to know History is to control power," and "History is the movement of all moving things and the knowledge of this movement; it is cognised change." Only as we know this movement, we are in a position to control that phase of the movement in which we are directly implicated. Otherwise, the moving situation fatally controls us. Knowledge of the relations of cause and effect in the historical world can alone save us from living in a dream-world. In the latter, consequences are taken as the results of wishes; in the historical world, he who wills the end must will the means.

Mr. Catlin then engages in a truly brilliant criticism of the various schools of history-writing: accumulation of facts, the humanistic treatment, subdivided into the homiletic and literary, the immersion or re-living theory of Croce, the Hegelian philosophy, the "scientific" historians. He then considers the general contrast of the utilitarian and poetic treatments of history. From each species he derives its contributing factor. He does full justice to the poetic and religious treatment of history—only the result is poetry and religious experience, not history, immediately appreciated values, not a method of control. Moreover, "to the precise degree to which History becomes out of touch with the practical problems of our own day, it approximates, if it is to remain valuable, to Poetry." History cannot become a science, but it is, provided that the historian is aware of what it is about, the source and only source of the material of the social sciences, especially politics. History must be selective, and selection implies a dominating purpose—which, as we have already noted, is control. "The rise of the demand to understand the course of events, the underlying system, is the complement of the attempt to build up an educated citizen body, and is a demand which cannot be treated with contempt."

Catlin, therefore, takes issue with those who hold that history cannot be a source of political instruction because it is concerned with unique, unreduplicable events performed by unique individuals as well as with those who make it a bare record of past events. Human nature exhibits a certain consistency in human behavior, and history exhibits situations which are sufficiently similar to one another to evoke recurrent ways of dealing with them. The content of historical events may be infinitely diversified, but it manifests also certain generic and constant forms, social expedients and policies. These three things, human nature (as revealed in psychology), environmental difficulties and social expedients, supply the conditions of a genuine political science. "For the social scientist the study of History is the study of human method."

Political science, like physical and economic science, demands abstractions, for only through these do the constant and recurrent forms emerge from the welter of diversified and ever-changing content. Psychology gives the key to the abstractions to be made and used. "Political man" is a justifiable abstraction. But the subject-matter of politics is not the state or states, an assumption which is a survival of the struggle for supremacy between church and state. Political processes are not those which grow out of the activities of some sixty states, but those exhibited in acts repeated countless times a day. The student of politics must discover what is the political act, an act which is commonplace and constantly recurring in the everyday processes of living. The abstraction which Catlin himself fastens upon as the source of the hypothesis without which scientific method is impossible is that "man in his political actions is moved by the desire for power or, more precisely, to execute his own will." The whole tenor of Catlin's treatment makes it clear that he regards economic science as much more advanced than political, and that he is in search of a concept which will have the scope and fertility which the abstraction of acquisitive man has manifested. It would be true, I think, to his spirit to say that politics is as much hampered by restriction to states and their governments as economics would be if it were confined to public finance. From this point of view, the economic parallel to Hocking's effort would be to try to show that all the activities of private human beings to obtain the relief, comfort, security and prestige which come from wealth, are, in ultimate analysis, merely phenomena of public finance.

I regret that limitations of space forbid following Catlin through his account of the place of politics among the social sciences, a discussion which deals mainly with its relations to sociology, anthropology and psychology.

The impression left upon me by this book is one of wholesomeness, like a refreshing breeze blowing through a close atmosphere. It is a book to be reckoned with by all students of social affairs. It is a curious coincidence that Catlin and Hocking both assume the same psychological foundation: will and will to power. Yet the two have built radically different structures upon the same basis. Both may be wrong, but only one can be right. Mr. Catlin saves his will to power from being mythological by conceiving will as desire to attain one's ends when others are implicated. But I sometimes wonder whether all human theorizing would not be furthered by an agreement wholly to eliminate the word "will," at least for a generation or two. It is a popular term, having no place even in psychological science save as something to be analyzed, as presenting a problem. Back of the question of execution of purposes lies that of their formation. Mr. Catlin can hardly be blamed for omitting in this particular treatise consideration of that theme. But it is not a question which can be ignored in the discussion of politics itself, however inappropriate it may be to a preliminary discussion of its methods and problems. It is a problem having a psychological phase, but it is also a problem of the social sciences. Does politics accept aims as given to it and consider simply their execution? If so, the abstraction of political man can perhaps be maintained, but only at the expense of ruling out considerations of the greatest human concern. And I wonder what some of the younger economists will have to say about the virtual assumption that economics has attained such scientific status that it may be taken as a model for a sister social science. But in spite of these reservations and others which might be made, the book should serve as a definite and fresh point of departure, not only for "politicists," but for all occupied with the problems and methods of the human sciences, of ultimate highest concern for human beings.

The Origin of the State by Robert H. Lowie.
New York: Harcourt, Brace and Co., 1927.

The student of the history of law and politics will find
this volume invaluable in supplying both data and understanding of their primitive condition. The book should become the
starting point of any further discussions of the problems connected with early political organization; its emphasis, as the title
indicates, falling upon the political rather than the juridical aspect. Lowie holds that unless we arbitrarily define the state in
terms of modern political entities, the evidence goes to show historic continuity of function and structure so that we are entitled
to speak of a state in connection with primitive societies. By
means of a rich and critical assemblage of evidence he shows the
inadequacy of the two chief types of theory which deny the as-
cription of political order to such groupings. While admitting
the value as a secondary contribution of Oppenheimer's contention that the state arose through conquest and exploitation of
the conquered, he convincingly exhibits the insufficiency of the
theory to cover all the facts, dwelling particularly on the evidence which shows that prior political organization and some
degree of administrative skill on the part of the conquerors are
involved in those states which on the surface corroborate Oppenheimer's theory. The other chief theory criticized is that advanced by Maine who would make personal bonds, connected
with blood relationship actual or imputed, the exclusive source
of organization in primitive groups. He proves, conclusively to
my mind, that the territorial tie was also operative and that the
bonds formed by local propinquity must be taken into account
even in dealing with the organizing and controlling force of the
blood tie. One chapter of the book, incidental to its main purpose, is a successful refutation of the theory which makes sov-

[First published in *Columbia Law Review* 28 (1928): 255.]

ereignty a universal characteristic of political organization. Another chapter, dealing with associations formed on the basis of sex, age, military or magic prowess, etc., shows their role in the constitution of political authority. In this discussion he qualifies a view previously advanced by him which would give these associations preponderating efficacy, while he now admits that they sometimes weaken territorial bonds.

Law in the Making by Carleton Kemp Allen.
New York: Oxford University Press, American
Branch, 1927.

This valuable work consists of lectures delivered at the
University of Calcutta in 1926. The preface informs us that the
lectures were originally entitled "The Sources of Law," but the
title was altered so as to make it clear that the book was not concerned with the literary and documentary sources, but with all
the forces that enter into making rules of law to be what they
are. The plan of the book thus calls for a discussion of the place
and operation of Custom, Precedent, Equity and Legislation. A
final chapter, "Subordinate and Autonomic Legislation" takes up
the processes of devolution, with, as is natural, especial reference
to Great Britain, by which legislative power has been delegated
to subordinate bodies; in other words, it considers Administrative Law. It will be noted that the scope of the book is complete
and well organized.

Mr. Allen in his preface says his chief indebtedness is to the
late Sir Paul Vinogradoff, and the reader will find constant evidence of the influence of this distinguished scholar and historian.
As is fitting when ideas are largely determined by the historical
school of jurisprudence, the first chapter is a penetrating and
solid criticism of the school of Austin according to which law
has only one "source," the will of the sovereign. In opposition to
this view, the role of custom is emphasized; the place of sovereignty is conceived to be that of a subordinate, although in
modern societies highly important, agency in the *enforcement* of
law. In the words of the author: "There is a difference between
considering law as the creation of a sovereign power, and considering the sanctioning power as the creation of law. We have en-
deavoured to show the necessity for regarding law as the product
of social forces; that does not in any way preclude us, as lawyers,

[First published in *Columbia Law Review* 28 (1928): 832–33.]

from requiring a sanction for law among these social forces, when they have reached an appropriate stage of development."

The chief law-making force, then, is Custom, and the origin of law is non-litigious. The main position of the book is well presented in a quotation from Vinogradoff: "It is not conflicts that initiate rules of legal observance, but the practices of every day, directed by the give-and-take considerations of reasonable intercourse and social co-operation." Convention rather than conflict is the source of law, just because social life is fundamentally agreement rather than dissension.

While I sympathize with the critique of Austinianism, it may fairly be doubted whether Mr. Allen has quite faced the ultimate issue. It might be retorted for example that while customs involving unity of social action precede dissensions and litigation, yet customs do not become laws in any juridical sense until they are authoritatively stated or formulated, and that the occasion of such statement is always a dispute. Customs themselves conflict, and the source of law may be in the need of adjudicating such conflicts rather than in the bare fact of customs themselves. In this case, a rule of law cannot be conceived as the *mere* reduplication in formal statement of antecedent custom, for it involves an element which is additive and in a sense, as viewed from the standpoint of prior custom, creative. To recognize a custom as authoritative and obligatory is to give that custom a new status; in a way it represents the beginning of a *new* custom. I do not think it paradoxical to say that while there would not be laws unless there were social customs, yet neither would there be laws if all customs were mutually consistent and were universally adhered to.

The point of these remarks is that something happens when a custom becomes a law, and that I do not find in Mr. Allen a clear statement of just what this something is. In the chapter on "Interpretation and Application of Custom," Mr. Allen traverses the ground involved in this question in a discussion of the function of jurists and judges in law-making. He is compelled here to face the question of whether customs are law until they are declared to be such by a competent juridical authority. It cannot be objected that he fails to recognize the importance of judicial interpretation and application. He states that the form and content of many existing customs are themselves derived from technical rules evolved by interpreters and tribunals. At the same time he asserts that custom must not be conceived to be purely a creation of judicial technique, since the relation between indigenous customary law and technical treatment of it is one of action and re-action. This statement may be admitted, but it seems to avoid the basic issue: Is any custom a rule of law until it has received some technical treatment for the sake of application? However, I do not wish to be hypercritical. The two chapters, no matter how this issue be decided, are of enormous value to a student in giving an account both of the historical development of custom in relation to civil and common law, and of various theories put forth regarding the matter. He gives an excellent treatment of Savigny's view that law is a product of the Volk-geist or inner "conviction" of a people, while custom, in the sense of actual habits, is but an outer badge or ear-mark of law, not its source. He also states fully the theory of Lambert and Koehler that it is by arbitral and judicial decisions that law is differentiated from morals. He gives a full body of material regarding the attitude of English courts towards customs. His own predilection for the view that custom is itself the original law-making force is seen, perhaps, in his treatment of cases where *apparently* the courts have declared that some custom is *not* law; for he tends to interpret the decisions to signify that the courts held that proof was lacking that the alleged custom was really a custom. Nevertheless, some of the decisions might also be cited, I think, to justify the reverse interpretation; namely, to indicate that in some cases judges regard the custom as so unreasonable, in technical interpretation, that they refuse to admit that any amount of evidence could prove it to be a custom. However, here as elsewhere, Mr. Allen gives the material on both sides so fully and fairly that the reader has in his own possession the grounds for reaching his own conclusions on disputed points.

I shall not attempt to follow the argument of the book through all the successive topics. Suffice it to say that with respect to precedents, equity and legislation, Mr. Allen gives both the factual historical material relevant to the topic, and also the chief theories which various schools of jurisprudence have put forth with respect to them. While the book does not profess to be a history of philosophical jurisprudence, the student will find in it a valuable introduction to the theories of the various schools, all the more valuable because the theoretical views are introduced in connection with the origin of some practical legal question. I do not think the reader will find anywhere else such an adequate and well balanced historical account of the various factors involved in the making of law, nor a more judicious statement of the views of important theoretical interpreters. If the book has a defect, it goes with its merits. It is so judicial and so aware of what may be said on both sides of controverted issues, that it sometimes leaves the impression of an attempt to combine opposed theories instead of offering a clear-cut decision between them.

Brave Gospel

An Adventure with Children by Mary H. Lewis. New York: The Macmillan Co., 1928.

Teachers and parents who are interested in learning about the meaning of progressive schools cannot do better than to read this spirited book. It is drawn to the life from the life of a school conducted by its author for twelve years. The title is enticing, and it conveys the spirit of the book. The emphasis does not fall upon pedagogical theory, save indirectly and by embodiment in actual work, nor upon studies and the subject-matter of the curriculum. Miss Lewis indicates that she may tell something about the latter on another occasion, but since there are many schools which are doing their academic work thoroughly, the emphasis here falls upon what can take place when children play and work together in a natural, simple, and wholesome environment. Besides, as she intimates, teachers are already only too willing to take their material and methods ready-made from the hands of others, while many theorists in teachers colleges, who do not teach children, are turning out subject-matter and methods to order. It was a happy thought to set forth that background of a community life in a free environment out of which, according to needs as they show themselves, subject-matter and method emerge in the very process of living.

Thus the book is the story of the drama of a developing life. It tells how children, teachers, subjects, methods of instruction, and discipline, grow together. The reader is enabled to share directly in the processes of development so that the zest and ardor of the director of the educational experiment, as she relives the life of the school, imparts itself to the reader. In spite, however, of the informal character of the exposition, it has structure and plan. The reader learns to appreciate through a living exhibition the value of imagination in education, the way in which teachers

[First published in *Saturday Review of Literature* 4 (1928): 1016.]

select and train themselves, the ways in which the cooperation of parents is enlisted, and the consequent education of adults as well as of children. The lesson of these values is conveyed by perception of what actually happens when children and teachers, sharing in common activities of work and play, carried on in simple, almost crude, surroundings, find themselves having to meet constantly new needs and to realize new opportunities.

The implicit message of the book is perhaps best stated in its closing words: "My faith is in the children. They who built the school and lived in it throughout those busy, happy years will demand for their own children an education no less stimulating, no less rich in opportunities for meaningful experiences, than was their own. To the children, then, may safely be entrusted the enlarged and perfected fulfillment of an adventure which is as unending and expanding as life." If I say that this passage tells the message of the book, it is because it sums up the story of an actual school in which life, growing under wise direction, is identified with education, and education is then found to be a brave and joyous adventure, instead of a drab task. And it enforces the lesson that it is the very nature of growth, when once it is initiated, to go on of itself. This power of a free and developing life to sustain and enlarge itself is, after all, our only ultimate security. Till we rid ourselves of our fears and learn to trust this power of growth in life itself, our efforts at reform in education as in other social affairs will be doomed to disappointment. This little book is a reinforcement of faith and courage.

Miscellany

Foreword in Paul Radin's
Primitive Man as Philosopher

Dr. Radin's work opens up an almost new field. It may not go contrary to the beliefs which are implicitly current among workers in the anthropological field. But even an outsider, like the present writer, can see that it surely introduces a new emphasis, fixing attention upon phases of the culture of primitive man which are usually passed over lightly, if they are not overtly denied. There are at least many premises and many conclusions which have gained popular currency which are incompatible with the material and interpretations which he presents. From the standpoint of the specialist in this intellectual territory, Dr. Radin's work is pioneering in quality; it introduces new perspectives in its assertion of the existence of a definite intellectual class, proportionate in numbers and influence to the "intellectuals" in any civilized group, and one which is possessed of ideas upon most of the themes which have formed the staples of philosophical discussion. It is easy to imagine his contribution becoming the centre, almost a storm-centre, of animated debate and heated controversy among the special students of primitive life.

In that discussion a layman like myself has no place. But no one concerned with the intellectual history of mankind, especially with the background of what has now become more or less conventionally set apart as philosophy, can fail to be intensely interested in the material which he has advanced. There are not lacking recent writers on the origins of philosophy who have dealt with its emergence from primitive speculations, especially from the material connected with religious beliefs and rites, and who have insisted upon the influence of the latter upon the formation of early philosophic notions. But in the light of Dr. Radin's material their views need reconsideration. For if he is even

[First published in Paul Radin, *Primitive Man as Philosopher* (New York: D. Appleton and Co., 1927), pp. xv–xviii.]

approximately right, philosophic origins are not to be sought for in the cruder and conventionalized forms which religious beliefs assumed among the populace at large, but rather in the interpretations of the small intellectual class, whose ideas may have been crude because of limitations of subject matter at their command, but which at least were bold, independent, and free within these limitations.

It may be worth while, even at the expense of a hasty traversing of ground which Dr. Radin has covered in detail, to point out some of the matters of the background of philosophic origins with respect to which the material of Dr. Radin demands either authoritative refutation or else a pretty thoroughgoing revision of notions which have become current. Among these points is the secondary and auxiliary place of supernatural and magical practices and beliefs in connection with practical achievement. If we trust the material, primitive man was in fact more "tough minded," more realistic in facing facts, than is currently believed. The student of morals and social philosophy must give serious attention to the weighty mass of evidence which is adduced to show that early man instead of being enslaved to the group to the point of absorption in it was in fact highly individualistic, within certain limits more so than modern civilized man. The extent to which early ethical judgments in the way of social condemnation were limited to special occasions instead of being generalized into judgments of character at large raises the question whether their moral standpoint was not in so far sounder than that which civilized "progress" has developed. The prevalent idea that the customs of the group provide automatic moral standards and rules receives a severe shock when we find that along with great freedom of "self-expression" there is equal emphasis upon responsibility for personal control of actions so as not to harm others. The conception that primitive man attributes an independence to the existence of the group comparable to that of the "external world" seems not only to do justice to the facts which the upholders of the incorporation theory rely upon, without falling into their excesses, but to be also a valuable contribution to any sociological theory. And these are only a few of the points with respect to which the material of the first part of Dr. Radin's work demands serious attention together with reconstruction of current beliefs as to the background and origin of later moral and social speculations.

For the abstract phases of philosophy the second part, entitled "The Higher Aspects of Primitive Thought," is equally significant. The titles of the chapters are themselves sufficient to indicate the precious nature of the material to those interested in the development of metaphysical speculation. Dr. Radin would doubtless be the first to deny that he is breaking entirely new ground in his presentation of the actual facts regarding aboriginal man's notion of what constitutes reality and human personality. But I do not know where one would turn for such a complete and convincing picture of the dynamic and qualitative way in which the world presented itself to the primitive speculator on existence. Under the influence of modern philosophic theories, it has been assumed that the object and world were first regarded as collections of sense-data, while the obvious inconsistencies with this notion have been accounted for as animistic and supernatural injections. Dr. Radin explodes this traditional notion. He makes it clear that objects and nature were conceived dynamically; that change, transition, were primary, and transformation into stability something to be accounted for. His account makes clear that effects, emotional and practical, were the material of the thought of real objects, and that thinkers, in their doctrine of an inner "form," stated in rational terms a notion which was expressed mythically by the mass, a notion which has marked affiliations with a persistent strain in the classic philosophic tradition.

To continue, however, would be merely to summarize what the book itself vividly presents. I only hope that the cases selected by way of illustration may serve to indicate to those interested in the development of philosophic ideas and to the larger number interested in the growth of the intellectual phase of human culture, the rich and provocative material which Dr. Radin has freshly provided.

Introductory Word in Sidney Hook's
The Metaphysics of Pragmatism

Variant developments in thought, scientific or intellectual, in their early stages suffer in statement and apprehension in two ways. These ways although logically opposed to each other are psychologically complementary. On the one hand, there is an exaggeration of the factor of novelty which creates an illusion of total breach of continuity. On the other hand, there is an injection into the new ideas of older conceptions which are irrelevant and the elimination of which is demanded by the new ideas. Because of the suppression of the continuities, and indeed the fulfillments, which are required to make the new fully comprehensible, and because of the insertion of the old notions which the new point of view makes untenable, it is not surprising that the introduction of any significant variation in thought is marked by a period of confused controversy in which both goal and road are obscured to participants on either side.

Yet it is antecedently certain that continuities there must be; the new idea must be generated out of the old; it has its basis in them; and in the end its justification is found in the completion and organization which it contributes to them;—its removal of their surds and inconsistencies. If the present is big with the future, it is certain that the past was big with the present. Any novelty, whether a practical invention or a departure in theory, which finally wins a place for itself gains not only a psychological familiarity due to wont and use, but a logical "naturalness," an inevitableness, because it is seen to carry on and fulfill what went before. Looking back from the vantage point of later time, this factor of development is so marked as easily to give rise to a false impression of a one-way evolution or unfolding from within. Thus it is that many theories which began as "perfect ab-

[First published in Sidney Hook, *The Metaphysics of Pragmatism* (Chicago: Open Court Publishing Co., 1927), pp. 1–5.]

surdities" or wilful eccentricities close their careers as obvious
common-places that only restate what everyone had always believed. Indeed, in their later stage, the virtual attitude of the former critic is often: "If that was what you meant all the time, why
didn't you say so?" The question is well meant. But its implication overlooks two facts. To develop an adequate statement
and understanding of a new view is all one with ability to see its
connections, continuities and completions of what went before.
Only miraculous creatures, goddesses springing full grown from
the head of Zeus, are exempt from a period of uncertain and precarious growth. The other fact overlooked is that the establishment of these continuities demand a recasting, a re-seeing, of old
beliefs, and the latter resist modification even more than refrac-
tory physical substances. In short, the perception of continuity
and fulfillment occurs only as old ideas undergo a subtle and pervasive modification. By the time a new conception has become a
version of "what everyone always believed," what everyone always believed has undergone purgation and transformation.

On the other hand, phases of the former beliefs which have to
be discarded if the new one is valid are unconsciously but surely
"read into" the new. Failure to see the continuities which do exist is compensated for by the assumption of identities which
must be read out. The basic method and common form of all dialectical refutation of new conceptions consists in first assimilating them in some respect to views already current and then
showing the logical contradiction between this assimilation and
other phases of the new idea. The critic thus convincingly demonstrates that the new view would be absurd if it were held in
terms of his own position. Just as it takes time to discover the
respects in which a new idea completes and organizes old beliefs,
so it takes time to detect and eliminate old elements which are so
taken for granted that they are unconsciously projected, to its
undoing, into the new. Gradually, often imperceptibly, an equilibrium is attained as eccentricities are smoothed into connections and engrained habituations are remade.

These remarks have been suggested to me by reading Dr.
Hook's work. The volume is noteworthy because, more than
anything on its subject with which I am acquainted, it expresses
an equilibrium which is consciously and deliberately sustained
between that newer movement which goes by the name of prag-

matism and instrumentalism and essential portions of classic thought. Dr. Hook sees at once, altogether and gladly, connections and revisions which in the ordinary course of discussion are seen only reluctantly and piecemeal. He has worked clear of the partial concessions and misunderstandings which accompany early stages of discussion, and placed himself securely on the further side, on a definite realization of both the reconstructions demanded and the continuities and completions effected, keeping both in view with an equal mind.

To develop this remark in detail would be only to attempt in a hasty and sketchy way what the book itself accomplishes with leisurely amplitude. But one point may be indicated by way of illustration. As is obvious from the mere names, "instrumentalism" made much of instrumentalities, and "pragmatism" much of action, practise. The projection of older ideas is seen in the fact that the ideas of tools and action were given a personal and subjective meaning. Instrumentalism was taken to signify that thought and knowledge exist only as means of accomplishing some private advantage, some external utility. The earlier stages of criticism show that instrumentalism was even defined as the doctrine that all knowing is subordinate to satisfying organic, animal needs. The idea of action was given a similarly isolated and private interpretation. What the criticisms really proved was the nature of the conceptions which were previously current as to instruments and action. When these conceptions were read into the new view, there was no difficulty in attributing to the latter a denial of all objective and "disinterested" thought. It took time to make it clear that what was genuinely new in pragmatism was precisely a denial of these conceptions, and the substitution for them of an objective conception of tools, purpose and action.

But Dr. Hook at the outset cut the discussion clear of all such encumbrances and irrelevant confusion. He makes it clear that "instruments" denote objects having a definite existential status and office, and that "action" does not cease to be continuous with the energies of nature when it is expressed in the behavior and habits of a living organism. There is then no difficulty in making it clear that thought, which in science deals with the objects which have the status of instruments, is itself a further tool of a distinctive type, and yet like other instruments, one set to operate in a common world of existences. There is an important sense in which all conclusive thinking is circular and is justified by its circularity. It brings us back at its close to the material which formed its starting point, enabling us to see it as a contributing and an enveloped member of an inclusive whole. This completer vision forms, I take it, the reality of what is termed synthesis. This consists in the perception of material previously isolated and fragmentary as a constituent of a related unity. The grasp which Mr. Hook has upon both the newer movement and the essential factors of classic thought enables him to achieve such a synoptic vision to a remarkable extent. His discussion is thus lifted far above the level of controversy which has attended so much of the consideration of pragmatism. It is possible for a reader by means of rigid definition of the terms "metaphysics" and "pragmatism," laid down inflexibly in advance, to hide his mind from the enlightenment which this book can convey. But the reader who permits his idea of the meaning of these words to grow with and from the actual subject-matter of the following pages will find in them, I am confident, a penetrating and illuminating union of the basic ideas in the newer movement with those of the classic philosophic tradition, a union in which equal justice is dealt to the truths which are carried over and completed in the new development and to the transformations in them which the new ideas exact.

Introductory Note in
Joseph Kinmont Hart's
Inside Experience

Of all things difficult to attain, understanding is perhaps the most difficult and the most important. When persons arrive at an understanding they come to agreement, and agreement is committal to a common cause: it is reciprocal engagement and mutual confidence. The bitterness of misunderstanding is indicated in the reproaches which attend it: charges of betrayal, intimations of bad faith. Mutual pleading of faith is more readily secured in appearance than in reality. It is possible only when there lies back of it a common store of experiences. Without resemblance of experiences, words have different meanings, and communication is a sham: ideas diverge even when their formula is the same. Yet, without understanding and that reciprocal committal and mutual faith which is its essence, any so-called society is but an aggregate held together by fear of danger or promise of profit. A community is constituted by those who communicate with one another, who agree with one another in action because they share in a common understanding.

The humane import of a philosophy of experience has its source in this dependence of social life upon reciprocal engagements; of the latter upon understanding; and of understanding upon a life experience of men and things. Experiences vary with temperament, with circumstances, with time and place, with every accident of contact. Were this diversity the whole of the story, however, communication would be but an exchange of external gifts, a trading of bribes, with a view to keeping an outward peace: social life would be but a mechanical equilibrium of repellent atoms. One cannot even understand himself, his own acts, beliefs, and purposes, save as he binds them into an un-

[First published in Joseph Kinmont Hart, *Inside Experience: A Naturalistic Philosophy of Life and the Modern World* (New York: Longmans, Green and Co., 1927), pp. xxi–xxvi.]

broken continuity with his past, save as he discovers some continuity of experience. To have a community of experiences with others is not only the condition of ability to understand them, but the understanding and assent of others which springs from this common background frees and deepens one's further understanding of himself.

For this reason, the realization of understanding and the creation of a community are supremely difficult. All intelligent speech signifies that a person has been able to eliminate the severing peculiarities that mark off his own experience and that of those addressed, and to find an experience which is common and comprehending. That, in turn, signifies a power to grasp the universal and objective—not easy to attain.

Yet men so crave the expansion and reinforcement which come from the agreements of understanding that they tolerate and invent all kinds of substitute semblances. Surrender to a passing contagion of emotion; the deliberate working up of a common fear and hate (as in war); respect for external conventions; the repetition of formulae of religious creeds and political platforms; familiarity with like circumstances, however trivial; conjunction in an undertaking wherein each at bottom is pursuing his own private gain; servile docility in dragooning opinions; fanatic imposition of fidelity to the same phrases and symbols: all these serve as such substitutes *for real understandings*. Yet reality is not mocked: the price of understanding, the obtaining and communicating of common experience, has not been paid. Any crisis reveals the hollowness of the apparent agreement. At bottom it rests on force, on the hope of personal gain, on the fear of private loss.

Hence, once more, the human need and opportunity of a philosophy which shall reveal the common foundations that underlie the superficial diversities of experiences, and which shall manifest the common patterns that are woven into their variety. Never was the need greater than to-day. Never before has there existed in the world so much of external contact and exchange. Steam and electricity have brought the ends of the earth together. Those who touch and mix bring with them experiences hardened into separation by unlikeness of traditions, customs and outlooks. Confusion abounds; external chaos and conflict are the signs of absence of inward understanding. The common creed which held western civilization in some sort of unity has disintegrated, and endures in name only, not in deed. The recrudescence of "fundamentalism" in religion and politics is as much an evidence of confusion and division as are the phenomena of overt uncertainty and disorganization. An exaggerated external conformity is demanded; belief is standardized and regimented, because we feel how thin and stretched are the bonds of union that come from mutual understanding, only. Our insistence upon uniformity is a compensatory reaction due to the absence of unity. As I have said elsewhere, the actual "philosophy" of our time is analogous to the check and balance theory of our political powers. This latter denotes the abandonment of hope of intrinsic cooperation and vainly attempts to secure harmony by assigning to unrelated powers such places and boundaries that each will at least prevent the undue encroachment of others. So, in our theory of life, we think by a policy of division and segregation and external checks to achieve order and wholeness. So, art, science, religion, industry and commerce, morals, politics, is each to have its own separate room, to carry on its business apart. Thus we think to build the human habitation fair and whole and render life a harmony!

When I say that such a situation creates a demand for a philosophy of experience, and provides it with its opportunity, I mean nothing so silly as that philosophy can itself effect integration and mutual interpenetration. That is something to be done by all the processes of living. But a vital philosophy is itself a criticism, a record and a prophetic indication. Therefore philosophy is a valuable, perhaps an indispensable auxiliary and guide in the coordination of the operations of living. As criticism it can uncover and sterilize the traditions, the ingrained habitual ideas, which are barriers to a wider shared experience. Uncovering traditions will not eliminate them; but it is hard to see how we can emancipate ourselves from them until they have been located and brought to light. As a record, a philosophy of experience can bring to light and illuminate enduring and comprehensive patterns of experience; it can grasp and retain in summary forms the identities and wholenesses which are so easily dissipated when experiences are rapid, multifarious, crowded into the hurly-burly hours. Philosophy may at least sketch a map and a chart which as an indication of unity may guide in effecting unification. In its prophetic office, philosophy may construct intellectually what Dr. Hart so happily calls a "dramatic highway." It may show the path to be followed in the delineation of the design, the contour and the perspective of a now disordered and confused experience.

Dr. Hart's book is welcome as a contribution to the task of revealing the structure of experience, and exhibiting its articulations. One difficulty under which philosophy labors is that in doing its work it can employ only the tools that already exist: words and ideas which have already been so specifically appropriated to particularistic and divisive functions as to make them unfit for their work. The way out, as Dr. Hart so clearly shows, is constant effort, renewed experiment, varied and cooperative approach. The task of revising our words, remaking our tools, even while they are actually at work, cannot be confined to those who are professionally and officially "philosophers." The candor, courage and sympathetic insight of minds which move outside any technical fold are needed. Dr. Hart's pages approach the task with liberality and generous imagination. If they are received in the spirit in which they are offered, a spirit free from petrifaction and wooden literalness, instinct with eager desire, devoted to the realities to which words at best can only point, solicitous only for the kind of assent and agreement which spring from converse with these realities, these pages cannot fail to be a noteworthy contribution to the promotion of that understanding which is the greatest of our needs.

Introduction to Roswell P. Barnes's
Militarizing Our Youth

Is the reader aware that there is in existence in this country a well-organized movement to militarize the tone and temper of our national life? Is he aware that militarism has already become a vested interest, economic as well as political and social? Is he aware that the effort of this vested interest to militarize the country is operating deliberately and knowingly through the medium of our schools and colleges? Is he aware that the vested interest resorts to methods of aspersion and overt attack in order to intimidate those persons and organizations who oppose its efforts to get a strangle hold on our schools and in order to prevent students from being influenced by the facts and arguments these opponents present? Is he aware that, by their own statements, their present intervention—not to call it by the name of interference—in education is regarded by the vested militaristic interest as simply the best substitute attainable at the present time for universal military service and as a step in creating conditions when conscriptive service will be adopted?

The following pages give material that enables anyone to make up his mind about these questions. The material is in the form not of the reckless aspersions in which the militaristic crowd freely indulges but in the form of facts, readily verifiable, most of them cited from official sources. It is doubtless this element of fact, undeniable fact, which so arouses the bitterness of the vested militaristic interest, and leads it in the words of one of its representatives, quoted in this pamphlet, to urge attack upon "subversive agitation" not only with "facts and figures" but with "venom and fury." The attack on the fifty-four persons who endorsed the previous (Lane) report of the society which sponsors

[First published in Roswell P. Barnes, *Militarizing Our Youth: The Significance of the Reserve Officers' Training Corps in Our Schools and Colleges* (New York: Committee on Militarism in Education, 1927), pp. 3–4.]

also the present report was certainly long on venom and fury, but short on facts and figures—except figures of speech.

The American people is not as yet sufficiently militarized to favor a movement for its complete assimilation of the military spirit. The danger is that it will not be aware of what is going on. Hence the importance, the supreme importance, of stating the facts which will enable our people to become aware of the present organized movement, and, in being aware, to check it. Hence also the venom and fury directed against those who have become acquainted with the facts and who are striving to give the American public a knowledge of them. Nothing will be as fatal to the success of the militaristic attempt as knowledge of the facts. To suppress the dissemination of this knowledge is the logical course for the militaristic interest to pursue. Their previous activity shows that it considers one of the most effective means of suppression to be zeal in discrediting those who make the facts known by any kind of disingenuous and misleading statement. The publication of the present report will doubtless lead to the renewal of statements of which Roosevelt's "short and ugly word" is the fitting appellation.

For our part, we invite the attention of the public to the *facts*, secure in the confidence of what the outcome will be if the attention of the public is once given them. But unless the facts are known and attended to, the outcome is by no means so certain. The militaristic movement is well organized, is energetically active, unrelentingly aggressive. It has a definite program and is taking definite steps for its execution. The nature of the program and of the steps in its execution are set forth on the authority of official documents in the pages of this pamphlet. Peoples do not become militaristic or imperialistic because they deliberately choose so to do. They become militaristic gradually and unconsciously in response to conditions of which militarism is the final consequence. Education of youth and the reflex of that education on parents and friends is an important part of the forces which have militarization for their consequence.

Of this situation the militaristic vested interest is well apprized. Are those who are opposed to the subordination of our civil policies to a warlike purpose equally aware of it? What are they doing and going to do about it?

Afterword in Charles Clayton Morrison's
The Outlawry of War

Mr. Morrison has covered the various questions involved in the outlawry of war so completely that I can only repeat in other words what he has said. And as his words are more eloquent and forceful than those at my command, to essay this task is superfluous! Why then do I accede to his request to append some words to what he has written? Chiefly because I am glad of the opportunity to ally myself in any possible way with the movement which he has so convincingly shown to be the only way to get rid of the curse of the war-system. There are three points to be especially emphasized in my remarks. Outlawry of war releases and makes articulate the international spirit of our own day. It liberates and organizes the moral factors of mankind. It exemplifies all that is fundamental and effective in the significance and function of law in human history and life.

I. Emancipation of the International Spirit

It is a commonplace that steam and electricity have made the nations of the world increasingly interdependent. They have drawn the peoples of the earth, for weal and for woe, closely together. Interdependence is a condition of many things better than those which mankind has achieved in the past. But interdependence in and of itself is not necessarily a good. A condition of good is not an achievement of good. For interdependence is also a condition of many new evils, and of the manifestation of old evils on a vaster scale. The barriers which once

[First published as a foreword in Charles Clayton Morrison, *The Outlawry of War: A Constructive Policy for World Peace* (Chicago: Willett, Clark and Colby, 1927), pp. vii–xxv; subsequently moved to end of book and retitled "Afterword."]

isolated peoples made it impossible for them to cooperate fruit-fully with one another; but they also rendered it impossible for them to fight and exploit one another. There was a time when the idea of impressing men in one continent and transporting them across an ocean that they might work as slaves in another was unthinkable. There was a time when wars were localized, re-stricted to neighbors. Now all nations are contiguous in effect; states from every continent on the globe took part in the last war, which was truly not just in name a world-war. Before the newer industrial regime, it was unthinkable that exploitation of backward nations should be undertaken for the sake of control of raw materials and finding of markets for manufactured goods. For half a century it has been a regular procedure. Interdepen-dence is an ominous as well as a promising fact. It is as yet un-determined to which side the balance will incline. What is to be done with our newly acquired internationalism, what it is going to do with us, is one of the few momentous issues of history.

While economic forces have brought about the present world internationalism, the results extend far beyond industry and commerce. They extend beyond the political area, whether dip-lomatic or military. It is a commonplace that the discoveries of science and the fruitions of art now quickly become the posses-sion of the whole world, and that the nations are sharers in a noble emulation. Of this aspect of internationalism we cannot say what we have said of our economic internationalism, that it is fraught with danger and threat of evil. But nonetheless there is a problem. We hear much of the "international mind" in these days. But "mind" has two meanings: there is mind in operation, mind incarnate in action; and there is mind which is but senti-ment and pious opinion, mind which denotes indulgence in in-effectual idealism, reverie and self-deception. Such international mind as now exists belongs largely to the latter kind. What chan-nels of operation has it which enable it to affect seriously the course of affairs? It is a fine thing in itself, and lends itself to elo-quent discourse. But it exists *by* itself, as in itself, in separation from the practical hurly-burly of the world. Aside from the valu-able satisfaction it affords the persons cultivated enough to have it, it is hard to point to any significant achievement to its credit.

Thus the question of liberating and making articulate the in-ternationalism of the modern world has two sides. It is matter of utilizing for good the economic interdependence of the peoples who inhabit the earth, and of making it possible for an international mind to function effectively in the control of the world's practical affairs.

It is submitted that outlawry of war is the means and the only means of transmuting existing internationalism in both these phases into a power for good in human life. The problem of utilizing international industry and commerce for the enhancement and bettering of human life is largely one of prevention. They may work for mutual advantage when they are prevented from operating to the one-sided advantage of strong states and to the detriment of weaker ones. It is the ever-present threat of the use of force by navy and army, on the part of nations strong in actual and potential equipment for war, which is the essence of that exploitation which is called economic imperialism. The effect of the war-system is not measured, moreover, by the wars which have been overtly waged for economic reasons in the last half-century. The war-system is in the background constantly in times of peace. It is the possibility of resort to armed force which controls to-day for the most part the relations of the industrially backward nations to those economically advanced. Any one who is in contact with inhabitants of the Orient knows how rapidly the sentiment has grown among them that force is the only thing the western powers respect and that therefore it behooves the eastern peoples to militarize themselves. Volumes could not say more as to the role of the war-institution, overt and latent, in deciding the form which economic internationalism now takes. Like the air we breathe the institution is bound up with all the facts of the present relations of nations. It is consequently almost impossible for the imagination to realize what the economic interdependence of people would become if the heavy hand of the war-system were removed. But think away the influence of that hand, ever-ready in the background, and the imagination, accustomed as it is to think in terms of the threat of force, will at least feel an enormous liberation, the lifting of an awful burden.

The removal of the same burden will enable the international mind to expand and take in those who are now ultra-nationalistic, and who think of patriotism not as public spirit but as antagonism, veiled or truculent, of one nation to others. What is even more important, it will enable the international mind thus released to become a working reality. It will cease to be a private indulgence, a mark of cultivation, a theme for the platform and the printed page. It will have a career of action opened in which it may freely and abundantly express itself. The intellectual, artistic and religious unities of mankind will have a free and fair field in which to flower and produce their fruit. They will be relieved of the enormous financial oppression which now weighs upon the tax-payer in every nation, an oppression due to the direct and indirect demands of the war-system. But this gain is negative and external compared with that which will accrue when men and women of all peoples find themselves able to think of themselves as active cooperators with those of other nations, emancipated from all the suspicions, jealousies, fears and hatreds which issue from the war-system only themselves to issue betimes in more wars. I confess to a sinking of the heart when observation reveals so many persons who believe in international good-will who are content to tinker with secondary projects, instead of building upon the foundation which will insure effective emancipation of the international spirit.

These considerations are general. They apply, however, with peculiar force to the American people. Our geographical isolation has since the war been petrifying into isolationism as a policy, as an idea. Our latent nationalist exclusivism shows signs of becoming an offensive militant nationalism. We are in danger of surrendering our traditional feelings of amity for an arrogant self-sufficiency. One factor which has produced this result is the fact that it has been so ardently preached to us that the key to and centre of all international cooperation is political cooperation with other nations, especially those of Europe, thus becoming part and parcel of what Mr. Morrison calls the European system. I do not see how any thoughtful person can deny that the campaign for the method of political alignment has not only not released international spirit, but has hardened tendencies toward isolationism. It has operated as far as it has had a significant effect to dry up our international idealism, or to divert it into futile and wasteful channels.

The reasons are not far to seek. Physical distance, geographical aloofness, counts. We have so large and rich a country of our own that appeals to mix in the politics of another continent leave us cold. We are all of us immigrants of varying dates. Many, perhaps most, came over here because there was something in the old world they wished to leave behind, to get rid of. The general disillusionment which followed the glowing hopes of a war to end war, the terms of the peace treaty, the more intimate and widespread knowledge of European politics, of the rivalries and diplomatic methods, have created an aversion to getting inter-mixed politically with Europe, an aversion of a kind which easily grows into a complacent holier-than-thou attitude. These condi-tions and others of the same general kind strengthen the idea that if incorporation in any form or guise within the political sys-tem of the old world is the only method of international coopera-tion, we will stay by ourselves, isolated, aloof, self-sufficient. It is this kind of situation which enables super-patriots and would-be witch-burners to use even the word "internationalism" as a term of reproach and abuse.

For our own country, especially, it would then be an enormous release to place our formal and official relations to the other countries of the world on a juridical basis. It would disentangle sentiment and opinion from danger of getting mixed in political matters which are not only remote from us but which are op-posed to our traditions and interests. As I write there has come into my hands a document which is the output of professional-ized militarists—and as Mr. Morrison points out, war as an in-stitution necessitates the cultivation of the militaristic spirit as a profession which carries on its business in times of peace. The document is issued in behalf of the "Military Departments of American Universities and Colleges." It is a deliberate attempt to cast discredit, by name, on more than fifty representative men and women of America, college presidents and teachers, philan-thropists, editors, United States senators, clergymen, all persons of some distinction, and some of them among the most worthy citizens of the country. Their crime is that they are interested in developing the spirit of peace and international cooperation in this country and opposing the Prussianizing of American institu-tions, particularly our schools. The evident desire is to intimi-date all opposition to militarism by identifying those who work for peace with bolshevist communism. Since these persons men-tioned are internationally minded, and wish to do something about it and not simply talk generalities, they are said to be either the unconscious dupes or the willing tools of the Third International.

The attack cannot be dismissed as trivial merely because it is ridiculous. The instance is submitted as a typical exhibition of the inevitable effect of the war-system in the first place in creating a professional group seated in high and influential positions who identify militarism with loyalty to the country; and secondly of putting in their hands a powerful weapon with which to repress all upholders of international good-will, friendship and cooperation. Until war is outlawed, the international mind will be forced back into a realm of sentimentality, ineffective aspiration, futile dreaming, because efforts to give it active expression will be represented as disloyalty to our own institutions. Detailed argument seems unnecessary. The reader is invited to consider the matter and see what method save mutual agreement to outlaw war will unite loyalty to national affairs and interests with full and abundant release of that amity and cooperation among nations, economic and spiritual, which constitutes internationalism.

II. Liberation of Moral Force

Mr. Morrison points out, as Mr. Levinson and others before him have done, that the war-system inevitably operates to generate moral division and paralysis. Nothing is more serious than conditions which compel masses of men to split into two antagonistic parts their moral beliefs and allegiances. There are a few persons who solve the difficulty by standing out against war on moral or religious grounds under all circumstances whatever. I have no word of reproach for them. But the masses of men never have been, and in my judgment, going by experience, never will be of this mould. We are nourished in the bosom of our own country; we owe to it indirectly if not directly our protection, security and opportunities for development. It is no easy matter in time of war to break these ties and to put ourselves in opposition to the expressed will of one's mother country. For these reasons millions of persons who live in the spirit of peace in time of peace feel bound to support their own country in time of war.

Law is on one side, domestic law and international law, and that law sanctions war and demands some degree of active participation in war; ordinary every-day conscience is against war, against organized killing and organized hatred. This dualism reaches deep and extends far and wide. There is one obvious remedy. Place law on the side of conscience. At present the lover of peace becomes the criminal, the outlaw, in time of war if he ventures to hold out for peace. Outlaw war, and the law is on the side of peace and moral conviction. The criminal, the man who sets himself in opposition to the law of his country and of nations, will then be the man who foments and instigates war. I can only express my surprise that clergymen, educators, public servants and others interested fail to see that the only way to emancipate, organize and consolidate the moral convictions and loyalties of citizens is to deal at the root with the cause which creates moral impotency and division, by placing law on the side of mankind's moral desires and beliefs instead of, as it is now, in opposition to them. This brings us to the third point.

III. The Function of Law

Mr. Morrison has repeatedly in the following pages called attention to the point of view of those who oppose or are indifferent to the outlawry movement because they misconceive the nature of law in general and the law against international killing in particular. There are even intelligent persons who state that they do not know what is meant by saying that war is now legal, and that it is an acknowledged and legitimized political institution for settling disputes. At first sight such a position may seem like inexcusable ignorance. In reality it indicates how a legalized state of affairs once it has been long established is taken for granted; it is so habitual, so matter of course, so thoroughly bound up with the course of affairs—in this case the course of international relationships—that it is not thought of. The thing which attracts attention is simply the occurrence of overt wars, which are then taken by some to be regular inevitable events like volcanic eruptions and earthquakes, and by others as deplorable incidents to be dealt with one by one.

It is the fundamental pervasiveness of war as the legalized

method of settling disputes among nations that causes these persons to be unaware of the fact that it is an established political institution. This statement is no more paradoxical than is the fact that we have no direct perception of other settled conditions, like the air we breathe, the physiological conditions of the body, but only of some disturbance in them. The first point then upon which to be clear with reference to the relation of law to war is that it is *not a question of having for the first time a connection set up between war and law, but a question of having law set against war instead of for it.* It is not just a matter of "passing" a law against war, of issuing a ukase, but the life-and-death matter of altering the system under which nations live. This is the essential meaning of Outlawry; no one who realizes this meaning will consider the relation of law to war to be a trivial matter. Let there be no mistake about this matter. All those whose profession and whose interests are bound up with the war-system see the point. Are those having an interest in having an orderly, cooperative system substituted for one of mutual fear, hostility and destruction, to be obtuse?

Another way of approaching the question of the relation of law to human conduct and relationships is to consider the historic development of law. Every student of history knows that there was a time when individuals were judges and executors in their own behalf in all cases of injuries received. The right of "self-help" was universal. Any person who was wronged or who thought he was injured was sovereign judge of what he should do to set the wrong to rights. There were no courts, no sheriffs, no representatives of the public to intervene. Blood feuds were the result. Gradually courts and public officials representing law developed. The settlement of disputes and the redressing of injuries was taken out of the hands of those directly concerned and who settled their disputes by force between themselves. Law intervened in behalf of pacification. *The historic role of law has been a means of "keeping the peace," of adjudicating disputes without recourse to violence.*

As between individuals, the duel was the last vestige of a regime once universal. When the duel was put under the ban of law, every form of dispute and conflict between individuals was taken out of the realm of settlement by force and brought under the rule of law. Disputes between nations are the one remaining form of human conduct where resort to settlement by violence, organized violence, is sanctioned by law itself, instead of being brought before a public tribunal, operating under uniform rules, for decision. The outlawry of war is thus no sporadic fiat, no gesture made on paper. It is the completion of the historic experience, the accrued wisdom, of mankind as to the most proper way of settling disputes and conflicts of interests. It applies to controversies between nations the method which has already been worked out to care for all other controversies which threaten to break the peace and order of social life. Considering that the consequences of settling disputes between nations by force far transcend in evil those which result from settling private and personal disputes by violence, it is strange that any one should fail to see that the relation of law to organized national violence is the most momentous of social issues.

To apply the current bias against over-legislation, against trying to make persons "good" by rules of law, to the outlawry of war is thus totally aside from the point. The analogy of the relation of law to war is not with sumptuary or prohibitory legislation, but to that law which provides that concrete conflicts of interest shall not terminate in recourse to destructive violence. To doubt the function of law in this latter respect is to contradict all human experience; it is to invite return to private anarchy in all phases of conduct. To regard the outlawry of war as mere prohibition of war, akin to issuing edicts against earthquakes, is the most lazy and superficial kind of thinking. Its essence is positive and constructive:—the provision of orderly methods, agreed upon between nations and to which their honor is publicly pledged, by which disputes may be settled without recourse to organized violence as the ultimate arbiter. When the method is once instituted no one will wish to return to the present method any more than any one would now propose to return to the primitive savage method of settling private disputes by private feuds, private wars. It will then stand out beyond a peradventure that our present method is a projection of barbarism into civilization, so that the barbarities of war, direct and indirect, are the necessary results of perpetuated barbarism. Instead of being trivial and episodic, the relation of law to war as a method of settling controversies is the issue of civilization against barbarism. The history of mankind is the proof of this statement.

Finally, the question of the function of law in respect to war rests upon the moral issue already touched upon. It is true that there is a great difference between law in fact, law in action, and words written upon paper. Unless there is a deep and widespread need for a public measure, a law is merely "passed" and then is passed over. I cannot imagine any sane human being denying that the existing status of international relationships with their frequent culmination in wars, establishes a need. If there is such a person I for one can no more argue with him than I could reason with a person who holds that bodily diseases create no need for measures of prevention and remedy. But there must be something more than a need. There must be an acute and general recognition of the need, a consciousness of trouble and evil, if the rule of law is actually to rule, and not be an idle pronunciamento. There must be a solid body of conviction and desire. The rule of law must render articulate an underlying solid body of belief and will. The denial of the efficacy of juridical methods of dealing with disputes between nations is thus at bottom a denial that there is at present among the peoples of the world—I say the peoples, not the diplomats, soldiers and politicians—a will to peace, a profound and enduring conviction of the evils of war.

Theoretically, this is possible. But one thing is certain. The proposal of the outlawry of war, with all that is contained within it, for the first time in history provides a means for discovering whether the will of the peoples is for war or peace. If the former, then wars will continue; no sensible person will waste his time and energy in tinkering with devices to get rid of them or to perfume and sugar-coat them. But let us at least find out what is the desire of the peoples of America and Europe. And I repeat, the attempt to discover this desire has never been made, for no simple, readily understood and fundamental method for uncovering their desire has ever been proposed, save the one for outlawing war. If their response is the will to peace, the outlawing of war will be the most decisive and comprehensive registration of the will of peoples that history has known. So much for the objection which rests on the futility of passing of laws.

I have written hypothetically, as one must till the trial is actually made. Before one indulges in any pessimistic forebodings as to the outcome, let one remember that hitherto the making of war and of the state of peace which under the war-system is only a truce between wars, has always been in the hands of officials, not of the peoples. The officials, no matter how well-intentioned personally, have been compelled to operate under the terms of the war-system, a system under which secret diplomacy and secret treaties, advancing of one's own nation at the expense of others, maintenance of the balance of power, recourse to intrigue combined with intimidating force, are bound to flourish. At present we are caught in the system, officials who make wars and peoples who suffer from them alike. The system creates the bonds which so tie our hands as to render efforts for peace ineffectual. I repeat what I have already said: As our objections to the plan spring mostly from the fact that our thinking is so colored by and subdued to the present system that our imagination of the future cannot escape from its influence, so our fears lest the peoples of the earth will not overwhelmingly manifest desire for the delegalizing of war spring from the fact that we conceive them to judge and act under the limitations and distortions imposed by the war-system.

I can only repeat in conclusion what Mr. Morrison has said, that the prime responsibility for commitment to the project rests upon the people of our own country. In the past our geographical situation and our economic resources have to a large extent protected us from being drawn into the war-system. We are now involved in its skirts and unless decisive measures are taken may readily become fully engaged in it without our conscious desire and plan. To save ourselves from being drawn in we must do something positive and decisive. In order to employ our relative immunity for the advantage of other peoples who are directly caught in its meshes, we must also do something. There is nothing the United States can do for Europe—and ultimately for Asia—half as important as to take part in freeing it from the shackles of the war institution. If we can assist in relieving Europe from that overhanging menace, Europe has the resources, material, intellectual and moral, to recover and take her place again as a leader in the friendly rivalry and cooperation of civilizations. Shall we rise in time to the opportunity to save ourselves from the risk which impends and to do for the rest of the world that which most needs to be done for the sake of enabling peoples to live and work together in amity? It is for the American people to answer, and their answer will be the reception given to the plan to cut the established alliance of law with war so as to put law decisively and irrevocably on the side of peace.

An Appreciation of Henry George

It was a happy thought of Professor Brown to select and arrange passages from Henry George's immortal work that give the gist of his contribution to political economy and social philosophy, while the pages which follow show that the task has been executed with a skill equal to the idea. The fact that Henry George has an ardent group of disciples who have a practical program for reform of taxation has tended to obscure from the recognition of students of social theory that his is one of the great names among the world's social philosophers. It would require less than the fingers of the two hands to enumerate those who from Plato down rank with him. Were he a native of some European country, it is safe to assert that he would long ago have taken the place upon the roll of the world's thinkers which belongs to him, irrespective, moreover, of adherence to his practical plan. But for some reason we Americans are slow to perceive and celebrate intellectual claims in comparison with the merits of inventors, political leaders and great industrialists. In the case of the author of *Progress and Poverty* the failure has doubtless been accentuated in academic circles by the fact that Henry George thought, wrote, and worked outside of them. And in the world at large, in spite of the fact that no works on political economy have had the circulation and reading obtained by his writings, discussion of the practical merits of his plan of reform of taxation has actually tended to blur his outstanding position as a thinker. This has been the case because the enormous inertia of social habit and the force of tremendous vested interests have depreciated his intellectual claims in order to strengthen opposition to his practical measures.

I do not say these things in order to vaunt his place as a

[First published in *Significant Paragraphs from Henry George's "Progress and Poverty,"* ed. Harry Gunnison Brown (Garden City, N.Y.: Published for the Robert Schalkenbach Foundation by Doubleday, Doran and Co., 1928), pp. 1–3.]

thinker in contrast with the merits of his proposals for a change in methods of distributing the burdens of taxation. To my mind the two things go together. His clear intellectual insight into social conditions, his passionate feeling for the remediable ills from which humanity suffers, find their logical conclusion in his plan for liberating labor and capital from the shackles which now bind them. But I am especially concerned in connection with Professor Brown's clear and well-ordered summary, to point out the claims which his social theory has upon the attention of students. No man, no graduate of a higher educational institution, has a right to regard himself as an educated man in social thought unless he has some first-hand acquaintance with the theoretical contribution of this great American thinker.

This is not the time and place, nor is there need, to dwell upon the nature of this contribution. Henry George is as clear as he is eloquent. But I cannot refrain from pointing out one feature of his thought which is too often ignored:—his emphasis upon ideal factors of life, upon what are sometimes called the imponderables. It is a poor version of his ideas which insists only upon the material effect of increase of population in producing the material or monetary increment in the value of land. One has only to read the third section of these extracts to note that Henry George puts even greater stress upon the fact that community life increases land value because it opens "a wider, fuller, and more varied life," so that the desire to share in the higher values which the community brings with it is a decisive factor in raising the rental value of land. And it is because the present system not only depresses the material status of the mass of the population, but especially because it renders one-sided and inequitable the people's share in these higher values that we find in *Progress and Poverty* the analysis of the scientist combined with the sympathies and aspirations of a great lover of mankind. There have been economists of great repute who in their pretension to be scientific have ignored the most significant elements in human nature. There have been others who were emotionally stirred by social ills and who proposed glowing schemes of betterment, but who passed lightly over facts. It is the thorough fusion of insight into actual facts and forces, with recognition of their bearing upon what makes human life worth living, that constitutes Henry George one of the world's great social philosophers.

A Tribute to Morris Raphael Cohen

Friends, it is perhaps natural on an occasion when we are commemorating—I will not say twenty-five years of history but twenty-five years of life—that our minds should be led backward, and so my mind has been running, as I sat here, into past years. I am perhaps older not merely than our guest, our honored guest, but than most of my colleagues here. So I have been led to recall, without derogation to the credit which my colleague, Mr. Woodbridge, has in bringing up Morris Cohen or that which belongs to Felix Adler, certain of his other early teachers: Josiah Royce, William James of Harvard, and that academic outlaw, Thomas Davidson.

I have been led to think of this living stream, into the current of which Morris Cohen was taken up, of which he became a part and which through him has passed on into the lives of so many others of us. I think not merely of these individuals, these personalities who cannot be present in the body but are certainly now present in the mind and spirit, not merely of Morris Cohen and some of the rest of us, but of all who have in any way come under his intellectual influence. I think also of the multitude of others in the past who have entered into his life and through his into the lives of those who are meeting here tonight, and into those of the countless other students of his who are not able to be here: of the scholars, rabbis, learned men of Russia and of the Orient. Perhaps, I, as an old man, am going too far back into the past, but it seems to me that the great significance of an occasion like this is that we may realize how real and how continuous are the influences which hold the intellectual and moral life of men together. These people, many of them from far lands and strange countries, have become in ways that none of us can realize—we

[First published in *A Tribute to Professor Morris Raphael Cohen, Teacher and Philosopher* (New York, 1928), pp. 17–20.]

do not even know the names of many of them—are even now a vital influence because of the candor, the intellectual energy, vigor and independence of a man like Morris Cohen.

If I were speaking of some persons I might seem in this emphasis upon the past to be derogating somewhat from Cohen's intellectual independence, but you all know him too well to give any such interpretation to my remarks.

It is not only that men like Josiah Royce, William James and Thomas Davidson, to mention only those who have gone, were themselves men of independence, who stood upon their own intellectual feet, men of very diverse views,—that they were, as the old New England phrase had it, not only men of character, but they were themselves characters, and so could not turn out any mere echo or phonographic repetition of their own views,—but that Morris Cohen has so amply demonstrated his own intellectual independence. In fact, I might almost say that the only thing I have against him is his undue fear lest somebody else agree with him.

It seems to me sometimes a little morbid; in another person almost inhuman. It is a wonderful thing that a person who is so thoroughly a democrat, and so thoroughly a believer in democracy, can have such a tremendous respect for minorities as Morris Cohen has. On the whole, the smaller the minority the more favorably it is looked upon by him. It is his candor, straightforwardness, his critical love of truth, as well as of scholarship, that we honor in him this evening. And because of this the stream of the past which is passing through him is a living stream. The thousands of pupils whom he has taught, so many of whom are here tonight to do him honor, so many of whom would gladly be here, have come here to participate in that spirit of candor, of straightforwardness, of honesty, without pretentious parade, which has marked his life.

Wherever there has been any oppression, there the oppressed have found a friend in Morris Cohen. Wherever there have been elements that were unpopular merely for some conventional reason, they have found a friend and a sympathizer in him. I am sure that consciously or unconsciously all of us, who have come here to do him honor this evening, have done it not merely from personal affection and from loyalty to a friend, but because we feel that in writing ourselves down his friend, we are in some measure also identifying ourselves with the friends of truth, the friends of freedom, the friends of that freedom which is both the parent and the progeny of truth, the friends of that truth which alone makes humanity free.

To the Chinese Friends in the United States

From time to time cases of our Chinese friends seriously involved in difficulties with the authorities here have come under the notice of individual members of this Committee. Not infrequently a good deal of hardship and at times no little injustice have been worked upon these people because of the discriminatory acts and attitudes of those charged with the administration of the laws. A real need was felt, therefore, for some organized effort to meet the situation. The direct outcome of this sentiment was the formation of the committee known as THE NATIONAL COMMITTEE FOR LEGAL DEFENSE OF CHINESE. Its purpose is specifically to secure to the Chinese of all classes in this country their full legal rights by providing access to adequate counsel and by any other related type of assistance it can give. The Committee also regards efforts to change discriminatory attitudes in the administration of the law as entirely within its scope.

It is plain that the Committee has a real task on its hands, because of both the difficult nature and the very large scope of its work. It is plain, too, that successful furtherance of its purposes must depend upon the combined support of every Chinese and every American who is interested in this new effort.

We have engaged Mr. John T. Find as executive secretary, and we earnestly hope that all our Chinese friends throughout the United States will cooperate with him and the members of this Committee either as individuals or as a group, to make this organization an effective instrument for promoting the legal interests of the Chinese people in this country and thereby strengthening the friendly relations between the United States and China.

[First published in *Chinese Student Bulletin* 1 (1928): 4.]

Appendixes

Appendix 1
Dewey's Naturalistic Metaphysics
By George Santayana

Readers of the *Journal of Philosophy* are doubtless studying, or have studied, Professor Dewey's recent book on *Experience and Nature*, certainly the weightiest and most incisive account he has given of his philosophy. In reviewing it, I may therefore be excused from attempting to sum up his chief contentions in his own language, considering especially that his language, as he himself says, is the chief or only obstacle to understanding him. Nor would the fairest paraphrase of his conclusions do him justice. Without the many pointed allusions and incidental insights that humanize his pages, without his constant appeals to the economy of the working mind, many of his positions would remain paradoxes, and it would be impossible to discover the scrupulous fidelity to facts, seen at a certain angle, which dictates his words, even when they seem most unintelligible. Here is a remarkable rereading of things with a new and difficult kind of sincerity, a near-sighted sincerity comparable in philosophy to that of contemporary painters in their painful studies. The intellect here, like the fancy there, arrests its dogmatic vision and stops short at some relational term which was invisible because it is only a vehicle in natural seeing. No wonder that these near elements, abstracted and focused in themselves, have a queer look. For my part, I am entirely persuaded of the genuineness and depth of Dewey's views, within the limits of his method and taken as he means them. He is, fortunately, not without an active band of followers who will be able to interpret and elaborate them in his own spirit. I am hardly in their case, and all I can hope to accomplish is to fix the place and character of this doctrine in relation to the points of view which I instinctively take or which seem to me, on reflection, to be most com-

[First published in *Journal of Philosophy* 22 (1925): 673–88. For Dewey's reply, see pp. 73–81.]

prehensive. And I will append such conclusions as I may provisionally reach on this subject to a phrase by which Dewey himself characterizes his system: *Naturalistic Metaphysics.* In what sense is this system naturalistic? In what sense is it metaphysical? How comes it that these two characters (which to me seem contradictory) can be united in this philosophy?

Naturalism is a primary system, or rather it is not a special system at all, but the spontaneous and inevitable body of beliefs involved in animal life, beliefs of which the various philosophical systems are either extensions (a supernatural environment, itself natural in its own way, being added to nature) or interpretations (as in Aristotle and Spinoza) or denials (as in idealism). Children are interested in their bodies, with which they identify themselves; they are interested in animals, adequate playmates for them, to be bullied with a pleasing risk and a touch of wonder. They are interested later in mechanical contrivances and in physical feats and adventures. This boyish universe is indefinitely extensible on its own plane; it may have heaven around it and fairyland in its interstices; it covers the whole field of possible material action to its uttermost reaches. It is the world of naturalism. On this material framework it is easy to hang all the immaterial objects, such as words, feelings, and ideas, which may be eventually distinguished in human experience. We are not compelled in naturalism, or even in materialism, to ignore immaterial things; the point is that any immaterial things which are recognized shall be regarded as names, aspects, functions, or concomitant products of those physical things among which action goes on. A naturalist may distinguish his own person or self, provided he identifies himself with his body and does not assign to his soul any fortunes, powers, or actions save those of which his body is the seat and organ. He may recognize other spirits, human, animal, or divine, provided they are all proper to natural organisms figuring in the world of action, and are the natural moral transcript, like his own feelings, of physical life in that region. Naturalism may, accordingly, find room for every sort of psychology, poetry, logic, and theology, if only they are content with their natural places. Naturalism will break down, however, so soon as words, ideas, or spirits are taken to be substantial on their own account, and powers at work prior to the existence of their organs, or independent of them. Now it is precisely such disembodied powers and immaterial functions prior to matter that are called metaphysical. Transcendentalism is not metaphysical if it remains a mere method, because then it might express the natural fact that any animal mind is its own center and must awake in order to know anything: it becomes metaphysical when this mind is said to be absolute, single, and without material conditions. To admit anything metaphysical in this sense is evidently to abandon naturalism.

It would be hard to find a philosopher in whom naturalism, so conceived, was more inveterate than in Dewey. He is very severe against the imagination, and even the intellect, of mankind for having created figments which usurp the place and authority of the mundane sphere in which daily action goes on. The typical philosopher's fallacy, in his eyes, has been the habit of hypostatizing the conclusions to which reflection may lead, and depicting them to be prior realities—the fallacy of dogmatism. These conclusions are in reality nothing but suggestions or, as Dewey calls them, "meanings" surrounding the passing experience in which, at some juncture, a person is immersed. They may be excellent in an instrumental capacity, if by their help instinctive action can be enlarged or adjusted more accurately to absent facts; but it would be sheer idolatry to regard them as realities or powers deeper than obvious objects, producing these objects and afterwards somehow revealing themselves, just as they are, to the thoughts of metaphysicians. Here is a rude blow dealt at dogma of every sort: God, matter, Platonic ideas, active spirits, and creative logics all seem to totter on their thrones; and if the blow could be effective, the endless battle of metaphysics would have to end for lack of combatants.

Meantime there is another motive that drives Dewey to naturalism: he is the devoted spokesman of the spirit of enterprise, of experiment, of modern industry. To him, rather than to William James, might be applied the saying of the French pragmatist, Georges Sorel, that his philosophy is calculated to justify all the assumptions of American society. William James was a psychologist of the individual, preoccupied with the varieties of the human imagination and with the possible destinies of the spirit in other worlds. He was too spontaneous and rare a person to be a good mirror of any broad general movement; his Americanism, like that of Emerson, was his own and within him, and perhaps more representative of America in the past than in the future. In Dewey, on the contrary, as in current science and ethics, there is a pervasive quasi-Hegelian tendency to dissolve the individual into his social functions, as well as everything substantial or actual into something relative or transitional. For him events, situations, and histories hold all facts and all persons in solution. The master-burden of his philosophy, which lends it its national character, is a profound sympathy with the enterprise of life in all lay directions, in its technical and moral complexity, and especially in its American form, where individual initiative, although still demanded and prized, is quickly subjected to overwhelming democratic control. This, if I am not mistaken, is the heart of Dewey's pragmatism, that it is the pragmatism of the people, dumb and instinctive in them, and struggling in him to a labored but radical expression. His pragmatism is not inspired by any wish to supply a new argument to support some old speculative dogma. Nor is he interested, like Nietzsche and Vaihinger, in a heroic pessimism, desperately living as if postulates were true which it knows to be false. He is not interested in speculation at all, balks at it, and would avoid it if he could; his inspiration is sheer fidelity to the task in hand and sympathy with the movement afoot: a deliberate and happy participation in the attitude of the American people, with its omnivorous human interests and its simplicity of purpose.

Now the philosophy by which Americans live, in contrast to the philosophies which they profess, is naturalistic. In profession they may be Fundamentalists, Catholics, or idealists, because American opinion is largely pre-American; but in their hearts and lives they are all pragmatists, and they prove it even by the spirit in which they maintain those other traditional allegiances, not out of rapt speculative sympathy, but because such allegiance seems an insurance against moral dissolution, guaranteeing social cohesion and practical success. Their real philosophy is the philosophy of enterprise. Now enterprise moves in the infinitely extensible boyish world of feats and discoveries—in the world of naturalism. The practical arts, as Dewey says, assume a mechanical unity and constancy established in the universe. Otherwise discoveries made to-day would not count to-morrow, inventions could not be patented, the best-laid plans might go astray, all work might be wasted, and the methods of experts could not be

adjusted more and more accurately to their tasks. This postulated mechanical system must evidently include the hands and
brain of the worker, which are intertwined inextricably with the
work done. It must also include his mind, if his mind is to be of
any practical account and to make any difference in his work.
Hence the implicit American philosophy, which it is Dewey's
privilege to make explicit, involves behaviorism. This doctrine is
new and amazing if taken to deny the existence of thought; but
on its positive side, in so far as it puts all efficient processes
on one level, it has been an implication of naturalism from time
immemorial. For a naturalist nothing can be substantial or
efficacious in thought except its organs and instruments, such as
brains, training, words, and books. Actual thought, being invisible and imponderable, eludes this sort of chase. It has always
been rather ignored by materialists; but it remained for American optimists to turn their scorn of useless thought into a glad
denial of its existence. This negative implication of behaviorism
follows also from the commonsense view that mind and body act
upon each other alternately; for when this view is carried out
with empirical rigor, it corrects the speculative confusion which
first suggested it. What it called mind turns out never to have
been anything but a habit in matter, a way people have of acting,
speaking, and writing. The actuality of spirit, mystically momentary, does not fall within the purview of this empirical inventory any more than the realm of truth, invisibly eternal. Men of
affairs, who can easily tell a clever man from a fool, are behaviorists by instinct; but they may scout their own conviction
when it is proposed to them by philosophers in paradoxical language. The business intellect, by the time it comes to theorizing,
is a little tired. It will either trust a first impression, and bluff it
out, or else it will allow comfortable traditional assurances in
these hazy regions to relieve it of responsibility.

Is Dewey a behaviorist? On the positive side of the theory, he
certainly is; and it is only when we interpret what he says about
ideas, meanings, knowledge, or truth behavioristically, that the
sense and the force of it begin to appear. Often, indeed, he seems
to jump the barrier, and to become a behaviorist in the negative
sense also, denying the existence of thought: because it would be
to deny its existence if we reduced it to its material manifestations. At least at one point, however, the existence of thought in

its actuality and spiritual concentration is admitted plainly. Not, indeed, on the ground which to most philosophers would seem obvious and final, namely, that people sometimes do actually feel and think. This consideration might seem to Dewey irrelevant, because actual feeling and thinking are accounted for initially, on his view, by the absolute existence of the specious or conventional world: they do not need to be introduced again among its details. An impersonal transcendental spectator, though never mentioned, is always assumed; and the spectacle of nature unrolled before him may be, and strictly speaking must be, wholly observable and material. There can not be any actual mind in experience except the experience itself. The consideration which nevertheless leads Dewey to graft something consciously actual and spiritual upon the natural world is of quite another sort. Essentially, I suspect, it flows from his choice of "events" to be his metaphysical elements (of which more presently); incidentally it is attached to the sympathetic study which he has made of Aristotle. Events, he thinks, have natural "endings," "culminations," or "consummations." They are not arbitrary sections made in the flux of nature, as if by geometrical planes passed across the current of a river. They are natural waves, pulsations of being, each of which, without any interruption in its material inheritance and fertility, forms a unit of a higher order. These units (if I may express the matter in my own language) fall sometimes into the realm of truth, when they are simply observable patterns or rhythms, and sometimes into the realm of spirit, as in animal perception or intent, when the complex tensions of bodily or social life generate a single sound, an actual pang, or a vivid idea. Mind at such moments possesses a hypostatic spiritual existence, over and above the whole behaviorist or pragmatic ground-work of mind: it has become conscious, or as Aristotle would say, has reached its second entelechy and become intellect in act. This hypostatic spiritual existence Dewey seems to recognize at least in esthetic contemplation; but evidently every actual feeling or idea, however engrossed in action or however abstractly intellectual, is in the same case. Such an admission, if taken to heart, would have leavened this whole philosophy; but Dewey makes it grudgingly, and hastens to cover it up. For instance, when he comes upon the phrase "Knowledge of acquaintance," a phrase intended to express just such instant innocent immediate perusal of essence, he refuses to understand it as it was meant, and says that acquaintance implies recognition and recognition familiarity; on the ground, I suppose, that people are called "acquaintances" when they bow to one another: and we are left with an uncomfortable suspicion that it is impossible to inspect anything for the first time. In another place we are told that consummations are themselves fruitful and ends are also means. Yes, but in what sense? Of course, no earthly flame is so pure as to leave no ashes, and the highest wave sinks presently into the trough of the sea; but this is true only of the substance engaged, which, having reached a culmination here, continues in its course; and the habit which it then acquired may, within limits, repeat the happy achievement, and propagate the light. One torch by material contact may kindle another torch; and if the torches are similar and the wind steady, the flames, too, may be similar and even continuous; but if anyone says that the visible splendor of one moment helps to produce that of another, he does not seem ever to have seen the light. It will therefore be safer to proceed as if the realm of actual spirit had not been broached at this point, and as if the culminations recognized were only runs or nodes discoverable in nature, as in the cycle of reproduction or in sentences in discourse. The behaviorist landscape will then not be split by any spiritual lightning, and naturalism will seem to be established in its most unqualified form. Yet in this case how comes it that Dewey has a metaphysics of his own, that cosmology is absent from his system, and that every natural fact becomes in his hands so strangely unseizable and perplexing?

This question, which is the crux of the whole system, may be answered, I think, in a single phrase: *the dominance of the foreground*. In nature there is no foreground or background, no here, no now, no moral cathedra, no centre so really central as to reduce all other things to mere margins and mere perspectives. A foreground is by definition relative to some chosen point of view, to the station assumed in the midst of nature by some creature tethered by fortune to a particular time and place. If such a foreground becomes dominant in a philosophy naturalism is abandoned. Some local perspective or some casual interest is set up in the place of universal nature or behind it, or before it, so that all the rest of nature is reputed to be intrinsically remote or dubious or merely ideal. This dominance of the foreground has always been the source of metaphysics; and the metaphysics has varied according as the foreground has been occupied by language or fancy or logic or sceptical self-consciousness or religious rapture or moral ambition. Now the dominance of the foreground is in all Dewey's traditions: it is the soul of transcendentalism and also of empiricism; it is the soul of moralism and of that kind of religion which summons the universe to vindicate human notions of justice or to subserve the interests of mankind or of some special nation or civilization. In America the dominance of the foreground is further emphasized by the prevalent absorption in business life and in home affections, and by a general feeling that anything ancient, foreign, or theoretical can not be of much consequence.[1] Pragmatism may be regarded as a synthesis of all these ways of making the foreground dominant: the most close-reefed of philosophical craft, most tightly hugging appearance, use, and relevance to practice today and here, least drawn by the lure of speculative distances. Nor would Dewey, I am sure, or any other pragmatist, ever be a naturalist instinctively or on the wings of speculative insight, like the old Ionians or the Stoics or Spinoza, or like those many mystics, Indian, Jewish, or Mohammedan, who, heartily despising the foreground, have fallen in love with the greatness of nature and have sunk speechless before the infinite. The pragmatist becomes, or seems to become, a naturalist only by accident, when as in the present age and in America the dominant foreground is monopolized by material activity; because material activity, as we have seen, involves naturalistic assumptions, and has been the teacher and the proof of naturalism since the beginning of time. But elsewhere and at other periods experience is free to offer different perspectives into which the faithful pragmatist will be drawn with equal zeal; and then pragmatic metaphysics would cease to be naturalistic and become, perhaps, theological. Naturalism in Dewey is accordingly an assumption imposed by the character of the prevalent arts; and as he is aware that he is a naturalist only to that

---

1. I can imagine the spontaneous pragmatism of some President of a State University, if obliged to defend the study of Sanskrit before a committee of Senators. "You have been told," he would say, "that Sanskrit is a dead language. Not at all: Sanskrit is Professor Smith's Department, and growing. The cost is trifling, and several of our sister universities are making it a fresh requirement for the Ph.D. in classics. That, Gentlemen, is what Sanskrit *is*."

extent and on that ground, his naturalism is half-hearted and short-winded. It is the specious kind of naturalism possible also to such idealists as Emerson, Schelling, or any Hegelian of the Left, who may scrupulously limit their survey, in its range of objects, to nature and to recorded history, and yet in their attitude may remain romantic, transcendental, piously receiving as absolute the inspiration dominating moral life in their day and country. The idealists, being self-conscious, regarded this natural scene as a landscape painted by spirit; Dewey, to whom self-consciousness is anathema, regards it as a landscape that paints itself; but it is still something phenomenal, all above board. Immediacy, which was an epistemological category, has become a physical one: natural events are conceived to be compounded of such qualities as appear to human observers, as if the character and emergence of these qualities had nothing to do with the existence, position, and organs of those observers. Nature is accordingly simply experience deployed, thoroughly specious and pictorial in texture. Its parts are not (what they are in practice and for living animal faith) substances presenting accidental appearances. They are appearances integrally woven into a panorama entirely relative to human discourse. Naturalism could not be more romantic: nature here is not a world but a story.

We have seen that the foreground, by its dominance, determines whether the empirical philosopher shall be provisionally a naturalist or shall try being something else. What now, looked at more narrowly, is the character of this foreground? Its name is Experience; but lest we should misunderstand this ambiguous word, it is necessary to keep in mind that in this system experience is impersonal. It is not, as a literary psychologist might suppose, a man's feelings and ideas forming a life-long soliloquy, his impressions of travel in this world. Nor is it, as a biologist might expect, such contact of sensitive animals with their environment as adapts them to it and teaches them to remember it. No: experience is here taken in a transcendental, or rather in a moral, sense, as something romantically absolute and practically coercive. There exists a social medium, the notorious scene of all happenings and discoveries, the sum of those current adventures in which anybody might participate. Experience is deputed to include everything to which experience might testify: it is the locus of public facts. It is therefore identical with nature, to the extent and in the aspects in which nature is disclosed to man. Death, for instance, should be set down as a fact of experience. This would not be possible if experience were something personal, unless indeed death was only a transition to another life. For so long as a man's sensations and thoughts continue, he is not dead, and when dead he has no more thoughts or sensations. But is such actual death, we may ask, the death that Dewey can have in mind? The only death open to experience is the death of others (here is a neat proof of immortality for those who like it); and death, for the pragmatist, simply *is* burial. To suppose that a train of thoughts and feelings going on in a man invisibly might at last come to an end, would be to place the fact of death in a sphere which Dewey does not recognize, namely, in the realm of truth; for it would simply be true that the man's thoughts had ceased, although neither he nor anybody else could find that fact in experience. For other people it would remain a fact assumed and credited, for him it would be a destiny that overtook him. Yet Experience, as Dewey understands it, must include such undiscoverable objects of common belief, and such a real, though unobserved, order of events. The dominant foreground which he calls Experience is accordingly filled and bounded not so much by experience as by convention. It is the social world.

How conventional this foreground is will appear even more clearly if we note the elements which are said to compose it. These are events, histories, situations, affairs. The words "affairs" and "situations," in their intentional vagueness, express very well the ethical nerve of this philosophy; for it is essentially a moral attitude or a lay religion. Life is a practical predicament; both necessity and duty compel us to do something about it, and also to think something about it, so as to know what to do. This is the categorical imperative of existence; and according to the Protestant tradition (diametrically opposed to the Indian) the spirit, in heeding its intrinsic vocation, is not alienated from earthly affairs, but on the contrary pledges itself anew to prosecute them with fidelity. Conscience and nature here exercise their suasion concurrently, since conscience merely repeats the summons to enter a field of responsibility—nature—formed by the deposit of its past labors. The most homely business, like the widest policies, may be thus transfused with a direct metaphysical inspiration; and although Dewey avoids all inflated eloquence on this theme, it is clear that his philosophy of Experience is a transcendental moralism. The other two terms, however, "events" and "histories," point to the flux of matter, although this is still gathered up and subdivided under units of discourse. "Event" is now a favorite word among philosophers who are addressed to the study of nature, but bring with them an empirical logic; and it well expresses that conjunction. An event does not involve a spectator, and does involve an environment on the same plane as the event: so far events belong directly to the flux of nature. At the same time an event is a change, and all the dialectic of change applies to the conception. Are events the crises between existence characterized in one way and existence characterized in another way? Or are events the intervals between such crises? But if these intervals, each having a somewhat different quality, were taken separately, they would not lodge in a common space or time; there would be no crises between them, no change, and (as I think would appear in the end) they themselves would have no existence. If events are to be successive, and fragments of the flux of nature, they must be changes in an abiding medium. In other words, an event, in its natural being, is a mode of substance, the transit of an essence. Moreover, natural events would have to be microscopic, because intervals containing no internal crisis, however long or even eternal they might seem sentimentally, could not be measured and would count as instants. This corollary is well fitted to remind us that nature laughs at our dialectic and goes on living in her own way. Her flux, like the flow of a river, is far more substantial than volatile, all sleepy continuity, derivation, persistence, and monotony. The most ordinary form of change in her—perhaps the only fundamental form—is motion; and it would be highly artificial to call the parts of a motion events where there are no crises and no intervals. Even night and day, unless we choose a particular point on the earth's surface for our station, are not events, since both are perpetual. It is apparently only on higher levels, genetically secondary, that nature produces events, where movement becomes rhythmical, and a culmination is followed by a breakdown and a repetition, as in animal birth and death. These secondary rhythms naturally attract the attention of a human observer, whose units of perception are all impressionistic and pictorial; he selects events from the vast continuities of nature because they go with rhythms in his own organism, with which his intuitions—the only vital culminations—are conjoined. Hence the empirical impression that nature is a series of events, although if they were mere events they could not be parts of nature, but only essences succeeding one another before vacant attention or in discourse; in other words, we should be in the mock world of psychologism.

The superficial level proper to empirical events becomes even more obvious if instead of calling them events we call them histories. The parts of nature seem events when we ignore their substance and their essence and consider only their position; anything actual is an event only, so to speak, at its margins, where it ceases to be itself. But before the parts of nature can seem to be histories, we must impose on them dramatic unities fetched from a far more derivative sphere. Histories are moral units, framed by tracing the thread of some special interest through the maze of things, units impossible to discriminate before the existence of passions and language. As there is a literary psychology which represents the mind as a mass of nameable pictures and describable sentiments, so there is a romantic metaphysics which hypostatizes history and puts it in the place of nature. "Histories" bring us back into the moral foreground where we found "situations" and "affairs." The same predicaments of daily life are viewed now in a temporal perspective, rather than as they beset us at any one moment.

That the foreground of human life is necessarily moral and practical (it is so even for artists) and that a philosophy which limits itself to clarifying moral perspectives may be a very great philosophy, has been known to the judicious since the days of Socrates. Why could not Dewey have worked out his shrewd moral and intellectual economy within the frame of naturalism, which he knows is postulated by practice, and so have brought clearness and space into the picture, without interposing any metaphysics? Because it is an axiom with him that nothing but the immediate is real. This axiom, far from being self-evident, is not even clear: for everything is "real" in some sense, and there is much doubt as to what sort of being is immediate. At first the axiom produced psychological idealism, because the proudly discoursing minds of philosophers took for granted that the immediate for each man could be only his own thoughts. Later it has been urged (and, I think, truly) that the immediate is rather any object—whether sensible or intelligible makes no difference—found lying in its own specious medium; so that immediatism is not so much subjective as closely attentive and mystically objective. Be it noted, however, that this admitted objectivity of real things remains internal to the immediate sphere: they must never be supposed to possess an alleged substantial existence beyond experience. This experience is no longer subjective, but it is still transcendental, absolute, and groundless; indeed it has ceased to seem subjective only because it seems unconditioned; and in order to get to the bottom and to the substance of anything, we must still ask with Emerson, What is this *to me*, or with William James, What is this *experienced as*. As Dewey puts it, these facts of experience simply *are* or *are had*, and there is nothing more to say about them. Such evidence flooding immediate experience I just now called mystical, using the epithet advisedly; because in this direct possession of being there is no division of subject and object, but rapt identification of some term, intuition of some essence. Such is sheer pleasure or pain, when no source or object is assigned to it; such is esthetic contemplation; such is pure thinking, the flash of intellectual light. This mystical paradise is indefinitely extensible, like life, and far be it from me to speak evil of it; it is there only that the innocent spirit is at home. But how should pragmatism, which is nothing if not prehensile, take root in this Eden? I am afraid pragmatism is the serpent; for there is a forbidden tree in the midst, the tree of Belief in the Eventual, the fruit of which is Care; and it is evident that our first parents must have partaken of it copiously; perhaps they fed on nothing else. Now when immediate experience is crossed by Care it suffers the most terrible illusion, for it supposes that the eventual about which it is troubled is controllable by the immediate, as by wishes, omens, or high thoughts; in other words, that the essences given in the immediate exist, generate their own presence, and may persist and rearrange themselves and so generate the future. But this is sheer superstition and trust in magic; the philosophy not of experience but of inexperience. The immediate, whether a paradise or a hell, is always specious; it is peopled by specters which, if taken for existing and working things, are illusions; and although they are real enough, in that they have definite character and actual presence, as a dream or a pain has, their reality ends there; they are unsubstantial, volatile, leaving no ashes, and their existence, even when they appear, is imputed to them by a hidden agency, the demon of Care, and lies wholly in being perceived. Thus immediate experience of things, far from being fundamental in nature, is only the dream which accompanies our action, as the other dreams accompany our sleep; and every naturalist knows that this waking dream is dependent for its existence, quality, intensity, and duration on obscure processes in the living body, in its interplay with its environment; processes which go back, through seeds, to the first beginnings of life on earth. Immediate experience is a consummation; and this not in esthetic contemplation alone, but just as much in birth-pangs or the excitement of battle. All its episodes, intermittent and wildly modulated, like the sound of wind in a forest, are bound together and rendered relevant to one another only by their material causes and instruments. So tenuous is immediate experience that the behaviorist can ignore it altogether, without inconvenience, substituting everywhere objects of conventional belief in their infinite material plane. The immediate is, indeed, recognized and prized only by mystics, and Dewey himself is assured of possessing it only by virtue of his social and ethical mysticism, by which the whole complex theater of contemporary action seems to him to be given immediately: whereas to others of us (who are perhaps mystical at other points) this world of practice seems foreign, absent from our better moments, approachable even at the time of action only by animal faith and blind presumption, and compacted, when we consider its normal texture, out of human conventions, many of them variable and foolish. A pragmatist who was not an ethical or social mystic, might explore that world scientifically, as a physician, politician, or engineer, and remain throughout a pure behaviorist or materialist, without noticing immediate experience at all, or once distinguishing what was given from what was assumed or asserted. But to the mystic, if he is interested in that world, it all comes forward into the immediate; it becomes indubitable, but at the same time vague; actual experience sucks in the world in which conventional experience, if left to dogmatize, would have supposed it was going on; and a luminous cloud of immediacy envelops everything and arrests the eye, in every direction, on a painted perspective; for if any object becomes immediate, whatever it may be, it becomes visionary. That same spiritual actuality which Dewey, in passing, scarcely recognized at the top of animal life, he now comes upon from within, and without observing its natural locus, lays at the basis of the universe. The universe, in his system, thereby appears inverted, the accidental order of discovery being everywhere substituted for the natural order of genesis; and this with grave consequences, since it is not so easy for the universe as for an individual to stand on its head.[2]

Consider, for instance, the empirical status of the past. The only past that ever *is* or *is had* is a specious past, the fading survival of it in the present. Now the form which things wear in the foreground, according to this philosophy, is their *real* form; and the meaning which such immediate facts may assume hangs on their use in executing some living purpose. What follows in regard to past time? That the survival or memory of it comprises all its reality, and that all the meaning of it lies in its possible relevance to actual interests. A memory may serve as a model or condition in shaping some further enterprise, or may be identified with a habit acquired by training, as when we have learned a foreign language and are ready to speak it. Past experience is accordingly real only by virtue of its vital inclusion in some present undertaking, and yesterday is *really* but a term perhaps useful in the preparation of tomorrow. The past, too, must work if it would live, and we may speak without irony of "the futurity of yesterday" in so far as yesterday has any pragmatic reality.

This result is consistent with the general principle of empirical criticism by which we are forbidden to regard God, truth, or the

2. A curious reversal of the terms "natural" and "ideal" comes about as we assume that the immediate is substantial or that it is visionary. Suppose I say that "everything ideal emanates from something natural." Dewey agrees, understanding that everything remote emanates from something immediate. But what I meant was that everything immediate—sensation, for instance, or love—emanates from something biological. Not, however, (and this is another verbal snare) from the concepts of biological science, essences immediately present to the thoughts of biologists, but from the largely unknown or humanly unknowable process of animal life. I suppose we should not call some of our ideas scientific if they did not trace the movement of nature more accurately and reliably than do our random sensations or dramatic myths; they are therefore presumably truer in regard to those distributive aspects of nature which they select. But science is a part of human discourse, and necessarily poetical, like language. If literal truth were necessary (which is not the case in practice in respect to nature) it would be found only, perhaps, in literature—in the reproduction of discourse by discourse.

material cosmos as anything but home vistas. When this principle is applied to such overwhelming outer realities, it lightens the
burden of those who hate external compulsions or supports;
they can henceforth believe they are living in a moral universe
that changes as they change, with no sky lowering over them
save a portable canopy which they carry with them on their
travels. But now this pleasant principle threatens the march of
experience itself: for if my ancestors have no past existence save
by working in me now, what becomes of my present being, if ever
I cease to work in my descendants? Does experience today draw
its whole existence from their future memories? Evidently this
can not be the doctrine proposed; and yet if it be once admitted
that all the events in time are equally real and equally central,
then at every point there is a by-gone past, intrinsically perfectly
substantial and self-existent; a past which such memories or continuations as may be integral to life at this later moment need
continue only very partially, or need recover only schematically,
if at all. In that case, if I ever find it convenient to forget my ancestors, or if my descendants find it advantageous to forget me,
this fact might somewhat dash their vanity or mine if we should
hear of it, but can not touch our substantial existence or the
truth of our lives. Grant this, and at once the whole universe is
on its feet again; and all that strange pragmatic reduction of yesterday to tomorrow, of Sanskrit to the study of Sanskrit, of truth
to the value of discovering some truth, and of matter to some
human notion of matter, turns out to have been a needless equivocation, by which the perspectives of life, avowedly relative,
have been treated as absolute, and the dominance of the foreground has been turned from a biological accident into a metaphysical principle. And this quite wantonly: because practice, far
from suggesting such a reduction, precludes it, and requires
every honest workman to admit the democratic equality of the
past and the future with the present, and to regard the inner processes of matter with respect and not with transcendental ar-
rogance. The living convictions of the pragmatist himself are
those involved in action, and therefore naturalistic in the dogmatic sense; action involves belief, belief judgment, and judgment
dogma; so that the transcendental metaphysics and the practical
naturalism of the pragmatist are in sharp contradiction, both in

logic and in spirit. The one expresses his speculative egotism, the other his animal faith.

Of course, it is not Dewey nor the pragmatic school that is to blame for this equivocation; it is a general heirloom, and has infected all that criticism of scholastic dogma on which modern philosophy is founded. By expressing this critical principle more thoroughly, the pragmatists have hoped to clear the air, and perhaps ultimately may help to do so. Although I am myself a dogmatic naturalist, I think that the station assumed by Dewey, like the transcendental station generally, is always legitimate. Just as the spirit has a right to soliloquize, and to regard existence as a strange dream, so any society or nation or living interest has a right to treat the world as its field of action, and to recast the human mind, as far as possible, so as to adapt it exclusively to that public function. That is what all great religions have tried to do, and what Sparta and Carthage would have done if they had produced philosophers. Why should not America attempt it? Reason is free to change its logic, as language to change its grammar; and the critic of the life of reason may then distinguish, as far as his penetration goes, how much in any such logic or grammar is expressive of material circumstances, how much is exuberant rhetoric, how much local, and how much human. Of course, at every step such criticism rests on naturalistic dogmas; we could not understand any phase of human imagination, or even discover it, unless we found it growing in the common world of geography and commerce. In this world fiction arises, and to this world it refers. In so far as criticism can trace back the most fantastic ideas—mythology, for instance—to their natural origin, it should enlighten our sympathies, since we should all have lived in the society of those images, if we had had the same surroundings and passions; and if in their turn the ideas prevalent in our own day can be traced back to the material conditions that bred them, our judgment should be enlightened also. Controversy, when naturalism is granted, can yield to interpretation, reconciling the critical mind to convention, justifying moral diversity, and carrying the sap of life to every top-most intellectual flower. All positive transcendental insights, whether empirical, national, or moral, can thus be honored (and disinfected) by the baldest naturalism, remaining itself international,

Bohemian, and animal. The luminous fog of immediacy has a place in nature; it is a meteorological and optical effect, and often a blessing. But why should immediacy be thought to be absolute or a criterion of reality? The great error of dogmatists, in hypostatizing their conclusions into alleged preëxistent facts, did not lie in believing that facts of some kind preëxisted; the error lay only in framing an inadequate view of those facts and regarding it as adequate. God and matter are not any or all the definitions which philosophers may give of them: they are the realities confronted in action, the mysterious but momentous background, which philosophers and other men mean to describe by their definitions or myths or sensible images. To hypostatize these human symbols, and identify them with matter or with God, is idolatry: but the remedy for idolatry is not iconoclasm, because the senses, too, or the heart or the pragmatic intellect, can breed only symbols. The remedy is rather to employ the symbols pragmatically, with detachment and humor, trusting in the steady dispensations of the substance beyond.

Appendix 2
Contemporary American Philosophy *
By Frank Thilly

The contemporary philosophies of the United States are largely characterized by their opposition to traditional idealism and their interest in the problem of knowledge, which is in many cases interpreted as a problem of action. The new movements derive their inspiration from the methods and results of natural science and seek, not always successfully, to avoid the metaphysical presuppositions of the older schools. The time-honored question of consciousness becomes the subject of their story, in the course of which we find the mind progressively stripped of its former qualities and functions until little is left of it but the name. Its requiem is sung by behaviorism and its emaciated form finally given over to materialism, the laughing heir, to be burned. An old trait of philosophy, however, remains: the new schools meet with vigorous criticism from each other as well as from the camp of speculative idealism against which they offer a united front. The interest in the problems though often narrow is always keen; and never before have our philosophical printing presses turned out such a mass of painstaking works as are being published in our country today. If it is true that war is the father of all things, we may confidently look forward to an era of fertility hitherto unknown in our brief intellectual history.

Let us turn first to the so-called realistic schools, both of which, in the new fashion, have published volumes representing their respective coöperative labors. 'Critical' realism follows largely in the wake of the older epistemologies, employing, however, a new and sometimes confusing terminology, which often leads one to forget that one is face to face with old acquaint-

* Read at the Sixth International Congress of Philosophy, at Harvard University, September 13–17, 1926.
[First published in *Philosophical Review* 35 (1926): 522–38. For Dewey's reply, see pp. 73–81.]

ances. Like the bygone realisms and idealisms, which were all more or less 'critical'—giving reasons for their faith,—the new critical realism carries the materials of a working philosophy in its kit: objects known, mental states, and the intermediary processes, such as ether waves, sense organs, and brain-processes, the mental states being generally reduced to epiphenomena. In order that there may be knowledge, something must be given; the nature of the object is said to be reflected in consciousness, given in sense or in thought: this revelation or symbol is the datum, quality-complex, character-complex, or essence. These qualities must have a bearer, for they must be somewhere even when they are not felt: 'the mental state' is such a bearer or vehicle of data. We seem to have here the tenuous ghost of the old soul-substance, many of whose functions it performs: indeed, we even find it endowed with causal efficacy.[1] The knower is confined to the data, the appearances or phenomena, to use the old language; he can never literally inspect the existent which he affirms and claims to know: the objects themselves do not get within our consciousness: between us all is "the unplumb'd, salt, estranging sea."[2] And so far as one can see, the theory can never bring us back to the solid land from which we stepped into its ship, but our faith in it is firm. We instinctively feel the appearance to be the character of real objects; the qualities are "imagined out there." We have the instinctive and irresistible feeling that what we have given, what we are aware of, is the object known itself. Moreover, pragmatism comes to our aid: we react to these data or qualities *as if* they had existence of their own. Everything is *as if* realism were true; and the *as if* is so strong that we may consider our instinctive and actually unescapable belief pragmatically justified.

According to Santayana we become conscious of a datum; or the appearance becomes a datum by a leap of intuition from the state of the living organism to the consciousness of some essence; and by another leap of faith and of action from the symbol actually given in sense or in thought to some ulterior existing object,[3] we instinctively feel these appearances to be the character of real

1. *Essays in Critical Realism: A Co-operative Study of the Problem of Knowledge*, 1920, p. 27.
2. *Ibid.*, pp. 196, 203, 24.
3. *Ibid.*, p. 183.

objects. Or, the datum is directly affirmed of the outer reality by an irresistible act of faith or action, or by the very pressure and suggestion of our experience. Have we not here a desperate effort to get the phenomena back again to their noumenal base, of which they were assumed to be the reflections in the first place?

And now as to the relevancy of the data: it is said that they must represent the character of the object "in some measure."[4] The object affirmed and intended is known in terms of the content presented to the knowing self. According to some critical realists, the content is relevant to the object in the sense that it contains its structure, position, and changes. "The content of knowledge offers us the fundamental categories, such as time, space, structure, relations, and behavior, in terms of which we think the world."[5] That is, more simply, knowledge is the recognized possession by the mind of the 'form' of the thing.[6] But how can we reach the form of the thing itself if the percipient can never get beyond the datum, if the gates to the existent physical object are closed to him? It is true, we are assured that what we perceive, conceive, remember, think of, is the outer object itself; but are we not also told that we have immediately present only subjective content? How can we know that the conception of our data, of our subjective content, in terms of categories, form, law, corresponds to the real world, the system of electrons, for example, which is never *perceived* by us? Besides, there is no agreement in the school as to what the essences really include; according to some of its members they embrace all possible qualities, primary, secondary, and tertiary; according to others, only some of the *primary* qualities.

We also find the teaching that essences have independent ideal existence, live in an independent logical sphere; they are not perceived but thought; they are universals, meanings; they become objects of intuition by accident. Even though these universals be derived from the data by the activity of thought, is it not fair to ask who or what does the thinking? In the last analysis Santayana explains them, as he explains all mental life, as the result of brain processes, as epiphenomena. The ideal logical realm in which philosophies are constructed, in which the leaps of intui-

4. *Ibid.*, p. 198.
5. *Ibid.*, pp. 200 f.
6. *Ibid.*, p. 218.

tion, faith, and action arrive, is an appearance of the nervous system. And yet this shadow-land of meaning which makes thought cognitive, also makes it practical. Intent is a mystery; it is not a mechanical force but an ideal pointing; and yet it is practical. How is this mystery solved? Behaviorism furnishes the answer: when thought is embodied in language, it becomes an agent in the physical world: the chasm between the symbol and the physical object is bridged by means of language, which is physical, but which like the Greek horse secretly carries meanings into the enemy's camp. We are deftly steered away from interactionism by such phrases as "thought supervenes," "language is merely an overflow of the physical basis of thought."[7] We are also told that science gives the mind dominion over matter by discovery of its form; thought is a part of nature but mechanically helpless; nevertheless ideas in a certain sense become directive in a mechanistic universe when they are conscious. How all this is possible on the theory of epiphenomenalism is a mystery.

The complaint has been lodged against the epistemologies of the past that they presuppose systems of metaphysics; and there has been a persistent demand for a 'voraussetzungslose Erkenntnistheorie,' a demand which our critical realists can hardly be said to have heeded. The neo-realists openly reject it; indeed, they insist on the emancipation of metaphysics from epistemology, declaring that the nature of things cannot be found in the nature of knowledge.[8] They reject all philosophies in which metaphysics is sharply divorced from the special sciences,— philosophies which make facts and laws of science dead abstractions, mere instrumental artifacts. Analysis is the method which will lead us to knowledge. It may be said, however, that their logic plays into the hands of their metaphysics and vice versa, as was also the case with Hegel; only, the logical method and the philosophy in harmony with it differ in these two schools. For the new realist the cosmos is an analyzable collection of static parts, while for Hegel, the old realist, it is a synthetic process of evolution. For both the universe is physical and logical. The new

7. *Reason in Science*, pp. 148, 24.
8. For the common platform of the school see *The New Realism: Coöperative Studies in Philosophy*, pp. 1–42.

realists accord full ontological status to things of thought (subsistences) as well as to physical entities (existences); things are real which do not exist, for to exist means to be in space and time. Hegel unites them in the living, acting, evolving *Begriff*, the concrete universal.

The new realists, then, presuppose a physical world of existences and a logical world of subsistences, both being real and analyzable into simples; analysis, however, does not destroy its object. Not only are the individual things independent of their being known, but the relations in which they stand to each other in no way change the object; that is, relations are external. This teaching follows as a logical consequence of the fact that a term, a concept, is eternally what it is, regardless of its relations. Therefore, relations, like objects, must be independent of knowing; and knowing can make no difference to the entity known and is not causally related to it. Moreover, the same object may belong to both the physical world and consciousness: its relation to consciousness does not change it. Analysis and conception are a means of access to reality: the reality is independent of the knowing it.

For this theory, says Spaulding, everything that can be known, or even not known, is a reality: not only physical things and mental processes, but universal truths, ideals, values, concepts, morality. Anything that can be thought, known, implied, imagined, even dreams, illusions and the like, are real, because all, as knowable, as concepts, are realities.[9] It would seem that the new realist gets rid of a whole host of problems by relegating the entire ideal, non-physical realm to the limbo of subsistence, which is real but does not exist in space and time: it belongs with the same cosmos as the physical only in that, like this, it can be known. The knower that knows logical constants also belongs with it, and may itself be known as the things that it knows, and analyzed. Moreover, cognition must take its place within the same plane as space, number, physical nature: when knowledge takes place, there is a knower interacting with things. In other words, we have a knower that not only knows physical things and their relations, thinks logically, analyzes and synthesizes,

9. See Spaulding, *The New Rationalism*, 1918; also: "Postulates of a Self-Critical Epistemology," *Phil. Rev.*, XVIII, pp. 615 ff.

constructs theories of science, but sits in judgment upon knowing, knows knowing just as it is.[10]

We have here a distinctly idealistic note, a note not at all out of harmony with epistemological realism as such: it is realistic in the sense that objects known are neither modified nor created by the act of knowing, and that no underlying reality is required to mediate the relationship between knowing and the object. By objects is meant anything that can be known, among them being included not only physical things but the whole world of concepts, thoughts as well as the thinker himself that knows them. This would leave the problem of the knower, of consciousness, of the mind, an open question; but the school proceeds to settle it by means of its one-sided method of analysis and the metaphysics which inevitably results from it. The knower which embraces all things known in its horizon must perforce itself be reduced to its lowest terms in order to satisfy the demands of science, which raises doubts against the fiction of a soul. Woodbridge declares that if we accept the conception of mind which flourished in the idealistic philosophies, it will be futile to assault the logical structure of idealism. We are therefore compelled to reduce consciousness to a state of 'innocuous desuetude': it must be either an object or a relation between objects in the realistic cosmos; for Woodbridge it is a relation. Just as things are held together in space, so they are held together in consciousness; only, in the continuum of consciousness they are held together in relations of meaning. Indeed, these connections hold them together: objects thus become representative of each other; in consciousness bread, for example, means nourishment, water the quenching of thirst. Consciousness is, therefore, nothing but such a 'meaningful' relation between objects; they are connected here in such a peculiar way as to become known. That is, when objects enter consciousness, meaning is added. We are also told that consciousness becomes aware of objects because of their meanings: when the linkage of meanings is destroyed, awareness diminishes.[11]

10. *The New Realism*, pp. 31 ff.
11. For Woodbridge see "The Field of Logic," *Science*, XX, pp. 587 ff.; "Problem of Consciousness," in *Studies in Philosophy and Psychology* (the Garman volume); "Nature of Consciousness," *J. of Phil.*, II, 119 ff.; "Consciousness and Meaning," *Psych. Review*, XV, pp. 397 ff.

This account of consciousness is nothing more than a statement of the fact that objects take on meaning in consciousness, that meaning is added: they acquire these meanings in virtue of being in consciousness together. They do not acquire them from consciousness; consciousness simply becomes aware of the meanings. And awareness of a fact is identical with awareness of it as meaning something: awareness *is* the manifold and irresistible meaning-connections which the things in the conscious situation have. Does this mean anything more than that to become aware of things is to become aware of what they mean; and that we should not become aware of things unless they meant something? Assuming all this to be true, is the story ended? Is it foolish to ask what it is that objects slip into and out of when they slip into and out of consciousness, and come out of as clean as they went in? Is it not proper to inquire how the meanings are added and subtracted in the slipping process, and where they come from? We do get an answer to these questions: consciousness is a function of the brain. Consciousness, we are told by Woodbridge, does not connect anything, synthetize anything; events get connected in the organism, and there arises this peculiar awareness of the connection. In other words, the highly differentiated organism is acted upon and acts upon the environment: this interaction is sensation, which is a natural event. Awareness of the sensation and its implications arises as a product of all these conditions; how we do not know. That is, awareness of the sensation is a relation of the organism to the stimulus, nothing more; the mystery of consciousness is supposed to be solved.

We are left here with the problem of consciousness unanswered; we receive no help by being told that it is a relation between an external stimulus and the nervous system. And Montague carries us no further: he simply develops the conception a little more scientifically. He accepts only one system of realities, the realities of space and time; there is no supernatural and super-spatial world. Consciousness is just a relation existing in a material world along with other relations; and like them it is describable ultimately in terms of the basic relation of space and time. It is finally explained in terms of potential energy in the brain: "when the potential energy at a nerve center is greater than the inflowing kinetic energy which is its cause, there exists a consciousness of the quality of that energy."[12] Here, again, we fail to obtain the slightest insight into the nature and meaning of consciousness; we receive instead a theory of its physiological basis or origin.

It must be pointed out in conclusion that the conception of consciousness as a relation between objects is by no means a necessary consequence of epistemological realism as such. The realist McGilvary, for example, defines consciousness as a "way of being felt together," a way of being experienced together, which must be taken at its face value. The way of being felt together is distinct from all other ways of togetherness; it is an ultimate fact not to be identified with anything else.[13] It is at this point that the way is opened to a real understanding of the problem of consciousness.

We come now to John Dewey, in whom the spirit of revolt is more vigorous and far-reaching than in any of his contemporaries. He utters his plague on both our traditional houses of rationalism and empiricism as well as on all the theories which conceive the universe in analogy with the cognitive side of human nature, whether as a mechanism or as a sensational or conceptual system. He protests against reducing man's beliefs, aversions, affections, to mere subjective impressions or effects on consciousness, to mere epiphenomena or appearances; against a block-universe, in which need, uncertainty, choice, and novelty would have no place. His chief concern is with human life and its interests, its values, and its works: "*Greift nur hinein ins volle Menschenleben, und wo ihr's packt, da ist es interessant!*" It is for this reason that his influence has spread far beyond his classroom; indeed, pragmatism, often in a distorted form, has become the most popular American philosophy of the day.

Dewey rejects what he calls the "idealistic fallacy," the view that *knowing* is the sole and genuine experiencing, that things are just and exclusively what they are *known* to be, a view which, he thinks, would make reflective thinking with logic as its norm the standard for experiential, religious, aesthetic, indus-

---

12. Montague, "Contemporary Realism and the Problem of Perception," *J. of Phil.*, IV, pp. 374 ff.; "Relational Theory of Consciousness," *ibid.*, II, pp. 39 ff.
13. "Experience as Pure and Consciousness as Meaning," *J. of Phil.*, VIII, pp. 511 ff.

trial, and social objects. Equally unsatisfactory to him is a philosophy which sets up intuition, immediate insight, mystical certainty of the real, and religious experience as a higher kind of knowledge. Against them all he places his own basal thesis that things are what they are experienced as, and that to give a just account of anything is to tell what a thing is experienced as. This is what he calls his unsophisticated realism; and the method of taking things in this unsophisticated way, as a starting-point, remember,—simply, directly, impartially,—is the genuine critical method, is critical empiricism. Now we not merely *know* things but experience them as desired and undesired, good and bad, beautiful and ugly, as just what they are; we love, hate, desire, fear, believe, and deny. We have to do here with active performances to and about things, with acceptances and rejections of things, with organic attitudes and dispositions.[14]

This critical method is applied to truth itself. We must frankly start out from the fact of thinking as inquiring, and purely external existences as terms of inquiry; and we must construe validity and truth on the basis of what they actually mean and do. We find that a meaning is true so far as it is tested through action that carries it to successful completion. "We call it verification when we regard it as a process, when the development of the idea is strung out and exposed to view in all that makes it true. As a process telescoped and condensed we call it truth." What Dewey tells us here is that an hypothesis that explains the facts or is verified, has been carried to successful completion and is accepted as true. In this sense the utility of the idea is the test of its truth. This thought is universalized to mean: human thinking satisfies human purposes, desires, it is an instrument in the service of the will, and its success in satisfying the will is its end and test. The finalities (atoms, concepts, God), therefore, have existence and import only as problems, needs, struggles, and instrumentalities of conscious agents and patients.[15] All this is true if it is not forgotten that among the human purposes is the will to know, to understand, to explain experience,—the immediate

14. See Dewey's *Experience and Nature*; also "Brief Studies in Realism," *J. of Phil.*, VIII, pp. 393 ff., 546 ff.; *Influence of Darwin on Philosophy*, pp. 242 ff.
15. See "Intellectualist Criterion of Truth," in *Influence of Darwin*, etc., pp. 112 ff.

experience, for example, of seeing the sun move. And Dewey's entire system is based upon this old conception of truth: the thinker must report experiences just as they are, impartially; he must distinguish between the different kinds of experiencing and put them into the classes where they belong, not where he would like to have them belong. And as an epistemologist he seeks to tell the old truth about the entire knowledge-situation, for "thinking with logic as its norm" guides him in the construction of his theory of knowledge.

The same old-fashioned thinking is employed by our philosopher in his study of the value-situation: he must report our value-experiences just as they are. There are immediate goods or values,—objects are wanted, desired, striven for,—and there are principles by which they may be appraised, regulated, and verified. That is, there are goods *de facto*, desired goods, and goods *de jure*, reasonable, desirable, 'real' goods. Conscience in morals, taste in the fine arts, convictions in belief pass insensibly into critical judgments. Knowledge is a means of illuminating and justifying goods, of liking and choosing knowingly, that is, in responsible and informed ways instead of ignorantly and fatalistically. The question at once arises: by what principles are our likings to be judged; what are these responsible and informed ways in which the likings must express themselves? What are the conditions and consequences which will help us to like them more? The rationalist's *summum bonum* in morals is said to be an abstraction while would-be naturalism's appeal to the strongest desire would land us in nihilism. Whither, then, shall we turn for a criterion of the desirable, the real goods? It is held that we learn their bearing by applying them, by seeking to realize their intent, their meaning: the better is what will do more in the way of liberating and increasing likings, values, of making goods more secure, more coherent, more significant in appreciation. In other words, the test of a liking is its capacity to free, increase, and secure other likings, that is all. Santayana's judgment that Dewey is "an inveterate naturalist" would thus seem to be well founded.[16] It might also appear that he is the philosopher *par excellence* of twentieth century Philistinism: now that "the requisite tools of physics, physiology, and economics are at hand," he

16. Santayana, "Dewey's Naturalistic Metaphysics," *J. of Phil.*, XXII, pp. 673 ff.

tells us, the work of criticism can be begun. This would be a mistaken judgment, however. We must not forget that Dewey the naturalist is also a sincere and ardent social idealist and a thorough-going optimist. "Social reform," he insists, "is conceived in a philistine spirit if it is taken to mean anything less than precisely the liberation and expansion of the meanings of which experience is *capable*. Nothing but the best, the richest, and the fullest experience is good enough for man." Positive concrete goods of science, art and social companionship are the basic subject-matter of philosophy as criticism; and only because such positive goods already exist is their emancipation and secured extension the defining aim of intelligence. The fact is that Dewey does not carry naturalism to its logical, materialistic conclusion because he has an abiding faith in human nature. This is what Santayana must mean when he characterizes his naturalism as "half-hearted and short-winded" and defines his attitude as "essentially a moral attitude or lay religion," or as a transcendental moralism. Indeed, it is not only in his practical philosophy that Dewey betrays his heritage: his entire conception of experience as experiencing reveals an idealistic flavor, for after all it is his psychology which supplies him with knowledge of the behavior of experience, of the knowing, feeling, willing acts or attitudes found in experience.

Indeed, there is something half-hearted in nearly all the new philosophies which have been described in the preceding pages. We note this, for example, in the apologetic treatment of mind or consciousness, which played such a leading rôle in the systems against which protest is now being raised. Mind has fallen from its high estate and is reduced to a mere relation between objects. The next step in its declining career would seem to be its elimination from serious discussion as either useless or non-existent; and this step is taken by the new science of behaviorism. It rejects the method of introspection and makes sensori-motor action, "human action and human conduct as a mechanical function of the environment and the reaction system," its object-matter. "To assume that these reactions are accompanied by consciousness," says Weiss, "is no more helpful in understanding behavior than it is to assume that if we knew whether atoms in a chemical reaction actually experience affinity, valence, warmth, cold, etc., we could explain chemical reactions." The behaviorist studies the stimuli and situations which act upon man and "the reactions which result from the operation of these stimuli upon a nervous system having certain acquired and inherited characteristics." Only in this way shall we reach objective, accurate, and verifiable results.[17]

In his article, "A Behavioristic View of Purpose," Perry has made a thoroughgoing attempt to apply the behavioristic method in the field of purposive human conduct.[18] He points out that behaviorism does not abandon consciousness but only the introspective theory of consciousness: "it regards the animal reflex or habit as a more elementary phenomenon than an introspectively discriminated intensity." Instinct and complex are organic dispositions or systematic arrangements which condition specific modes of performance. What is called purpose is likewise just the particular set or tendency or disposition of an organism. Determination by the future does not mean determination by an antecedently existing idea of a future result but the action of a present disposition that is correlated with future consequences. It is the set of the nervous mechanism that is responsible for the action which we call teleological, intelligent.

It seems plain that the entire behavioristic enterprise would be impossible if there were no consciousness to fall back upon at every step; and we are not surprised that some members of the school hesitate to abandon it. The behaviorist translates into terms of nervous disposition and action what he believes to be taking place in an actual conscious situation, in which the agent observes, thinks, plans, contrives. The behaviorist is himself a thinking, contriving animal, and knows how he goes about solving practical problems: otherwise there would be no behavioristic theory of human conduct. Even if he were able to do without a consciousness as an active factor in conduct, he would still need it as a fund to draw upon to meet his obligations as a behaviorist.

This, however, would not prevent us from studying action from the outside or from calling acts of adjustment intelligent in

17. A. P. Weiss, "The Relation between Physiological Psychology and Behavior Psychology," *J. of Phil.*, XVI, pp. 626 ff.
18. *J. of Phil.*, XVIII, pp. 85 ff. See also, in criticism of Behaviorism: Lovejoy, "Paradox of the Thinking Behaviorist," *Phil. Rev.*, XXX, pp. 135 ff.; "Pragmatism and the New Materialism," *J. of Phil.*, XIX, pp. 5 ff.; Pratt, "Behaviorism and Consciousness," *J. of Phil.*, pp. 596 ff.

a Pickwickian sense, as we might do in the case of a plant or even of a machine. Perry sticks to this text when he declares that the introspective psychologist regards mind as something that supervenes, while the behaviorist regards it as something that intervenes as an arc or circuit of the general causal nexus. Intelligence is for him an observable fact, in this sense. If this is so, we ask with Lovejoy, what are the observable facts in the case of the planning action in which we find entities which are not real parts of the material world? A past or possible future state of the material world is not at the moment when it is represented in the experience of the planner a part of the real material world. The content of my memories or expectations is not as such present in the existing bodies and objects, not a part of the general causal nexus. Nothing, however, will prevent the behaviorist from fishing in dark waters; he has his neural sets to fall back on: whatever is revealed in consciousness will be translated into terms of the intervening arc.

In behaviorism consciousness, mind, either finds its occupation gone or gives up the ghost. Similar tendencies to depreciate consciousness have already been noted in other philosophies of the day; and it is not surprising that the charge of materialism has been lodged against many of their representatives.[19] It is hard to justify such an indictment because the new materialisms, like their nineteenth-century ancestors, are not rigorously developed systems of metaphysics. We may, however, characterize as naturalistic the theories which identify conscious intelligent action with mere neural sets and neural adjustments as well as those which explain consciousness as the effect of the mechanism of the brain. To regard the living human organism as the locus of consciousness is not materialism unless the organism is in turn reduced to a mere physical mechanical system.

Among the critical realists Sellars and Santayana have been singled out as fair targets in the camp of materialism. For Sellars consciousness is one variant of the cortex of the brain, neural activity being the other; psychical entities are peculiar characteristics of the neural wholes and inseparable from them. "Consciousness is the brain become conscious." It is existentially present to that part of the cortex which is functioning, and the

19. See Lovejoy, "Pragmatism and the New Materialism," and Pratt, "The New Materialism," *J. of Phil.*, XIX, pp. 337 ff.

brain's space is its space. Both parallelism and interactionism are rejected in name, apparently in order to satisfy science; and the problem is craftily solved by letting the variant consciousness "literally assist the brain to meet new situations": it surveys, selects, combines, and guides behavior. So far we have nothing but a soft-speaking but full-fledged interactionist dualism. In order, however, to make such assistance possible, consciousness becomes an extended manifold, evidently on the principle that the 'assisting' cause must be like its effect. We are finally frankly told that "consciousness is physical and extended, but is not a spatial part of the brain." [20] This is, of course, a consistent materialism; it saves the soul by making it an inseparable physical assistant of the brain: consciousness can do nothing without neural action, and in certain cases neural action can do nothing without consciousness. But in that case must not this physical and extended consciousness be a part of the universal mechanical system, and if so, how can it be a 'variant' except as the ether-wave is a variant from the air-wave?

Santayana, too, has been ranked among the materialists. It is true, his essences are ideal, not mechanistic; they are neither states of the mind nor physical existences but meanings. Nevertheless, they are the products of organic processes, automatically generated by them,—the product of structure in the world,— epiphenomena; and by themselves they are mechanically helpless. And it is only through "the overflow of the physical basis of thought," as we have seen, that they can become efficient in the mechanical universe. But if these ideal essences are part and parcel of the universe and can become helpful by their mere presence to the physical basis of thought, how can the universe be a mere mechanical system? And if the universe is such a mechanical system, how shall we account for the ideal essences; how can they be automatically generated by organic processes? If Santayana is a materialist, he is only a half-hearted one; he refuses to sacrifice his essences to the system.

It would be a laborious task to attempt a classification of the various neo-realists with respect to their materialistic leanings. The whole spirit of the school with its non-physical world of subsistences, its universe of thought and meaning, it seems to

20. "Is Consciousness Physical?" *J. of Phil.*, XIX, pp. 690 ff.

me, is opposed to a mere mechanistic interpretation of reality. Two souls, however, are lodged in its corporate heart: it has a wholesome respect for the logical entities and an abiding trust in natural science. We hear that the knower, which as known belongs to the sphere of subsistence, is also some variety of agency homogeneous with the environment, on the same plane as space, number, physical nature. That is, the thinker is of the earth earthy but his thoughts are in the non-physical land of thoughts, and both dwell together in the same cosmos of knowableness. Then there is the teaching that consciousness is a relation between objects, which has a materialistic sound; but it is sometimes merely intended as a non-committal way of saying that in consciousness objects have meanings, which is itself a bare statement of fact and merely opens up the whole problem. To other realists, however, it means that consciousness is a relation between the organism and the physical energies, as has already been pointed out in the case of Montague, whose doctrine may fairly be called materialistic, or energistic. But even here potential energy spends its idle hours by becoming conscious, and brings a rift into the mechanistic lute.

And now, in conclusion, what shall we say of these new philosophies as a whole? They have been characterized as closet-philosophies removed from life and its works, as immersed in specialistic problems and employing a technical terminology that is a hindrance rather than a help, each coöperative group swearing by its official tenets in its specific jargon, like the old scholastic orders. There is some truth in these complaints; they are complaints, however, which are not new in the history of thought. It must not be forgotten that we are living in the reign of Science, and that popular monarchs are always feared and obeyed, be they theological, metaphysical, or positivistic. The new theories seek to make their peace with the new science, and the terms offered by them have often been over-generous. But the enterprise has not been unprofitable, for, after all, the interest has been centered upon the old fundamental questions, which have been honestly examined and discussed, often from new and suggestive angles. And in spite of the most painstaking efforts to explain consciousness away by dressing it in new clothes and giving it new names, it still remains as a fundamental problem. It is, therefore, impossible to ignore the so-called idealistic philosophy, which has itself kept in intelligent touch with all the new movements and does not fail to appreciate the particular contributions which they have made. It, too, begins with the frank recognition of objective reality, accepts the world of objects and of selves as given, and studies the world of experience; indeed, what else could it study? And it finds that to be an object is to stand in relation to a subject, in a judgment-relation. Our objects are always objects of knowledge, and our knowledge is knowledge of objects. Another thing: the knowing attitude is not the only attitude of the person. Mind includes will and purpose; it is teleological, it interprets according to means and ends. The pragmatists are right in emphasizing this phase of consciousness; their error consists in subordinating it to mere practical ends. One of the ends of the mind is just to know, to understand; and such knowing has both practical and theoretical value. Again, analysis is a most important function of knowledge, but so is synthesis: the mind aims at unity not only in things but in itself; it cannot remain sane unless it is at one with itself. Neo-realism leaves us with a collection of fragments—physical things, meanings, relations, logical entities—which some one must attempt to put together again. Perhaps its work of destruction in the philosophical China shop has been worth while; at any rate it has left some pieces that can be utilized in the work of reconstruction that is bound to follow. And when pragmatism has performed its mission of emphasizing the importance of life in its larger aspects, it will perhaps tell us *how* to live; it will enter the fields of art and literature and politics and ethics and point us to a new culture and real civilization. This is what the great thinkers from Plato down have attempted to do for us; their efforts may be failures but what better has pragmatism to put in their place? Life is too short for us to learn in a life-time by our own individual experience what to do even with the pragmatic yard-stick in our hands. Do we not need a Moses to lead us out of the wilderness?

Appendix 3
Some Meanings of Meaning in Dewey's
Experience and Nature
By Everett W. Hall

Meaning is plural. So it is with the meaning of meaning. It would be an injustice to the empirical spirit of Dewey to presuppose, at the very outset of our inquiry, that his interpretation of the nature of meaning (or rather, of meanings) is a singular and stable affair. No, we must expect uncertainty and fluctuation. After all, the important thing, as Dewey says, in any critical undertaking, is richness of meaning rather than truth (especially if we add the adjective "fixed" to this last). So we will at least begin by adopting Dewey's spirit. We will accept the denotative method and simply point to this and that meaning of meaning as they happen or precisely as they are presented to us in *Experience and Nature*. We will treat all his meanings of meaning as equal, since they are all immediately "had" by the casual reader. If this leads us to an evaluation within Dewey's own use we will admit it only reluctantly.

Perhaps the first character to impress us is that meaning is restricted, it is not to be referred to all reality (or, more precisely, it occurs within nature). There is, it seems, a world (or a level) of meaningless natural or physical events to which meanings are added. Dewey tells us that events "acquire" meanings. "A directly enjoyed thing adds to itself meaning . . ." (p. 167), ". . . events come to possess characters . . ." (p. 174), ". . . universals, relations, meanings, are of and about existences, not their exhaustive ingredients. The same existential events are capable of an infinite number of meanings" (p. 319). He speaks of "converting physical and brute relationships into connections of meanings," for on the merely animal level that which procures satisfaction is not yet an object or "thing-with-meanings" (p. 370). All this seems perfectly clear as well as important, for it marks

[First published in *Journal of Philosophy* 25 (1928): 169–81. For Dewey's reply, see pp. 81–91.]

off Dewey's position from that of idealism. But, empirically enough, Dewey does not leave us here. He feels constrained to point out that natural events themselves are relational, are cases of interaction, are not only sources of later "added" meanings, but are themselves vague, immediate, non-articulated meanings. But more of this in the sequel.

Delving further into meaning as restricted and as only a part of nature we find other characteristics. We are told that meaning is restricted to social communication and social communication is restricted to linguistic behavior. Language gives rise to socially shared activity, to participation, and this *is* meaning. Thus Dewey tells us that language "created the realm of meanings" (p. 168). "Meanings do not come into being without language, and language implies two selves involved in a conjoint or shared undertaking" (p. 299). "Language is a natural function of human association; and its consequences react upon other events, physical and human, giving them meaning or significance" (p. 173). Now this, again, is definite enough, but, true to the empirical spirit, Dewey does not stick to it in any hard and fast dialectical fashion. On occasion, Dewey is not loath to extend the sphere of meaning to the non-human and the non-social, to physical interactions preceding the rise of language and communication, to qualities in their non-communicable and indefinable immediateness. "Meanings are objective because they are modes of natural interaction; such an interaction, although primarily between organic beings, also includes things and energies external to living creatures" (p. 190). "Apart from language, from imputed and inferred meaning, we continually engage in an immense multitude of immediate organic selections. . . . We are not aware of the qualities of many or most of these acts; we do not objectively distinguish and identify them. Yet they exist as feeling qualities, and have an enormous effect upon our behavior. . . . They give us our *sense* of rightness and wrongness, of what to select and emphasize and follow up, and what to drop, slur over and ignore, among the multitude of inchoate meanings that are presenting themselves. They give us premonitions of approach to acceptable meanings, and warnings of getting off the track. Formulated discourse is mainly but a selected statement of what we wish to retain among all these incipient starts, following ups and breakings off" (pp. 299, 300). Here we at least seem to have meaning antecedent to language and discourse and the social participation based in such.

But we must hasten on with our description of the meanings of meaning. Another important interpretation is that meanings refer simply to consequences, the future, possibilities, what is to come. "What a physical event immediately is, and what it *can* do or its relationship are distinct and incommensurable. But when an event has meaning, its potential consequences become its integral and funded feature. When the potential consequences are important and repeated, they form the very nature and essence of a thing. . . . Since potential consequences also *mark* the thing itself, and form its nature, the event thus marked becomes an object of contemplation; as meaning, future consequences already belong to the thing" (p. 182). But Dewey even goes further at times and identifies meaning with awareness of consequences. "Commonsense has no great occasion to distinguish between bare events and objects; objects being events-with-meanings. . . . Events have effects or consequences anyway; and since meaning is awareness of these consequences before they actually occur, reflective inquiry which converts an event into an object is the same thing as finding out a meaning which the event already possesses by imputation" (p. 324). If we waive the question as to whether consequences must be anticipated, we again seem to have a perfectly definite interpretation of meaning. The meaning of anything (or better, of any event) lies in its future, in that which succeeds it. But we are not left here. We are also told that meaning refers to the present and the past. To dwell a moment on the latter we need only to point out Dewey's emphasis on conditions, antecedents, causes, and their rôle in meaning to make this clear. "The proposition that the perception of a horse is valid and that a centaur is fanciful or hallucinatory, does not denote that these are two modes of awareness, differing intrinsically from each other. It denotes something with respect to causation, namely, that while both have their adequate antecedents, the specific causal conditions are ascertained to be different in the two cases. Hence it denotes something with respect to consequences, namely, that action upon the respective meanings will bring to light (to apparency or awareness) such different kinds of consequences that we should use the two meanings in very different ways. . . . Since conditions in the two cases *are* different, they operate differently" (p. 322). This example, though recognizing the place of "conditions" (i.e., prior conditions) as well as consequences in meaning, might seem to reduce the former to the latter. This can hardly be said of the following, however: "The union of past and future with the present manifest in every awareness of meanings is a mystery only when consciousness is gratuitously divided from nature and when nature is denied temporal and historic quality. When consciousness is connected with nature, the mystery becomes a luminous revelation of the operative interpenetration in nature of the efficient and the fulfilling" (pp. 352, 353). That is, we seem here to be told to look for meaning in total "histories," in immanent temporal wholes rather than in the future or consequential alone.

An interpretation closely connected with the last is that meanings are tools. On this basis any method or means of attaining desired consequences would be a meaning. Language, being one of the most widespread and delicately varied of tools, would consequently be a chief form of meaning. "As to be a tool, or to be used as means for consequences, is to have and to endow with meaning, language, being the tool of tools, is the cherishing mother of all significance" (p. 186). Yet we are told that meanings are both instruments and *also* immediate ends, fulfillments. Hence we are led to wonder whether their distinguishing characteristic is that they are tools. "Communication is uniquely instrumental and uniquely final. It is instrumental as liberating us from the otherwise overwhelming pressure of events and enabling us to live in a world of things that have meaning. It is final as a sharing in the objects and arts precious to a community, a sharing whereby meanings are enhanced, deepened and solidified in the sense of communion" (pp. 204, 205).

And this brings us to another distinction that Dewey emphasizes, namely, that between meaning as reference and meaning as immediate sense. By meaning as reference Dewey seems to mean a situation where the symbol and the symbolized, the sign and the thing signified, are quite external and where meaning is directly appreciated as a reference to some character outside that which means or refers. Dewey sometimes calls this cognitive or intellectual meaning. On the other hand, "sense" refers to meaning directly given, where there has been no analysis into sign and the signified. We have even here a reference, a relation, an interdependence, but it is of elements in a whole rather than of two wholes looked upon as quite external to each other. There is reference, but not awareness of reference as such. Dewey sometimes speaks as though "signification" or meaning as cognitive reference were due to a problem and its solution, whereas "sense" or immediate meaning does not. The following may serve to present his distinction: "The qualities of situations in which organisms and surrounding conditions interact, when discriminated, make sense. Sense is distinct from feeling, for it has a recognized reference; it is the qualitative characteristic of something, not just a submerged unidentified quality or tone. Sense is also different from signification. The latter involves use of a quality as a sign or index of something else, as when the red of a light signifies danger, and the need of bringing a moving locomotive to a stop. The sense of a thing, on the other hand, is an immediate and immanent meaning; it is meaning which is itself felt or directly had. When we are baffled by perplexing conditions, and finally hit upon a clew, and everything falls into place, the whole thing suddenly, as we say, 'makes sense.' In such a situation, the clew has signification in virtue of being an indication, a guide to interpretation. But the meaning of the *whole* situation as apprehended is sense" (pp. 260, 261).

But we are not done with our denotative duties even yet. We must not close this empirical survey until we have pointed out one more character or type of meaning, one which really brings us back to the beginning of our list. Meaning is simply one form of interaction—namely, interaction between an organism (Dewey does not always say human, but we may perhaps assume the adjective) and an extra-organic environment. "The qualities [direct meanings—in this case, sensations] never were 'in' the organism; they always were qualities of interactions in which both extra-organic things and organisms partake. When named, they enable identification and discrimination of things to take place as means in a further course of inclusive interaction. Hence they are as much qualities of the things engaged as of the organism" (p. 259). Thus we can readily see that meaning has its prerequisites and that it is a restricted sort in a larger world of events. "Organic and psycho-physical activities with their qualities are conditions which have to come into existence before mind, the presence and operation of meanings, ideas, is possible.

They supply the mind with its footing and connection in nature; they provide meanings with their existential stuff" (p. 290).

The reader is by now very exacerbated. Why such a collection of quotations? And, further, do you mean to imply that all these meanings of meaning you think you have distinguished are mutually exclusive? But patience. The empirical method is to blame for all this. I have been trying merely to describe, to point out. Who am I that I should lay down *a priori* rules as to the significance we shall place on Dewey's words? I have tried to let them speak for themselves. If they are somewhat incoherent and diversified on the one hand and if they suggest a possible unification and reduction on the other, we must solve our problem by appeal to some other procedure—the denotative one has tried and has failed to point out what we want. So it is with fear and trembling and only because of the importunate demands of my reader that I venture forth on somewhat of an evaluation and criticism. Dewey's interpretations of meaning have now been "had." They present a mixture of stability and uncertainty—a problem. Intelligence awakes and demands a (possible) solution.

II

First of all let us put thrifty miserliness aside, let us cast many of the different meanings overboard. We will have plenty of labor making port with only a few and even those in emaciated form. And of those left, let us first of all consider meaning as consequent to language and a matter of the social sharing of action to which language gives rise.

No one would be so foolish as to deny that language does help in community of action (although there certainly may be community of action without language), nor that language is always and intimately bound up with meaning. But what bothers me is: Is meaning to be *restricted* to language and the shared activity to which it gives rise? In the first place, it does not seem quite legitimate to restrict meaning to socially shared activity. The nonactive, the active but not socially shared would seem to be characters of the real world. Are they simply meaningless? And even in distinctly shared activities, are there not always non-shared and non-communicated features, and are these forthwith to be relegated to the realm of the meaningless? Is there any meaning which gets completely and exhaustively shared with other people? Is not every communication maimed and partial if not in some measure downright false when compared with the meaning which one is trying to communicate? Dewey maintains that there is a distinction between non-shared and shared activity. Yet this distinction must be meaningless, for if it had meaning it would be included entirely in one of the pair distinguished. In short, he can not legitimately say anything about the non-shared, for saying would be a sharing and thus would destroy the very nature of the non-shared (if we can talk about the nature of that which is meaningless). But perhaps Mr. Dewey would tell us that all this dialectical quibbling is foolish. There is such an "event" as non-shared activity and it has meaning not only after it has become an object involving a social sharing, but before; i.e., a meaning can be a merely *potential* sharing. Well and good, then, our objection is admitted.

Let us turn to the language side of it. Can meaning be restricted to linguistic behavior? First, to take an empirical and personal case: I have always liked sailing, but have never taken the time to verse myself in nautical terminology. I remember once when the tack of the mainsheet was not drawn tightly enough, with the consequence that there were diagonal wrinkles from the foot to the luff for quite a ways up. I saw those wrinkles and I appreciated what the trouble was, but I did not know the names for the portions of the sail involved. When I tried to express myself I discovered how difficult it was and how many circumlocutions were necessary in order to put my meaning in words. I had no terminology directly applicable to the portions of the sail I wished to designate. The meaning of those wrinkles likely involved much incipient or imaginal linguistic behavior on my part. But the unique *point at stake* not only involved more than language (and thus transcended language); it could not be turned over into language without torture and a good deal of pointing. And I am inclined to think that the situation would have meant something to me even though I had not desired to communicate to someone else concerning it. The illustration may not be worth much. But there are other characters in experience than what we mean by language. If this were not so it would be nonsense to restrict meaning to language. Now are these other characters meaningless? Probably Dewey would answer: No, but their meaning lies in their linguistic usage, which, of course, changes them. We are in the same predicament as before. If meanings transcend language, then language is not the exhaustive nature of meaning. But if they do not, then we are forced to admit either that there is no reality other than language, or that there is meaningless reality. Dewey, I think, would accept this latter alternative and call such meaningless reality, "existence." But I am still so dense that I can not understand why the contrast between language and the non-linguistic (or meaning and existence) is meaningless.

The point I have been trying to make is a simple one. If you *restrict* meaning to the linguistic and to the socially shared you can only do so by asserting the reality of the non-linguistic and the non-shared. Now to claim or to imply reality would seem to involve, whether explicitly or implicitly, the attribution of some sort of character or nature. To say that this realm of bare existence or the meaningless is simply "had" does not get out of the difficulty. For had-ness is a case of meaning. Mere immediate presence, givenness, hypostatized particularity, are all meanings, natures. In short, the limitation of meaning is itself a meaning, and the exclusion of meaning from any portion of reality means something. But more of this anon.

Let us turn to the identification of meaning with the future, with consequences. This interpretation has peculiar force. Although we do not need explicitly to distinguish and separate that which means and that which is meant in order to have meaning (as Dewey admits), yet whenever we are challenged to think of our meaning we do discover these two elements, and such a discovery involves a temporal process. Now inasmuch as we ordinarily go, in this process, from that which means to that which is meant, and inasmuch as we usually identify meaning with the meant, it seems quite natural to say that the meaning of anything is its future, or the later elements in the series of events.[1] Now this at first sight seems to do well enough even when we mean the

---

1. I shall not discuss specifically the notion that meaning is a tool or means. It often is. But again we have a restriction which will not strictly hold up. Dewey recognizes this in saying that culminations are meanings. I might also suggest that Dewey's non-teleological series (his natural events, causes-effects, termini, etc.) are also cases of meaning. The argument is the same.

non-future; when, for example, the thing meant is past. For must we not reproduce this past situation in order to mean it, and thus is not what is meant the reproduction which, in relation to our symbol, is future? But we have a "nigger in the wood-pile." It is quite true that we may mean a future reproduction and even that we never can refer to a past (or to any temporal situation) without also involving a reference to a future. But how can we distinguish a reproduction from that which is not such? A reproduction, however much of the future it involves, *also* refers to a past and is what it is because it is not merely future. In short, meanings often (I personally believe always) bear a reference to that which is past, and however indirect you make that reference you will have to deal with it sometime.

But I hear protests. What I mean, says Dewey, is not that the past is meaningless and that we never refer to it, but that it only has significance in so far as it makes a difference in the future, in so far as it modifies consequences. But Dewey has already admitted that every difference of antecedence makes a difference of consequence. Now it may be that the most important thing in a given meaning centers around the future, but this is far from saying that the meaning is the future or merely in the future. Rather, we must recognize that some meanings at least (and I believe every meaning) involve a temporal unity of both past and future (and I may add, present). It is the same problem as before. Do you mean anything by restricting meaning to the future? If you do, then you have a meaning outside the realm to which meaning is restricted. Perhaps past differences are explored because of consequential differences. But they are still in some sense past and their importance for the future does not reduce them to the future, nor does it give us a merely one-way dependence.

I wish to evaluate briefly one other use (or perhaps I had better here say possible use) of meaning for Dewey. This one is perhaps the most inclusive of all, but it is one which Dewey does not himself definitely speak of as the nature of meaning. I refer to the so-called denotative or pointing method itself. We are told that in the last analysis we can designate what we mean only by pointing to it. This certainly is a matter of reference, is, in fact, an attempt to give us reference in its lowest and most irreducible form. But just what is designated by this pointing?

We will pass by the question of the relation of pointing to language, whether it antedates language, is included within language, or is the more inclusive, language being merely an elaboration. But this much seems clear, Dewey feels that in pointing we have got at the heart of reference (and thus of meaning). It is meaning at its simplest. Yet even here we have complexity. There seems to be on the one hand a pointing and on the other something pointed to. Let us consider the former. I think the analogy of the pointed finger is very definitely in Dewey's mind. Is the finger necessary for the pointing? Or, more generally, can you have a pointing unless you have that which is pointed? Must you not have a starting point (as well as terminus)? Dewey does not say, but we may answer for him. Yes, pointing is always *from* as well as *to*, it is directional, selective. It is always a case of a limited perspective having its footing in a relatively definite location—in a part, not in the indiscriminate whole of reality.

So far, I'm inclined to think Dewey would agree, although this is a mere guess. But how about that which is pointed to? Here Dewey will perhaps speak for himself a little more definitely. These things meant or denoted appear to be immediate experiences which we simply have or enjoy. I confess I do not know what sort of thing this "simply having" is. It becomes especially difficult to decipher when we are told that it has relations, occurs in a continuum with other experiences, is qualitative, and on occasion is even allowed to possess meaning. To say that it is just what it is and we have got to take it as such (because it is ineffable) may lead to hard words, but is scarcely a help to one who, gropingly, is really trying to understand. Perhaps there is something the matter with my introspective powers, but somehow I can not seem to locate any absolutely ineffable immediates in my own experience, though I am sure there is a taste of ineffability flavoring *all* of them (as I tried to say when I questioned whether any experience or meaning is completely communicable). I wonder if simply pointing at them would not destroy some of the absoluteness of their ineffability? But let us not stray too far from the issue. If I get Dewey straight, what he is trying to say about whatever it is that is pointed to is that it remains itself somehow independent of the pointing. That which is denoted exists not only apart from its being denoted, but even as a denoted something it is still the same as it was before entering that relation. Even while being pointed to it is still independent of the pointing. I do not think I am mistaken as to Dewey's position here. For if pointing modified the thing pointed to, then we could never point out, exactly, the original experience just as it was "had" (as Dewey insists).

So even in meaning as denotation we come back to the same story. Namely, we find that meaning is a restricted sphere that finds itself in a larger environment. The same simple question arises. Must not the distinction between these two itself have meaning? Can one designate in *any* fashion that which is absolutely independent of all designation?

But I hear an objection. I am told I have not distinguished between two standpoints, namely, between that of observing a mere existence and the mere existence itself, or between an experience for a spectator or in memory and that experience as it is directly "had." I am perfectly willing to admit the distinction, but I hasten to add that it means something. And I also feel inclined to believe that, because it is a distinction, it must involve an identity. If the non-observed experience or immediate existence is to be anything but an absolutely unknowable, empty somewhat (nay, even here we are ascribing some sort of nature to it), if it is to be admitted as anything at all, it must possess some relative identity, at least, with the designated, observed, meaningful experience from which it is distinguished. Dewey would seem to recognize this when he assumes that you can later designate an experience which originally was simply "had." But we can not assert a (relative) identity where there is no common character in any sense. (And we might well ask if we have not got meaning wherever there is a common character running through differences.) The realm of existence can not be *merely* different from the realm of observed and designated experience. There may very well be a difference of emphasis in the nature of existence and in the nature of meaning, but this would lead us to say that they are simply two aspects of every experience and of all reality. Neither can be absolutely independent of the other. There is no realm of existence from which all meaning can be excluded.

All this appears to be merely negative. It has opposed Dewey's stand. Yet we can not leave without a positive statement. I sincerely believe there is significance and value in Dewey's contention that meaning is restricted. And so, starting from the empirical, we have been led to the critical, and now (horror of horrors!) we are going to plunge into the dogmatical. Well, take it or leave it. Nevertheless, I am going to present, very crudely, an outline of my own doctrine of meaning.

III

I want to start with a hint from Dewey, from a distinction he makes within the realm of meaning. "There is thus an obvious difference between mind and consciousness; meaning and an idea. Mind denotes the whole system of meanings as they are embodied in the workings of organic life; consciousness in a being with language denotes awareness or perception of actual events, whether past, contemporary, or future, *in* their meanings, the having of actual ideas. The greater part of mind is only implicit in any conscious act or state; the field of mind—of operative meanings—is enormously wider than that of consciousness. Mind is contextual and persistent; consciousness is focal and transitive" (p. 303). This distinction between the contextual and the focal which with Dewey is a relatively insignificant distinction between two kinds of meaning, I intend to make central in the very meaning of meaning. My thesis is simply this: that which means (the symbol) is always a focal aspect of a larger contextual whole which is its meaning (in the sense of that which is meant or is symbolized).

We have seen how meaning can not be completely confined within any limited portion of reality. Yet I think Dewey is right in his feeling that, whatever be its limits, meaning does in its nature involve a partiality. What Dewey failed to do was to appreciate how *both* these elements are bound up in meaning; he failed to grasp the relation of the meaning in the sense of the symbol or that which refers to the meaning in the sense of the meant. We always mean (refer to) some identity in difference or whole. But we are always satisfied with a relatively few features of that whole, providing we feel that they somehow give us the core.

Take definitions. They give us meanings in the sense that they give us essential elements. These essential elements are sufficient, ordinarily, for our dealings with the vastly more complex whole of which (so far as our definition is good) they are the focal features. Take the definition of book. We would probably agree on including printed pages bound together having a certain minimum size and perhaps possessing outside covers. But the total thing meant ultimately by book carries us step by step into an overwhelming contextual whole involving all sorts and kinds of books, innumerable concrete details reaching out in every direction.

Take words. The main difficulty here in applying our view is that the symbols we find in language, once we analyze them, seem so arbitrary. Their naturalness is simply a matter of familiarity growing out of social custom. Think of the word "cat." Any other sound or combination of sounds would seemingly fit in with that four-legged creature which the word symbolizes. But the point is that, for us, this particular sound has become a real part of the total whole involved. The symbol is not a self-contained whole external to and set over against another self-contained whole which is its meaning. No, the symbol is a true part of the meaning and ordinarily is about all of the meaning we get hold of except for the sense that there *is* more and that, were we challenged, we could go to and explore this larger whole in some detail. So when we are talking about a cat (whether in particular or in general) the main thing we have is the sound or sight of the word, plus a greater or less fringe of shifting imagery. But we are always sure that there is a more, and that what we have is a part of it, although a vicarious part truly functioning for the whole. Thus words (and symbols in general) are peculiarly treated as the whole meaning, while yet they are recognized to refer beyond themselves. Their reference is not a pointing to something external, but is their own vicarious partiality.

But this analysis is not to be restricted to language. In fact it is the very arbitrariness of symbols in language which lends false color to the notion that the meaning (that which refers) and the meant are separate and external. Here is a sailor. He is out in a storm at night. He hears above the roar a whine, a shriek, a crack. He can not see, but he knows what has happened aloft. Those sounds mean, just as truly as any language, that a sail has been blown out of its bolt ropes. Clearly the sign or symbol is here not external to the signified. Or take another case. A man walking through a forest hears a groan. It is not simply so much noise, it has a startling meaning in that lonely place. A doctor understands the meaning of every slightest change in the breathing of his patient suffering from pneumonia. A smile means gladness, a drooping face and tear-stained cheek mean sorrow. Need I go on? Is it not clear that in each of these the symbol is truly an aspect which brings a larger whole to a focus? The symbol is that part of the whole thing meant which passes muster for the whole, with which the whole is peculiarly identified.

In every case of meaning concrete details in the nature of that which is meant are implied, but ignored. Now by existence, I think, we always in some sense mean a total, detailed context in all its concreteness. But, of course, we never get this, we can only approximate. Thus we never can completely go from a symbol to its full meaning (that which is meant), to the total existence to which it refers. Yet wherever we stop we feel the element of arbitrariness in the cessation. We are always in the realm of meaning because every whole we experience indicates and bears with it a larger context. What happens then to existence? Sometimes it is made an unknowable somewhat outside all experience. Sometimes it becomes synonymous with the mere fact of detailedness wherever found. This latter is the most popular today. Differences are put on their own, and thus existence often comes to be equated with mere particularity and our result is a specificism.

I think we come nearer the mark, however, when we realize that meaning and existence are relative terms. Existence refers to the fact of differentiation within any whole. Meaning refers to the fact that every whole is more peculiarly involved in and dependent upon some of these different features than others and thus that these parts, in thus summing up and focalizing the whole, can "represent" the whole. But they could not do so were they all. They are both sufficient and insufficient. Their sufficiency is due to their value and centrality, their vicarious nature. Their insufficiency is due to their larger setting upon which they depend and whose nature they bear, but do not exhaust.

Thus Dewey is right when he treats meaning as restricted, but he is also wrong. For he does not realize that it is a restriction which enlarges. He fails to recognize the identity which all meaning presents—the identity of the partial and the complete.

Appendix 4
Divergent Paths to Peace
By James T. Shotwell

Sir: Professor Dewey's recent article in the *New Republic*, commenting on the Kellogg offer of a treaty to renounce war, leads one to the conclusion that proponents of the outlawry of war tend to concentrate upon their own dogma to such an extent as to be indifferent to the exact significance of other proposals upon the same problem. There is little value in arguing on deductions when there is a complete disagreement as to the basis of fact upon which they rest. The attempt to draw the distinction between aggression and defense as stated by Professor Dewey is not to be found in any serious proposal of those attempting to secure a practical definition. This will be rather readily apparent to most readers. But there is a further confusion which seems to be widely shared and which, therefore, does need clearing up.

An acceptance of an agreement as to what is legitimate defense and what is aggression does not necessarily involve acceptance of an obligation to put down aggression. The enforcement of peace is quite another problem from that of the definition of defense or aggression. The distinction between these two problems of an enforcement and definition was clearly set forth in the very first document which attempted the definition of aggression. The "Draft Treaty of Disarmament and Security" of the Geneva Committee in 1924 defined aggression, but refused to accept the obligation to suppress the aggressor. According to that plan, the aggressor was simply to be regarded as having forfeited the rights and privileges it enjoyed under international law, leaving each nation free to treat the "outlaw" according to the individual interests of the various signatories or in accordance with their other obligations. The literature which has grown up about this suggestion ought to be sufficiently familiar to the "out-

[First published in *New Republic* 54 (1928): 194. For Dewey's article to which this is a reply, see pp. 163–67; for Dewey's rejoinder, see pp. 168–72.]

lawry" proponents to prevent such major misunderstandings. But for fear some reader draws a mistaken inference from this reference to the 1924 proposal, it should be pointed out that it is not the same as that proposed by Mr. Borah in his article in the *New York Times* in answer to M. Briand's hesitancy. Mr. Borah has nothing to say concerning the forfeiting of rights and privileges by an aggressor, because he does not know how to distinguish the aggressor from the defendant. Unless some such distinction is drawn, however, we either cannot renounce war, or, if we do, we renounce war in favor of universal anarchy.

Appendix 5
China and the Powers:
I. What Hope for China?
By William Crozier
Major General (Retired), United States Army*

The dramatic events which took place in China during
the two years commencing with the shooting by the police of
Shanghai of some members of a Chinese mob on May 30, 1925,
and the very considerable effort of certain foreign Powers to
come to terms with China on the tariff and extraterritoriality
questions, as represented by the conferences on these subjects
at Peking in 1925 and 1926, had their customary effect in this
modern world, which demands to know all about everything
which takes place; and high-class newspaper men from everywhere flocked to China to satisfy the demand. These writers reported well the contemporary events, the circumstances leading
up to them, and the conditions in the country, so that there is
no need to describe to the reading public the state of disorder,
civil war and semi-anarchy which prevails in the distracted "Republic" of China. Nor is there reason for relating in detail incidents illustrative of this state, such as the executions without
trial of political opponents, of editors of newspapers and of financial speculators charged with depressing the paper currency
issued by war lords—with nothing behind it—as well as innumerable small fry, like disorderly soldiers—many of them all
undoubtedly guilty of offenses of high or low degree, but none
having had anything like what we would call a judicial ascertain-

* General Crozier has seen active service in China and has paid several lengthy
visits to that country, both under the Monarchical and under the Republican régime. The following article is written as a result of his recent sojourn of more
than a year there, whence he returned to Washington in January. He was delegate
to the Peace Conference at The Hague in 1899; Staff Officer in the Field in the
Philippine Insurrection of 1899–1900; Chief Ordnance Officer with the Peking
Relief Expedition against the Boxers in 1900; President of the United States
Army War College in 1912 and 1913; Chief of Ordnance for sixteen years before
and during the World War until December, 1917, and subsequently a member of
the American War Council, part of that time in France and Italy.
[First published in *Current History* 28 (1928): 205–12. For Dewey's reply, see
pp. 196–98.]

ment of guilt, or even, usually, a pretense of such process. These things are understood.

There has been a general tendency in recent accounts and discussions regarding China to go back to the revolution of 1911, when the Empire was overthrown, and to show the failure of the attempts to set up in its place an orderly Government, called a Republic, which could properly administer the affairs of the State, the failures resulting in disorderly conditions which would perhaps account for the apparently contemptuous official disregard of what the Occident considers the elementary rights of man. The Government of China has always been from the top down, with no accountability on the part of any official to those below him, but only to those above, and in the case of the Emperor to Heaven only! The administration of the Government was, therefore, what it has been everywhere else under similar circumstances, in the interest of those doing the governing and not in that of the governed. And that is still the case among the many war lords, North and South, despite the high-sounding phrases imported from the West, including Russia, France and the United States, about equal rights and liberty.

In theory all the land of China belonged in former times to the Emperor, and the theory was reduced to practice whenever in his uncontrolled judgment the occasion called for it. If the proper official considered that a piece of private property was needed for public use it was summarily taken, in the name of the Emperor, though usually, it is true, with some compensation. But this was given only in gratuitous consideration for injured feelings, not in acknowledgement of a right, and it was generally much below the value of the property. The Rev. John Macgowan relates an illuminating incident of a period as late as the introduction of the telegraph into China. An objecting owner placed himself in the hole which had been dug for a pole and declared that he would die rather than let the pole be erected. Of course, he had special reasons for such radical conduct, which were connected with the nearby graves of his ancestors. But he quickly changed his mind when it was explained to him that the line was being run at the express command of the Emperor, who, he was reminded, had the power to order him and his wife and children "to be seized and to be cut into a thousand pieces, and none would question his right to do so."

But the everyday economic exploitation of the masses was in taxation, as it always is where economic exploitation is arbitrarily practiced, and this was levied and collected under a most pernicious system. The Governors of provinces were required to forward certain fixed sums to the capital, either in money or kind, but no limit was placed upon the amount which they might collect from their provinces; and as they were given no salaries, but usually had to pay officials or court favorites for their appointments, and moreover had no permanent security of tenure, they were under not only the necessity for providing for the current expenses of their establishments but also the temptation to secure as promptly and as liberally as possible provision for their own future. They followed in their provinces the same system as was practiced with themselves, calling for stated amounts from the district magistrates who, in turn, collected what they liked or were able to extract from subordinate political divisions. And so it went on down the line to the disreputable body of men who were the tax-gatherers, in direct contact with the people. The tax-gatherers, like others, without salaries, and also having purchased their positions, had the privilege of getting what they could out of the poor villagers, as long as they kept within certain forms of the law.

The land tax, for example, was often not unfairly assessed; but all sorts of ways were found for increasing the amounts collected. One way was to let the time for payment go by without notice and then to come down on the delinquent with a perfectly outrageous and arbitrarily fixed fine for delay, which the victim would be too ignorant and too terrified to combat. It would be useless to appeal to the mandarin, for his sympathies and those of all the officials of his court were with the tax-gatherer. They were all participants in the extortions. And the experienced observer cited above tells us that by chicanery and deception, by lies unspeakable, and by false accusations that would bring men within the covetous grasp of mandarins, extortions were exacted that would bring misery and wretchedness upon the homes of the poor, which means the large majority of the population. The clothes upon their backs and the little utensils in which their food was cooked would be taken from the country people if they had no other property with which to meet the rapacious demands.

Tyrannized Masses

The civil list was a very simple matter. There were practically no charges upon the national treasury for local administration, which took care of itself in the way described. And another witness, a British Consular officer of many years' experience in different parts of the interior, tells us that law and order could be maintained with a small number of troops because the people had no weapons and "the great bulk of the population was kept under, constrained to be content with a bare subsistence as the reward of constant toil, and the rabble was constrained to starve."

This picture of the economic relations of the masses with their officials has its counterpart in the personal relations. Oriental philosophy has produced many fine precepts for the government of the relations of man with his fellow man; but out in China the official is not a fellow man. He is a very superior being, who is himself the judge in the matter of any offense committed against him, with no responsibility to the people. And in judging the offense, too, as well as in other trials of accused persons, he has had time-honored freedom to make as full use as he liked of the bamboo and other forms of torture in order to facilitate proceedings by stimulating the memory or the inventive faculties of the accused. These inflictions, although not punishments adjudged after conviction but mere incidents of the trial, would often tear the flesh of the victims in such manner as to leave them invalids for months.

But the bamboo was not reserved for use in connection with judicial proceedings only. Lord Macartney tells us in the diary of his mission in Peking, in the last part of the eighteenth century, that men were seized without ceremony along the route and made to tow the boats of the mission up the Peiho, and purveyors were directed to furnish provisions and other supplies for their use, with prompt application of the bamboo for any failure of service or supply. He tells us also that when his ships needed native pilots for coming up the coast two men were summarily ordered by the local mandarin to accompany his fleet, in complete disregard of their pleas that they had not been engaged in piloting for years and that their business would be ruined if they were forced suddenly to leave.

The British Consul described the prisoners consigned to an old-world jail, after proceedings of the judicial character above indicated, heavily shackled with chains that clanked as they moved, crowding up to the bars, dreadful spectres of humanity, for all the world like wild beasts in a cage, some of them vicious by nature, and the rest brutalized by an inhuman penal system. The prisoners were brutes and the jailers were no better.

Such is the system under which the Chinese people have always lived. But it is not to be inferred that the Chinese officials were a cruel set, inflicting wanton suffering with malice or cynical indifference. They were not. The Chinese are a kindly race, reasonable in the affairs of life and tolerant of small shortcomings. They have many very human virtues, are famous for the veneration of their parents, their affection for their children, and their devotion to the whole family membership. But the officials are what their kind all over the world have always been when unrestrained in the control of relations between themselves and their subordinates. They have consulted their own interests and those of the ones close to them and have never hesitated at the exercise of any amount of severity in overriding what we call human rights, both economic and personal.

The Chinese people have never had the right to a speedy public trial for offenses charged, have never been secure in their persons, houses and effects, have never enjoyed the privilege of life, liberty and the pursuit of happiness, and have been helpless to obtain these blessings for themselves. Sages have enunciated rules for wise and considerate government by the ruler, who evolved from the patriarch, and he from the head of the family; and the Chinese magistrate, exercising locally legislative, executive and judicial power, has been called the father of his people. But human nature is not proof against license.

Civil Rights

In America civil rights have been so long established in routine and accustomed practice that we have forgotten the long travail and the bloody struggles through which they were acquired. There is nothing to keep the process present in our thoughts, and it is only when we consult the history of the Western European races that we realize these things have never been handed down from above as a gracious concession of autocracy but have been conquered bit by bit from reluctant authority. From the Magna Charta, wrung by force from King John in 1215, in which was granted freedom from taxation without representation and the right of trial according to law, to the Declaration of Independence, with its comprehensive statement that all just powers of government are derived from the consent of the governed, the successive steps toward government of the people, by the people and for the people have been painfully won by the force of the people's own power.

This power is, in the main, the power of numbers in intelligent combination, the most elementary power in the world. Two men can whip one if they have the intelligence and the motive to combine against him. And this is the only kind of power that little people have against concentrated authority, which has no difficulty in organizing and arming to beat them in detail. But the Chinese people have never had the faculty of combination, because they lack the prime essential, the ability to intercommunicate freely, to form public opinion and common sentiment for inspiring them to concerted action with mass strength.

There is nothing in combined action which is foreign to their capacity, for they have practiced village democracy for centuries, reaching common conclusions upon the matters within the limited competence of the village authorities; and the authorities have acted in responsibility to the governed numbers, looking downward for the approval which could be easily given or withheld. But when the field is wider, and the word of mouth will not carry freely among the members of the body politic, a certain amount of education must come in, so that the written word may supplement the spoken, and an avenue of intelligence be opened to the popular mind through which it may be empowered to effect the union, achieve strength, and may also learn to avoid such use of its power as would involve destruction, instead of promotion, of the people's common interests.

An overwhelming proportion of the Chinese people is illiterate and densely ignorant. The percentage of illiteracy has been variously estimated. There are no statistics. But shortly before the overthrow of the Empire the Chinese Government, in connection with one of its schemes of reform, estimated that after its educational project should be in operation for six years the number of illiterates would be reduced to 99 per cent. of the population! This is probably overstated; but, being a Chinese governmental estimate, it does not err through motive. Other students of China have placed the illiterates at 98½ and still others at 97 per cent. At all events it is enormous.

When, therefore, in 1912, certain self-constituted officials proclaimed the Chinese Republic, and the American Government hastened to offer recognition and congratulations on the institution of a system similar to its own, our people, having forgotten how their own free Government had been acquired, failed to realize that the only thing which could be said with certainty of the new Government was that it could not possibly operate in accordance with its scheme. For the scheme, of course, vested the ultimate political power in the people, and the Chinese people are utterly incapable of exercising such power.

No one can have a clear title to an office in China, for the people are incapable of giving it, and any Government that is established must be some kind of usurpation. And this is what all the Governments have been since the overthrow of the Manchus. The late leader of the Nationalist Party, Dr. Sun Yat-sen, realized this, and placed militarism as the first step in the program by which a real republic is to be established, after which is to follow tutelage of the people, and then democracy. That is to say, there is to be military usurpation of political power from the other militarists who are now exercising it in different sections of the country; then the new usurpers are to prepare the people to replace them in the exercise of control, and then they are to give up the power (obtained by fighting) with the profit and importance accompanying it. And the leaders, according to Dr. Sun's program, are to do all this without any compulsion from below, which the people are as yet confessedly unable to exercise. They are to do it beause they are a different kind of militarist from those whom they are to replace or from those the world has heretofore produced!

When it is stated thus, in the light of history and of reasoning upon human nature, we can see what chance there is of any early success for Dr. Sun's program. And, indeed, we have already seen some of the results of its operation—in the considerable section of China where the Nationalist forces have secured authority.

The Old Adam has appeared among the leaders, and personal profit and rivalry for power are repeating the distressing history of the past sixteen years.

So we must believe that if China is to be regenerated by her own efforts and her people relieved from exploitation by their native rulers it must be by the educative process, giving power to the governed who exact accountability from officials, by which alone the task has been accomplished in all other parts of the world where popular liberty prevails. And this will certainly come about eventually, because the spark of education has been lighted in China, and it can never be put out. But as to how long it will take, and as to how much suffering incident to the struggle there will be in the meantime, the experience of our own race is not reassuring. Although China, with the help of our example, can traverse the arduous course in less time than it took us by the method of trial and error, still the spirit wilts in contemplation of the weary generations which must be required for success against installed power, under the handicap of the disturbed conditions which blight the growth of education.

Is there no way of accelerating the process from the outside? And, in conscience, is not that part of the world where the thing has been better worked out called upon to try and help the Chinese people?

We are told by well-meaning persons that the Chinese people have a right to work out their own salvation in their own way and that it would be wrong to interfere in their internal affairs. But who are the Chinese? Are they the 2 per cent. who exercise an autocratic and profitable rule over the others? Or are they the inarticulate 95 per cent. who have nothing to say in the matter and never have had? If we have any duty or responsibility in the premises, to which group is it? Or have we any at all? By staying out and keeping our hands off we leave the 2 per cent. free to fight among themselves for the control of all the others, and to force as many of the latter into the mêlée as they can arm and equip, while harrying the remainder with the miseries of civil war. The only justification which we admit for making use of our strength is the defense of our own interests, of the lives and property of our nationals. But what idealism is there in this plea when dealing with a weak and backward people? Is the selfish reason the only one to which we will grant any validity?

But we are also told that the task of assuming charge of China against the united opposition which we would encounter from all the factions which are now fighting each other would be too big; that the game would not be worth the candle; and that it could not be prosecuted to success in any case, for it would involve endless guerilla warfare with the irreconcilable 400,000,000 of China's hostile population. Let us look at the situation for a moment.

China's armed forces are loosely estimated at some 2,000,000 men, whose sole present occupation is fighting each other or plundering the unarmed people. And this is the limit of her numerical possibility, for the task of armament and supply, particularly of ammunition, is already too much for her warring chiefs, even with the considerable assistance which she receives from abroad, in finished product, raw material and technical help, notwithstanding the quasi-embargo. The numbers are formidable, and if efficiency were maintained in reasonably like degree, they would be sufficient to deter any thoughtful soldier from advising his Government to undertake military operations against them, away off there in China.

The Chinese are much better armed than they have been in any of their previous clashes with outside Powers, and far better organized and drilled. They know more about the use of modern weapons; and they have never lacked courage when they recognized an occasion for its display. Some of them have exhibited discipline and endurance of a high order in campaigns, and, although very little fighting generally accompanies their military operations, their advances and retreats, and their occupation and abandonment of position, they have shown on more than one recent occasion that they are capable of maintaining a pitched battle with a tenacity which is evidenced by a high percentage of casualties. But their training scarcely extends beyond the duties of the infantry soldiers, and in that it is practically limited to elementary close and open order drill and manoeuvre, and the use and care of the rifle and the pistol. Their ammunition supply is too limited to permit the target practice necessary for any proficiency in marksmanship, and for the same reason they cannot have the training required for familiarizing the detachments with the operation of their automatic arms. It is doubtful if any number of them worth considering could keep a machine gun in action, even if the quality of their ammunition would permit anybody to do so.

Some of the arsenals can manufacture trench mortars, and this simple weapon they can use to some extent; but they do not manufacture field artillery; their supply of modern guns is very limited; and their officers lack the scientific training without which it is impossible to utilize the range and power of this important arm. Their aviation service is almost non-existent. They have a few planes, still fewer native pilots, and their planes are rarely in the air. They have nothing like the organization and equipment for the constant overhauling and repair which are needed to keep an aviation service going, and they have no means of renewing their supply of planes and parts except from abroad. They have no dirigible balloons whatever. They have few tanks, no gas masks and no gas service, and no means of manufacturing in quantity either the masks or the gas. They have a few motor cars and motor trucks, and they can drive these very well and keep them in reasonable repair; but the number in the entire country is too small for adequate military service, and they have never manufactured any themselves.

China has been overcome and completely taken possession of more than once in her history. The last occasion was the Manchu conquest, in which Peking was occupied in 1644, and a dynasty was set up which ruled the country with absolute power for two and a half centuries. The military advantages which enabled the Manchus to achieve this success were better organization, better fighting spirit and more robust physique. They had no superiority of weapons. The use of gunpowder had been known in the Orient for several centuries; and in the Occident the matchlock, firing by a burning or glowing match brought in contact with a primed touch-hole by a trigger, had been developed to the point of exercising a significant influence on infantry combat. But in China neither side had many firearms of any kind, and both were armed in the main with swords, bows and arrows, and other primitive weapons. In the manufacture of these the Chinese were probably better off than the Manchus, being more advanced in all the arts of civilization. Of course, the Chinese outnumbered the Manchus many times. Notwithstanding the great inferiority in numbers of the Manchus, the latter established a complete rule of force over all China, maintaining it for a number of years, at first by means of armed garrisons stationed at important points throughout the country. But as time went on and obedience became a habit, the Manchu Emperor was accepted as the evident instrument of Heaven whose favor he enjoyed, in accordance with the usual Chinese acceptance of fate; and the garrisons of "Banner Men" fell into desuetude and ultimately degenerated into useless pensioners, a charge upon the public funds.

So far as the military problems of taking control in China are concerned, it ought to be simpler now for any first-class Power than it was for the Manchus in the seventeenth century, and for a combination of Powers Chinese resistance should present no difficulty whatever. Japan alone has less disparity of numbers than the Manchus had, and her superiority of armament and organization over those of China is far greater. The World War brought home to the man in the street the supreme military value of industrial power. No lesson of the war was more widely inculcated than this one. And in this vital element of military strength China is incomparably further behind the Occidentally civilized world than she was in comparison with her victorious opponent of 1644. She has made some progress, it is true, but it is a bare beginning: she is still hopelessly outclassed.

It is probable that there is no force in China that could stop a single American division in organized military operations, and a force equivalent to eight or ten divisions could dissipate and reduce to military impotence every serious unit in the country, effecting a complete occupation, which could be maintained as long as necessary. The purely military task would be so easy as to justify search for the most benevolent way of performing it.

As to guerilla warfare, in which would be exhibited the universal hostility of an implacable populace, and which would require for its control such diffusion of an occupying force as to augment greatly the numbers needed for regular operations, nothing of the kind would be probable. The maintenance of such warfare calls for sacrifices and strenuous efforts, and a spirit which can be sustained only by resentment against the pressure of injurious tyranny, or by an intense patriotism, which the Chinese masses do not have. There is an exotic nationalism of "New China," but Dr. Sun Yat-sen himself has said that his people in general do not possess national feeling, which must be inculcated in them. The task of arousing it, however, in the face of a beneficent rule which would really consider the interests of the people would be great, and those seeking to arouse it would have to labor continuously against the Chinese popular disposition to acquiesce in a régime under which they are permitted quietly to pursue their vocations. There is plenty of evidence of the small amount of force which is necessary to put down Chinese uprisings, even where there is a genuine grievance; and with improvement of previously unsatisfactory conditions the native common sense of the Chinese race can be relied upon to make the inculcation of belief in a false grievance too difficult for the continuous success of the agitator. The "Red Spears," it is true, and other similar peasant organizations have been a serious annoyance to the armies of warring militarists in Central China; but these people have been harried to near death by the soldiery, their crops and animals taken, their homes looted and their women ill treated; and in desperation, with nothing left to lose, they have taken to reprisals against their tormentors, of which not the least unfortunate effect is to leave them addicts of the bandit habit for an indefinite time.

A word about the boycott: This has been claimed by Mr. Eugene Chen, of Nationalist notoriety, to be an invincible weapon in the hands of his countrymen; and there has been a disposition to admit the claim by foreigners who have been impressed by the effect on the Japanese of the boycott of 1919 against the occupation of Shantung, and by that of 1925–26 against the British of Hongkong, following the shooting incidents of May 30 and June 23. But these manifestations were directed by organizations of individuals who were probably incited and certainly encouraged by the constituted authorities, and who followed the methods of picketing, punishment and other forms of violence which have become classical in the coercion of "black-legs" in labor disputes both in the East and the West. So that it is impossible to say with what degree of spontaneity the boycotts were sustained. The British of Hongkong are firmly of the opinion that if the pickets had been restrained from the confiscation of British goods and the imposition of enormous blackmail upon vessels which visited Hongkong, making the whole movement a very profitable one for them, and if the Cantonese had not been able to obtain supplies of goods of other nationalities, the keenness of the merchants for trade and of the people for supplies would have made the boycott futile. The possibility of success of a widespread boycott against a Power or group of Powers effecting an occupation of China is more or less speculative, but the success of an attempt which would be officially discouraged and in which methods of intimidation would be prevented cannot be argued from the experience of 1919 and 1925, in which these methods had full play and official sympathy.

There remains to be considered the agency by which intervention might be attempted—the so-called Treaty Powers. Of these those which have the greatest interest in a stable and well governed China, and which at the same time can contemplate the expense without at once finding it prohibitive, are Great Britain, France, America and Japan. The Power which is so situated as to make the task the easiest for her is, of course, Japan; and the one which could best afford to undertake it is America. But we know that the American people would not think of sanctioning such a proceeding by either their own Government or any other. They would consider it not only morally and ethically wrong and militarily impracticable, on grounds which I have been examining above, but they would be distrustful of the spirit in which it would be undertaken and carried through. They would have no confidence in the altruism with which even our own Government would take up a trusteeship of the Chinese people and administer it in the sole interest of the wards, as political minors, until these could be trained to take over the management of their own estate, and they would be quite certain that shady financiers or even well-intentioned business men naturally solicitous about their own interest would exert such an influence on the administration of China as to give it altogether too much of the character of an exploitation of the Chinese people in the interests of foreigners. Americans would not trust our own public opinion to exert itself in behalf of remote wards.

It is charged by thoughtful Chinese, as well as by their political radicals, that the advantages given to foreigners by the "unequal treaties" are already oppressively used, to the economic and political detriment of the Chinese people; and there is an uncomfortable measure of truth in the charge. Friends of China assert that the unjust treatment would be accentuated with the enlarged opportunity for selfishness which would be afforded by complete control, and they are quite sure that there would be no self-imposed restriction of control which would limit it, as it should be limited, to the least degree which would accomplish its purpose, and would prompt the greatest possible utilization of native personnel and other Chinese agencies of administration.

There is also an element of the Treaty-Power population which admits no such duty to the peoples of the uttermost parts of the earth as would call upon them to make the effort and the sacrifice which would be required to free these people from the oppression and the exploitation of their own rulers and to shorten their course toward the consent of the governed. They are impressed by the expense of the undertaking, not believing that better trade conditions would more than return it, and they recoil from the risks and the bloodshed which might be involved. Altruism is all very well, but charity begins at home, and there is such a thing as quixotism. The first duty of the Government is to its own people, and the first duty of the people is to themselves, their respective fathers of families already burdened with expenses enough, their mothers and their soldier sons.

Finally, there is the difficulty of international cooperation; the mutual jealousies and distrust of the Treaty Powers, each thinking of its own selfish interests and determined that no other Power shall secure such control of China's railways or commercial water routes, or what not, or such influence in the administration of her Government as would give an advantage to its own nationals. There are many who contend that these international suspicions would prevent any efficient cooperation in the task of regenerating China, either in her own interest or in that of the intervening Powers, and that the Powers would still more strongly negative consent to consign the task to any single Power. The difficulties which are now encountered in securing accord upon any matter in which the various Powers are interested are numerous enough.

It may be that these objections are well taken; that the Treaty Powers, either jointly or separately, fail to constitute an instrumentality of sufficiently high class for the performance of such an advanced duty as the extension to politically incompetent peoples of the benefits of the device of trusteeship. Although this device is the best that statesmanship has worked out for the protection and the tutelage of the immature within the State, it is quite possible that the world is not yet good enough for the safe recognition of the existence of the national minor. But in that case it were best that we should recognize the true reason for pursuing the "Hands Off China" policy. It is not that it would be ethically wrong or practically impossible to do otherwise, but that we cannot trust ourselves or our neighbors with the delicate duty of laying a kindly hand on the shoulder of a backward nation and guiding it with firmness along the trail which we know because we have been over it.

Chinese industry, thrift, intelligence, eagerness to learn, hospitality to Western material and political civilization are such as to afford abundant encouragement to the belief that a period of tutelage need not be long if only a fair start could be given to an evolutionary development of the power of the governed. And for a civil leadership the native intelligentsia, some of it highly educated, affords a very fair amount of fine and worthy personnel. But the start is held back, and a revolutionary character is forced upon the development by the inability of any one to invent an argument which would appeal to the possessor of arbitrary power as a reason why he should voluntarily accept, and even cultivate, a restriction of his power in the interest of those under his rule. The militarist naturally prefers to fight for his preferential position as long as he can make war personally profitable.

It may be that we Occidentals cannot do anything in the premises. It is a pity if that is so. But, at all events, let us not make a merit of refusal to lend a hand to free a floundering people from cruel exploitation by the unrestrained human nature of their native rulers, because, singly or collectively, our nations are neither fit nor willing to do so.

Notes

The notes here, keyed to the page and line numbers of the present edition, explain references to matters not found in standard sources.

170.5   Capper resolution] Senator Arthur Capper introduced into the Senate a resolution, prepared by James T. Shotwell, professor of history at Columbia University, to widen the Briand proposal. Although S. O. Levinson urged Capper to reword it, Capper introduced it in its original form, indicating it could be changed in a committee hearing. For a full account, see John E. Stoner, *S. O. Levinson and the Pact of Paris* (Chicago: University of Chicago Press, 1943).

224.26–27   one of the leaders of the new education] William Brickman notes in his edition of *John Dewey's Impressions of Soviet Russia and the Revolutionary World: Mexico—China—Turkey* (New York: Columbia University Press, 1964) that this educator is evidently Stanislav Teofilovich Shatskii (Schatzsky) whom Dewey discusses in chapter 6 of *Impressions.*

269.3   Miss Blake] Probably Katherine Devereux Blake, noted educator and author.

270.15   Mr. Linville] Henry R. Linville, first editor of the *American Teacher* magazine and a founder of the American Federation of Teachers. For a full account, see William Edward Eaton, *The American Federation of Teachers, 1916–1961* (Carbondale: Southern Illinois University Press, 1975).

271.19   Lusk Law] In his *The Decline of American Liberalism* (New York: Atheneum, 1967), Arthur A. Ekirch, Jr., says, "In the immediate postwar period, the most conspicuous instance of state illiberalism occurred in New York, where on March 26, 1919, the legislature set up a joint committee of six, under the chairmanship of Senator Clayton R. Lusk, to investigate radical and seditious activities and report back to the legislature.

Although only an investigating, and not a prosecuting, body, the Lusk Committee in its search for materials proceeded to stage a series of spectacular and illegal raids upon radical organizations. On the basis of its activities and charges, five Socialist assemblymen, duly elected by the people to represent their districts in the state legislature, were denied their seats and expelled from the Assembly chamber.

"The Lusk Committee also instigated the prosecution of various radical leaders and was responsible for two new school laws. The first of these laws required a loyalty oath of all teachers and directed the expulsion of any teachers deemed guilty of advocating 'a form of government other than the government of the United States or of this state.' The second law required all private schools to be licensed by the state and stipulated that no license would be granted to a school 'where it shall appear that the instruction proposed to be given includes the teaching of the doctrine that organized governments shall be overthrown by force, violence or unlawful means.'" The laws were later repealed.

279.25   West Chester Normal School incident] Twelve members of the faculty were dismissed by President Andrew Thomas Smith for making allegedly unpatriotic utterances before the Liberal Club of the school, after their defense of free speech and criticism of President Calvin Coolidge's stand in the Nicaraguan situation had brought forth protests from the local American Legion. The controversy centered on the dismissal of Dr. Robert T. Kirlin and Professor John A. Kinneman.

315.37   editor] C. K. Ogden, editor of the series International Library of Psychology, Philosophy and Scientific Method.

346.30   (Lane) report] Winthrop T. Lane's *Military Training in Schools and Colleges*, 1926.

Checklist of Dewey's References

This section gives full publication information for each work cited by Dewey. When Dewey gave page numbers for a reference, the edition he used was identified exactly by locating the citation. Similarly, the books in Dewey's personal library (John Dewey Papers, Special Collections, Morris Library, Southern Illinois University at Carbondale) have been used to verify his use of a particular edition. For other references, the edition listed here is the one from among the various editions possibly available to him that was his most likely source by reason of place or date of publication, or on the evidence from correspondence and other materials, and its general accessibility during the period.

Adler, Mortimer. *Dialectic*. New York: Harcourt, Brace and Co., 1927.

Allen, Carleton Kemp. *Law in the Making*. New York: Oxford University Press, American Branch, 1927.

Ayres, C. E. *Science: The False Messiah*. Indianapolis: Bobbs-Merrill Co., 1927.

Barnes, Roswell P. *Militarizing Our Youth: The Significance of the Reserve Officers' Training Corps in Our Schools and Colleges*. New York: Committee on Militarism in Education, 1927.

Bastian, Adolph. *Der Mensch in der Geschichte*. Leipzig: O. Wigand, 1860.

Beard, Charles A., ed. *Whither Mankind: A Panorama of Modern Civilization*. New York: Longmans, Green and Co., 1928.

Borah, William. "One Great Treaty to Outlaw All Wars." *New York Times*, 5 February 1928, sec. 9, p. 1.

Bosanquet, Bernard. *Science and Philosophy and Other Essays*. New York: Macmillan Co., 1927.

Brown, Harry Gunnison, ed. *Significant Paragraphs from Henry George's "Progress and Poverty."* Garden City, N.Y.: Doubleday, Doran and Co., for the Robert Schalkenbach Foundation, 1928.

Buchanan, Scott. *Possibility*. New York: Harcourt, Brace and Co., 1927.

Catlin, George Edward Gordon. *The Science and Method of Politics*. New York: Alfred A. Knopf, 1927.

Crozier, William. "China and the Powers: I. What Hope for China?" *Current History* 28 (1928): 205–12. [*The Later Works of John Dewey, 1925–1953*, edited by Jo Ann Boydston, 3:417–31. Carbondale and Edwardsville: Southern Illinois University Press, 1984.]

Dewey, John. *Experience and Nature*. Chicago: Open Court Publishing Co., 1925. [*Later Works 1*.]

————, and Tufts, James H. *Ethics*. New York: Henry Holt and Co., 1908. [*The Middle Works of John Dewey, 1899–1924*, edited by Jo Ann Boydston, vol. 5. Carbondale and Edwardsville: Southern Illinois University Press, 1978.]

Dickinson, Zenos Clark. *Economic Motives*. Cambridge, Mass.: Harvard University Press, 1922.

Dimnet, Ernest. *The Art of Thinking*. New York: Simon and Schuster, 1928.

Frankfurter, Felix. "Mr. Justice Holmes and the Constitution." *Harvard Law Review* 41 (1927): 121–64.

Frazer, James George. *The Golden Bough*. 12 vols. 3d ed., rev. London: Macmillan and Co., 1911–25.

Fuller Report. See The Sacco-Vanzetti Case

George, Henry. *Progress and Poverty*. New York: D. Appleton and Co., 1880.

Goldenweiser, Alexander A. *Early Civilization*. New York: Alfred A. Knopf, 1922.

————, and Ogburn, William Fielding, eds. *The Social Sciences and Their Interrelations*. Boston: Houghton Mifflin Co., 1927.

Hall, Everett W. "Some Meanings of Meaning in Dewey's *Experience and Nature*." *Journal of Philosophy* 25 (1928): 169–81. [*Later Works* 3:401–14.]

Harrison, Jane Ellen. *Prolegomena to the Study of the Greek Religion*. Cambridge: At the University Press, 1908.

Hart, Joseph Kinmont. *Inside Experience: A Naturalistic Philosophy of Life and the Modern World*. New York: Longmans, Green and Co., 1927.

Hays, Arthur Garfield. *Let Freedom Ring*. New York: Boni and Liveright, 1928.

Hippocrates. *Collected Works*. Vol. 1. Translated by William Henry Samuel Jones. New York: G. P. Putnam's Sons, 1923.

Hobhouse, Leonard Trelawney. *Morals in Evolution: A Study in Comparative Ethics*. 3d rev. ed. New York: Henry Holt and Co., 1915.

Hocking, William Ernest. *Man and the State*. New Haven: Yale University Press, 1926.

Hoernlé, R. F. Alfred. *Idealism as a Philosophy*. New York: George H. Doran Co., 1927.

Holmes, Oliver Wendell. *Collected Legal Papers*. New York: Harcourt, Brace and Howe, 1920.

Hook, Sidney. *The Metaphysics of Pragmatism*. Chicago: Open Court Publishing Co., 1927.

Jastrow, Morris. *Aspects of Religious Belief and Practice in Babylonia and Assyria*. New York: G. P. Putnam's Sons, 1911.

Kallen, Horace Meyer, ed. *Freedom in the Modern World*. New York: Coward-McCann, 1928.

Karlgren, Anton. *Bolshevist Russia*. Translated from the Swedish by Anna Barwell. New York: Macmillan Co., 1928.

Kirkpatrick, John Ervin. *The American College and Its Rulers*. New York: New Republic, Inc., 1926.

Kohler, Josef. A series of articles upon "Recht" in various primitive peoples, in the *Zeitschrift für vergliechende Rechtswissenschaft*, XI, XIV, XV.

Kropotkin, Petr Alekseevich. *Ethics: Origin and Development*. Translated from the Russian by Louis S. Frieland and Joseph R. Piroshnikoff. New York: L. MacVeagh, Dial Press, 1924.

———. *Mutual Aid*. New York: Alfred A. Knopf, 1919.

Lenin, V. I. *Collected Works*. Vol. 23. New York: International Publishers, 1926.

Letourneau, Charles. *L'Évolution de la morale*. Paris: L. Battaille, 1894.

Levinson, Salmon O. "The Legal Status of War." *New Republic* 14 (1918): 171–73. [*Middle Works* 11:388–92.]

Lewis, Mary H. *An Adventure with Children*. New York: Macmillan Co., 1928.

Locke, John. *An Essay concerning Human Understanding*. In *The Works of John Locke*, vol. 1. 10th ed. London: J. Johnson, 1801.

Lowie, Robert H. *The Origin of the State*. New York: Harcourt, Brace and Co., 1927.

Lunacharsky, Anatoli. *Die Volksbildung in der Russischen Sozialistischen Föderativen Sowjetrepublik*. Moscow: Staatsverlag, 1928.

Maine, Henry. *Early Law and Custom*. London: J. Murray, 1891.

Maspero, Gaston. *Dawn of Civilization: Egypt and Chaldaea*. Edited by A. H. Sayce. Translated by M. L. McClure. New York: D. Appleton and Co., 1894.

Merz, Charles. *The Great American Band Wagon*. New York: John Day Co., 1928.

Morrison, Charles Clayton. *The Outlawry of War: A Constructive Policy for World Peace*. Chicago: Willett, Clark and Colby, 1927.

Mumford, Lewis. *The Golden Day: A Study in American Experience and Culture*. New York: Boni and Liveright, 1926.

New York World. "The Search for Security." 3 December 1927, p. 10.

———. "A Diplomatic Fiasco." 12 January 1928, p. 14.

———. "Mr. Kellogg to M. Briand." 14 January 1928, p. 10.

———. "The Conversation between Mr. Kellogg and M. Briand." 11 April 1928, p. 12.

Noble, Edmund. *Purposive Evolution: The Link between Science and Religion*. New York: Henry Holt and Co., 1926.

Ogburn, William Fielding, and Goldenweiser, Alexander, eds. *The Social Sciences and Their Interrelations*. Boston: Houghton Mifflin Co., 1927.

Ogden, C. K., and Richards, I. A. *The Meaning of Meaning: A Study of the Influence of Language upon Thought and of the Science of Symbolism*. New York: Harcourt, Brace and Co., 1923.

Oppenheimer, Francis J. *The New Tyranny: Mysticism, Scepticism*. New York: Albert and Charles Boni, 1927.

Page, Kirby, ed. *Recent Gains in American Civilization*. New York: Harcourt, Brace and Co., 1928.

Petrie, William Matthew Flinders. *Religion and Conscience in Ancient Egypt*. New York: Charles Scribner's Sons, 1898.

Post, Albert Hermann. *Afrikanische Jurisprudenz*. Oldenburg and Leipzig, 1887.

Radin, Paul. *Primitive Man as Philosopher*. New York: D. Appleton and Co., 1927.

Rée, Paul. *Die Entstehung des Gewissens*. Berlin: C. Duncker (C. Haymons), 1885.

Richards, I. A., and Ogden, C. K. *The Meaning of Meaning: A Study of the Influence of Language upon Thought and of the Science of Symbolism*. New York: Harcourt, Brace and Co., 1923.

The Sacco-Vanzetti Case: Transcript of the Record of the Trial of Nicola Sacco and Bartolomeo Vanzetti in the Courts of Massachusetts, and Subsequent Proceedings, 1920–7. Mamaroneck, N.Y.: Paul P. Appel, 1969. [Contains a facsimile reprint of the Fuller Committee Report.]

Santayana, George. *The Realm of Essence*. New York: Charles Scribner's Sons, 1927.

———. "Dewey's Naturalistic Metaphysics." *Journal of Philosophy* 22 (1925): 673–88. [*Later Works* 3:367–84.]

Schmidt, Leopold Valentin. *Die Ethik der alten Griechen*. Berlin: W. Hertz, 1882.

Sharp, Dallas Lore. "Education Goes Ahead." In *Recent Gains in American Civilization*, edited by Kirby Page. New York: Harcourt, Brace and Co., 1928.

Sherrington, Charles S. *The Integrative Action of the Nervous System.* New Haven: Yale University Press, 1923.

Shotwell, James T. "Divergent Paths to Peace." *New Republic* 54 (1928): 194. [*Later Works* 3:415–16.]

Smith, William Robertson. *Lectures on the Religion of the Semites.* London: A. and C. Black, 1894.

Spencer, Herbert. *Principles of Ethics.* New York: D. Appleton and Co., 1914.

———. *Principles of Sociology.* New York: D. Appleton and Co., 1923.

Steinmetz, Sebald Rudolf. *Ethnologische Studien zur ersten Entwicklung der Strafe.* Leiden: S. C. von Doesbergh, 1894.

Thilly, Frank. "Contemporary American Philosophy." *Philosophical Review* 35 (1926): 522–38. [*Later Works* 3:385–400.]

Thomas, Norman. "Advances in the Quest for Peace." In *Recent Gains in American Civilization*, edited by Kirby Page. New York: Harcourt, Brace and Co., 1928.

Tufts, James H. *On the Genesis of the Aesthetic Categories.* University of Chicago. The Decennial Publications, first series, 3:3–14. Chicago: University of Chicago Press, 1903.

———, and Dewey, John. *Ethics.* New York: Henry Holt and Co., 1908. [*Middle Works* 5.]

Tugwell, Rexford Guy. *Industry's Coming of Age.* New York: Harcourt, Brace and Co., 1927.

Veblen, Thorstein. *The Instinct of Workmanship and the State of the Industrial Arts.* New York: Macmillan Co., 1914.

Ward, Paul William. *Sovereignty.* London: G. Routledge and Sons, 1928.

Weeks, John H. *Among Congo Cannibals.* Philadelphia: J. B. Lippincott Co., 1913.

Wells, H. G. *The Outline of History.* Garden City, N.Y.: Doubleday, 1920.

Westermarck, Edward Alexander. *The Origin and Development of the Moral Ideas.* 2 vols. New York: Macmillan Co., 1906–8.

Wundt, Wilhelm. *Ethics: An Investigation of the Facts and Laws of the Moral Life.* 3 vols. Translated by Edward Titchener, Julia Gulliver and Margaret Floy Washburn. New York: Macmillan Co., 1902–7.

———. *Philosophische Studien.* Vol. 4. Leipzig: W. Engelmann, 1888.

Index